MW00608525

"Lee Martin McDonald is world famou ~~of the biblical canon. In the present book,~~ ___ focuses on the Jesus story. In light of the advances in perceiving the evidence of eyewitness accounts in the Gospels and the fact that oral tradition is not always untrustworthy, Lee wisely points out the vast amount of reliable historical information in the Gospels, although they were primarily composed to defend the faith and win converts (*kerygmata*). Lee assesses the importance of the Dead Sea Scrolls for comprehending Jesus' time and his unique message and astutely includes not only the so-called apocryphal gospels but also the Jewish traditions about Jesus. Lee writes with skill, insight, and spiritual energy. His insight that Jesus' message proves 'we are significant enough to be loved' will be moving for many readers, as well as the notion that the biblical Jesus is also the Christ of faith. This book is highly recommended for classes and all who find Jesus' story riveting and compelling."

—**James H. Charlesworth**, director and editor, Princeton Dead Sea
Scrolls Project; George L. Collord Professor of New Testament
Language and Literature, Princeton Theological Seminary

"*The Story of Jesus in History and Faith* is perhaps the best technical survey of Jesus research now in print. It is at once exhaustively thorough, painstakingly fair, and enormously readable. This is simply a great book that will serve scholars and students alike who need to become current on virtually every critical issue surrounding the Gospels, the life of Jesus, and the intersection of history and faith."

—**Gary Burge**, professor of New Testament,
Wheaton College and Graduate School

"In what must be regarded as a tour de force in Jesus studies, Lee McDonald has picked up the gauntlet thrown down by David F. Strauss in the nineteenth century, effectively challenging his two dichotomies: that the Jesus of history must be divorced from the Christ of faith, and that the historicity of the Fourth Gospel is decimated by that of the Synoptics. As a fourth quest for Jesus seeks a way to include the Gospel of John, this book will play a pivotal role in restoring the critical integration of history and faith regarding the greatest subject of both fields: Jesus."

—**Paul N. Anderson**, professor of biblical and Quaker studies,
George Fox University; author of *The Riddles of the Fourth Gospel*

"Lee McDonald writes as a veteran scholar with a depth of experience in both the church and the academy. *The Story of Jesus in History and Faith* distinguishes itself by offering readers a learned and carefully nuanced discussion of what history is, how it is written, and what relevance it has for our understanding of Jesus. McDonald skillfully leads his readers through all of the important topics and questions, including the historical reliability of the New Testament Gospels and the miracles, death, and resurrection of Jesus. Careful reading of this book will profit believers and skeptics alike. I am pleased to recommend it."

—**Craig A. Evans**, Payzant Distinguished Professor
of New Testament, Acadia Divinity College,
Nova Scotia, Canada

"Lee McDonald has provided a wide-ranging compendium of useful information on the study of the historical Jesus, including an account of the life, death, and resurrection of Jesus that engages the major critical issues. This material will be well suited to students at various levels of engagement. This is vintage McDonald."

—**Stanley E. Porter**, president, dean, and professor
of New Testament, McMaster Divinity College,
Hamilton, Ontario, Canada

"McDonald surveys the broad range of issues and sources in historical Jesus research in a way that is irenic toward all sides. Rather than pursuing a partisan line he writes as an independent observer and yet with sensitivity to the scholars with whom he disagrees."

—**Craig Keener**, professor of New Testament,
Asbury Theological Seminary

The Story of
JESUS
in History
and Faith

||||||||||||||||||||||||||||||||||||||||||||||||||

LEE MARTIN McDONALD

B

Baker Academic

a division of Baker Publishing Group
Grand Rapids, Michigan

© 2013 by Lee Martin McDonald

Published by Baker Academic
a division of Baker Publishing Group
P.O. Box 6287, Grand Rapids, MI 49516-6287
www.bakeracademic.com

Printed in the United States of America

Library of Congress Cataloging-in-Publication Data
McDonald, Lee Martin, 1942–
    The story of Jesus in history and faith / Lee Martin McDonald.
        pages cm
    Includes bibliographical references and index.
    ISBN 978-0-8010-3987-4 (pbk.)
    1. Jesus Christ—Historicity. I. Title.
BT303.2.M397 2013
232.9′08—dc23   2013007792

13   14   15   16   17   18   19   7   6   5   4   3   2   1

To my many colleagues and friends
in the Institute for Biblical Research who trusted me
as their president from 2006 to 2012

Contents

||||||||||||||||||||||||||||||||||||||||||||||||||||||

Preface

IIIIIIIIIIIIIIIIIIIIIIIIIIIIIIIIIIIIIIIIIIIIIIIIIIIIIIIIIIIIII

A colleague who is quite familiar with the history of historical Jesus research recently asked why I saw the need to write yet another book on this subject! He indicated to me that everything that can be known has already been said many times over. I mentioned to him that much is now known about Jesus that has only emerged in the last decade, some of which is the result of recent archaeological discoveries, and some the result of reassessments of some of the ancient data that has been circulating among scholars for more than a generation. Also, most of those who write on this subject more often than not write for scholars and ignore those in the church or students in college or seminary who are looking at the "historical Jesus" for the first time. While an emerging picture of Jesus is gaining favorable responses from many biblical scholars, this is still a story that needs to be told to students, pastors, and educated laypersons in churches. Much of the new and emerging picture of Jesus has formed as a result of a better understanding of the Jewish context in which Jesus lived than was possible to know in previous generations.

It is not inappropriate to ask, however, why after two thousand years of study we are still resolving problems in our understanding of the origins of the Christian faith and especially of its founder. This volume is not an arrogant attempt to correct all of the previous stories about Jesus, but rather an attempt to offer an introduction to nonspecialist readers who are not familiar with what is going on in life of Jesus biblical research today. I would suggest here that those who are exploring this subject for the first time may well want to ignore the many footnotes in this volume and simply try to get a "feel" for the subject. The footnotes are for those who are more advanced in their study of Jesus and who want to know and perhaps research some of the critical literature and arguments circulating among scholars. Also, while I have put in several important Greek or Hebrew words, they are both transliterated and translated so readers without those language skills can be familiar with some important technical terms that help in our investigation of the story of Jesus.

I should also remind readers that because so many books have been written about Jesus, there is no way to give each of them serious consideration in a study this size, or for that matter even in multivolume works on Jesus. I have chosen instead to limit myself to some of the most recognized critical resources that have had the greatest influence on recent discussions about Jesus and his career. Readers will observe that I accept the New Testament Gospels as the primary and most reliable sources for knowing about Jesus. Some scholars have given greater priority to some of the so-called noncanonical or nonbiblical gospels than those in the New Testament. I will say here and below that those sources tend to offer nothing new or of much value; rather, they tend to be more sensational and reflect sectarian perspectives. The critical literature about the story of Jesus is commonly referred to as "secondary" literature, and ancient sources are regularly referred to as "primary" sources. The former literature aims at interpreting the latter.

My primary focus in telling the familiar story about Jesus is to provide something for serious students who are unfamiliar with the critical issues that surround this story and to do this *within the context of faith*. The reader will quickly see that I acknowledge the limitations of historical inquiry, but also the limitations of a faith perspective. Happily, as we will see, we are not obligated to choose between these two, but we can gain much from both perspectives. I will acknowledge here and elsewhere that, on the one hand, the Jesus discovered through strictly critical historical research, with all of its historical assumptions, cannot account for the emergence of the early church and its faith, let alone offer a coherent portrait of Jesus. On the other hand, seeing Jesus only through the eyes of faith and a simple reading of the Gospels, while satisfying to many people of faith, often means ignoring a better understanding of who Jesus was and seldom viewing him in the most appropriate Jewish historical context.

In the following chapters, we will first look carefully at the notion of history and historical inquiry and how historical methodology has been applied to the story of Jesus. This is a pivotally important step since it is here that we can best understand why competent scholars examine the same ancient sources about Jesus and yet disagree on their interpretations of his story. What are the best criteria to use in examining the ancient sources, and what assumptions are most appropriate in studying the story of Jesus? Before looking at the most important questions in the story of Jesus, we will also examine the primary sources from which scholars gather pieces of data that enable them to explore various aspects of the life of Jesus. Besides the major events and teachings of Jesus as presented in the Gospels, there are many other areas on which reasonable scholars can agree, but they are not as important in constructing a picture of Jesus in his historical context as the ones we will discuss below. As we look at the story of Jesus, readers will observe that we spend more time on some areas than on others, and that is because they are generally considered to involve more important historical issues that also have a bearing on Christian faith about Jesus. For example, I spend considerably more time on the death, burial, and resurrection of Jesus than on the other areas.

I will from time to time refer to both historical and faith perspectives throughout this study, and I will be using the word "story" throughout to reflect on both historical and faith perspectives about Jesus. At the conclusion of our focus, I will emphasize the importance of both perspectives for understanding Jesus of Nazareth. At the end of this volume, I have also provided a very select bibliography of some of the most important resources that will aid students and pastors in their further study.

I want especially to thank James Ernest for his participation in this venture and the many good suggestions he has offered that will make this a more useful contribution. He and his Baker Academic colleagues have helped to make this a much better work than it would have been otherwise. Their careful evaluation of my manuscript reflects well on their commitment to excellence in their many notable publications. I have learned much from them in several publishing ventures that I have had with Baker Academic over the years. Any mistakes or errors in research and publication remain my own responsibility.

I have dedicated this volume to my many colleagues and friends in the Institute for Biblical Research. I have learned much from them over the years, and, as the readers will see, I have relied heavily on their many contributions to Jesus research. Many of our members are internationally known for their academic and publishing achievements. Some of them are *the* noted experts in their fields, and their work is regularly reflected in my own research and writing. They have honored me with their trust as president of the Institute from 2006 to 2012, and I count it a privilege to have been their colleague for the past thirty-eight years. It is therefore out of my sincere appreciation for them that I dedicate to them this volume.

Abbreviations

||||||||||||||||||||||||||||||||||||||||||||||||||

Papyri

P.Egerton	Egerton papyrus	P.Oxy.	Oxyrhynchus papyri
P.Lond.	Greek papyri in the British Museum	Sel.Pap.	*Selected Papyri*

Old Testament Pseudepigrapha

1 En.	*1 Enoch (Ethiopic Apocalypse)*	T. Jos.	*Testament of Joseph*
		T. Jud.	*Testament of Judah*
Jos. Asen	*Joseph and Aseneth*	T. Sim.	*Testament of Simeon*
Pss. Sol.	*Psalms of Solomon*		

Dead Sea Scrolls

1QapGen	*Genesis Apocryphon*	4Q246	*Apocryphon of Daniel*
1QH	*Thanksgiving Hymns*[a]	4Q521	*Messianic Apocalypse*
1QM	*War Scroll*	11Q5	*Psalms Scroll*[a]
1QpHab	*Pesher Habakkuk*	11QPs	*Psalms Scroll*[a]
1QS	*Rule of the Community*	11QT	*Temple Scroll*[a]
3QHym	*Hymn Scroll*	CD	Cairo Genizah copy of the *Damascus Document*
4QFlor	*Midrash on Eschatology*[a]		
4Q159	*Ordinances and Rules*		

Mishnah, Talmud, and Related Literature

b.	Babylonian Talmud
m.	Mishnah
t.	Tosefta
y.	Jerusalem Talmud

'Abot	*'Abot*	'Erub.	*'Erubin*
'Arak.	*'Arakin*	B. Bat.	*Baba Batra*

B. Qam.	Baba Qamma	Pesaḥ	Pesaḥim
Ber.	Berakot	Qidd.	Qiddušin
Giṭ.	Giṭṭin	Roš Haš.	Roš Haššanah
Ḥag.	Ḥagigah	Šabb.	Šabbat
Ker.	Kerithot	Sanh.	Sanhedrin
Ketub.	Ketubbot	Soṭah	Soṭah
Meg.	Megillah	Sukkah	Sukkah
Menaḥ.	Menaḥot	Taʿan	Taʿan
Naz.	Nazir	Yad.	Yadayim
Ned.	Nedarim	Yebam.	Yebamot
Peʾah	Peʾah	Yoma	Yoma (= Kippurim)

Targumic Texts

Frg. Tg.	Fragmentary Targum	Tg. Neof.	Targum Neofiti
Tg. Isa.	Targum Isaiah	Tg. Onq.	Targum Onqelos

Other Rabbinic Literature

ʾAbot R. Nat.	Avot of Rabbi Nathan	Midr. Pss.	Midrash on the Psalms
Deut. Rab.	Deuteronomy Rabbah	Num. Rab.	Numbers Rabbah
		Pesiq. Rab.	Pesiqta Rabbati
Exod. Rab.	Exodus Rabbah	Qoh. Rab.	Ecclesiastes Rabbah
Gen. Rab.	Genesis Rabbah	Sipre Deut.	Sipre on Deutoronomy
Kallah Rab.	Kallah Rabbati	Sipre Num.	Sipre on Numbers
Lam. Rab.	Lamentations Rabbah		

Apostolic Fathers

Ign. Smyrn.	Ignatius, To the Smyrnaeans	Ign. Pol.	Ignatius, To Polycarp
		Mart. Pol.	Martyrdom of Polycarp

New Testament Apocrypha and Pseudepigrapha

Acts Pil.	Acts of Pilate	Gos. Pet.	Gospel of Peter
Gos. Heb.	Gospel of Hebrews	Gos. Thom.	Gospel of Thomas

Greek and Latin Works

Cicero

De Repub.	De republica

Didymus

In Psalm.	Commentary on the Psalms

Clement of Alexandria

Strom.	Miscellanies

Eusebius

Hist. eccl.	Ecclesiastical History

Homer

Od.   Odyssey

Irenaeus

Haer.   Against Heresies

Jerome

De viris
illustribus   De viris illustribus
In Eph.   Commentary on
Ephesians

Josephus

Ag. Ap.   Against Apion
Ant.   Jewish Antiquities
J.W.   Jewish War
Life   The Life

Justin

1 Apol.   First Apology
Dial.   Dialogues with Trypho

Livy

Livy   History of Rome

Origen

De princ.   First Principles
In Jer. hom.   Homilies on Jeremiah
Or.   Prayer

Ovid

Fast.   Fasti
Metam.   Metamorphoses

Philo

De Iosepho   De Iosepho
Flaccus   Against Flaccus

Philostratus

Apoll. Tyana   Life of Apollonius of
Tyana

Pliny the Elder

Nat.   Natural History

Plutarch

Num.   Numa
Rom.   Romulus

Ptolemy

Geog.   Geography

Seneca

Polyb.   Ad Polybium de consolatione

Suetonius

Augustus   Divus Augustus

Tacitus

Ann.   Annals

Tertullian

Apol.   Apology

Secondary Sources

ABD	Anchor Bible Dictionary
ABRL	Anchor Bible Reference Library
AGJU	Arbeiten zur Geschichte des antiken Judentums und des Urchristentums
ANF	Ante-Nicene Fathers
ANRW	Aufstieg und Niedergang der römischen Welt: Geschichte und Kultur Roms im Spiegel der neueren Forschung. Edited by H. Temporini and W. Haase. Berlin, 1972–

BAR	Biblical Archaeology Review
BETL	Bibliotheca ephemeridum theologicarum lovaniensium
CBQ	Catholic Biblical Quarterly
CRINT	Compendia rerum iudaicarum ad Novum Testamentum
CSR	Christian Scholar's Review
DSD	Dead Sea Discoveries
ETL	Ephemerides theologicae lovanienses
ExpTim	Expository Times
HTR	Harvard Theological Review
ICC	International Critical Commentary
IDB	The Interpreter's Dictionary of the Bible
JBL	Journal of Biblical Literature
JSP	Journal for the Study of the Pseudepigrapha
JSJSup	Supplements to Journal for the Study of Judaism in the Persian, Hellenistic, and Roman Periods
JTS	Journal of Theological Studies
JSNTSup	Journal for the Study of the New Testament: Supplement Series
LCL	Loeb Classical Library
NEAEHL	The New Encyclopedia of Archaeological Excavations in the Holy Land. Edited by E. Stern. 4 vols. Jerusalem, 1993
NIDB	New Interpreter's Dictionary of the Bible
NICNT	New International Commentary on the New Testament
NovT	Novum Testamentum
NovTSup	Supplements to Novum Testamentum
NT Apo	New Testament Apocrypha
NTS	New Testament Studies
NTTS	New Testament Tools and Studies
OBS	Oxford Bible Series
OGIS	Orientis graeci inscriptiones selectae. Edited by W. Dittenberger. 2 vols. Leipzig, 1903–1905
PL	Patrologia latina [= Patrologiae cursus completus: Series latina]. Edited by J.-P. Migne. 217 vols. Paris, 1844–1864
SBLDS	Society of Biblical Literature Dissertation Series
SBLRBS	Society of Biblical Literature Resources for Biblical Study
SBT	Studies in Biblical Theology
SecCent	Second Century
SP	Sacra pagina
TJ	Trinity Journal
TS	Theological Studies
TynBul	Tyndale Bulletin
WBC	Word Biblical Commentary
WUNT	Wissenschaftliche Untersuchungen zum Neuen Testament

Introduction

||||||||||||||||||||||||||||||||||||||||||||||||||||||

Without question, the most influential person in human history is Jesus of Nazareth. No other political or religious leader has gained more followers than Jesus, and no one else has influenced the origin of more religious communities (churches) and educational and humanitarian institutions, including hospitals, than Jesus. Likewise, no other person in human history has been written about or proclaimed more than Jesus. From the church's beginnings, biblical scholarship has tried to understand and explain this phenomenal person. Those books that have focused on him and the implications of following him are among the largest collection of religious artifacts in the world. The church owes its origin and development to its beliefs about him, so we must conclude that no other person in history can be more important for the church than Jesus of Nazareth.

But who was Jesus and what can we know about him? Christians are often puzzled by this question since they regularly read their Scriptures and believe that Jesus was born of a virgin, grew up in the region of Galilee, was baptized by John the Baptist, enlisted a group of twelve disciples to aid him in his ministry, preached the kingdom of God, healed many, was transfigured on a high mountain, was celebrated as the coming Messiah as he entered Jerusalem, "cleansed" the temple of money changers, was subsequently arrested, tried, crucified, and buried, rose from the dead, and, before he ascended to heaven, commissioned his disciples to make more disciples. He is regularly confessed as Lord, Christ, Son of God, and Son of Man. After some two thousand years, pastors around the world continue to teach and preach the story of Jesus and its implications for Christian living.

This abbreviated summary of Jesus' life, ministry, and fate is, of course, presented in the New Testament Gospels, so what is all of the fuss about?

Why are there so many confusing stories going on about him every year in the media, generally about a month or so before Christmas and about a month or so before Easter? Why are there so many questions about Jesus, and why do the critics not simply read their Bibles and recognize what Christians around the world already know? Such questions are easier posed than answered. Since the eighteenth century scholars have regularly debated the identity of Jesus. They do not approach the Bible in the same way that church members regularly do—namely, as a sacred and authoritative book—and admittedly they have seldom taken the time to explain why they conclude what they do about Jesus to those in the church. These scholars often come to the Bible pursuing a different agenda than the agenda that Christians around the world have, and they certainly have a different perspective on history and historical inquiry. Since the time of the Enlightenment,[1] which emphasized independence from the authority of the church in favor of critical inquiry, historians and philosophers began to develop perspectives about miracles and the supernatural that excluded their consideration, except to say that they emerged in the "pre-enlightened" world of the biblical times, and that such notions, though common then, must be rejected now.

Since those times many biblical scholars have bought into the common presuppositions of the Enlightenment and have tried to account for the phenomenon of Christian faith and the origin of the church in naturalistic ways. That is, they often see considerable amounts of myth and legend in the Bible and assume that it must be "demythologized" so that its many myths about the origin of the world and the miracles of God's intervention in human history can be completely laid bare, explained, and reinterpreted. Only then can the message of the Bible be adequately understood. Once that step has taken place, they contend, the story of Jesus and the emergence of the church and the church's Bible can be more adequately understood.

This view has many proponents who have produced a virtual plethora of books trying to account for the origin of the church without what they believe are the mythical trappings about the supernatural intervention of God in human affairs. As yet there is no consensus among biblical scholars on how to account for the biblical stories about Jesus and the emergence of early Christianity. I will say more about the variety of explanations of the biblical story about Jesus in the opening chapters of this book, but for now I will only mention that biblical scholars seem to be increasingly divided in terms of what

1. The Enlightenment was a European intellectual movement of the seventeenth and eighteenth centuries that was influenced especially by the philosophers Descartes, Locke, Newton, Kant, Goethe, Voltaire, Rousseau, and Adam Smith. Several theologians also joined this movement and began to apply their new methodologies of historical inquiry to the biblical literature.

they believe they can rationally affirm about Jesus. Biblical scholars today are often divided into two camps, namely "minimalists" and "maximalists." The former scholars do not see much historical credibility in the Bible's message about Jesus or early Christian beginnings. The latter scholars are known for arguing that the biblical message has far more historical credibility than the minimalists have considered possible. Since the early nineteenth century, there have been three major historical "quests" for understanding and interpreting the story of Jesus. The so-called "third quest" is now under way, and many contemporary scholars believe that there is much more in the biblical story that can be affirmed as historically credible than was considered possible a generation ago.

I will discuss later what the third-quest scholars' assumptions and conclusions are as well as the value of their findings for the church today, and I will acknowledge here that those who have always approached the Bible as divinely inspired Scriptures may find this a challenging subject. There is much that we can learn about Jesus and early Christian faith from critical historical scholars; for example, they can affirm without objection the biblical reports that Jesus grew up in Nazareth, that he was baptized by John the Baptist, and that he died by crucifixion in the first century AD at the direction of Pontius Pilate. As we will see, there is even more than this that is widely acknowledged as historically credible. Historical scholars have provided considerable useful detail about the manner and commonality of crucifixions in the ancient world, as well as how persons were buried in the first century. That information cannot be unimportant for understanding Jesus and what he faced at the end of his life, but the church's historic position that Jesus died for our sins is well beyond the scope of a historian's inquiry. Similarly, while historians can affirm that many of Jesus' followers accepted him as their anticipated Messiah and Son of God, they cannot state that Jesus was in fact the Messiah and Son of God. That is beyond their scope of inquiry.

Are Christians today at the mercy of historical inquiry? By no means, though results of careful historical inquiry will be shared in the rest of this volume that have considerable value for Christians and their understanding of their faith. Since Jesus is the central figure for all of Christianity, whatever we can learn about him cannot be considered unimportant. Nevertheless, Christian faith does not, in the final analysis, depend on the latest results of historical scholars. It ultimately depends on a strong belief that God has acted in the life, ministry, and fate of Jesus and that this activity has considerable value for faith.

In antiquity the big question about Jesus was whether he was God or a divine personality. Many in antiquity did not accept him as such or as having a special relationship with God, but many did. While some have argued that acceptance of Jesus as Messiah was widespread by the end of the first century, the evidence does not support that assumption. By the end of the first century AD, it is estimated that there were somewhere in the neighborhood of one hundred and twenty-five thousand Jews and Gentiles who had accepted Jesus as their Messiah and Savior. Considering that there were some sixty million residents in the greater Mediterranean world by then and between six and seven million Jews, the Christian population was quite small. By the fourth century those numbers had changed considerably, but the Jewish population still far outnumbered the Christians until approximately the seventh or eighth century. Nevertheless, by the early second century the Christian witness had grown considerably and was on its way to becoming a significant religious witness in the ancient world.

Today universities and theological seminaries focus for the most part on what we can know from a historical-critical perspective about Jesus, but less attention is given to the relevance of this for Christian faith. Since faith is an essential ingredient in all of Christianity, does *faith* have a role in this inquiry? Is there a way to bring history and faith perspectives together?

It is widely recognized that the Bible was written by and for believers in God who openly acknowledge God's activity in history. This was and continues to be an important presupposition for both Jewish and Christian faith, but, regardless of how much one is devoted to God or what the Bible has to say, this alone does not make one competent to understand the historical context of early Christianity or the various religious and political groups that are identified in that context. I will assume throughout this study that Christian faith is considerably enhanced by a better understanding of the historical context in which Jesus lived, ministered, and died and in which faith in him emerged. Our knowledge of Jesus' story is also greatly enriched by careful historical research and inquiry.

PART ONE

History and the Historical Jesus

1

History, Historical Inquiry, and the Historical Jesus

||||||||||||||||||||||||||||||||||||||||||||||||||||||

Since the church's beginning, Christianity has anchored its faith in a God who acts in history, especially in remarkable events such as the exodus of the Jews from Egypt and the resurrection of Jesus from the dead.[1] However, since the time of the Enlightenment in the seventeenth and eighteenth centuries, and the consequent development of a new methodology for examining history, this belief has become the focal point of numerous debates. Does God work in phenomenal ways that can be observed, detected, or experienced through sensory perceptions? Does the God of the Bible who acts in history even exist? Did the miracles mentioned in the Bible actually occur, or were they simply the product of a primitive worldview that modern individuals can no longer accept? Again, does God intervene in the natural nexus by raising someone from the dead or in other ways by suspending or contravening the laws of nature? Are all such notions to be attributed to a primitive pre-enlightened age when mythological thinking was commonplace?

It is quite remarkable that many of the studies on the Jesus of history show a lack of awareness of how historians do history and the major assumptions of historical inquiry.[2] For that reason, before we begin a study of

1. Some of the following is a summary and updating of an earlier chapter written on this subject that appeared in Lee Martin McDonald and Stanley E. Porter, *Early Christianity and Its Sacred Literature* (Peabody, MA: Hendrickson, 2000), 1–22.
2. Several recent investigations of the story of Jesus do show some awareness of the notion and practice of history, as well as historical-critical methodology, such as Robert L. Webb, "The Historical Enterprise and Historical Jesus Research," in *Key Events in the Life of the Historical*

the "historical" Jesus, our initial attention will focus on the nature of history and historical inquiry.

The Conflict between History and Faith

Since the Enlightenment, the notion of God's activity in human affairs has been questioned and increasingly doubted. Since then a significant number of scholars have questioned whether miracles occur and whether the remarkable activity and fate of Jesus actually happened. At the same time biblical scholars presented a new methodology for understanding the Bible that raised questions about traditional notions regarding miracles and divine activity in human affairs. New criteria were employed that challenged the biblical worldview of a God who acts in history and in phenomenal ways. The new approach to biblical traditions was troublesome to many Jews and Christians. The goal in applying a new historical methodology to biblical traditions appears to have been to make biblical faith more credible and acceptable to modern society, but this had a significant impact on traditional biblical beliefs.

Church Responses to the Enlightenment

As one can readily imagine, many debates ensued within the church. Some theologians responded by claiming that the results of a historical inquiry that in principle or in practice ignores the activity of God in human affairs cannot be a valid tool of biblical inquiry, nor can the church trust its results. However, many theological scholars, including F. C. Baur, Ernest Rénan, Friedrich Schleiermacher, David Strauss, and others, looked for ways to wed biblical and religious thought to contemporary critical thinking. The results of their inquiry had a mixed and uneasy reception in churches. Some biblical scholars concluded that the biblical picture of divine activity in history was mythological; that is, it came from an earlier and more primitive worldview (German, *Weltanschauung*) that was no longer tenable in the modern age. They wanted

Jesus: A Collaborative Exploration of Context and Coherence (ed. D. L. Bock and R. L. Webb; Wissenschaftliche Untersuchungen zum Neuen Testament 247; Tübingen: Mohr Siebeck, 2009), 9–94. See also the extensive and helpful discussion of the notion and practice of historical inquiry in Michael R. Licona, *The Resurrection of Jesus: A New Historiographical Approach* (Downers Grove, IL: InterVarsity, 2010), 29–198; Gerd Theissen and Annette Merz, *The Historical Jesus: A Comprehensive Guide* (Minneapolis: Fortress, 1998), especially 90–121; Scot McKnight, *Jesus and His Death: Historiography, the Historical Jesus, and Atonement Theory* (Waco: Baylor University Press, 2005), 3–76; and Charles W. Hedrick, *When History and Faith Collide: Studying Jesus* (Peabody, MA: Hendrickson, 1999), especially 1–28.

to anchor Christian faith in a *historical* person, Jesus of Nazareth—not in one who was a miracle worker, who died for the sins of the world, and who was raised from the dead, but rather in one who was a great teacher of ethics and wisdom.

This "liberal" picture of Jesus drew converts within the church, but most Christians continued to reject it. How could Christians account for the transformation of the disciples after the death of Jesus and the birth of the Christian faith using the newly established historical methodology that denied, in principle at least, God's miraculous activity in Jesus, especially his raising Jesus from the dead?

Rudolf Bultmann

In the twentieth century, no New Testament theologian challenged the traditional understanding of Christianity more than the German scholar Rudolf Bultmann. His application of the new strict historical-critical methodology to the biblical writings had the result of denigrating the prominent miracles of God recorded in Scripture. He argued that the true stumbling block of Christian faith was the cross (1 Cor. 1:23) and not its affirmation of the supernatural in history. For him, God acted in a hidden way in the death of Jesus that called his followers to give up all worldly security in order to find security in God alone. He questioned the relevance for modern society of talk about supernatural activity in history and attempted to translate the message of the New Testament into meaningful twentieth-century language. For Bultmann, God acts in "hidden ways" that are not discernible to the scrutiny of historians, but rather to the eyes of faith. The cause-and-effect events of the natural order are not interrupted by supernatural divine activity, but rather God has revealed himself to those who hear his call that comes through the preaching about Jesus who was crucified. A natural historian would have only seen an injustice done to a figure of history, but to those with faith, it was the place where the God who acts in hidden ways supremely acted in history. Bultmann's goal, however well he achieved it, was aimed at identifying the true "stumbling block" of the Christian message and to present it with clarity to his generation. He did not believe that the true stumbling block of Christian faith could be its focus on miracles and the supernatural elements in the church's traditional message, but rather on the message that God calls one to abandon all worldly security and, in radical obedience, surrender to the Christ who comes to us in the preaching of the cross and who reveals authentic Christian living.

Bultmann was without question a historian *par excellence* as well as a philosophical theologian and New Testament scholar. Rarely can anyone be proficient in all three, but Bultmann was; and it is precisely at the point where Christian faith and history intersect that Bultmann brought all three of his interests together to engage modern thinkers in a careful understanding of the Christian message. Whether or not he adequately understood the church's Easter message or handled the New Testament traditions that confess the resurrection of Jesus will be explored later. As a historian, he challenged Christians of his generation to rethink the viability of their confession of God's activity in history and to rethink the kind of history in which God does act. He was especially helpful in clarifying some of the major challenges that the church faces in the growing secular society where Christians live.

For Bultmann, God's hidden acts, as in the case of the assurance of one's salvation that comes through hearing the preached Word of God, often come in the various circumstances of life when God speaks in ways that are hidden to others. Bultmann asked the church to speak honestly when it speaks historically about God's activity. While not denying the activity of God in history, he maintained that such activity is not verifiable through the historian's method of inquiry, nor does it involve a violation of the natural order of events such as we see in the Bible. All such talk, he said, is mythological and grows out of a pre-enlightened view of the world. On the other hand, rather than rejecting the so-called myth in the Bible, that is, the supernatural activity of God in history, Bultmann chose to reinterpret it in terms of human self-understanding. In other words, the belief in the supernatural interventions of God in history was the ancient person's way of concretizing the "otherworldly" activity of God in terms of "this worldly" experiences. Ancient persons encountered the activity of God in their personal experience of life, but they articulated it in mythological terms that were familiar to them. When properly interpreted ("demythologized"), the activity of God could be seen as a new and authentic self-understanding.

He believed that all events of history are open to the historian's craft, and, if there is no empirical historical way to affirm, say, the resurrection of Jesus from the dead, then the church had to find an alternative way to confess its faith in the Christ who comes to us in the proclamation of the gospel. He concluded that the results of historical inquiry are the same for the Christian as for the non-Christian, and maintained that Christian faith can never be tied to the ever-changing results of historical inquiry. For him, the Christ according to the flesh, or the Jesus of historical inquiry, is largely irrelevant for Christian faith (2 Cor. 5:16).

The implications for traditional Christian faith that stem from the application of modern historical methodology to the study of the life of Jesus were of little concern to Bultmann. What the historian does with the traditional or biblical Jesus was of no consequence to him. He could say that he "let it [the traditional picture of Jesus in the Gospels] burn peacefully, for I see that that which burns is all fantasy-pictures of the life-of-Jesus theology, that is, the Christ according to the flesh. But the Christ according to the flesh is irrelevant for us; I do not know and do not care to know the inner secrets of the heart of Jesus."[3] For Bultmann, the manner in which the Easter faith arose in the disciples "has been obscured in the tradition by legend and is not of basic importance."[4] In a highly publicized essay, he stated unequivocally that "an historical fact that involves a resurrection from the dead is utterly inconceivable!"[5] He concluded that the ancient worldview that made room for angels, demons, miracles, and resurrections was outdated and no longer tenable for Christians in the twentieth century, adding that "it is impossible to use the electric light and the wireless [radio] and to avail ourselves of modern medical and surgical discoveries and at the same time to believe in the New Testament world of spirits and miracles."[6] Referring to the similar conclusions of existentialist philosopher Karl Jaspers, Bultmann argued emphatically that "he is as convinced as I am that a corpse cannot come back to life or rise from the grave."[7] For Bultmann, Christian faith in the resurrection meant that "death was not swallowed up into Nothing, but that the same God, who is always coming to us, also comes to us in our death. In this sense, faith in the resurrection is the criterion for whether someone is a Christian or a non-Christian."[8] In terms of Jesus' resurrection, he could only conclude that Jesus was raised in the apostles' faith.

After Bultmann

Although many modern theologians disagree with Bultmann's conclusions, no one can doubt that he raised pivotal questions about our understanding of history that need to be answered *prior* to our investigation of the New Testament. More than any other biblical scholar of the twentieth century, Bultmann has shown that our worldview plays a significant role in the conclusions we draw from an investigation of the New Testament.

Others after Bultmann applied modern historical criticism to the Bible with equally radical consequences. Because of this, it is essential that we focus briefly on modern historical assumptions and how their application to the message

---

3. R. Bultmann, *Essays: Philosophical and Theological* (trans. J. C. G. Greig; London: SCM, 1966), 101.

4. R. Bultmann, *Theology of the New Testament* (trans. K. Grobel; London: SCM, 1951), 1:44.

5. R. Bultmann, "The New Testament and Mythology," in *Kerygma and Myth* (ed. H.-W. Bartsch; trans. R. H. Fuller; New York: Harper & Row, 1961), 1:39.

6. Ibid., 5. See also 13–15.

7. R. Bultmann, "The Case for Demythologizing," in *Kerygma and Myth*, 2:184. See also 1:8.

8. R. Bultmann, "Is Jesus Risen as Goethe?" in *Der Spiegel on the New Testament* (ed. W. Harenberg; trans. J. H. Burtness; London: Macmillan, 1970), 236.

of the New Testament can have an important impact on the results of our investigation. Is modern historical methodology adequate for evaluating or appropriating the fact and significance of God's work in history, especially the biblical testimony about divine intervention in history through the suspension or contravention of the laws of nature?

Before answering this question, we must first decide what history is and how historians operate today, and seek to understand the contemporary philosophies of history including the methodologies used in examinations of the past. These matters need clarification since the assumptions and methodologies historians bring to biblical inquiry largely determine what conclusions they will draw.

History, Science, and Historical Inquiry

In what follows we will briefly consider the commonly accepted principles and assumptions of contemporary historical inquiry and their impact on an understanding of God's activity in the story of Jesus and the foundational events for understanding Christian preaching. I will subsequently ask whether there is an approach to history that is credible and allows for the possibility of a faith in a God who acts in history.

The Meaning and Subject of History

The word "history" (derived from the Greek *historia, historeō*) originally referred to "learned" or "skilled" inquiry or visitation with the purpose of coming to know someone. It came to refer to an account of knowledge about someone or something. Today, the term is largely used in reference to a study of *human* activity in its social environment. Often "history" is used to distinguish reality from myth or legend, that is, whether something really happened.

In universities today, history departments are commonly located in the social science departments, and history is now inseparable from describing past actions of human beings. While nature can be a part of history if it affects human behavior, as in the case of earthquakes, diseases, or tornados, the primary concern of historians is human behavior. Natural events can affect the course of human history, but they are not the primary focus of historians. As R. G. Collingwood has argued, historical explanations are essentially attempts to account for human behavior—namely, things done in the past by human beings.[9] For him, history is "(1) a science, or an answering of questions;

9. R. G. Collingwood, *The Idea of History* (Oxford: Oxford University Press, 1946), 9.

8

(2) concerned with human actions in the past; (3) pursued by interpretation of evidence; and (4) for the sake of human self-knowledge."[10] Walsh limits the historian's field even further by saying that the historian is concerned only with the *past* actions of humankind that are no longer open or available to direct inspection.[11] Natural scientists are interested in "what happens," and this is one of the distinguishing marks between the scientist's subject and that of the historian. Historians are not *primarily* interested in "what happens" or in establishing rules that govern the present and the future.

Historians are not naturally philosophers or "prophets" of history who enjoy the vantage point of surveying the entire historical process to find out what future possibilities might be. They do not naturally interpret current events and what the future will be like based on what they believe has happened in the past.[12] In a strict sense, history is limited to the study of humanity's past, and predictions about the future or even the present do not properly lie within historians' field of inquiry.[13] Karl Jaspers agrees with this and claims that historical science is confined to the past and that "the course of history as a whole knows no necessity. 'It had to come' is not a scientific [historic] sentence."[14] It is largely the memory of past experience that has been preserved in written records and is most logically studied in chronological dimensions. Within chronological developments, one can subdivide history into geographical locations, political developments, cultural contexts, and other areas of human interest.[15]

In the nineteenth century, historical positivists ushered in an important development in historical inquiry, concluding that history was essentially the ascertaining of facts, sifting through them, and *then framing general laws from them*. Collingwood defined "historical positivism" *as a philosophy* acting in the service of natural science whose duties included the ascertaining of facts obtained by sensuous perception. Following historical analysis, laws are framed by the inductive method, and from this a positivistic historiography arises. The

10. Ibid., 10–11.
11. W. H. Walsh, *An Introduction to Philosophy of History* (London: Hutchinson, 1967), 19.
12. P. Gardiner argues this point in *The Nature of Historical Explanation* (London: Oxford University Press, 1968), ix.
13. It is here that A. Toynbee has received his strongest criticism. He begins his ten-volume work *A Study of History* endeavoring to be a historian of preceding civilizations; but he gradually lapses into the role of a prophet of what will take place in subsequent civilizations. See criticisms of Toynbee on this point in Walsh, *Introduction*, 160–64.
14. K. Jaspers, *Philosophical Faith and Revelation* (trans. E. B. Ashton; London: Darton, Longman & Todd, 1967), 186.
15. R. V. Daniels, "History: (1) Methodology," in *Encyclopedia Americana* (New York: Americana Corporation, 1971), 14:226.

rules the positivists used to ascertain these facts are basically twofold: first, there is an analysis of the sources in question to determine earlier and later elements in the material, thereby enabling historians to discriminate between more and less trustworthy portions; and, second, internal criticism is applied to determine how the author's point of view—or distortions—might have affected his or her statement of the facts.[16] In their research, positivists never fully carried out their ambition beyond the ascertaining of facts. Their notion of history and historical research, however, has continued to this day only slightly varied. They defined historical knowledge as the reality of the past, whose reality is found in facts, whose essence is obtained through historical processes. Generally speaking, historians today regularly follow the broad outlines of the positivists and examine the past to understand better humanity's development and present condition *and to understand themselves in their social environment.*

History, from the perspective of the positivists, is also concerned only with events that happen within the space-time continuum. Events in the spiritual realm, whether real or imagined, are not proper subjects for historical inquiry. Historians *as historians* have no tools whereby they can measure such events, and their inquiry is scientific only insofar as it is a form of measurement. Historians assess the evidence for or against a given event and measure the credibility of the surviving evidence whether preserved in stone, parchment, paper, or even items of an archaeological nature as in the case of etchings on a wall, broken potsherds, or other items left behind by humans. Such things do not belong to the intangible sphere of spirit.[17]

But does the historian stop there? According to Gardiner, historians have the obligation to act as interpreters of history and to attempt to describe and assess past events *in light of their present understanding and experience of the laws of nature*, such as the uniformity of nature.[18] Walsh agrees that historians answer questions about the meaning and purpose of historical events along with their description of them, but adds that a historian's value judgments only "slant" history; they do not determine its details.[19] In regard to biblical events, however, this "slanting" often does significantly influence the details that are described related to the event. For instance, the denial of the reality of miraculous events does affect the outcome of a historian's conclusions about the past.

It is this philosophizing aspect of the historian's task that Stephen Neill understands as the cause of many debates among theologians on the subject of biblical history. He is opposed to the use of philosophical assumptions

16. Collingwood, *Idea of History*, 126–30.
17. W. Wand, *Christianity: A Historical Religion?* (London: Hodder & Stoughton, 1971), 23.
18. Gardiner, *Nature*, 70–112.
19. Walsh, *Introduction*, 180–84.

that function as criteria for discerning the reality and interpretation of past events.[20] Neill correctly claims that it is naive to think that historians function without assumptions, and he realizes that this is the place where differences and difficulties arise in biblical interpretation. Historians who are open to the activity of God in history will no doubt interpret the biblical narratives differently than those who in practice ignore divine activity in human affairs. The evidence examined can be the same, but their interpretation and assessment varies because of the assumptions they bring to their inquiry.[21]

After sifting through primary sources and prioritizing them in terms of which ones are more or less reliable, historians draw conclusions about their understanding, plausibility, and consistency.[22] Determining the historical circumstances or context of ancient texts is often accomplished by comparing pieces of information with one another accompanied by other available external evidence on the same topic. Finally, historians offer a synthesis of the data obtained in which they form a reconstruction of how an examined event is believed to have occurred. Not infrequently the available evidence does not allow historians to draw firm conclusions, so at that point historians make informed and careful conjectures that involve their own personality, personal experience, moral values, and historical assumptions. Because they make arguments and statements that can be rationally assessed, they are at their best when they clarify their own historical framework and assumptions about what happens in history as they form their conclusions.

Historians differ in their conclusions not because they have their heads buried in the sand but because of what they bring to their inquiry. Ancient historians, for example, may have wondered whether Jesus himself was raised from the dead, but modern historians question whether anyone was raised from the dead. Can those who think historically and critically today accept any ancient belief in resurrection from the dead? Willi Marxsen, for instance, claims that modern individuals "simply must (in spite of the unequivocal belief of those narrators and early readers [of the Bible]) raise the question of historicity and then answer this question in accordance with *our own* historical judgment and knowledge."[23] Marxsen, having answered in advance the

---

20. S. Neill and N. T. Wright, *The Interpretation of the New Testament 1861–1986* (rev. ed.; Oxford: Oxford University Press, 1988), 301–2.

21. That such disputes are not confined to biblical scholars is well illustrated in the recent work of R. S. Bagnall on the use of papyri in historical understanding. See his *Reading Papyri, Writing Ancient History* (London: Routledge, 1995).

22. See Daniels, "History," 229.

23. W. Marxsen, "The Resurrection of Jesus as a Historical and Theological Problem," in *The Significance of the Message of the Resurrection for Faith in Jesus Christ* (ed. C. F. D. Moule; trans. D. M. Barton and R. A. Wilson; London: SCM, 1968), 16–17.

question of whether any person can be raised from the dead, rejects in advance the resurrection of Jesus as a historical event. Is it therefore reasonable to make a decision about past reported events before investigating them? Harvey says yes, and clarifies his view as follows:

> When dealing with an event so initially improbable as the resurrection of a dead man, the two-thousand-year-old narratives of which are limited to the community dedicated to propagating the belief and admittedly full of "legendary features, contradictions, absurdities, and discrepancies," how could a critical historian argue that since much can be said for it and no convincing evidence against it, it is probably historical?[24]

Léon-Dufour asks, however, whether historians can approach historical evidence objectively for any event if they have already rejected its possibility in advance.[25] This "prior understanding" (German, *Vorverständnis*) is what Gardiner had in mind when speaking about the temptation of the historian to ask the big questions first, and having answered them, then to "deal with the subject along a course set by those answers."[26]

Historians have not yet developed a set of universally accepted criteria for judging the historicity of events, although many operate as if they have. What leads to disagreements among historians is what is at the heart of current debates about the biblical story of Jesus. What we bring with us to our work affects our conclusions. What we bring to our investigation is not found in the sources themselves, but in our own peculiar interests, philosophies, and worldviews. In this sense, there is always a subjective element in historical inquiry. This subjective element, says Walsh, is the limiting factor in any truly *scientific* investigation of the past.[27] All history, he claims, is always written from a particular point of view that includes a certain moral outlook.[28]

Paul Tillich describes the historian's "historic consciousness" as "one cause of the endless differences in historical presentations of the same factual material." He says that because it is impossible to sever historical consciousness from the historian, and because there is no history without factual occurrences, there is no history without the reception and interpretation of factual occurrences by historical consciousness.[29] Tillich argues that all historical documents,

24. Harvey, *Historian*, 109.
25. X. Léon-Dufour, *The Gospels and the Jesus of History* (ed. and trans. J. McHugh; London: Collins, 1968), 254.
26. Gardiner, *Nature*, xi.
27. Walsh, *Introduction*, 169–87.
28. Ibid., 182.
29. P. Tillich, *Systematic Theology* (Digswell Place: James Nisbet, 1968), 3:321–22.

whether legend, chronicle, or scholarly report, are interpreted through one's own philosophical framework, which includes

> the selection of facts according to the criterion of importance, the valuation of causal dependences, the image of personal and communal structures, a theory of motivation in individuals, groups, and masses, a social and political philosophy, and underlying all of this, whether admitted or not, an understanding of the history in unity with the meaning of existence in general.[30]

Walsh reminds us of the difficulty of justifying the moral outlook and judgment of one investigator over another.[31] Assumptions and moral outlook do not alter the sources historians investigate, but conclusions about what the sources mean cannot always be independently verified through a careful examination of them. If historians refuse to accept the moral outlook or worldview of others, they may be unreasonable or naive but not necessarily ignorant of the facts. Worldviews are exceedingly difficult if not impossible to substantiate or support.

The practice of historical inquiry, in a strict sense, is not a science. Natural scientists observe phenomena that under observation *can be repeated* in order to discover certain laws that can be detected about the behavior of all such phenomena in the same given circumstances. Historians, on the other hand, cannot separate themselves from evaluating past events within their own worldview about the laws that govern the universe. They are primarily concerned with describing past events and their relevance for human self-understanding. Jaspers rightly observes that the role of a historian's subjectivity and framework or worldview in the scientific study of history is a limiting factor in modern historical research and the historians' choice of theme, period of investigation, and research. For him, the historian's craft is always something like a work of art on a scientific basis in the sense that the historian must accept the limitations that science imposes on the subject.[32] In other words, the writing of history involves both personal subjectivity and also critical assessment of the limited artifacts of history. This leads to the major assumptions that have been developed and employed in modern historical inquiry.

Assumptions of Modern Historiography

What assumptions do modern historians use in their investigations of the past? Facts do not speak for themselves, but are interpreted in large measure

30. Tillich, *Systematic Theology*, 3:372.
31. Walsh, *Introduction*, 182–85.
32. Jaspers, *Philosophical Faith*, 187.

13

from assumptions drawn from personal experience and perceptions of scientific inquiry. The most common historical assumptions include the following:

1. *Autonomy*. One of the revolutions of thought prompted by the Enlightenment had to do with a division between authority and autonomy. Immanuel Kant saw the Enlightenment as autonomy from authority. It was humanity's release from all authority that gave historians and philosophers freedom to think without direction from another.[33] Reason overthrew the old shackles of religious or state authority. Prior to the Enlightenment, understanding of the past was largely accomplished by means of testimony. Historians knew the past often by accepting or rejecting their sources. Keener rightly observes, however, that ancient historians and philosophers did not automatically believe everything that was reported to them, and at times were quite discriminating in their assessments of ancient historical reports.[34] Nevertheless, the assessment is correct that much of history was written based on the acceptance or rejection of the sources ancient historians examined.

Collingwood has labeled the earlier form of knowledge essentially a "scissors and paste" history.[35] Insofar as one accepts the testimony of an authority and treats it as historical truth, that person, he claims, "obviously forfeits the name of historian; but we have no other name by which to call him."[36] Before the Enlightenment, the function of the historian essentially was that of compiling and synthesizing testimonies of so-called authorities or eyewitnesses. Historians were primarily (though not exclusively) editors and harmonizers of their sources. Examples of this can be seen in Eusebius's *Ecclesiastical History* (early to mid-fourth century AD) and Sozomen's *Ecclesiastical History* (fifth century AD). In both cases it is obvious that their historical assumptions included a belief in God and their acceptance of the miraculous intervention of God in human affairs—assumptions that were also held by the authors of the sources that they used in writing their histories. Collingwood concludes that these kinds of works were useful, but not actually history, since there is little criticism, interpretation, or reliving of past experience in one's own mind in them.[37] Modern historians are not so loyal to their sources that they don't see when their sources failed to do justice to the subject matter. The principle of autonomy is an essential part of the historian's task in relation to biblical interpretation. Harvey explains that "one must, to be sure, listen to

33. See Harvey's *Historian*, 39, for a more detailed explanation of this principle.
34. Craig S. Keener, *Miracles: The Credibility of the New Testament Accounts* (Grand Rapids: Baker Academic, 2011), 1:87–96.
35. Collingwood, *Idea of History*, 282.
36. Ibid., 256.
37. Ibid., 204.

and wrestle with Paul, but . . . one cannot assume that even Paul spoke only in the spirit of Christ, for other spirits also come to expression through him."[38] Although historians cannot function apart from their sources, their sources do not dictate their conclusions. In this sense, autonomy is an accepted principle used by most modern historians and many contemporary biblical scholars.

2. *A Closed Causal Nexus.* Although seldom acknowledged, one of the most commonly accepted assumptions of historical inquiry is that history is a closed continuum of cause-and-effect events. This prevailing perspective on history arose in the Enlightenment era, and nineteenth-century positivists refined it. It is regularly assumed that history is a constant state of immanent interconnections of cause and effect. Each event emerges out of and is understood in relation to the natural historical context in which it appears. Macquarrie says this means that "although there may be distinctive events, and even highly distinctive events, all events are of the same order, and all are explicable in terms of what is immanent in history itself. Thus there can be no divine irruptions or interventions in history."[39] He adds that the result of the application of this principle on the activity of God in history is that God reveals himself, but "his activity is immanent and continuous. It is not the special or sporadic intervention of a transcendent deity."[40] Although an event may qualify and transform the future course of history in significant ways, it never appears within the historical process as an inexplicable bolt from the blue.

This view of history has obvious consequences for traditional notions about the activity of God in history and leads to a denial of the existence of God[41] and supernatural interventions in history. This assumption of a closed universe logically concludes that *all* historical events are of the same order and have natural (intramundane) explanations, even if they cannot immediately be explained. They are an uninterrupted series of events that are continuous with one another, and cannot be explained apart from one another. The net result of the application of this principle to Christianity is that it becomes a relative religion. Macquarrie, following Ernst Troeltsch, said that this path would make Christianity reside "within the sphere of religious and human history as a whole, and no absolute claim can be made for it. The life and work of Jesus Christ himself may be a very distinctive event, but it cannot be absolute or final or of a different order from other historical events."[42]

38. Harvey, *Historian*, 40.
39. J. Macquarrie, *Twentieth-Century Religious Thought* (London: SCM, 1970), 143.
40. Ibid.
41. Gordon D. Kaufman, "On the Meaning of 'Act of God,'" *Harvard Theological Review* 61 (1968):175–201, here 187, draws this conclusion.
42. Macquarrie, *Religious Thought*, 143.

3. *The Principle of Analogy*. Modern historians investigate their subjects on the basis of analogy. Analogy essentially means that historical knowledge relies upon what is known in order to find out what is unknown. It assumes that history is repetitive, constant, and of the same order. What is absolutely unique either does not occur in history or is absolutely unknowable. Historians can discern past events only if they find some connection between them and modern-day events with which they are familiar.[43] Macquarrie claims that in historical analogy we assume all events of the past are analogous to events that we ourselves experience in the present. Historians regularly assume that events that are analogous to their own experience are more likely to be true than those events for which they can find no analogy.[44]

What historians know about the repetition of nature, its constancy, and the general laws within which nature operates helps them understand the scope of history. Therefore, since knowledge can only proceed from the known to the unknown, an event cannot be considered historical in the technical sense if it is without analogy to other events in history. Gardiner acknowledges that historians cannot ignore certain laws that govern the field of historical inquiry.[45] Braaten, however, challenges this principle because it essentially says that history cannot reflect anything new—it can only discover what it already knows, and history therefore has little to say.[46] He contends that history must be open to the unique, but he does not adequately answer how that which is absolutely unique can be knowable. Christian theology has often responded that what is absolutely unique is knowable if it has been revealed to us by God, but that is a difficult concept for a historian *as a historian* to investigate. Christians regularly contend that God has uniquely revealed himself to us through his Son, Jesus Christ (John 10:30–38; 1 John 4:9). The notion of revelation may be the Christian's best defense for the uniqueness of Jesus and of God's activity in raising him from the dead, but historians as historians have no ability to treat or assess uniqueness in the same manner as Christian theologians.

4. *Probability*. It is difficult to find any discussion of the principle of probability among those who investigate the historian's craft, but most historians appear to assume it to be true. This is what Gardiner calls a commonsense explanation.[47] When historians use common sense, they make use of their own experience and contemporary scientific information. There are many stories that we regularly conclude are myth or unfounded legends based on our own

43. Braaten, *History*, 44.
44. Macquarrie, *Religious Thought*, 142.
45. Gardiner, *Nature*, 45.
46. Braaten, *History*, 44–46.
47. Gardiner, *Nature*, 5–23.

experience and knowledge about what is probable. For instance, given what we know about probability, it is unlikely that a cow can jump over the moon, that an ax head can float on the water, or that a dead person who has been buried three days can rise to life. The bedrock of the principle of probability is one's sensory perception, personal experience, and reflection on historical investigations of the past. The implications of this principle for traditional Christian beliefs are obvious. Most of us have not experienced the phenomenal or the so-called unique miraculous activity, or a God who intervenes in natural history the way that we read about such activity in the Bible.

The biblical reports about healing or nature miracles appear implausible since generally they are not a part of modern human experience. Few scholars today doubt that Jesus was a miracle worker in the sense that he was able to perform various kinds of healings for individuals in need, but this has analogy in the history of human experience. There is much more skepticism about nature miracles, such as walking on the water and stilling a storm, or raising a person from the dead. Scholars today who examine healing phenomena often account for them by attributing them to some psychosomatic ability or something that is not completely clear but nevertheless still accountable within the natural sphere of activity and will one day be better understood. As we will see below, remarkable healing stories are quite common in antiquity but also in modern history, and they are generally understood as as-yet-unexplained natural phenomena.

Historical Assumptions and the Acts of God in History

When the above assumptions or principles are applied in biblical inquiry, major consequences emerge, especially in regard to passages that focus on divine intervention in history such as creation, parting the waters of the Red Sea, and resurrections from the dead. If the common assumptions of modern historians are applied to the chief tenets of biblical faith, the consequences are considerable. Biblical assertions about God's unique and supernatural events in history must either be discarded or understood in different ways—such as what they say about human existence. This, of course, affects Christian belief about the activity of God in this world and human affairs. The New Testament makes clear that the stumbling block of the cross was overcome on Easter morning when Jesus was raised from the dead and appeared to his disciples. Such activity is beyond analogy and the historian's experience, and if the above historical assumptions are valid, many Christian beliefs about the activity and fate of Jesus appear invalid. If one accepts common historical assumptions as appropriate guides for interpreting the biblical story of Jesus, the conclusions one draws about Christian faith will be remarkably different from those of modern historians. Did God raise Jesus from the dead or not?

If the subject of history is humanity in its social environment, and if there is no divine intervention in history, then, as Jürgen Moltmann rightly concludes, "on this presupposition the assertion of the raising of Jesus by God is a 'historically' impossible and therefore a 'historically' meaningless statement."[48] The remarkable activity of God in the story of Jesus must be rejected since the biblical writers acknowledge an open continuum wherein God, who is separate from nature, performs redemptive deeds within nature in order to make his will known to humankind.

There are no analogies in the historians' experience to the resurrection of Jesus that enable them to accept as historical such an event. Since historians proceed from the known to the unknown, and since there are no analogies to the resurrection of Jesus, then historians regularly conclude that it did not occur. There are other resurrections mentioned in the Bible, but they are resuscitations in which a person survives death and returns to physical life to die again; for example, Lazarus (John 11:38–44), Paul bringing back to life a child that had died (Acts 20:9–12), or Elisha raising a woman's son to life (2 Kings 4:32–37). Early Christians always viewed Jesus' resurrection as unique (1 Cor. 15:20). If the New Testament writers are correct, God's participation in raising Jesus from the dead has no parallels. Historians, however, have no objective criteria that can enable them to assess unique events. What is without analogy is beyond *historical* inquiry.

There are no known *natural* or *rational* causes in the circumstances surrounding the death of Jesus that could give rise to a resurrection. Jesus was arrested, beaten, crucified, and buried. His disciples abandoned him and fled, and were understandably filled with despair and gloom over the loss of one who they believed was Israel's promised Messiah. In those circumstances, there is nothing in the experience of historians, or in known natural laws, that leads them to conclude that a resurrection would be forthcoming. Indeed, what historians know through experience and natural law leads them to conclude that Jesus' life ended finally, tragically, and completely at the cross.

Finally, it is simply not probable under any known circumstances that dead persons will rise from the grave after three days. Traditional Christianity and even popular modern defenders of the faith often argue that Jesus was not simply just another man, but rather the unique Son of God, so it is improbable that death could contain such a person. Against this line of thinking is historians' inability to establish Jesus' uniqueness through historical methodology.

48. J. Moltmann, *Theology of Hope* (trans. J. W. Leitch; London: SCM, 1969), 174.

There are no known categories of thought available to them that enable them to affirm faith statements about Jesus as "Lord," "Christ," "Son of Man," or "Son of God." Interestingly, New Testament writers do not conclude that Jesus was raised from the dead because he was unique or had a special relation with God; rather, his uniqueness and special relationship with God are seen in his resurrection from the dead (e.g., Acts 2:32–36; Rom. 1:3–4; Phil. 2:5–11)! The contemporary apologetic arguments for the resurrection of Jesus based on his uniqueness, while clever, are not rooted in the New Testament message.

Modern historical assumptions present a significant challenge to biblical perspectives. Jürgen Moltmann agrees as he concludes: "In face of the positivistic and mechanistic definition of the nature of history as a self-contained system of cause and effect, the assertion of a raising of Jesus by God appears as a myth concerning a supernatural incursion which is contradicted by all our experience of the world."[49] When viewed from the perspective of modern historical assumptions, miraculous events are regularly classified as myth or legend, but not reality.

Contemporary theologians must determine whether there are limitations in modern historical methodology and whether there are real events of the past that are simply not discernible through this methodology. Those who confess that Jesus has been raised from the dead, the quintessential affirmation of the Christian faith, must wrestle with the complexity of the relationship between history and faith. The Gospel writers, and indeed all New Testament writers, were interested in the story of Jesus, in what he did or said, and they also acknowledged that Jesus cannot be understood apart from the Easter faith that they proclaimed. The resurrection of Jesus is the presupposition for Jesus becoming the object of Christian preaching.[50] Long ago, George Ladd aptly addressed the problem:

> The critical historian, as historian, cannot talk about God and his acts in the Incarnation, the Resurrection, and the Parousia; for although such events occur within the history of our world, they have to do not merely with the history of men, but with God in history; and for the historian as historian, the subject matter of history . . . is man. Therefore the historical-critical method has self-imposed limitations which render it incompetent to interpret redemptive history.[51]

The New Testament writers affirm God's activity in history and supremely in his activity in the story of Jesus' life and fate. There is a theological as well as historical way to understand and appropriate that activity today, and

49. Moltmann, *Theology of Hope*, 177.
50. W. Marxsen, *Anfangsprobleme der Christologie* (Kassel: Gutersloher Verlaghaus, 1960), 51.
51. G. E. Ladd, "The Problem of History in Contemporary New Testament Interpretation," in *Studia Evangelica* (ed. F. L. Cross; Berlin: Akademie, 1968), 5:99.

I will return to this topic at the end of this volume, but for now, we will ask about ways that biblical scholarship in modern times describes the distinction between "the historical Jesus" and "the Christ of faith."[52]

Historical Inquiry and the "Historical Jesus"

Is the "historical Jesus" of historical-critical scholarship opposed to the Christ of the church's faith? To some extent, the answer is yes! There is no historical means by which we can acknowledge the church's affirmation of Jesus as Lord or that he died for the sins of the whole world. On the other hand, the historical Jesus—that is, the Jesus that historians can reconstruct from historical sources based on their critical assumptions—likely never existed. The various pictures of the historical Jesus in contemporary research cannot adequately account for the origins of the Christian faith and the emergence of the early church. Scot McKnight is quite right when he concludes that "any method designed to help us 'find Jesus' has to be more than some scientific criterion. I think this because human intention, which is what historical Jesus studies are really all about, cannot be reduced to a science."[53] Some other dimension besides scientific historical inquiry is also needed. Historical investigations of the Gospels and other literature of antiquity have often had many positive results that enable moderns to understand more clearly the dimensions of the Christian faith that were preached and handed on in the church, and even more about Jesus than was previously known, but is that alone enough to lead one to accept the church's confessions about Jesus? There is much about the context of early Christianity that remains unclear when viewed only through the eyes of faith, and those who labor in historical research often clarify the historical context of early Christianity and do the church a great favor. However, there are still limitations in what the historian can recover.

The scholarly distinction between the Jesus of history and the Christ of faith, as we will see below, continues to be an important issue for Christian faith today.[54] Is the Jesus of historical-critical research the object of the church's faith? Of course not! That figure is more often than not the product of fanciful and

---

52. A recent and valuable contribution to an examination of the notion and practice of history and the problems that it poses for Christian faith is Webb's "Historical Enterprise," in Bock and Webb, *Key Events*, 9–94. He also offers a recent collection of sources that describe the scope of historical inquiry and historical-critical methodology.

53. McKnight, *Jesus and His Death*, 44. His discussion of the criteria that are used for determining the authentic sayings and deeds of Jesus on pp. 42–46 is convincing and germane to our discussion.

54. This topic is discussed at length in the amazingly comprehensive (3,330 pages) new set of volumes on the historical Jesus by Tom Holmén and Stanley E. Porter, eds., *Handbook for the Study of the Historical Jesus* (4 vols.; Leiden: Brill, 2012).

wishful thinking by scholars who have rejected the biblical Jesus in favor of one that best fits their own historical bias. Craig Evans has written a very telling volume that challenges many of these so-called historical portrayals of Jesus of Nazareth and their handling of the ancient sources, especially the Gospels.[55] Is the Christ of the church's confession a mythological fictional figure? Is he simply a charismatic Jewish wisdom teacher who lived in Palestine some two thousand years ago and attracted a large following as a result of his teaching, preaching, miraculous healings, exorcisms, and other deeds, who told of God's impending judgment and kingdom, and claimed to have a special relationship with God, but died tragically after a short period of ministry? Historians are challenged in deciding which portrait of Jesus to accept based on their own awareness of the past, experience of nature, scientific knowledge, and inquiry into the ancient sources that tell his story, but the church does have an answer.

Faith in Jesus as the Christ is faith in a historical phenomenon in the sense that Christian faith is centered in God's activity in a historical person who lived and died in Palestine in the first century. Because of this, Christians cannot avoid having a serious interest in historical questions. Their concern with history is an important strength of Christian faith, but faith in a God who acts in history also exposes Christianity to the risks and uncertainty of historical-critical research. Christianity cannot exist as a community of people who affirm timeless truths and have a disconnection from whatever happened or happens in history. Christian faith is directly related to historical events—namely, to a person who lived, ministered, and died in historical circumstances that are often as clear to the historian as to the believer. Historical inquiry can often sharpen our focus on the life of Jesus of Nazareth, which is relevant for Christian faith, but the self-imposed limitations of that approach are regularly at odds with the claims and beliefs of Christians. Faith, however, realizes that appropriation of God's activity in Jesus cannot be found in the historical-critical dimension, but through faith alone. This will become more obvious in our next section.

Quests for the "Historical Jesus"

Before focusing on the sources for the study of the story of Jesus and the primary aspects of his life, I will say something about the history and background of this "life of Jesus research" that has developed into an industry all its own.

---

55. See Craig A. Evans, *Fabricating Jesus: How Modern Scholars Distort the Gospels* (Downers Grove, IL: InterVarsity, 2006). See also Philip Jenkins, *Hidden Gospels: How the Search for Jesus Lost Its Way* (Oxford: Oxford University Press, 2003), where he makes similar comments about some of the strange ways the message of and about Jesus has been distorted in modern biblical scholarship.

Scholars regularly write and talk past one another when they discuss the story of Jesus, and it is here especially, as we saw above, where history and faith collide. Although laypersons in churches are often unaware of this field of research and the inbuilt conflicts connected with it, historical Jesus studies (or "life of Jesus research," or *Leben Jesu Forschung*) nevertheless play a significant role in most centers of academic theological study today. Examinations of Jesus' life and ministry from a modern (often positivistic) *historical* perspective are regularly at odds with traditional Christian perspectives, that is, the so-called "Christ of faith" of the church's confession. Given the historical assumptions discussed above, how can one be historically credible without diminishing the value of the Christ who is experienced through faith? To answer that question, we need to understand what has been going on in life of Jesus research, including its strengths and limitations. As we have noted above, some events in Jesus' life are not *historically* credible—that is, some are reported in the Gospels that do not match the experience of critical historians and are loaded with theological implications. This does not mean that they did not happen, but that they are beyond the scope of *historical* inquiry.

So, what are scholars talking about when they focus on the "historical Jesus"? Some scholars have concluded that the Jesus of the church's confession is "unreal"—a product of legend and mythology—and they look for other ways to account for the story of Jesus in the Bible. The "real" Jesus for them is a human being who lived and died in antiquity, without all of the ecclesiological accretions added to him over the centuries that made him the object of the church's worship and confessions. According to them, the real Jesus did not walk on water, did not believe that he was the Messiah, and certainly was not resurrected. Who then was this "historical Jesus"?[56] I will respond to that shortly, but I should not get too far ahead of the story. The answer will become clearer as we survey briefly the widely recognized four phases of scholarly quests to discover the identity of the Jesus of history.

The First Quest for the Historical Jesus

The term "historical Jesus" became common parlance among biblical scholars following Albert Schweitzer's now-famous book *The Quest for the Historical Jesus*,[57] in which he described the results of the various historical

56. A good discussion of the problem is in C. Stephen Evans, *The Historical Christ and the Jesus of Faith: The Incarnational Narrative as History* (Oxford: Clarendon Press, 1996), 1–46 and 170–202.

57. The English title of the translated 1906 German edition was *The Quest for the Historical Jesus: A Critical Study of Its Progress from Reimarus to Wrede* (New York: Macmillan, 1910); it was republished as *The Quest for the Historical Jesus* (ed. John Bowden; London: SCM, 2000).

attempts from the mid-eighteenth century to the early part of the twentieth century to discover who Jesus was, what he said, and what he did from a historical-critical perspective. These so-called empirical approaches to the story of Jesus, later labeled a "quest," reflected the positivistic understanding of history that developed out of the Enlightenment. In the early twentieth century, Albert Schweitzer described these attempts to recover the historical Jesus, as he "actually was," as a dead-end street that did not capture the essence of Jesus. Schweitzer effectively ended the first quest for the "historical Jesus" when he observed that those who wrote lives of Jesus were in effect writing their own stories rather than the story of Jesus.

Hermann Samuel Reimarus (1695–1768) is commonly identified as the founder of the first historical quest, even though it was actually begun earlier by the English Deists, who denied divine intervention in human and worldly affairs after creation was complete. Reimarus was one of the most influential early contributors to this quest, but because he rightly feared the reaction to the publication of his conclusions that denied the supernatural origins of Christian faith and relativized the Christ of the church's confession, his findings were not published until after his death by his student and friend, the German philosopher Gotthold Lessing (1729–1781).[58] Reimarus's emphasis on a portrayal of Jesus that was influenced by modern historical methodologies that denied in principle the supernatural intervention of God in history strongly affected the later work of David Friedrich Strauss (1808–1874), who advanced Reimarus's earlier positions. Strauss called for an investigation of the life of Jesus that assumed that the Gospels were filled with myth and could no longer be trusted as accurate reflections of what Jesus said, what he did, and who he was.[59] Another important and similar voice in early historical Jesus research was Joseph Ernest Rénan (1823–1892) whose *Life of Jesus*, like that of Strauss, created no small stir among traditional Christian theologians and church leaders by drawing similar conclusions.[60]

Besides these highly influential scholars, others also pursued the ever-elusive historical Jesus, especially F. C. Baur (1792–1860), Heinrich Julius Holtzmann

---

The German title was *Von Reimarus zu Wrede: Eine Geschichte des Leben-Jesu-Forschung* (Tübingen: Mohr, 1906).

58. H. S. Reimarus, *Reimarus: Fragments* (trans. R. S. Fraser; Philadelphia: Fortress, 1970). This work originally appeared as *Von dem Zwecke Jesu und seiner Jünger: Noch ein Fragment des Wolfenbüttelschen Ungenannten; Fragment 7* (ed. G. E. Lessing; Braunschweig: n.p., 1778).

59. D. F. Strauss, *The Life of Jesus Critically Examined* (trans. G. Eliot; 3 vols.; London: Chapman, 1835; repr., Philadelphia: Fortress, 1972). The German title was *Das Leben Jesu kritsch bearbeitet* (2 vols.; Tübingen: Osiander, 1835, 1836).

60. E. Rénan, *The Life of Jesus* (trans. C. E. Wilbour; London: Trübner, 1864). The original title was *La Vie de Jésus* (Paris: Michel Lévy Frères, 1863).

(1832–1910), Johannes Weiss (1863–1914), William Wrede (1859–1906), Martin Kähler (1835–1912), Adolf von Harnack (1851–1930), and, finally, Schweitzer himself (1875–1965).[61] It has been estimated that some one hundred thousand lives of Jesus were written during the eighteenth, nineteenth, and early twentieth centuries, sixty thousand of which were published in the nineteenth century alone.[62]

Most of these "lives of Jesus" were written from a historical perspective that was opposed to the church's belief in the uniqueness of Jesus and was closed to the notion of the intervention of God into human affairs. The biblical narratives about Jesus' actions were seen as myth and consequently dismissed. These scholars found ways to explain away or deny the miracles of the Bible, especially the activity of God in creation, the exodus, and the resurrection of Jesus from the dead. Their biggest challenge was to explain how the Jesus they constructed gave rise to the transformation of the disciples, the conversions of James and the apostle Paul, and the emergence of the early church. Who would have crucified their Jesus and why? Their underlying assumption was that the Jesus "of history" was a more reliable foundation for the church's faith than the traditional Christ of the church's confession. The alternative to the historical Jesus, for these writers, became the "Christ of faith," as Martin Kähler called him[63]—in other words, the Jesus of the church's confession, who the early disciples believed had performed miracles, who had a unique relationship with God, who was crucified for the sins of the world, who was raised from the dead, and who will come again to usher in the kingdom of God.

Kähler's compelling work influenced subsequent historical Jesus studies by effectively calling into question the limitations of the newly formed historical-critical methodology and its negative assumptions that were applied to the study of the life of Jesus. He denied the distinction between the historical Jesus and the Christ of faith, arguing that the former, or the real Jesus, was known only through the proclaimed Christ who is presented in the church's proclamation. Unfortunately, Kähler's work was not translated into English until 1964, and it had little effect on English studies before its translation. For Kähler, the primary sources for this Jesus were the canonical Gospels, and he rejected the notion that Christian faith was dependent upon the ever-changing results of negative historical inquiry.

61. For a bibliography of early historical Jesus research, see C. A. Evans, *Life of Jesus Research: An Annotated Bibliography* (NTTS 13; Leiden: Brill, 1989).

62. These figures come from Hugh A. Anderson, *Jesus* (Englewood Cliffs, NJ: Prentice-Hall, 1967), 16.

63. Martin Kähler, *The So-Called Historical Jesus and the Historic, Biblical Christ* (trans. C. E. Braaten; Philadelphia: Fortress, 1964). The original title was *Der sogenannte historische Jesus und der geschichtliche, biblische Christus* (Leipzig: Deichert, 1892).

The eighteenth-, nineteenth-, and early-twentieth-century scholars who sought to identify the historical Jesus introduced modern historical and philosophical assumptions about history into their research. Their influence was enormous and significantly affected the emergence of what later was called "liberal theology." For example, Friedrich Schleiermacher (1768–1834) argued that faith's foundation could no longer be located in the church's dogma, or in a tenuous historical foundation, but rather in the realm of feeling and experience.[64] Scholars today appear more aware of their historical assumptions than were those in the eighteenth and nineteenth centuries. Many then believed that they were writing purely objective history without philosophical assumptions. The common assumption then was that if one could somehow reconstruct the historical Jesus separated from all of the actions attributed to him by those of pre-enlightened faith (miracles, resurrection from the dead, divine titles, and other "mythological" elements added by the early church), then it would be possible to recover the essence of Jesus, and that this "historical" Jesus would somehow have positive significance for the church. These scholars believed that church dogma throughout history tended to obscure the Jesus of antiquity and present mostly the Christ of the church's faith. They tried to understand Jesus apart from the miracle stories in the Gospels and the accounts of his resurrection from the dead, and looked for explanations of how he came to be confessed as Lord by the church. Their Jesus was essentially viewed as a religious sage who gave new ethical teaching to his followers (e.g., the Sermon on the Mount).

The problem with this enterprise, again, was how to account for the large following of Jesus and why anyone would want to crucify him. In order to explain this, Schweitzer suggested that central to the life and teachings of Jesus was a radical, apocalyptic eschatology; namely, that Jesus fully expected the imminent advent of the kingdom of God. Schweitzer stated that Jesus was simply wrong at this point and concluded that the kingdom did not come as Jesus had hoped and proclaimed. For him, it was impossible to understand Jesus apart from this perspective. Subsequent studies of Jesus sought to minimize the role of apocalyptic eschatology in Jesus' thinking and claimed instead that for Jesus the kingdom of God had manifested itself in his ministry ("realized eschatology") without reference to a future coming kingdom. Even today, some scholars continue to deny the importance of this apocalyptic eschatological perspective[65] in Jesus.

---

64. See A. C. Thiselton's discussion of Schleiermacher in his *New Horizons in Hermeneutics* (Grand Rapids: Zondervan, 1992), 204–36.

65. This view held that the end of the ages was soon to come with a violent overthrow of this world's kingdoms by God and his messiah. The righteous would then be blessed, and the wicked would be judged by God.

Although Jesus certainly taught that in some sense the kingdom of God had been realized in his ministry (Matt. 12:28; Luke 4:18–29; 11:20), still the fullness of that kingdom for Jesus was yet to come (Matt. 6:10; Mark 9:1; 14:25). Many scholars today recognize the tension in Jesus' teaching between the "already" and the "not yet" of the kingdom of God, but most acknowledge that the notion of a coming kingdom of God that would bring judgment and blessing was also an important part of Jesus' teaching. John the Baptist was clearly an apocalyptic thinker who focused on preparation for the coming kingdom of God, and most scholars recognize that Jesus' ministry was begun in conjunction as well as in sympathy with John's ministry and teaching and had a similar focus on preparation for a coming kingdom of God (see Mark 1:14–15). If the most influential person in Jesus' formative ministry, John the Baptist, was an apocalyptic thinker, and Jesus' earliest followers also adopted this perspective (and no one seems to deny this), it is at least plausible that Jesus also held that same perspective. No one doubts that Jesus also believed that in some sense the coming kingdom had also been realized in his ministry. It is less plausible that Jesus' followers misunderstood him at this point than that he was a Jew who was highly influenced by the apocalyptic thought current in his day.

The "No Quest" for the Historical Jesus

As a result of the work of Schweitzer and that of Rudolf Bultmann, the importance of the quest for the historical Jesus, especially in terms of biographies of Jesus, was significantly minimized and essentially abandoned for several decades by many leading Continental scholars following Bultmann. But were there other scholars who wrote about Jesus during and following Bultmann? Yes, of course, but liberal scholarship largely did not write definitive biographies on the life of Jesus at that time, though many substantial studies on Jesus did emerge, including Joachim Jeremias's well-known *Parables of Jesus* (German, *Die Gleichnisse Jesu*, 1947) and his *Eucharistic Words of Jesus* (German, *Die Abendmahlsworte Jesu*, 1949), as well as the substantial work of the notable and still-read T. W. Manson (*The Sayings of Jesus*, 1949) and C. H. Dodd (*The Parables of the Kingdom*, 1961). When James M. Robinson wrote his *New Quest for the Historical Jesus* (1959), this so-called "new quest" was essentially a continuation of the quest that other scholars had been carrying on without interruption before, during, and after the Bultmann era. But because Bultmann was such a dominant New Testament scholar in the twentieth century, his perspective significantly affected other scholars and his disinterest in the historical Jesus led others to speak of a "no quest" period. Dale Allison, a leading historical Jesus scholar, is quite correct, however, when he argues that historical Jesus scholarship did not cease during or after the Bultmann era, despite the fact that the majority of Jesus scholars today continue to refer to a "no quest" period.[66] The most important scholars who championed this so-called "no quest" position included Karl Ludwig Schmidt, Martin Dibelius, Bultmann, and Friedrich Gogarten—scholars who flourished between the 1920s and the 1950s and also developed a form-critical analysis of the Gospels. They concluded that the pursuit of the historical Jesus would not be profitable since the object of the church's faith was never the Jesus of history, but rather the Christ of faith. Bultmann, for example, contended that the *fact* of Jesus (his "thatness") was the presupposition for Christian faith, but he disregarded the importance of the historical details of Jesus' ministry and life.[67] Shelter from the radical conclusions of the earlier historians was found in the Christ of the church's proclamation. For Bultmann, God is always subject, and never the object of Christian theological inquiry. Consequently, any information gleaned by critical historical inquiry was largely irrelevant for Christian faith. Bultmann was strongly influenced by Martin Kähler, and agreed with him that Christian faith cannot depend upon the ever-changing uncertainties of historical research. He went further than Kähler, however, and maintained that any historical information about Jesus other than his "thatness" was irrelevant for Christian faith. Although Bultmann and others did not call the Jesus of the church's faith the "unhistorical Jesus," Jesus in essence became an unhistorical figure and was identified as the mythical Jesus (or Christ of faith) of the early church's faith and hopes. Bultmann rightly rejected the idea that the "Jesus of history" (the historian's Jesus) was the object of the church's hope, but he did not conclude that the "real Jesus" was the Jesus of the church's proclamation. For him, this Jesus (Christ) was a mythological figure who needed to be "demythologized," that is, reinterpreted in appropriate modern existential categories that could be grasped by the current generation. For Bultmann, the activity of God comes in the preaching of the cross and the risen Christ. Easter faith, he claimed, was the disciples' interpretation of the significance of the cross that was disclosed to them by

66. Dale C. Allison, *Resurrecting Jesus: The Earliest Tradition and Its Interpreters* (New York: T&T Clark, 2005), 4–9.

67. The classic statement is the opening line of Bultmann's *Theology of the New Testament*, 1:3 (italics added): "*The message of Jesus* is a presupposition for the theology of the New Testament rather than a part of that theology itself." See also his *Jesus and the Word* (New York: Scribner, 1934, 1958); *Jesus* (German; Tübingen: J. C. B. Mohr, 1926); and *Jesus Christ and Mythology* (German, 1958; English, 1960; repr., London: SCM, 2012).

God. The identity of Jesus in Bultmann's work is vague, and his "Christ" appears to be little more than a cipher or symbol that (not "who"), like in Karl Jaspers' thought, initiates faith.

The "New Quest," or Second Quest, for the Historical Jesus

The attempt to transfer interest from history to theology that was characteristic of Bultmann's approach, and indeed the interest in distinguishing early Christianity from Jesus himself, was one of the results, if not the aim, of the form-critical approach that had largely abandoned the original quest for the historical Jesus. But not all of Bultmann's students were as skeptical as he was about the value of historical inquiry for Christian faith or what could be known historically about the Jesus of history. In particular Ernst Käsemann,[68] along with Günther Bornkamm, Ernst Fuchs, and James M. Robinson, held that if historical information about Jesus was obtainable, it could not be irrelevant for Christian faith. Most scholars agreed that Christianity made historical claims about events that reportedly took place in history, and that they are inextricably connected with a person who lived and died in Palestine in the first century. Several of Bultmann's students believed that considerably more historical data about Jesus than his "thatness" is knowable, and they began the so-called "new quest" for the historical Jesus, which lasted roughly from the 1950s to the 1970s.

Several criteria in this new or "second" quest were employed to discover and identify historical aspects of Jesus' life. Central to this new quest was the criterion of dissimilarity; namely, that the stories that were more likely to be true about Jesus were those that isolated him from those elements that were common to Judaism of that day or those that were common in early Christianity that advanced the early church's agenda. In other words, this criterion aimed at eliminating early Jewish influences on Jesus as well as Christian beliefs about him, assuming that they were later additions, and arguing that the real Jesus was the one "stripped of dogmatic accretion."[69]

According to Dunn, this liberal quest wanted to portray Jesus "as a teacher of timeless morality" who was a "good example," as "the first Christian [rather] than the Christ."[70] This goal was perhaps best articulated earlier by Norman Perrin, who concluded, "Liberal scholarship . . . accepted the

---

68. In 1953 Ernst Käsemann delivered a lecture contradicting his teacher, Bultmann. The essay is published in English as "The Problem of the Historical Jesus," in his *Essays on New Testament Themes* (trans. W. J. Montague; SBT 41; Naperville, IL: Allenson, 1964), 15–47.

69. See James D. G. Dunn, *Jesus Remembered* (Grand Rapids: Eerdmans, 2003), 38–39.

70. Ibid., 39.

full burden of historical-critical scholarship without hesitation and without reserve, believing that the historical core of the gospel narratives, when reached, would reveal Jesus as he actually was, and that he would then be revealed as worthy of honor, respect and imitation, revealed as the founder of a faith which consisted in following him and his teaching closely and purposefully."[71]

There does not appear to have been the slightest thought in this second quest that the Jesus of history himself may have initiated the christological formulations that were circulating about him in the early church. In other words, these historical Jesus scholars refused to accept that the church's views about Jesus may have come from Jesus himself! Those confessions were all deemed to be late additions to his story and could therefore be dismissed.

Another important criterion that followed from dissimilarity was "coherence," that is, other data about Jesus in the ancient traditions that cohered with the criterion of dissimilarity was also likely to be authentic. That criterion was followed by "multiple attestation"; namely, material attested in multiple ancient sources is likely to be authentic. The Gospel of John, because of its openly high Christology, was generally excluded from any consideration as a reliable witness to the historical Jesus. We will assess these and other criteria below.

In this second quest, the emphasis on the differences between the historical Jesus and the Christ of the emerging church continued. These scholars, unlike their form-critical predecessors, recognized that although the material of the Gospels did not clearly disclose the life situation (*Sitz im Leben*) of those who transmitted the Gospels, nevertheless their quest showed that the Gospel traditions had been selected and modified to fit the interests of Jesus' later followers. To the credit of some of those scholars, how could it have been otherwise? The story of Jesus was relevant not only to the needs of the community that first received it and to the communities of faith that passed it on, but they recognized that the evangelists (now regularly called redactors or editors) geared their message to meeting those varying needs by what they selected and edited or redacted. This new or "second" quest seemed more interested in the connection between *kerygma*, or Christian proclamation, and history, since biblical faith at least was in Jesus of Nazareth, a historical figure. The value of the historical information obtained by these "second questers" using the criteria noted above is contested within the scholarly community today.

71. Norman Perrin, *Rediscovering the Teaching of Jesus* (London: SCM, 1967), 214.

The "Third Quest" for the Historical Jesus

In the 1980s, several scholars who were not satisfied with the results of the first and second quests began to look again at the historical sources to see if they could establish even more facts about Jesus that historians could reasonably accept and that would be helpful in clarifying the historical identity of Jesus. Although many scholars saw this as a "third quest,"[72] others saw it as simply a continuation of the second quest, but with many more participants coming from a wider diversity of backgrounds. Some scholars in this "third quest" have drawn generally negative conclusions about the most significant events advanced in the Gospels (the miracles especially), but others have perhaps argued for more than is knowable through the historical methodologies they employ. To some extent, both groups of scholars in this so-called third quest have shown a tendency to ignore what their contemporary opponents say about Jesus. Many of these recent studies continue to receive considerable attention in the popular media,[73] especially in the now annual discussions of Jesus that take place in various televised programs before Christmas and Easter. It often appears that the more radical the conclusions drawn, the more attention is given by the news media.

The so-called third-quest scholars, who are often negative toward the traditional and confessional portraits of Jesus in the canonical literature, include Morton Smith, John Dominic Crossan, Burton Mack, Marcus Borg, and Bart Ehrman. Several of these scholars have been associated with the well-known Jesus Seminar organized by Robert Funk. Borg prefers to make a distinction between the pre-Easter Jesus (= the historical Jesus) and the post-Easter Jesus (= the Christ of the church's faith). He does not deny the reality of the latter, even though he rejects the uniqueness of Jesus and interprets his ministry and teaching as he does other religious persons throughout history. Borg challenges the authenticity of many of the traditional affirmations about Jesus' person and activity and about 80 percent of the sayings attributed to him in the canonical Gospels.[74] Several of the scholars within this group have focused more on the short, pithy sayings of Jesus (aphorisms and apothegms) pretty much in isolation from their historical contexts. Richard Horsley has rightly been critical of this way of viewing Jesus through isolated,

---

72. See Neill and Wright, *Interpretation of the New Testament*, 379.

73. See, for example, D. van Biema, "The Gospel Truth?" *Time*, April 8, 1996, 52–59; K. L. Woodward, "Rethinking the Resurrection," *Newsweek*, April 8, 1996, 60–70; J. L. Sheler, M. Tharp, and J. J. Seider, "In Search of Jesus," *U.S. News and World Report*, April 8, 1996, 46–53.

74. M. Borg, *Meeting Jesus Again for the First Time: The Historical Jesus and the Heart of Contemporary Faith* (San Francisco: HarperCollins, 1994), 15–16, 20–24; *Jesus in Contemporary Scholarship* (Valley Forge, PA: Trinity Press, 1994), 160–79.

pithy statements and labels this process of identifying the historical Jesus as forced and focused on self-absorption, characteristic of those obsessing over the individual and viewing Jesus outside of his concrete historical and literary contexts. He calls this process of inquiry "narrow, distorting, and indefensible in terms of historical inquiry." He adds that "sayings do not mean anything in isolation from a context. Nothing much is communicated in isolated aphorisms. Jesus cannot possibly be understood except as embedded in both the movement he catalyzed and the broader context of Roman imperial Palestine."[75]

More typical of this so-called "third quest" is the renewed focus on Jesus as a Jew within the first-century Jewish Palestinian milieu. Two scholars who have provided valuable studies that interpret Jesus' life and ministry from a historical perspective within the context of first-century Judaism are Geza Vermes and E. P. Sanders.[76] Vermes has been credited with initiating this third quest with his *Jesus the Jew* in 1973. If there is one significant difference between current life of Jesus studies and those of previous generations, it is the emphasis on interpreting Jesus within the context of Judaism.[77] A problem emerged, however, because some studies assumed that the rabbinic Jewish traditions of the second to the sixth centuries AD reflected the practices of Judaism in the time of Jesus. This later focus on rabbinic Judaism tended to examine Jewish history anachronistically, that is, positing that what was true of Judaism of the second century (after the destruction of the temple in AD 70 and the Bar Kochba rebellion in AD 132–135) was also

75. Richard A. Horsley, "The Dead Sea Scrolls and the Historical Jesus," in *The Scrolls and Christian Origins* (vol. 3 of *The Bible and the Dead Sea Scrolls*; ed. James H. Charlesworth; Waco: Baylor University Press, 2006), 38.

76. Geza Vermes, *Jesus the Jew: A Historian's Reading of the Gospels* (Philadelphia: Fortress, 1973), and *The Religion of Jesus the Jew* (Minneapolis: Augsburg Fortress, 1993); E. P. Sanders, *Jesus and Judaism* (Philadelphia: Fortress, 1985), and *The Historical Figure of Jesus* (New York: Penguin, 1993). See also Donald Hagner's important study of Jewish attempts to see Jesus within a first-century Jewish context in his *The Jewish Reclamation of Jesus: An Analysis and Critique of the Modern Jewish Study of Jesus* (Grand Rapids: Zondervan, 1984). He also shows how contemporary Jews often ignore the Jesus of early Christianity (14, 38). This can also be said of other contemporary historical Jesus studies. More recently, and interestingly, Daniel Boyarin, in *The Jewish Gospels: The Story of the Jewish Christ* (New York: New Press, 2012), assesses the New Testament Gospels and Jesus himself as well as his teachings as being best understood within the Palestinian Jewish context in the time of Jesus. He even concludes that early Christian views that Jesus is the divine Messiah are no more than an expression of widely held *Jewish* views about the identity of the coming messiah.

77. See, for instance, J. H. Charlesworth, ed., *Jesus' Jewishness: Exploring the Place of Jesus in Early Judaism* (The American Interfaith Institute; New York: Crossroad, 1991) for a collection of interfaith essays that explore this question.

true of Judaism before those events. More recently, scholars have focused on the "Judaisms" of the first century that were contemporary with Jesus. For example, there has been considerable focus on the Judaism reflected in the Qumran community that produced the Dead Sea Scrolls and that of Philo of Alexandria, and to some extent the work of the Jewish historian Josephus as well.

Discussion of Jesus from a historical-critical perspective that also respects the faith dimensions of New Testament literature and the Jewish context in which Jesus lived includes the work of John P. Meier, James H. Charlesworth, Bruce Chilton, James D. G. Dunn, Craig A. Evans, Craig Keener, Ben Witherington III, and N. T. Wright, as well as Raymond E. Brown, Ben F. Meyer, and A. E. Harvey.[78] These scholars do not ignore historical investigation, but generally agree that the basis for the church's faith cannot be established by it. Luke Timothy Johnson, in an important evaluation of the conclusions about Jesus drawn by those in the now famed Jesus Seminar, summarizes the positions of the "minimalists" (only a minimal amount of historical data can be known about Jesus from the Gospels) and questions their negativity.[79] He exposes and vigorously challenges some of the Jesus Seminar's commonly held perspectives, including their (1) favoring several noncanonical texts over the canonical Gospels as primary sources for knowing who Jesus was; (2) ignoring the rest of the canonical writings (especially Acts of the Apostles and the writings of Paul) as important sources; (3) emphasizing the social aspects of Jesus' ministry rather than his religious interests; (4) rejecting the most important "theological" confessions of the traditional church; and (5) whether implied or explicitly stated, claiming that *historical* knowledge is normative for faith and theology. Johnson emphasizes the lack of self-criticism among some of these scholars and an uncritical preference for the noncanonical writings over the canonical Gospels in their reconstruction of Jesus.[80]

---

78. From a different perspective, the rabbinic scholar Jacob Neusner evaluates Smith's, Crossan's, and Meier's work on the historical Jesus with important conclusions about the whole enterprise of trying to understand the biblical Jesus from a historian's perspective. See his chapter, "Who Needs 'the Historical Jesus'?," in his *Rabbinic Literature and the New Testament: What We Cannot Show, We Do Not Know* (Valley Forge, PA: Trinity Press, 1994), 169–84.

79. Luke Timothy Johnson, *The Real Jesus: The Misguided Quest for the Historical Jesus and the Truth of the Traditional Gospels* (San Francisco: HarperCollins, 1996), esp. 20–27, 54–56. For similar arguments about the weaknesses of the criteria and historical approaches of those in the Jesus Seminar, see also Craig A. Evans, *Fabricating Jesus*, 34–51.

80. For a similar challenge of the weakness of the Jesus Seminar approach, see also the perceptive works of Evans, *Fabricating Jesus*, and Ben Witherington III, *The Jesus Quest: The Third Search for the Jew of Nazareth* (Downers Grove, IL: InterVarsity, 1997).

Meier similarly rejects what he believes are negative and unwarranted conclusions of the Jesus Seminar and contends, with Johnson, that there is much that is historical (or true) about Jesus in the Gospels and in the rest of early Christian literature, and that this material cannot be irrelevant for Christian faith.[81] Both insist, however, that faith in the Christ of the church's proclamation does not depend upon what one can or cannot know about Jesus through the means of modern historical research.

The most important issues that emerge in this "third quest" concern Jesus' relationship with the Judaism of his day, his self-conscious identity and sense of mission, the factors that led to his death, and those that gave rise to the emergence of the early church.[82] Noting the controversy and lack of agreement among scholars on these and other items, John Dominic Crossan raises the question of the propriety of much that has been termed *historical* investigation of the life of Jesus. In a telling comment that has often been repeated among scholars, he writes:

> Historical Jesus research is becoming something of a scholarly bad joke. There were always historians who said it could not be done because of historical problems. There were always theologians who said it should not be done because of theological problems. And there were always scholars who said the former when they meant the latter.[83]

Crossan further cites Daniel Harrington's seven emerging images of the so-called historical Jesus that reflect Jesus' Jewish background; namely, that Jesus is either a political revolutionary, a magician, a Galilean charismatic, a Galilean rabbi, a Hillelite (or proto-Pharisee), an Essene, or an eschatological prophet. Crossan admits that all of these pictures of Jesus are not compatible with solid historical evidence, and acknowledges that there apparently can be as many pictures of Jesus as there are exegetes who interpret him against his background. He concludes that this "stunning diversity is an academic embarrassment" and that "it is impossible to avoid the suspicion that historical Jesus research is a very safe place to do theology and call it history, to do autobiography and call it biography."[84] His comments, though now dated, are nonetheless still relevant in this conversation. Crossan concludes that Jesus

81. See J. P. Meier, "Reflections on Jesus-of-History Research Today," in Charlesworth, *Jesus' Jewishness*, 84–107.

82. N. T. Wright, *Who Was Jesus?* (Grand Rapids: Eerdmans, 1992), 17–18, has a helpful discussion of these issues. See also his "Quest for the Historical Jesus," *ABD* 3:796–802.

83. John Dominic Crossan, *The Historical Jesus: The Life of a Mediterranean Jewish Peasant* (San Francisco: HarperSanFrancisco, 1991), xxvii.

84. Ibid.

was essentially a Jewish peasant Cynic philosopher, but Crossan himself has contributed to the strange state of affairs in Jesus research by insisting on the priority of several noncanonical sources over those in the New Testament canon to create his image of Jesus. He chooses noncanonical material that most in the academic community have considered secondary at best and, in all probability, spurious. He disregards the reliability of most of the New Testament writings, and especially ignores the contributions of Paul and Acts as sources for the study of the historical Jesus. He also proposes that behind the second-century apocryphal *Gospel of Peter* lies a *Cross Gospel* that he thinks was written sometime in the middle of the first century, and that this *Cross Gospel* is the source of the passion narrative in all four canonical Gospels. Meier argues conversely that the *Gospel of Peter*, along with Crossan's *Cross Gospel*, are later sources that undoubtedly depend upon the canonical Gospels, rather than the other way around. Crossan generally values the apocryphal *Gospel of Thomas*, the Egerton papyrus (P.Egerton 2), the *Gospel of Peter*, and Morton Smith's allegedly discovered *Secret Gospel of Mark* over the canonical Gospels, but all of these noncanonical sources have dubious support, and most likely depend on the canonical Gospels. According to Meier, there is nothing in these materials that can serve as a legitimate source in the quest for the historical Jesus.[85]

Jacob Neusner, a prominent rabbinic scholar, seems puzzled that so many scholars in the Christian community prefer a historical approach to their Christian faith and on purely historical grounds not only make claims about who Jesus was, but also conclude who he was not. He asks:

> Why [do some Jesus scholars] insist that there is a kind of knowledge about Jesus that not only conforms to the kind of knowledge we have about George Washington but also distinguishes between the epiphenomena of piety and the hard facts of faith? "Who he really was" also means "who he really was not." I cannot point to another religion besides Christianity that has entertained in the intellectual centers of the faith a systematic exercise in learning commencing with unfaith; certainly not Islam, as Salman Rushdie's awful fate has shown, and certainly not Judaism, where the issues of theological learning—Talmud study and scripture study, for example—do not confuse secular history with the pattern of religious truth or ask Moses to submit to the mordant wit of Voltaire.[86]

---

85. J. P. Meier, *A Marginal Jew: Rethinking the Historical Jesus* (ABRL; Garden City, NY: Doubleday, 1991), 1:114–39, offers a careful analysis of these apocryphal texts and concludes that those who use these sources to reconstruct the historical Jesus, namely Crossan, Koester, and Robinson, "are simply on the wrong track" (123).

86. See J. Neusner, *Rabbinic Literature and the New Testament* (Valley Forge, PA: Trinity Press, 1994), 171; see also his much longer argument on pp. 171–78.

As I launch our study of some of the significant events in the story of Jesus following the two chapters on the primary sources for this study, I am under no illusion that what we can reasonably determine from a historian's perspective is *essential* for Christian faith, but I do agree that it has considerable value, even if it is not yet clear what the full value of the *historical* investigations of the origins of Christian faith might be. Christianity is a historical religion in the sense that Christians believe that God has acted in human history, and because of this historical inquiry cannot be irrelevant to Christian faith, even if that faith is not and cannot be completely dependent upon the ever-changing conclusions of historical inquiry. Nevertheless, there is a growing tendency among historical Jesus scholars to say quite freely that they believe we can know a good deal about the Jesus of history. Sanders, for instance, concludes that "the dominant view today seems to be that we can know pretty well what Jesus was out to accomplish, that we can know a lot about what he said, and that those two things make sense within the world of first-century Judaism."[87]

In this book, I am unashamedly starting with the premise that God has acted in Jesus in a unique manner unparalleled in human history and that, in him, something remarkable has been accomplished for all humanity. I also affirm that what we can know about Jesus is considerable, and I offer the following chart that reflects five perspectives that show considerable overlap in a number of areas. Later, in the conclusion of this volume, I will offer another list that I think is also a reasonable though not exhaustive list of things that a careful historian may also affirm.[88] Before considering the sources for examining the story of Jesus, it is important to list the widely credible facts established about Jesus through historical inquiry and also to focus briefly on the criteria that are most commonly used today in historical-Jesus research.

---

87. See Sanders, *Jesus and Judaism*, 2.

88. A very helpful discussion of the history of modern historical Jesus research is in Gerd Theissen and Annette Merz, *The Historical Jesus: A Comprehensive Guide* (Minneapolis: Fortress, 1998), 2–16. They have five phases in their survey beginning first with Reimarus and Strauss, then the old liberal quest of the nineteenth and early twentieth century, followed by the "no quest" or collapse of the quest for almost fifty years due to the influence of Bultmann and Karl Barth. The fourth phase is the "new quest" that begins in the 1950s with Ernst Käsemann and other Bultmann students, which is followed by the final phase, the so-called "third phase." I acknowledge below their helpful discussions of the various essential events and teachings of Jesus. Another helpful discussion of the various phases of the quest for the historical Jesus is Maurice Casey's *Jesus of Nazareth: An Independent Historian's Account of His Life and Teaching* (New York: T&T Clark, 2010), 1–99. He suggests more historical credibility for the Jesus traditions in the Synoptic Gospels than do many with a more skeptical bent.

Table 1.1

Scholarly Lists of Credible Facts about Jesus

E. P. Sanders[a]	J. H. Charlesworth[b]	Luke Timothy Johnson[c]	Funk & Jesus Seminar[d]	N. T. Wright[e]
1. Jesus was born ca. 4 BC, at the approximate time of the death of Herod the Great.	1. Jesus was a Jew.	1. Jesus was a human person (Paul, Hebrews).*	1. Jesus of Nazareth once existed.	1. Jesus spoke Aramaic, Hebrew, and probably Greek.
2. He grew up in Nazareth of Galilee.	2. His earliest followers had historical interest in him.	2. Jesus was a Jew (Paul, Hebrews).*	2. He began as a disciple of John the Baptist.	2. He summoned people to repent.
3. Jesus was baptized by John the Baptist.	3. His mission and teachings are Jewish.	3. Jesus was of the tribe of Judah (Hebrews).	3. He left John and launched his career as an itinerant sage.	3. He made use of parables to announce the kingdom of God.
4. He was a Galilean who preached and healed.	4. Jesus can be studied in light of the early church and the Judaism of his day.	4. Jesus was a descendant of David (Paul).	4. Jesus was an itinerant teacher in Galilee.	4. He accomplished remarkable cures, including exorcisms, as demonstrations of the truth of his proclamation of the kingdom.
5. He called twelve disciples.	5. Jesus led a renewal movement.	5. Jesus' mission was to the Jews (Paul).*	5. Jesus proclaimed the kingdom of God (God's imperial rule) in parables and short, pithy sayings.	5. Jesus shared in table fellowship with a socially and religiously diverse group, including those whom many Torah-observant Jews would regard as "sinners."
6. Jesus taught in small villages and towns, avoiding larger cities.	6. Jesus' attack against money changers was a major factor leading to his arrest and crucifixion.	6. Jesus was a teacher (Paul, James).*	6. He attracted a large following in Galilee and surrounding regions.	
7. Jesus confined his activity to Israel.	7. His disciples, except Judas, came from Galilee, and his mission is interpreted in light of views of messiah current there.	7. Jesus was tested (Hebrews).*	7. He was a charismatic healer and exorcist (cured some sick people and drove out what were thought to be demons).	

(continued on next page)

E. P. Sanders[a]	J. H. Charlesworth[b]	Luke Timothy Johnson[c]	Funk & Jesus Seminar[d]	N. T. Wright[e]
8. Jesus ate a final meal with his disciples.	8. Jesus was a devout Jew concerned with keeping the law.	8. Jesus prayed using the word *Abba* (Paul).	8. He was put to death by the Romans ca. 30 CE.	
9. Jesus engaged in a controversy about the temple.	9. Jesus was aware of noncanonical writings.	9. Jesus prayed for deliverance from death (Hebrews).		
10. Jesus was arrested and interrogated by Jewish authorities, apparently by orders of the High Priest.	10. He only quoted from *some* Hebrew Bible books.	10. Jesus suffered (Paul, Hebrews, 1 Peter).		
11. Jesus' disciples abandoned him after his arrest.	11. He was influenced by apocalyptic and eschatological thought.	11. Jesus interpreted his last meal with reference to his death (Paul [by implication in Tacitus and Josephus]).		
12. Jesus was crucified outside Jerusalem by the Roman authorities.	12. Jesus' parables are Jewish with parallels in later rabbinic writings.	12. Jesus underwent a trial (Paul).*		
13. His disciples said they "saw" him after his death.	13. His notions of purification are in keeping with later rabbinic traditions and in the *Temple Scroll* at Qumran, not like wealthy aristocrats in Jerusalem.	13. Jesus appeared before Pontius Pilate (Paul).*		
14. This led the disciples to believe Jesus would return and found a kingdom.	14. Sociology, anthropology, and branches of psychology have valid roles in interpreting Jesus.	14. Jesus' end involved some Jews (Paul).*		
15. After his death Jesus' followers continued as an identifiable movement.	15. Jesus was unusual because he claimed power and authority.	15. Jesus was crucified (Paul, Hebrews, 1 Peter).*		

(continued on next page)

E. P. Sanders[a]	J. H. Charlesworth[b]	Luke Timothy Johnson[c]	Funk & Jesus Seminar[d]	N. T. Wright[e]
16. Some Jews persecuted parts of the new movement (Gal. 1:13, 22; Phil. 3:6).	16. He thought of himself in terms of current messianic and eschatological perspectives.	16. Jesus was buried (Paul).		
17. This endured at least to a time near the end of Paul's career (2 Cor. 11:24; Gal. 5:11; 6:12; cf. Matt. 23:34; 10:17).	17. He performed many healing miracles.	17. Jesus appeared to witnesses after his death (Paul).		
	18. He began his ministry with John the Baptist and couched his message in similar eschatological terms.			
	19. Jesus clashed with popular religious groups in Palestine (Pharisees, Sadducees, Zealots, Essenes).			
	20. Jesus could be offensive in his dealings with and responses to individuals.			

a. Sanders, *Jesus and Judaism*, 11; *Historical Figure of Jesus*, 10–11.

b. J. H. Charlesworth, "Jesus Research Expands with Chaotic Creativity," in *Images of Jesus Today* (Valley Forge, PA: Trinity Press, 1994), 5–15.

c. Johnson, *Real Jesus*, 121–22. Facts marked by an asterisk (*) are also attested in noncanonical sources.

d. Robert Funk and the Jesus Seminar, *The Acts of Jesus: What Did Jesus Really Do?* (San Francisco: HarperSanFrancisco, 1998), 171. There is a more extensive summary of this on pp. 527–34.

e. These are in N. T. Wright, *Jesus and the Victory of God* (Christian Origins and the Question of God 2; Minneapolis: Fortress, 1996). They are also summarized in M. A. Powell, *Jesus as a Figure in History* (Louisville: Westminster John Knox, 1998), 154–55. Wright also accepts as historical most if not all items in the other lists here.

Criteria of Authenticity

Most New Testament scholars today agree that it is necessary to assess each ancient source about Jesus of Nazareth, including each act or teaching attributed to him, in order to determine its authenticity and connection with the historical Jesus. However, the same scholars do not agree on what criteria to use in order to establish or deny authenticity. It is generally recognized that the writers of the Gospels, although they were not unprejudiced scholars of history, nevertheless were significantly interested in the truthfulness of the stories that they reported. They were not dishonest persons.

On the other hand, most New Testament scholars recognize the relevance of much of what is in the Gospels to the early churches. Some scholars contend that whatever in the Jesus story was relevant to the early churches was later invented and placed on the lips or in the life of Jesus. The events of Jesus' life and ministry were obviously important to the early Christians, and those events became the earliest canon or authoritative base for Christian preaching, teaching, and behavior in the first-century churches as well as in the second century. For example, Paul cites the words of Jesus as support for his comments about relationships between husbands and wives (1 Cor. 7:10) and distinguishes his own words from those of Jesus in a manner that shows that Jesus' words were clearly more authoritative (1 Cor. 7:12; 11:23). In the book of Acts, Paul cites the words of Jesus to support his comments to the Ephesian elders (Acts 20:35). Not only were the things that Jesus said important to the early Christians; it was also significant to them that Jesus could raise the dead, heal lepers, make a blind person see, and deal with everyday circumstances of life such as paying taxes. When the churches faced challenges at a later time, this information was especially encouraging to them.

"Seven Pillars of Scholarly Wisdom"

There are a number of perspectives about the Gospels that some contemporary biblical scholars have accepted that question the authenticity of many traditional positions. Funk and Hoover have called them the "Seven Pillars of Scholarly Wisdom" and identify them as the following: (1) there is a distinction between the historical Jesus and the Christ of faith in the church's confession; (2) the Synoptic Gospels are closer to the historical Jesus than the Gospel of John, which focuses on a "spiritual" Jesus; (3) the Gospel of Mark was written before Matthew and Luke and used by them in their stories of Jesus; (4) both Matthew and Luke also depend on a source commonly called "Q" (from the German, *Quelle* = "source"); (5) the so-called eschatological Jesus, who focused on the coming kingdom of God and quickly approaching end of this age, is to be rejected in favor of a "non-eschatological Jesus," who spoke in aphorisms (short, pithy sayings) and parables about the presentness of God's rule; (6) there is a distinction between the oral culture in which Jesus lived and spoke in "short, provocative, memorable, oft repeated phrases, sentences, and stories" and the later written and longer tradition; and, finally, (7) the burden of proof for authenticity is on the scholar since the biblical narratives are embellished by mythic elements derived from the church's faith in Jesus.[89] Funk and Hoover are aware of the criticism that scholars often create a Jesus in their own image, so they adopted the cautionary dictum, "beware of finding a Jesus entirely congenial to you."[90] Many scholars reject several of the above "Seven Pillars," especially items 1, 5, 6, and 7, and advances have been made when these "pillars" have been questioned. However, I agree with Funk and Hoover that there is a tendency among scholars to produce a Jesus who is remarkably congenial to them.

The task of determining the authenticity of a reported event or teaching in the Gospels is a difficult process because scholars do not yet agree on the criteria by which decisions can be made. What are the most commonly accepted criteria by which one can determine the authenticity of Jesus traditions? Wherein does the burden of proof lie when determining the authenticity of a story?

Dissimilarity, Coherence, and Multiple Attestation

As mentioned above, biblical scholars have used several well-known criteria to establish authentic Jesus traditions. I will simply list here the three best-known criteria and then assess their strengths and weaknesses. (1) The *principle of dissimilarity* (or discontinuity) claims that those traditions that are neither an expression of Jewish piety or beliefs, nor an expression of early Christian piety or beliefs, are more likely authentic. (2) The *principle of coherence* states that a tradition is more likely to be authentic if it coheres with the hard-core facts about Jesus already established through the application of the principle of dissimilarity. (3) The *principle of multiple attestation* contends that a tradition found in several ancient sources is more likely to be authentic. In the last case, McArthur argues that when three (or four) Gospel writers agree on a tradition, the burden of proof lies with those who deny that tradition's authenticity. He admits, however, that this does not necessarily establish or negate a tradition.[91] More recently, some scholars have employed

89. R. W. Funk and R. W. Hoover, *The Five Gospels: The Search for the Authentic Words of Jesus* (New York: Macmillan, 1993), 2–4.

90. Ibid., 5, and Crossan, *Historical Jesus*, xxvii, cited above, and the consequent scholarly embarrassment (xxviii).

91. H. K. McArthur, "The Burden of Proof in Historical Jesus Research," *ExpTim* 82 (1971): 119. See also his "Basic Issues: A Survey of Recent Gospel Research," in *In Search of the Historical Jesus* (ed. H. K. McArthur; New York: Scribner, 1969), 139–44, and his "Introduction" to the same volume, pp. 3–20. For a more recent discussion of these and other criteria, see C. A. Evans,

noncanonical sources such as the *Gospel of Thomas*, the Egerton papyrus (P.Egerton 2), and other sources to establish authenticity.[92]

None of these criteria can finally determine authenticity, but if a tradition is attested by several strands (multiple attestation), the burden of proof rests with those who deny its historicity.[93] A strong attestation, for example, would be a combination of Mark, Q, and John.

Problems with Dissimilarity

Many of the third-quest scholars have rejected the criterion of dissimilarity because it isolates Jesus from his environment and dismisses the early church's interest in knowing what Jesus was actually like. This criterion does establish a unique Jesus who is isolated from his Jewish context and unremembered in the Christian community that acknowledged him as Lord and founder of their community of faith. However, it cannot have much value since it prefers a *unique* Jesus instead of the *typical* Jesus who lived in Palestine and presumably learned from his Jewish environment.[94] Gerd Theissen and Dagmar Winter offer an alternative criterion that makes far more sense to the current and emerging generation of Jesus scholarship and turns dissimilarity on its head. They contend that a more "plausible" tradition about Jesus is one that understands him within the context of Judaism *and* within the teachings that the early church remembered about him. Theissen and Winter assert that the criterion of dissimilarity has significant problems associated with it, and argue instead that the most informed and plausible picture of Jesus comes from assessing him both within his Jewish context and how he was remembered in early Christianity.[95]

"Authenticity Criteria in the Life of Jesus Research," *CSR* 19 (1989): 6–31; and his *Fabricating Jesus*, 46–51, and their application in 137–57. These and other criteria are discussed in detail in Meier's *Marginal Jew*, 1:167–95; and in Dunn, *Jesus Remembered*, 81–92, and McKnight, *Jesus and His Death*, 42–46.

92. On the nature and use of these noncanonical sources, see J. H. Charlesworth and C. A. Evans, "Jesus in the Agrapha and Apocryphal Gospels," in *Studying the Historical Jesus: Evaluations of the State of Current Research* (ed. B. Chilton and C. A. Evans; Leiden: Brill, 1994), 479–533.

93. These and other criteria are presented in G. Theissen and D. Winter, *Quest for the Plausible Jesus: The Question of Criteria* (trans. M. E. Boring; Louisville: Westminster John Knox, 2002). They argue contextual plausibility and the plausibility of effects in the early church.

94. It is interesting that the noted Jewish scholar Daniel Boyarin argues persuasively that the teaching of Jesus and the New Testament perspective of an anticipated messiah were all Jewish perspectives in the first century. See his *The Jewish Gospels: The Story of the Jewish Christ* (New York: New Press, 2012).

95. Theissen and Winter, *Quest for the Plausible Jesus*; see especially their critique of the criterion of dissimilarity on 19–23, but also 27–76. Their defense of the criterion of plausibility is discussed at length and in a compelling fashion on 172–225. I am in full agreement with this

Since Jesus was a first-century Jew, one would expect that his teachings would reflect his Jewish heritage, and this is indeed the case. The Lord's Prayer (Matt. 6:9–13), for example, is a typical Jewish prayer. Characteristically Jewish is also Jesus' teaching that all of the law hangs on loving God with all one's heart and soul and mind and one's neighbor as oneself (Matt. 22:37–40).[96]

Jesus was acknowledged as the founder and Lord of the early church. Without him, there would be no church! It follows, therefore, that Jesus' actions and teachings were remembered in the early churches and provided for them an authoritative base for Christian preaching and teaching. It is reasonable to assume that the early followers of Jesus would have preserved authentic traditions about him.[97]

The Criterion of Embarrassment

Another criterion frequently employed by the third-quest scholars is the criterion of embarrassment. This criterion posits that the early church would not have included embarrassing material in its sacred traditions unless it was authentic. It is not likely that a religious movement that confessed Jesus' sinlessness would have invented the stories about his baptism by John the Baptist (Mark 1:9–11; Matt. 3:13–17; Luke 3:21–22), since John's baptism was one of repentance. This is not the kind of story that followers of Jesus would have invented—rather, they would have tried to explain it, as we see in Matthew 3:14–17, or not reported it at

---

revised assessment of the criteria for authenticity. The criterion of dissimilarity is also discussed and challenged by S. E. Porter, in *The Criteria for Authenticity in Historical Jesus Research: Previous Discussion and New Proposals* (JSNTSup 191; Sheffield: Sheffield Academic Press, 2000). He has updated this work in his "Reading the Gospels and the Quest for the Historical Jesus," in *Reading the Gospels Today* (ed. S. E. Porter; McMaster New Testament Studies; Grand Rapids: Eerdmans, 2004), 27–55.

96. Helpful summary discussions of the well-known criteria used in establishing the "authentic Jesus" are Dunn, *Jesus Remembered*, 78–85; John P. Meier, "Criteria: How Do We Decide What Comes from Jesus?," in *The Historical Jesus in Recent Research* (ed. James D. G. Dunn and Scot McKnight; Winona Lake, IN: Eisenbraun's, 2005), 123–44; Theissen and Merz, *Historical Jesus*, 115–21; and McKnight, *Jesus and His Death*, 42–46.

97. N. T. Wright discusses the criterion of dissimilarity and its opposite, which he calls "double similarity," in *Jesus and the Victory of God*, 131–33. What this means is that if something that Jesus did or said is clearly in the Jewish tradition from which he emerges and is likewise reported in early Christianity, then it is likely to be genuine. This, of course, is similar to the criterion of plausibility set forth by Theissen and Winter. This is also similar to multiple attestation. John P. Meier has rightly criticized the criterion of dissimilarity precisely because it isolates Jesus both from his cultural milieu and from those who followed him. It only gives us a picture of the unique Jesus, but not the typical Jesus. See his discussion of this in *Marginal Jew*, 1:167–75. He argues that the principles of embarrassment (see the following section), multiple attestation, and coherence have legitimacy and place the burden of proof on those who deny the authenticity of the report or claim in the Gospels. Like many others, he has considerable disagreement with those who overemphasize dissimilarity.

all, as in the case of John 1:24–34. Similarly, stories about the early church leaders (Jesus' disciples, the Twelve) forsaking Jesus and running away when Jesus was arrested (Mark 14:50 and parallels) would hardly have been invented by a later church community. Along with that, why would the early churches invent a story about the earliest leader of the church denying he knew Jesus during the time of his trial (Mark 14:66–72 and parallels)? The same could be said about Jesus' cry on the cross (Matt. 27:46; Mark 15:34), which is not found in Luke or John. It is also highly unlikely that Jesus' rejection by the Roman and Jewish authorities resulting in his death would be passed along if it were not authentic.[98] The unflattering story of Jesus' disciples James and John coming to him in an almost childish manner, seeking places of prominence in his kingdom (Mark 10:35–45), cannot have been a later invention of followers of Jesus seeking to advance their image in Jewish or even non-Jewish communities. Jesus' family seeking to restrain him because it was reported that he might be deranged is another example of an unflattering story (Mark 3:21, see vv. 31–34) that the church would not have invented since it is a kind of story that needs considerable explanation. Such stories in the earliest traditions about Jesus surely support the historical reliability of the Gospel reports. There is nothing in such stories about Jesus or his disciples that would make it advantageous for the church to circulate them unless they accurately reflected what happened. There are other criteria that have been set forth, but they have not received the same acceptance or publicity as those mentioned above.[99]

Evaluating the Criteria

Dunn is not convinced that the criteria of authenticity are that reliable and says that they fail to offer an accurate reflection of the Jesus who lived and ministered in Palestine in the first century. He is more impressed by the

98. S. E. Porter has discussed these criteria in considerable detail in his *Criteria for Authenticity*, 28–123.

99. Meier lists other secondary or dubious criteria that he says cannot be relied upon to establish authenticity, but that some scholars in the past have employed to determine the authenticity of Jesus traditions. These include emphasizing (1) Aramaic (a tradition found with traces of Aramaic grammar, style, and vocabulary, as opposed to Greek), (2) Palestinian environment (sayings and deeds of Jesus that reflect the Palestinian environment), (3) vividness of narration (events and sayings that supply concrete details that are not germane to the event or saying itself), (4) tendencies of the developing Synoptic tradition (an attempt to plot tendencies in Matthew and Luke), and (5) historical presumption (the burden of proof is with those who deny that the leaders of the church would mislead the early Christians by reporting things that did not happen in the life of Jesus). Meier, *Marginal Jew*, 1:177–83. Both Evans and Meier have applied many of these primary and even secondary criteria to the miracle stories of Jesus, and both conclude that the miracle tradition, however it was to be accounted for, was an actual part of the ministry of Jesus. See C. A. Evans, "Life-of-Jesus Research and the Eclipse of Mythology," *TS* 54 (1993): 3–36, and Meier, *Marginal Jew*, 2:617–31.

expanded focus of the third-quest scholars, which includes a broader historical context for understanding Jesus. He is also impressed with the considerable attention that has been given to the relevance of the Dead Sea Scrolls, especially how they have "broken open the idea of a monolithic, monochrome Judaism, particularly as set over against the distinctiveness of newly emerging Christianity."[100] Dunn acknowledges the value of examining the rabbinic traditions in the second to the sixth centuries since they occasionally reflect historic Jewish positions from the first century. He also finds the apocryphal and pseudepigraphal literature from the time before and during the New Testament era useful in clarifying the context of Jesus and early Christianity and helping interpret the New Testament writings themselves. Dunn also appreciates N. T. Wright's criterion of "double similarity,"[101] which says a tradition is given added credibility if it can be seen within first-century Judaism and as a starting point of something in later Christianity.[102] This, of course, is similar to Theissen and Winter's criterion of plausibilit,y noted above.[103]

I am inclined to accept multiple attestation, coherence, embarrassment, and plausibility as important criteria for investigating the historical Jesus. I also agree that the broader context is more fruitful in discerning the authentic Jesus, and it includes not only the Greco-Roman and Jewish contexts, but the Dead Sea Scrolls literature as well as the so-called apocryphal and pseudepigraphal writings. I acknowledge that I am predisposed to accept the canonical Gospels as our earliest and most reliable reports about Jesus, despite their several differences. They all have an authentic core of Jesus' teachings and activities, including a reliable report about his fate. They are plausible and offer the earliest interpretations of the story of Jesus, clarifying why the early Christians spoke of him as Son of God, Son of Man, Lord, and Messiah. Their interpretation of Jesus is rooted in the earliest known stories about him in both history and faith.

---

100. Dunn, *Jesus Remembered*, 89, and see his discussion and evaluation of the criteria employed in the second and third quests in 78–92.

101. Ibid., 91. See also 91n132.

102. Wright, *Jesus and the Victory of God*, 132. Wright also challenges the criterion of double dissimilarity (Jesus cannot be like his Jewish context or what the early Christians remembered of him), much like Theissen and Metz's criterion of plausibility (see above) does, and contends that the authentic Jesus is also "decisively *similar* to both the Jewish context and the early Christian world" (italics his), and at the same time importantly *dissimilar*—in the sense that we must look earlier and not to the later Christian texts that clearly modified or expanded the Jesus tradition.

103. In Chris Keith and Anthony Le Donne, eds., *Jesus, Criteria, and the Demise of Authenticity* (London: T&T Clark, 2012), several well-known New Testament scholars challenge the traditional criteria used to establish the authentic Jesus of history. Their perspectives are well known from their previous work, but this volume signals a possible significant shift in the direction of future historical Jesus studies that is much in line with the various criteria discussed here.

Faith and Evidence

Of course, historians as historians will never be able to affirm the christological affirmations or interpretations about Jesus in the church's earliest documents, but it is important that Christians know their faith in Jesus is not contrary to the available evidence from antiquity. The church's teachings about Jesus have never been only about what historians can affirm or accept about him. Those who have experienced faith in Jesus as Lord generally have fewer problems acknowledging the message of the New Testament about him. This experience often is a distinguishing factor among biblical scholars today, though it is almost never discussed. Luke Timothy Johnson is one of the few biblical scholars to undertake a study of religious experience in the New Testament and its value for understanding the message of the New Testament about Jesus.[104] That experience, I suggest, enables one to be more open to the activity of God *in history*. We cannot expect historians who adopt the usual historical assumptions discussed above to draw the same conclusions, but we can learn much from them. There is much to be gleaned from a historical-critical approach to the story of Jesus, but there is still much more beyond that! I freely acknowledge that this additional element has affected my own approach to the story of Jesus. The story about Jesus has been passed on in the churches from the beginning of the church by those of faith and for the faithful, and much can be gleaned from the biblical traditions within that perspective. It does not follow that such persons were or are also dishonest in what they wrote or that they significantly distorted the message about Jesus. I will address this matter more in the last chapter.

In our pursuit of the Jesus of history, or historical reality about him, we cannot easily dispose of using common sense, or fail to recognize some of the many challenging places where the Gospels appear to be at odds with each other. Careful historical inquiry brings a greater capacity for understanding the Jesus of the New Testament. The Jesus of history, as scholars have reconstructed him, never existed, and the *real* Jesus cannot be fully known by employing criteria that ignore the activity of God in his earthly journey.

---

104. Luke Timothy Johnson, *Religious Experience in Earliest Christianity* (Minneapolis: Fortress, 1998). He focuses on the living Jesus who comes to us through faith and contends that this Jesus is significantly more important than the dead Jesus of the various historical quests. See also his *The Creed: What Christians Believe and Why It Matters* (New York: Doubleday, 2003), 1–65; and *Living Jesus: Learning the Heart of the Gospel* (San Francisco: HarperOne, 2000). This matter is also helpfully addressed by Brevard Childs in "On Reclaiming the Bible for Christian Theology," in *Reclaiming the Bible for the Church* (ed. Carl E. Braaten and Robert W. Jenson; Edinburgh: T&T Clark, 1995), 1–17. He rightly underscores the importance of interpreting the Bible in the context of faith (9–11 and 16–17).

PART TWO

Sources for Studying the Historical Jesus

2

The Gospels

Their Relationships and Reliability

‖‖‖

Most New Testament scholars agree that the canonical Gospels are the most important sources we have for investigating the story of Jesus. The Gospels are not unbiased or neutral reports, but they offer a sufficiently reliable portrait of Jesus along with an interpretation of who he was. The Gospel writers present Jesus as the pivotal personality in all of history and, along with the Jewish Scriptures, the central authority in the lives of those who followed him. Their stories about him purposefully invite their readers to faith and confidence in him, and in this sense the authors of the Gospels present an inextricable mixture of history and faith. Some of their stories about Jesus' activities and teachings can be reasonably argued as historically reliable, but the interpretations of Jesus' activities and teachings often speak in categories of divine activity. In other words, history and faith are not always distinguished in the Gospels. The thought never occurred to the writers of these stories, whom we call "evangelists," to keep history and faith separate. What they said about Jesus they also believed was true, but they go beyond what is typical in an ancient biography or history. For them Jesus was not only involved in human history, but also a divine figure who transcends history and is the Lord of humanity. It is clear that the evangelists' theological concerns were central to the message they told, but they also present many features about Jesus that many historical scholars today believe are credible.

49

Approaching History and Faith in the Gospels

Historians regularly distinguish between history and interpretation, but the evangelists did not. For them, the realities for both were the same. What they said about Jesus they believed was true! Not only did Jesus grow up in Nazareth in humble circumstances, but he was a wise teacher, healed many physical infirmities, hungered, thirsted, and died a tragic death (all of this is history); he was also the Christ who came to bring God's kingdom on earth, he was the anticipated messiah, he died for the sins of humanity, he was raised from the dead, he is coming again, and he is the Lord and Savior of the church (all of this is faith). For the early Christians, Jesus has a special relationship with God, and who he was and what he said and did has great benefit for all of humanity.

The evangelists did not present a complete story of all that Jesus did and said, but rather what they believed was sufficient for readers to exercise faith in him (John 20:30–31). We know almost nothing about Jesus' childhood and can only surmise from the historical context a few things that are likely true about his adolescence and young adulthood. Only two evangelists (Matthew and Luke) say anything about his birth, and they have significantly different stories—although with overlapping "punch lines." They aimed more specifically at setting forth those aspects of Jesus' life and fate that encourage readers and hearers to follow Jesus as the anticipated and longed-for Christ who would bring God's hope and salvation to humanity. This information is of a theological nature or faith perspective and is found throughout the Gospels. There is considerable evidence in both biblical and nonbiblical sources that points to Jesus' crucifixion under the authority of Pontius Pilate, but Mark, for instance, also says that he gave his life as a ransom for many (Mark 10:45). This is similar to what Paul said earlier, namely that "Christ died for our sins" (1 Cor. 15:3).

It is safe to say that we have no purely *historical* report about Jesus in the New Testament—that is to say, no report only concerned to present the facts about Jesus without interpretations for Christian faith. The Gospels were all written after Easter and by followers of Jesus, although they also report stories about Jesus that likely circulated in Palestine about him *before* his death. As we will see below, some of the sayings of Jesus are likely preserved in the so-called Q material, that is, sayings of Jesus that may predate his death and are common to Matthew and Luke, but are not found in Mark. Scholars regularly identify these sayings of Jesus with the letter "Q" (from the German "*Quelle*," meaning "source"). Nevertheless, we cannot expect to find in the Gospels unbiased critical historical reports, but rather affirmations of faith in telling the stories about Jesus. The evangelists tell the story of Jesus *in history and in faith*. These four New Testament sources provide our most important information about Jesus, but, as we will see in the next chapter, there are other ancient nonbiblical sources that often reflect some stories about Jesus that are reported in the Gospels.

In contemporary investigations of the Gospels, scholars have discerned other sources that the evangelists used in telling the story about Jesus. Some of those sources may have circulated in the early churches orally as "remembrances" of what Jesus said and did (or "memoirs," a term used by Justin Martyr in the middle of the second century [*1 Apol.* 64–67]), but some of these stories were likely written down in the middle of the first century and also circulated in the churches. Some of them likely circulated in Palestine *even before the death of Jesus*, and those stories and teachings were later incorporated into the Gospels. Since it is obvious that Jesus was popular among the Jews in Palestine, it should not be surprising that some of what he taught and did was written down even before he died. The Gospels were all written some thirty to sixty years after the death of Jesus, but it is virtually certain that the early churches taught many of the stories in the Gospels from their beginning (Acts 2:42; Gal. 3:1–5).

Scholars have long recognized that Matthew and Luke made considerable use of the Gospel of Mark. It is possible that much (not all) of the material common to Matthew and Luke that is not in Mark (the Q material listed below) was initially circulated orally and subsequently put in writing. Besides this, there are some stories and teachings found only in Matthew that are regularly designated "M" (e.g., Matthew's birth story, his reference to earthquakes at the death and resurrection of Jesus, and others). There are also some stories about Jesus and some of his teachings that are found only in Luke (for example, his birth story, some sixteen parables not found elsewhere, and others) and commonly designated "L" material. Luke himself lets us know at the beginning of his story about Jesus that many others have attempted to write about him (Luke 1:1–4). While we can only guess which materials he had in view, it is at least likely that Luke had Mark and Q in view. Most, if not all, of these other sources that Luke mentions are now lost, but they clearly informed the stories about Jesus that the evangelists later employed in writing their Gospels.

The Gospel of John, however, is considerably different from the Synoptic Gospels (Matthew, Mark, and Luke)—with only an 8 percent overlap. Its author likely did not use the same resources for telling his story, but was probably aware of Mark and perhaps much more (John 20:30). Many historical Jesus scholars have tended to ignore the Gospel of John as a reliable source of knowledge about Jesus. For instance, a gathering of more than one hundred biblical scholars from credible institutions, following the lead of Robert Funk, formed what came to be known as "the Jesus Seminar," determined to produce authentic traditions about Jesus, and they largely ignored the testimony of the

Gospel of John. They also expanded their sources to include the *Gospel of Thomas*. Their primary aim was to study the ancient sources, both biblical and nonbiblical, that told the story of Jesus in order to discern what Jesus actually said and did. They set forth criteria, discussed earlier, that they believed enabled them to identify what could be established as the historical core of the story about Jesus. They concluded that less than 20 percent of the sayings attributed to Jesus in the canonical Gospels are authentic and that the majority of sayings attributed to him were "embellished by mythic elements that express the church's faith in him" rather than authentic sayings of Jesus.[1] The "devil was in their details," of course, and those details were connected to the criteria they used to identify their "historical Jesus." It is well known now that their decisions were made on the basis of a vote using colored beads that members put into a container indicating their confidence, or lack thereof, in the authenticity of the various sayings of Jesus. Their model was based on the red-letter Bibles that listed the sayings of Jesus in red ink. When they acknowledged that Jesus had actually said what was reported of him in the Gospels, members placed a red bead into a container. If there was some doubt, but it was still likely that Jesus said it, the fellows voted by placing a pink bead in the container. If there was considerable doubt, but not final certainty, a gray bead was used in the voting, and if they were certain that Jesus never said it, then a black bead was used in the voting. Prior to their voting, they discussed and often debated the various sayings and deeds attributed to Jesus in the Gospels and elsewhere. Many of their votes did not get a 100 percent approval or disapproval. Again, the final votes showed that the *majority* of the fellows of the Jesus Seminar only recognized the authenticity of about 20 percent of the sayings of Jesus. Many internationally recognized biblical scholars are more positive in their assessment of the sayings and deeds attributed to Jesus in the Gospels, but many of them have also expressed various levels of confidence in the authentic sayings and deeds of Jesus in the Gospels.[2]

1. R. W. Funk and R. W. Hoover, *The Five Gospels: The Search for the Authentic Words of Jesus* (New York: Macmillan, 1993), 2–5.

2. I note here that when the Jesus Seminar began, I initially participated as a Fellow and even voted on some of the Jesus sayings that were being examined. I made more use of the red beads than did several others, but was nonetheless welcomed and treated with respect. I did not agree with their criteria (especially the criterion of dissimilarity) for establishing authentic sayings of Jesus. After dropping out of the group, I was later invited two times to address them on issues related to canon formation and was treated with kindness and respect by Robert Funk and his colleagues in the 1990s and recently during the Society of Biblical Literature meetings in Chicago. Some of their members disagreed with what I presented, but some said that they agreed with my views on the origin of the Bible. I continue to have contact with several members of the Jesus Seminar, who remain friends despite some of our differences in our approach to the story of Jesus and in our conclusions.

What Are the Gospels?

In the New Testament, the word "gospel"[3] was first used in reference to the "good news" that was proclaimed about Jesus the Christ (Mark 1:1; 1 Cor. 15:1–2). In the second century, the term was subsequently applied to the genre of writings (the Gospels) that focus on the story of Jesus' life, ministry, and fate. The length of Jesus' ministry was perhaps only one to three years at the most. Only Matthew and Luke have reports about his birth, and only Luke has a short story about Jesus' childhood—when he and his parents visited Jerusalem and the temple—and summary comments about his youth (Luke 2:40–52). The evangelists were quite selective in what they included in their reports.

Aims of the Gospels

The Gospels were produced not only to tell the story of Jesus with obvious calls to faith in him, but also to address the challenges and needs that the early churches were facing at the time the Gospels were written. Those challenges are often reflected in their narratives, and it is understandable that the evangelists would preserve and include those stories and traditions that were most helpful to the needs of the early churches. For instance, why would an evangelist preserve what Jesus had to say about divorce unless there were issues related to divorce facing some of the early churches? Divorce has little to do with the overall focus of the evangelists on preparing for the kingdom of God and doing the mission of Jesus the Christ. There is little doubt that Jesus would have addressed such matters, but they would not likely be included in the Gospels unless there was some situation in the early churches that such stories addressed. This does not suggest that the Gospel writers invented stories about Jesus, but rather that they were selective in what they reported. By around AD 150–160, Justin referred to "gospels" in conjunction with the memoirs or remembrances of the apostles, stating: "the apostles in the memoirs which are called gospels" (*1 Apol.* 63.3), and he goes on to cite Matthew and Mark.

The Word "Gospel"

The word "gospel" itself, however, was not invented by the early Christians, but, prior to the time of Jesus, already had a long history in the Old

---

3. The Greek noun for "gospel" is *euangelion*, meaning "good news," and its verb form, *euangelizomai*, means "to preach or proclaim good news" or "to preach glad tidings." The English translation of the noun form, "gospel," comes from the old English *godspel*, from *god*, meaning "good," and *spel*, meaning "news" or "story."

Testament and in Greco-Roman literature. For example, in the LXX (the Greek translation of the Old Testament Scriptures), the verb form *euangelizomai* ("to preach [or proclaim] the good news") was used in both the second and third parts of Isaiah (40:9; 52:7 [see Rom. 10:15]; and in 61:1, which is cited by Jesus in Luke 4:18) and the verbal form or noun ("proclaiming good news" or "joyful news") is found in 2 Samuel 4:10; 18:22, 25. The feminine form, *euangelia*, is found in 2 Samuel 18:20, 27; and 2 Kings 7:9.[4] Mark began his Gospel with the words, "the beginning of the good news [*tou euangeliou*] of Jesus the Christ."[5] This "good news" also inspired Luke to write his story of Jesus who proclaimed the good news concerning the coming kingdom of God (see his use of this term in Luke 1:19; 2:10; 3:18; 4:18; 7:22; 8:1; 9:6; 16:16; 20:1). Later his focus changes to a proclamation of the good news *about Jesus* (Acts 11:20), referring not to a book, but rather to the coming of the good news about the life, ministry, passion, and resurrection of Jesus that had already been proclaimed in the early churches for some years or more before Luke began to write.

The New Testament's use of this term is more in line with that of the Greco-Roman community than it is with the Old Testament writers. The early Christians often borrowed various terms, practices, and popular notions from their pagan counterparts, especially when those terms and concepts helped them convey a vivid understanding of their faith to their contemporaries. The term *euangelion* was used to announce the good news of victories by leading figures in antiquity, as well as to refer to great events in the life of an emperor or king. An ancient inscription containing this word was discovered at Priene, an ancient city on the western coast of Asia Minor (modern Turkey, south of Ephesus) that dates to around 9 BC. The inscription was used in celebration of the birth of Caesar Augustus (Octavian) and indicates that divine Providence has sent him as a "savior" to bring wars to an end and peace and good news ("glad tidings" = *euangelia* and *euangelion*) to the whole world. For our purposes, the relevant part of the Priene inscription is as follows:

> Everyone may rightly consider this event as the origin of their life and existence. Providence has marvelously raised up and adorned human life by giving us Augustus . . . to make him the benefactor of mankind, our saviour, for us and for

4. For a discussion of this text and its translation, see H. Koester, *Ancient Christian Gospels: Their History and Development* (Philadelphia: Trinity Press, 1990), 1–4.
5. There is some question whether "Son of God" was originally a part of Mark 1:1, as these words are missing in some early citations of Mark 1:1 and are in brackets in the leading Greek New Testaments (Nestle-Aland 27th and 28th editions and in the UBS 4th edition). Their original presence in Mark 1:1 is doubtful.

those who will come after us. But the birthday of the god [Augustus] was for the world the beginning of the joyful messages [*euangeliōn*] which have gone forth because of him.[6]

The earliest Christian communities welcomed the Gospels and passed them on to others, communicating in them that "good news" is found in Jesus the Christ (not the Roman emperor) and in Jesus' message about God's rule. The imperial propaganda about the Roman emperor may have influenced the early Christians and given them a useful term for telling their story about the "good news" in and about Jesus. Paul uses *euangelion* similarly when he says in Romans 1:1 and 2 that he himself had been set apart for the "good news" (or "gospel") of God, promised beforehand through the prophets regarding God's Son. Paul expanded the use of the term to designate God's activity in the death and resurrection of Jesus (1 Cor. 15:1–5) and in his coming, or *parousia* (1 Cor. 15:23–28).[7] Early Christian preaching and teaching focused on Jesus and especially on the presence of the kingdom of God in his words and deeds. When Mark began his story of "good news" of and about Jesus, those after him agreed that Jesus' life and teaching, including his death, resurrection, and anticipated soon return, constituted good news. Other gospels were written after Mark, some of which are now known only in fragmentary form or in brief quotations in the early church fathers, but all purport to tell portions of the story of Jesus.

Sources for the Life and Teachings of Jesus

Again, the most indispensable sources for reconstructing the life and teachings of Jesus are the New Testament Gospels, although recent studies about Jesus regularly reflect also some nonbiblical references that help in forming a historical picture of Jesus. Some biblical scholars regularly cite the *Gospel of Thomas*, P.Egerton 2, the *Dialogue of the Savior*, and other nonbiblical sources in their historical Jesus research.

There *may* also be some authentic sayings of Jesus preserved in several noncanonical traditions, including in various early church fathers, ancient biblical manuscripts, and fragmentary and apocryphal sources.[8] These sayings

6. The entire Greek text of the Priene inscription is printed in *OGIS* 458 (2.48–60).

7. See Koester, *Ancient Christian Gospels*, 4–6 and 6–23, for a discussion of the origins and use of the term "gospel" (*euangelion*) in antiquity as well as its use in designating a literary genre of the New Testament.

8. A useful collection of these sources is in J. K. Elliott, *The Apocryphal New Testament: A Collection of Apocryphal Christian Literature in an English Translation* (Oxford: Clarendon, 1993), especially 3–163.

of Jesus are generally referred to as the "agrapha," that is, sayings of Jesus that are not in the canonical Gospels. There are some 266 of these sayings, but their value for understanding Jesus is disputed even though some of them may be authentic reflections of things that Jesus actually said.[9] These sayings became more familiar to scholars through Joachim Jeremias's *The Unknown Sayings of Jesus*,[10] a small but important source that both lists and discusses these sayings. Jeremias believed that of the much larger list, only eighteen of them deserve special consideration.[11] He concluded that the majority of them are legendary inventions that bear the marks of forgery and sometimes fantasy.[12] Otfried Hofius later claimed that even Jeremias's conclusions were too generous. He argued that only ten of the agrapha need be taken seriously, and of these only four or five are likely authentic to Jesus.[13] These extracanonical sayings of Jesus no doubt functioned as authoritative scripture in the communities that possessed them, even though they did not become a part of the church's sacred Scripture collection. Do these sayings provide an independent tradition or source for scholars to reconstruct the life and teaching of Jesus? There is little agreement here among the scholars, but, more and more, there is an acknowledgment that *some* authentic sayings of Jesus likely do exist in the noncanonical sources, *but they simply do not add much to what is already known*. John Meier, for example, adds that if all eighteen of the sayings selected by Jeremias were authentic, they would still add nothing to our understanding of Jesus found in the Gospels and that a "great deal of effort over dubious material produces absolutely no significant new data." For him, further considerations of the agrapha are simply not worth his effort.[14] As one can see from the above samples, it is difficult to find anything of significance in the agrapha that advances our understanding of Jesus.

9. W. D. Stroker, *Extracanonical Sayings of Jesus* (SBLRBS 18; Atlanta: Scholars Press, 1989), offers the text of 266 of these sayings without evaluating sufficiently their contents or attributing authenticity or inauthenticity to them. He is probably right in concluding that some of these sayings are independent of the canonical Gospels, but he suggests that those in the *Gospel of Thomas* are earlier than those sayings in the canonical Gospels (1n2). Not a few scholars would dispute that claim.

10. Joachim Jeremias, *Unbekannte Jesuworte* (1947; 3rd ed., Gütersloh: Bertelsmann, 1961); English, *The Unknown Sayings of Jesus* (1957; 2nd ed., London: SPCK, 1964). More recently the agrapha have been discussed by Otfried Hofius, "Isolated Sayings of Jesus," *NT Apo* (ed. Wilhelm Schneemelcher; 2nd ed.; Louisville: Westminster John Knox, 1991), 1:88–91. They are conveniently listed and discussed in James H. Charlesworth and Craig A. Evans, "Jesus in the Agrapha and Apocryphal Gospels," in *Studying the Historical Jesus: Evaluations of the State of Current Research* (ed. Bruce Chilton and Craig A. Evans; NTTS 19; Leiden: Brill, 1998), 479–533.

11. J. Jeremias, *Unknown Sayings of Jesus*, 42.

12. Ibid., 26–42.

13. Otfried Hofius, "Unknown Sayings of Jesus," in *The Gospel and the Gospels* (ed. Peter Stuhlmacher; Grand Rapids: Eerdmans, 1991), 336–60.

14. Meier, *Marginal Jew*, 1:114 and 142n10.

Agrapha: Sayings of Jesus outside the Gospels

Otfried Hofius lists the following as worthy of serious consideration. The ones he considers authentic are marked with an asterisk (*).

1. "As you are found, so will you be led away [sc. to judgment]." (*Syriac Liber Graduum, Serm.* 3.3; 15.4)

2. "Ask for the great things, and God will add to you what is small." (Clement of Alexandria, *Strom.* 1.24.158)

3. "Be competent [approved] money-changers!" (*Ps. Clem. Hom.* II 51.1; III 50.2; XVIII 20.4)

*4. "On the same day he [Jesus] saw a man working on the sabbath. He said to him: 'Man, if you know what you are doing, you are blessed; but if you do not know, you are accursed and a transgressor of the law!'" (Luke 6:5 in D [= Codex D])

*5. "He who is near me is near the fire; he who is far from me is far from the kingdom." (*Gos. Thom.* §82; Origen, *In Jer. hom.* lat. III. 3; Didymus, *In Psalm.* 88.8)

*6. "(He who today) stands far off will tomorrow be (near to you)." (P.Oxy. 1224)

*7. "And only then shall you be glad, when you look on your brother with love." (*Gos. Heb.*, according to Jerome, *In Eph.* 5.4)[a]

8. "The kingdom is like a wise fisherman who cast his net into the sea; he drew it up from the sea full of small fish; among them he found a large (and) good fish; that wise fisherman threw all the small fish down into the sea; he chose the large fish without regret." (*Gos. Thom.* §8)

9. "How is it then with you? For you are here in the temple. Are you then clean? ... Woe to you blind who see not! You have washed yourself in water that is poured forth, in which dogs and swine lie night and day, and washed and scoured your outer skin, which harlots and flute girls also anoint, bathe, scour, and beautify to arouse desire in men, but inwardly they are filled with scorpions and with [all manner of ev]il. But I and [my disciples], of whom you say that we have not [bathed, have bath]ed ourselves in the liv[ing and clean] water, which comes down from [the father in heaven]." (P.Oxy. 840 §2)

10. "And never be joyful, save when you look upon your brother in love." (*Gos. Heb.* §5; compare Jerome, *In Eph.* 3 [on Eph. 5:4])[b]

a. Hofius, "Isolated Sayings," 91.

b. Ibid., 90. Similarly, Meier, *Marginal Jew*, 1:112–14. For other examples, see Hofius, "Unknown Sayings," 336–60; Charlesworth and Evans, "Agrapha and Apocryphal Gospels," 489; and Daniel J. Theron, *Evidence of Tradition* (Grand Rapids: Baker, 1957; repr., 1980), 96–99.

Again, the Gospels are our earliest and most reliable records available for telling the story of Jesus, but they do not offer a complete reconstruction of his life. Even a casual reading shows that a full biography was never intended. There are numerous gaps in the story and only a few inferences about his life and various influences before he began his ministry. The Gospel writers were quite selective in what they had to say about Jesus and simply focused on his ministry, teachings, death, and resurrection. A simple outline of Jesus' ministry and fate is discernible in the Gospels, but the chronology often varies. Also, only a handful of the stories about him are in all four Gospels. There are places where the stories about Jesus overlap in substance and even in the words the evangelists use. Most scholars agree that the Gospels offer authentic information about Jesus and have pivotal significance for understanding his identity and mission.

Some New Testament scholars contend that the evangelists more often offer reflections of the life of the early Christian community than accurate reports of Jesus' life, but this assumes that what they wrote was false or contrary to what Jesus actually said or did. Apparently some of the details in Jesus' life were not as important to the evangelists as they are to modern scholars who piece together various events that make up the story of Jesus. There are several important differences in their stories, such as the length of Jesus' ministry, when he "cleansed" the temple, or when he conducted the Last Supper. Some of these differences likely reflect the evangelists' theological perspectives and preferences, as we see in the cases of the earthquakes at the death of Jesus and at his resurrection in Matthew, or in the location of the appearances of Jesus in either Galilee (Matthew and Mark) or Jerusalem (Luke and John).

Literary Relationships

What relationships exist between the Gospels, and what level of reliability should we expect from them? Some scholars prefer to force harmonizations rather than allow each evangelist's message to emerge in its own right,[15] but most New Testament scholars today focus on the perspective, historical setting,

15. The early Christian churches resisted a mid-second-century attempt to harmonize the four New Testament Gospels into one gospel that eliminated their differences. Tatian, a student of Justin (ca. 150–160), constructed his harmonization of the Gospels known as the *Diatessaron* (Greek, "through four") and sometimes "the Gospel of the Mixed," and eliminated the differences in them. By rejecting the *Diatessaron*, the majority of churches concluded that the voice of each evangelist needed to be heard, acknowledging that the *Diatessaron* ran the risk of obscuring the intended message of each evangelist. The *Diatessaron*, however, was quite popular among many Christians in the East for centuries.

and message of each Gospel, giving careful attention to date, authorship, occasion, aim, message, and historical reliability.[16] In what follows we will look at *some* of these issues but focus our primary attention on the relationships and reliability of New Testament Gospels as witnesses to the story of Jesus.

The Synoptics and Their Relationships

The first three Gospels are regularly called the "Synoptic" Gospels because they offer a similar picture and sequence of the events of Jesus' life and because they often overlap not only in the events and teachings presented, but even in the wording. By the third century they were sometimes placed side by side in parallel columns in order to view them together, hence, "Synoptic" Gospels. Students of the Gospels would do well to make use of a synopsis of the Gospels that allows them to see at a glance the similarities and differences in the stories the Synoptics tell.[17]

The problem of accounting for the parallels in the first three Gospels, as well as for their differences, is commonly known as the "synoptic problem." Earlier most scholarly attention focused on harmonizing the differences in the canonical Gospels, but more recently considerable effort has been directed toward accounting for the many similarities in the Gospels and what sources the evangelists used in telling their stories about Jesus. Biblical scholars are now showing less interest in harmonizing the Gospel narratives than in accounting for their similarities and differences and what they tell us about the perspectives of the writers.

In regard to their relationships, a revolution in Gospel criticism occurred in the nineteenth century when biblical scholars began to recognize again that the Synoptic Gospels were not written independently of one another. While this was not new and could be dated back to the time of Augustine, if not earlier, a modern consensus emerged that Mark was the first Gospel and that Luke and Matthew made considerable use of Mark in producing their Gospels. Further, after noting many parallels in Matthew and Luke that are not in Mark, some scholars concluded that both Matthew and Luke used a common source now commonly referred to as "Q" (from the German *Quelle*, meaning "source") or the "Sayings Source." Scholars continue to disagree on whether this "Q" source was a written document or a common oral tradition,

---

16. Those wanting to know more about these issues should consult the most recent major New Testament introductions (see bibliography for a listing of them).

17. The most useful synopsis of the Gospels displays the Greek text and English translation on facing pages: Kurt Aland, ed., *Synopsis of the Four Gospels: Greek-English Edition of the Synopsis Quattuor Evangeliorum* (12th ed.; Freiburg, Germany: German Bible Society, 2007).

or some combination of both, but most agree that this source existed and was used by Matthew and Luke.

In antiquity, the most common accounting for similarities among the Synoptic Gospels was that Matthew wrote first and Mark and Luke made use of Matthew. Augustine argued that Mark simply abbreviated Matthew (*Cons.* 1.2.4, PL 34.1044). Origen earlier came to the conclusion that since the Spirit gave perfect memory to each of the Gospel writers, the differences between them were because of the "theological purposes" of Mark and Luke that were often highly subtle in nature (see his *Commentary on Matthew*, fragment of book 2, preserved in *Philoc.* 100.6 and 11.2–3, 6; and also in *Princ.* 1, Preface, 8).[18] In the eighteenth century more theories about these relationships began to emerge.

In 1764, H. P. Owen argued that Matthew was written first, Luke used Matthew, and Mark was written last using both Matthew and Luke.[19] In this way, the tradition of Matthean priority was maintained, and this pattern was essentially followed by J. J. Griesbach of Germany in 1783 (now known as the Griesbach Hypothesis).[20] By the nineteenth century, long-established beliefs about the priority of Matthew were changing and Markan priority began to emerge. B. F. Westcott advanced the theory that each of the four canonical evangelists appealed to both oral and written traditions independently of one another,[21] but his view did not prevail among biblical scholars. Chief among the early proponents of Markan priority were K. Lachmann and H. J. Holtzmann.[22] Lachmann, in a variation of Westcott's thesis, argued that Mark made use of earlier sources in constructing his Gospel than did Matthew and Luke and that his Gospel was thus closer to the original narrative. This led others, especially Holtzmann, to conclude that Mark was written first and that Matthew and Luke used Mark in the areas that all three Gospels have in common. He argued that Matthew and Luke, independent of one another, made use of an earlier form of Mark (called *Ur-Markus*), plus an additional

---

18. R. M. Grant (*An Historical Introduction to the New Testament* [New York: Harper & Row, 1972], 110) has commented upon the astuteness of this observation especially for the time in which it was written.

19. H. P. Owen, *Observations of the Four Gospels* (1764).

20. J. J. Griesbach, *Commentatio qua Marci Evangelium totum e Matthaei et Lucae commentariis decerptum esse monstratur* (1789), translated in *J. J. Griesbach: Synoptic and Text-Critical Studies 1776–1976* (ed. and trans. J. B. Orchard and T. R. W. Longstaff; Cambridge: Cambridge University Press, 1978).

21. B. F. Westcott, *An Introduction to the Study of the Gospels* (London: Macmillan, 1851; 6th ed., 1881).

22. K. Lachmann, "De ordine narrationum in evangeliis synopticis," *Theologische Studien und Kritiken* 8 (1835), 570–90; H. J. Holtzmann, *Die synoptischen Evangelien: Ihr Ursprung und geschichtlicher Charakter* (Leipzig: Engelmann, 1863).

source (Q). With modifications, Holtzmann's position has held sway among most biblical scholars. Some biblical scholars continue to affirm Matthean priority,[23] but it is generally agreed that Mark wrote the first Gospel, that Matthew and Luke made use of Mark, expanding Mark to some degree for their own purposes, and that they also used another source designated Q. This is generally known as the "Two-Document Hypothesis."

The Q Tradition/Document

Students of the New Testament reading critical literature on the Synoptic Gospels often read about "Q." As we noted above, Q is simply a convenient scholarly reference to those passages that are in Matthew and Luke, but not Mark. Scholars use the designation to identify a source used by Matthew and Luke in the writing of their Gospels. As we will see, for many scholars the scope of Q and its form (written and/or oral tradition) are still uncertain. The references to the Q passages have a Luke reference but with Q in front instead of Luke, as in Luke 4:2–13 = Q 4:2–13. The passages in Q are as follows:

The "Q" Source Material*

"Q" (Luke)		Matthew
1. 3:7–9, 16–17	John's Preaching	1. 3:7–12
2. 4:2–13	Jesus' Temptation	2. 4:2–11
3. 6:20–23, 27–30, 32–36	Sermon on the Plain 1	3. 5:3–6, 11–12, 39–42, 45–48
4. 6:37–38, 41–49	Sermon on the Plain 2	7. 7:1–5, 16–21, 24–27
5. 7:1–10	Centurion from Capernaum	9. 8:5–13
6. 7:18–35	John's Question; Jesus' Reply	13. 11:2–19
7. 9:57–60	Nature of Discipleship	10. 8:19–22
8. 10:1–12	Sending out Discourse	11. 9:37–10:15
9. 10:13–15, 21–22	Cries of Woe and Joy	14. 11:21–23, 25–26
10. 11:1–4	Lord's Prayer	5. 6:9–13
11. 11:9–13	Concerning Prayer	8. 7:7–11
12. 11:14–23	Beelzebub Controversy	15. 12:22–30
13. 11:24–26	Return of the Evil Spirit	17. 12:43–45
14. 11:29–32	Against Sign Seeking	16. 12:38–42
15. 11:33–35	Sayings on Light	4. 5:15; 6:22–23

23. W. R. Farmer, *The Synoptic Problem: A Critical Analysis* (New York: Macmillan, 1964) and *New Synoptic Studies: The Cambridge Gospels Conference and Beyond* (ed. W. R. Farmer; Macon, GA: Mercer University Press, 1983); and M. Goulder, *Luke—A New Paradigm* (JSNTSup 20; Sheffield: JSOT Press, 1989), 1:3–26.

"Q" (Luke)		Matthew
16. 11:39–52	Against the Pharisees	19. 23:4, 23–25, 29–36
17. 12:2–10	Exhortation to Confession	12. 10:26–33
18. 12:22–34	Anxiety and Possessions	6. 6:25–33, 19–21
19. 12:39–46	Watchfulness	22. 24:43–51
20. 13:18–21	Mustard Seed and Leaven	18. 13:31–33
21. 13:34–35	Lament over Jerusalem	20. 23:37–39
22. 17:22–37	Parousia Discourse	21. 24:26–28, 37–41
23. 19:11–28	Parable of the Talents	23. 25:14–30

*This chart comes from W. G. Kümmel, *Introduction to the New Testament* (trans. H. C. Kee; Nashville: Abingdon, 1975), 65–66. Note Matthew's order in the right column. The Annotated Scholars Version of *The Complete Gospels* (ed. R. J. Miller; Sonoma, CA: Polebridge, 1992), 253–300, is more complete. See also the introduction to this material on 248–52.

Although the existence of Q is widely acknowledged, there is still much that we do not know about it; for example, it is not clear whether Mark knew or used such a source in the places where Mark, Matthew, and Luke agree.[24] Some scholars argue that Q was probably a collection of Jesus sayings not connected to an Easter story, just as we see in the *Gospel of Thomas*, and that it was written before Mark. As we will see below, Dunn contends that much of this material was likely collected and written down *before* the death of Jesus and later incorporated in the Gospels.[25] In other words, it is possible that many of the traditions about Jesus that are in the Q material circulated in oral or written form *before* the death of Jesus, which likely accounts for its lack of an Easter tradition.

There have been long and continuous debates among scholars on the shape of the so-called Q document.[26] The most important objections to the existence

24. For a more complete discussion of this, see H. Conzelmann and A. Lindemann, *Interpreting the New Testament: An Introduction to the Principles and Methods of New Testament Exegesis* (trans. S. S. Schatzmann; Peabody, MA: Hendrickson, 1988), 57–59.

25. J. D. G. Dunn, *Jesus Remembered* (Christianity in the Making 1; Grand Rapids: Eerdmans, 2003), 881–93; see also his "Q[1] as Oral Tradition," in *The Written Gospel* (ed. Markus Bockmuehl and Donald A. Hagner; Cambridge: Cambridge University Press, 2005), 45–69.

26. Grant, *Historical Introduction*, 113–14, gives several reasons to doubt the existence of a completely written document such as Q and maintains that Matthew and Luke drew upon a common reservoir of oral tradition, though some may have been in written form. Long ago, Austin Farrer leveled some strong arguments against the existence of Q and against claiming that Luke used Matthew's Gospel. He maintained that it is easier to assume the use of a known source, namely Matthew, than to accept the existence of an unknown source, namely Q ("On Dispensing with Q," in *Studies in the Gospels* [ed. E. E. Nineham; Oxford: Blackwell, 1955], 55–86). T. R. Rosche, "The Words of Jesus and the Future of the 'Q' Hypothesis," *JBL* 79 (1960): 210–20, accepts the priority of Mark, but not necessarily the existence of Q.

of Q as a written source include the following: (1) Q may have been a fluid layer of oral tradition because the wording of the sayings in Q varies considerably between Matthew and Luke, and (2) both Matthew and Luke take up and incorporate the Q material into their Gospels in a different sequence, as we see in the Sermon on the Mount in Matthew 5–7 and the Sermon on the Plain in Luke 6 and throughout that Gospel. Conzelmann counters these concerns with four important points: (1) despite the differences, there are substantial agreements in word order in the Gospels; (2) if Q were nothing more than scattered oral traditions, it is amazing that there is so much in common from this tradition in both Matthew and Luke; (3) the Q material has *generally* (not completely) been adopted in the same order in both Matthew and Luke; and (4) the several "doublets" of sayings of Jesus in Matthew and Luke have their origin in each writer's selections from the same source (see, for example, Luke 8:16–18 and compare with Mark 4:21–25; then compare this with the doublet in Luke 11:33, which is also found in Matt. 5:15).[27] The majority of New Testament scholars today agree that Q did exist in written form, or mostly so, though there is little agreement on the precise boundaries of that document.

How does one account for the material common in both Matthew and Luke? There are only two options that have gained considerable attention, namely that Luke drew freely upon Matthew for his Gospel, or that Matthew and Luke made use of a common sayings source (written but possibly also oral). Matthew and Luke's close following of Mark's sequence, their use of most of his words, and the significant differences in sequence and verbal association when they do not follow Mark suggest that they did not draw from one another. Luke, for instance, would likely have been as faithful in following Matthew as he was when he followed Mark. However, if Matthew and Luke had made use of a *written* Q document, it seems that they would have used it with the same consistency with which they used Mark's Gospel, but that is not the case. The Q verbal similarities in Matthew and Luke constitute some 230 verses, and these similarities suggest that Matthew and Luke both drew upon a common *written* source, but the differences also suggest that they made use of a common *oral* tradition that was circulating among Jesus' followers. Some scholars are optimistic that they can establish the original content and order of Q, including its date around AD 50,[28] but others are less optimistic.

27. Conzelmann and Lindemann, *Interpreting the New Testament*, 55–57.
28. H. C. Kee, *Jesus in History* (New York: Harcourt, Brace & World, 1970), 64–66. T. W. Manson suggests that Matthew the apostle was the author of the Q document, a theory similar to the one that first suggested the idea of Q. Papias's statement regarding the *logia*, or sayings, of Jesus being collected by Matthew led to the concept of Q (Eusebius, *Hist. eccl.* 3.39.16). Cf. T. W. Manson, "Studies in the Gospels and Epistles," in *In Search of the Historical Jesus* (ed.

Some Synoptic scholars contend that the oral stage of transmission of the story about Jesus (before the Gospels were written) was not as fluid as other scholars have supposed. Although direct dependence has not been clearly established, the use of rabbinic techniques for transmission of the oral tradition by the early Christian teachers has been ably demonstrated.[29] Several scholars have shown how the early Christian churches made use of well-defined oral traditions similar to those used in rabbinic Judaism. In the early third century AD, rabbinic Jews codified Jewish oral traditions that had been passed on by various techniques from the first and second centuries AD. Early Jewish Christians may have learned similar techniques of transmission as part of their catechetical training, involving repetition and memorization of short, well-organized thoughts. The New Testament has several examples of this, for example, Romans 10:9; 1 Corinthians 15:3–8; and 1 Timothy 3:16. Gerd Theissen offers examples from antiquity reflecting a strong emphasis on oral tradition, especially noticeable in Socrates's method of training. He also refers to a well-known quotation showing Papias's (ca. AD 140) preference for oral traditions circulating about Jesus over written traditions (Mark and Matthew?), namely, "For I did not suppose that information from books would help me so much as the word of a living and surviving voice" (Eusebius, *Hist. eccl.* 3.39.4, LCL). He illustrates in Matthew 28:19–20 and Luke 10:16 how Jesus' teaching was passed on orally at first rather than in written form. He cites other examples indicating that Paul knew and used oral tradition about Jesus in the church (see 1 Cor. 7:10–11; 9:1–14; 11:23–26).[30] Some Jesus traditions probably existed in small units that were apparently detachable and applicable to different contexts, such as the teaching of the "first and the last" in Matthew 19:30; 20:16; and Luke 13:30, reflecting two very different settings.

H. K. McArthur; London: SPCK, 1970), 32. See also John S. Kloppenborg, *The Formation of Q: Trajectories in Ancient Christian Wisdom Collections* (Studies in Antiquity and Christianity; Philadelphia: Fortress, 1987); and his more recent Kloppenborg, ed., *Conflict and Intervention: Literary, Rhetorical, and Social Studies on the Sayings Gospel Q* (Valley Forge, PA: Trinity Press, 1995); Robert J. Miller, ed., *The Complete Gospels* (rev. ed.; San Francisco: HarperSanFrancisco, 1994), 249–52; see also the sane and very valuable discussion of Q and its origin in early Christianity in Dale C. Allison Jr., *The Jesus Tradition in Q* (Harrisburg, PA: Trinity Press, 1997), especially his opening chapter, 1–66, but the specific illustrations in the rest of the volume are of considerable help also; and, finally, Graham N. Stanton, *The Gospels and Jesus* (OBS; Oxford: Oxford University Press, 1989), 86–90.

29. See Birger Gerhardsson, *Memory and Manuscript: Oral Tradition and Written Transmission in Rabbinic Judaism and Early Christianity with Tradition and Transmission in Early Christianity* (The Biblical Resource Series; Grand Rapids: Eerdmans, 1998), esp. 71–78 and 194–323; and his more recent *The Reliability of the Gospel Tradition* (Peabody, MA: Hendrickson, 2001); R. Riesner, *Jesus als Lehrer: Ein Üntersuchung zum Ursprung der Evangelien-Überlieferung* (3rd ed.; WUNT 2.7; Tübingen: Mohr-Siebeck, 1988).

30. Gerd Theissen, *The Gospels in Context* (trans. L. M. Maloney; Minneapolis: Fortress, 1991), 3–4.

In Paul's epistles there is no reference to or awareness of existing earlier-written Gospels. Paul only acknowledges oral traditions (e.g., 1 Cor. 11:23; 15:3; Phil. 2:6–11), and there is no evidence for the existence of written traditions prior to his letters. The fact that he appealed to tradition (*paradosis*) being passed on to him (1 Cor. 15:3–7), or to his own encounter with the risen Christ as the source of his gospel (Gal. 1:11–12, 15–16) rather than written sources, is an argument against the existence of written Gospels prior to Paul's ministry. If there were written sources about Jesus in existence prior to Paul's ministry (Luke 1:1–4), there is no evidence that they were in general circulation, since no particular references are made to them.

A "Q Community" and the Historical Jesus

One of the more intriguing issues in the quest for the historical Jesus concerns the use of the so-called "Gospel of Q." For some time now, several New Testament scholars have argued that Q was a document separate from other canonical sources and reflects an earlier and separate stage of the community of Jesus when his followers did not call themselves "Christians." Some scholars assume that because there is no reference to the death and resurrection of Jesus in the Q material, that the producer(s) of Q was (were) uninformed or unconcerned about these traditions. In other words, it is argued that there was an early community of followers of Jesus who did not know the passion and Easter traditions, which, they claim, are reflections of a *later* community of Jesus' followers. This supposed community of Q followers of Jesus only possessed sayings of Jesus, the wisdom teacher. The events and perspectives that are at the heart of the canonical Gospels, they say, are missing from this earlier source or tradition used by both Matthew and Luke that is now called Q. This notion has led some scholars to conclude that New Testament teachings about the death and resurrection of Jesus were a later development. In other words, such notions are not reflective of the earliest followers of Jesus. This view, if true, is of course a remarkable perspective that is clearly out of step with historic Christianity.

Supporters of this position appeal to the *Gospel of Thomas*, which is a collection of sayings of Jesus without a narrative that connects them and which contains no passion or resurrection narratives. The *Gospel of Thomas* is preserved in Coptic and was not known until the discovery of the gnostic library at Nag Hammadi, Egypt, in 1945.[31] There is considerable scholarly

---

31. Three Greek papyrus fragments (P.Oxy. 1, 654, 655) had been found at the end of the nineteenth and the beginning of the twentieth centuries, but they were not known to come from this document until the entire document was found in 1945.

debate regarding the dating of this document; namely, whether it originated in the middle of the first century, as some argue, or in the early, middle, or even late second century, and whether it depends on the canonical Gospels or preceded them and was independent of them. If the *Gospel of Thomas* dates from *before* the canonical Gospels (so the argument goes), then there is support for the Q hypothesis that there was a community of followers of Jesus who did not have or know of a passion or resurrection narrative. The *Gospel of Thomas* and Q would represent a form of early Christianity that is distinct from the traditional model that is reflected in orthodox Christianity.

Second-century gnostic Christians, who denied the physical incarnation of Jesus and also his bodily resurrection from the dead, understandably adopted the *Gospel of Thomas* at a time when the incarnation and resurrection were openly challenged. For instance, the author of 1 John calls into question the emerging Docetic (Greek, *dokeō* = "appear" or "seem") heresy that Jesus only appeared to have a physical body. He claimed that those who denied that Jesus came in the flesh were not of God (1 John 4:2). There is no evidence that such a brand of Christianity existed before the end of the first century, and it is never addressed in the earlier New Testament writings. It is not clear, therefore, that the *Gospel of Thomas* is a reasonable parallel with the supposed Q source.

Even if the *Gospel of Thomas* contains several authentic sayings of Jesus (some scholars claim that as many as twenty-two of these sayings are authentic, but most do not acknowledge that many), they are nevertheless packaged in a document that is, to say the least, strange. Its bizarre conclusion about women having to become males in order to be fit for the kingdom of heaven does not reflect first-century Christianity![32]

There are a number of other serious difficulties with the Q community positions of this thesis, not the least of which is that there is no known first-century form of Christianity without some reference to the death of Jesus and his resurrection from the dead, and none is acknowledged by Paul or in the rest of the New Testament.[33] All of the New Testament writings assume the death of Jesus and his resurrection. The hypothesis that a Q community

32. See, for instance, *Gos. Thom.* 114, which says, "Simon Peter said to them [the disciples and Jesus], 'Let Mary leave us, for women are not worthy of life.' Jesus said, 'I myself shall lead her in order to make her a male, so that she too may become a living spirit resembling you males. For every woman who will make herself a male will enter the Kingdom of Heaven'" (*The Other Bible* [ed. and trans. W. Barnstone; San Francisco: HarperSanFrancisco, 1984]), 307.

33. It has been argued that 1 Cor. 15:12–20 suggests such a community, but in fact it only refers to some Corinthians who questioned the church's teaching about the resurrection of the dead, so Paul reminds them that if the dead do not rise, then Christ is not risen. His argument is *not* that Christ has not been raised, therefore the dead do not rise. Again, no known community of followers of Jesus in the first century denied the existence or importance of his death and resurrection.

existed before all others is commonly associated with Burton Mack, who assumes that the canonical literature was at best wrong about Jesus, and, at worst, fraudulent in its depiction of him.[34] The difficulty with Mack's view is that there is no record of any followers of Jesus who denied his passion and resurrection prior to or during the ministry of Paul. No existing documents demonstrate the existence of such a community (Q notwithstanding), and the only "copy" of Q that we have is in two sources (Matthew and Luke) that have a passion and resurrection narrative! Secondly, there was simply not sufficient time for such a tradition to emerge before the conversion of Paul, nor is there any evidence for the existence of such a community before, during, or shortly after the time of Paul. Few would deny that Peter and the Twelve were part of the inner circle of Jesus, and the band of twelve disciples/ apostles was closer to him than any others. After stating that Christ "died for our sins" and "was raised the third day," Paul indicates that the risen Christ appeared first to Peter, then to the Twelve, then to some five hundred followers of Jesus, then to James and the rest of the apostles, and last of all to himself (1 Cor. 15:3–8). This tradition that Paul received shows many signs of having been circulated orally prior to the time when Paul received it.[35] Paul received this tradition from others, or by revelation (Gal. 1:15–16), and he claims that the earliest followers of Jesus also acknowledged it. Paul states that he was in harmony with the earliest followers of Jesus and, by pointing out that this is what Peter, the Twelve, James, and the rest of the apostles preached and what the Corinthians believed (1 Cor. 15:3–11), he shows that his faith was anchored in the earliest traditions of the church. Paul aligned himself with the earliest understanding of the Christian proclamation and with those who were the earliest followers of Jesus and in his inner circle, and he claims that they centered their faith on the resurrection of Jesus from the dead. Had the case been otherwise, it would doubtless be reflected somewhere in the New Testament writings themselves, but this is nowhere to be found. To hold that a community of followers of Jesus (a "Q community") existed that did not accept that Jesus died for sins and was raised from the dead suggests that Paul was either

---

34. B. Mack, *The Lost Gospel: The Book of Q and Christian Origins* (San Francisco: Harper, 1993), esp. 42–49 and 245–50. For a careful response, see E. Linnemann, *Is There a Synoptic Problem? Rethinking the Literary Dependence of the First Three Gospels* (trans. R. W. Yarbrough; Grand Rapids: Baker, 1992), 177–85, who argues the time factor cogently. Linnemann and Farmer are well known for their arguments against the existence of a Q document.

35. Symmetry is seen in the four statements that are introduced by the Greek word *hoti* = "that" in each of the clauses of vv. 3–5, the balances between the "then . . . then" (Greek = *eita - epeita*) in vv. 5–8, and the balances of emphases in vv. 3–5 between 3 - 3 - 1 and in vv. 5–8 between 2 - 1 and 2 - 1. This is evidence of a tradition arranged for easy memory and transmission in oral form.

mistaken or not telling the truth. Neither Paul nor the other New Testament and early church writers hesitated to speak against what they considered to be divergent views in the church or anything else that they considered to be an affront to the Christian faith, such as when they later dealt with Docetism, Gnosticism, and the like.[36] If something like a Q community ever existed, it was marginal at best and played no significant part in the formation of early Christianity. The conversion of Paul took place sometime around AD 33–35 at the latest (Gal. 1:11–17), and he claims that his gospel was acknowledged by the leadership ("pillars") of the church in Jerusalem (Peter, James, and John), and that he and his gospel were accepted by them in Jerusalem (Gal. 2:2–10). Paul's gospel is compatible with the passion and resurrection stories of the canonical Gospels. The Gospels were all written some thirty to seventy years at the most after the death of Jesus, and they clearly reflect earlier traditions about Jesus, but nothing that shows that after his death such a Q community ever existed. There is simply not enough time for the church's traditions to change so radically—as the existence of a Q community presupposes.

The above being said, that no post-death and post-resurrection community of followers of Jesus is known that rejected notions of his passion (Mark 10:45) or his resurrection, did such a community exist *before* Jesus died? Were there early followers of Jesus who knew nothing of his forthcoming death and resurrection? Yes, of course! The Gospels all reflect that crowds of people followed Jesus during his ministry, and that they were impressed with his teaching and healing miracles. The impact of Jesus upon his followers and others around him during his preaching and teaching in Galilee is well known, and it is certainly possible that many of his teachings were written down by his early followers and later incorporated into the post-Easter Gospels.[37]

Dunn has argued convincingly that a number of the teachings and stories about Jesus were circulating among his followers even *before* his death. He answers the troubling issue about the Q material—namely, that it does not

---

36. This line of argument is also discussed in Andreas Lindemann, "Is there a Gospel of Q?" *Bible Review*, August 1995, 20; and in more detail in the more recent "The Sayings Source Q and the Historical Jesus," Colloquium Biblicum Lovaniense 49 (2000), *ETL* (4.2000), 549–59; and Andreas Lindemann, ed., *The Sayings Source Q and the Historical Jesus* (BETL 158; Leuven: Leuven University Press / Peeters, 2001). See also Eta Linnemann, "The Gospel of Q—Fact or Fantasy?," *TJ* 17 NS (1996): 3–18; and her *Is There a Synoptic Problem?* She challenges the Q community hypothesis that is central to the Jesus Seminar leaders.

37. Dunn, *Jesus Remembered*, 881–84, argues this point convincingly. See also his updated and convincing argument along the same lines, in which he argues for the authenticity of the oral traditions circulating about Jesus prior to his death, in *A New Perspective on Jesus: What the Quest for the Historical Jesus Missed* (Acadia Studies in Bible and Theology; Craig A .Evans and Lee Martin McDonald, series eds.; Grand Rapids: Baker Academic, 2005), 79–125.

include a death or resurrection report. Q does not contain such a tradition because most or all of that material was circulating among Jesus' followers *before* the cross and resurrection. Stories about him were circulating during his earthly ministry. Dunn rightly contends, "Jesus made an impact on those who became his first disciples, well before his death and resurrection. That impact was expressed in the first formulations of the Jesus tradition, formulations already stable before the influence of his death and resurrection was experienced."[38] This "living tradition" he claims was passed on orally by Jesus' disciples from the beginning and was recalled in the earliest days of the beginning of the church. It is not clear when some of that tradition was written down, but it is not impossible that Jesus was remembered both before and after his death and resurrection. It is certainly possible that some of what was remembered about him before his death was written down before the emergence of the canonical Gospels. What was remembered about him before his death no doubt formed at least much of the core of the oral tradition about him after his death and was likely at the heart of much of the early church's teaching about him (Acts 2:42).

How Jesus impacted his early followers before his death had to be sufficiently influential to cause them to leave family and positions and follow him as the one they all believed was going to initiate the kingdom of God. Why should anyone think that this impact was soon forgotten after Jesus' death and resurrection? His followers even argued before his death over who would have leadership roles in that coming kingdom (Mark 10:35–45). Following his death, when all hopes about Jesus and the kingdom he had proclaimed seemed dashed, the resurrection reinspired his followers to follow him and to advance his mission as well as to continue passing on to others the stories or traditions about Jesus that had been circulating earlier.[39] After Jesus' resurrection, what he said and what he did before his death, including what he said about his death and resurrection, were all considered very important for the life and witness of the early church, especially for their mission objectives, worship, and teaching ministries.

But why would anyone follow one who bore the scandal of a crucifixion, and how could anyone overcome the scandal of his rejection and crucifixion? In other words, what caused the tragedies that befell Jesus to be understood in a new way and appropriated by those who followed him? It is difficult to understand how the early Christians could have perpetuated the story of a crucified, despised, humiliated, and rejected religious leader, apart from the

---

38. Dunn, *New Perspective on Jesus*, 77.

39. See also Dunn's more extensive discussion about what was remembered about Jesus by his disciples in *Jesus Remembered*, 173–254.

hope and renewal that came with their belief in his resurrection. It was Paul's belief in the resurrection of Jesus that led him to emphasize the importance of the death of Jesus (1 Cor. 1:22–25; 15:3–20) and enabled him to overcome the ridicule of a crucified leader. After his resurrection, the early Christians remembered the events and teachings of Jesus and used them in their worship and instruction. These traditions were handed on in the churches because they met the missional, liturgical, and instructional aims of the early community of believers. Many of these traditions were included in the New Testament Gospels.

It cannot be demonstrated that Paul's view of the death and resurrection of Jesus influenced the other writers of the New Testament or that he was the source of a tradition that was in some way contrary to the views held by the earliest followers of Jesus. On the contrary, Paul and other New Testament and early church writers express their awareness of the death and resurrection of Jesus because it was central to the earliest strands and core of their faith.

Advocates of Q continue to make more of its existence than is warranted by the evidence. There probably was an additional source (or sources) to which Matthew and Luke appealed, some of which were written down,[40] and some of the material that Matthew and Luke have in common may well have been oral tradition preserved by the followers of Jesus and circulated orally in churches almost from the beginning (hence the variations in portions of the material they hold in common). Some of that oral tradition likely circulated among Jesus' followers even *before* his death, as Dunn has shown. If Q represented another community of Jesus' followers without a passion or Easter tradition, that was never acknowledged by anyone in antiquity. To postulate a post-death-of-Jesus kind of Christianity that restricted itself to an appreciation of the sayings of Jesus, even the subversive or alternative wisdom sayings (as Marcus Borg puts it),[41] is completely unwarranted.[42]

There are several other assumptions about Q that have no supporting evidence as yet, but that are regularly made by scholars who advocate a Q community of Jesus followers. Johnson lists the most important of these as the following: (1) the material common to Matthew and Luke comes from the same

40. Graham Stanton makes the point that due to the exact verbal parallels in many of the Q passages, at least some of the Q material was written down. See his *Gospel Truth: New Light on Jesus and the Gospels* (Valley Forge, PA: Trinity Press, 1995), 66–76.

41. M. Borg, *Meeting Jesus Again for the First Time: The Historical Jesus and the Heart of Contemporary Faith* (San Francisco: HarperCollins, 1994), 70.

42. For further arguments against this use of Q to postulate a supposed strange and different community of followers of Jesus that existed before Paul, see W. R. Farmer, *The Gospel of Jesus: The Pastoral Relevance of the Synoptic Problem* (Louisville: Westminster John Knox, 1994), as well as Linnemann, *Is There a Synoptic Problem?*, and also her "Is There a Gospel of Q?," 18–23, 42–43.

single source; (2) what is contained in the source as we now have it is all that it ever contained; (3) the original form of Q can be determined by omitting the alterations of it primarily in Matthew but also in Luke; (4) the source as it presently exists constituted the entire literature of a specific community of followers of Jesus; (5) it is possible to detect stages in the development of Q; (6) each of these stages is thematically unified; (7) stages of development or redaction correspond exactly to the community's social development; and, finally, (8) the group that read this document was an early form of a Jesus movement that was unaffected by the Jerusalem church and the Pauline "Christ cult." Johnson contends not only that there is not one shred of evidence for any of these assumptions, but that if they were true, they would leave the question of Christian origins unanswerable, since this would leave the Christian church without an impressive founder or any "founding experience."[43]

At best, Q appears to be a convenient descriptive title for material that is common to Matthew and Luke but not found in Mark. Nothing more or less is required from the evidence available. It is possible that parts of it came from a written source, but the evidence that all of it was written is lacking. The evidence that all of Q came from the same source, or that we have all of that source now (two of the weightiest assumptions of the advocates of the Q community), is lacking. Dunn and other scholars have already turned the Q community hypothesis on its head and have allowed us to think more seriously about the impact that Jesus made on those who followed him *prior* to his execution.[44] The vast majority of New Testament scholars today reject the notion of a post-Easter Q community, and with good reason.

Gospel Relationships

We have discussed how the Synoptic Gospels reflect a common relationship that is best understood by Mark being the first written Gospel and Matthew and Luke depending on Mark, as well as the Q materials that were either written or oral in form, or both. It is possible that John was familiar with the Gospel of Mark, as a few scholars have suggested, but that has not been clearly established. John is so different in his presentation of Jesus that we will have below a more extended discussion of the relevance and reliability of his Gospel. Many historical Jesus scholars have long ignored John's Gospel, and I will suggest below that there is good reason to take another look at what John has to offer.

43. Luke Timothy Johnson, *The Real Jesus: The Misguided Quest for the Historical Jesus and the Truth of the Traditional Gospels* (San Francisco: HarperSanFrancisco, 1996), 52–53.
44. Dunn, *Jesus Remembered*, 41–44, 147–49, 231–38, and elsewhere as noted above.

Long ago B. F. Westcott tabulated the parallels between the Gospels, and his results are still quite helpful for understanding the overall situation. These are as follows:

Gospel of	Peculiarities	Coincidences
Mark	7%	93%
Matthew	42%	58%
Luke	59%	41%
John	92%	8%

The most commonly accepted explanation for these close affinities, called the "Four Source Theory," mentioned above, suggests (1) Mark wrote the first Gospel. (2) Matthew and Luke used Mark and even altered Mark for their own purposes. (3) Matthew and Luke also used other sources, especially Q, that is, material in Matthew and Luke not found in Mark. The verbal and sequential parallels between Matthew and Luke in the so-called Q passages are not always as close as in the portions that they have in common with Mark. They are sufficiently close, however, to call either for dependence of one evangelist on the other or for both drawing upon a common source, now identified as Q. (4) It is further argued that the unique portions of Matthew and Luke, that is, their genealogies, birth narratives, and material found only in Matthew or Luke, come from Matthew's peculiar source or sources (commonly designated "M") and Luke's peculiar source or sources (commonly designated "L").[45] These relationships are regularly diagrammed as follows:

John's Gospel, as we saw in the chart above, is considerably different from the Synoptic Gospels in many of the stories it presents, but it is like them in some very important areas, such as agreement on Jesus' ability to attract large crowds through his teaching, preaching, and miracles, and also his triumphal entry into Jerusalem, arrest, crucifixion, burial, and resurrection. We will focus on what they have in common and their reliability below. Before that, we will summarize briefly the arguments for Mark's priority and then consider the reliability of the Gospels' message about Jesus.

Although the earliest witness to an event is not always the most reliable, its value is clearly enhanced by its closer proximity to the events it reports. It is

45. The term *Sondergut* (German, "proper material") is often used of that material in each Gospel that is peculiar to it.

also commonly argued that the subsequent sources tend to expand the stories in the earlier ones, and a case in point might be that the resurrection narratives are considerably longer in Matthew, Luke, and John than in Mark and contain greater emphasis on theological significance in the stories. Scholars often question the reliability of the longer narratives because expansions suggest later additions by the early churches to the authentic Jesus traditions. Did the expanded stories distort or enhance the story of Jesus? Those questions cannot be adequately dealt with here, but they are dealt with in considerable detail in more recent discussions listed in the bibliography.

Several factors point to Mark's priority and Matthew's and Luke's dependence on Mark: (1) With the exception of three short reports (Mark 4:26–29; 7:31–37; 8:22–26) and three short narratives (Mark 3:22–28; 9:49; 14:51–65), the whole of Mark is in Matthew and Luke. It is easier to explain the absence of these few passages in Matthew and Luke than it is to explain why Mark, if he wrote subsequent to them, would omit the vast sections of Matthew and Luke such as the birth, genealogy, expanded baptism and temptation stories, and the Sermon on the Mount (or Plain in Luke). It is easier to explain Matthew's and Luke's omission of a few portions of Mark. Kümmel has pointed out that 8,189 of the 10,650 words in Mark are in Matthew and Luke (Matthew employing 7,768 of them, and Luke using some 7,040). Matthew and Luke coincide extensively in the material they have in common with Mark, and this cannot be explained by Mark's omission of vast sections of Matthew or Luke.[46] (2) Matthew and Luke agree with each other *in sequence* only so far as they agree with Mark. In the Q material they have in common they do not follow the same sequence, as in the Sermon on the Mount (Matt. 5–7), which appears in various other locations throughout Luke. (3) There is strong agreement in wording in the material the Synoptics have in common, even though there is a tendency in Matthew and Luke to change Mark's simpler Greek to a more sophisticated Greek and to correct his oversights, as in Mark's attributing to Isaiah a quotation from Malachi 3:1 (cf. Mark 1:2 with Matt. 3:3 and Luke 3:4). They also make changes in Mark's grammar.[47] It is easier to understand why Matthew would have improved Mark than it is to understand why Mark would have changed Matthew to something less sophisticated. Craig A. Evans adds the issue of propriety, referring to Mark's reference to the weaknesses of the disciples (cf. Mark 4:38 with Matt. 8:24; also cf. Mark 8:17–21 with Matt. 16:9–12, omitted in Luke). Jesus' family's concern

46. Kümmel, *Introduction*, 57.

47. Such as where Mark uses the so-called present tense of a verb in a past narrative setting, such as "he says" (*legei*) instead of "he said" (*eipen*), which is changed to a more usual narrative tense by Matthew and Luke (cf. Mark 2:12 with Matt. 9:7 and Luke 5:25; Mark 4:10 with Matt. 13:10 and Luke 8:9; and Mark 16:8 with Matt. 28:8 and Luke 24:9).

about his stability (Mark 3:21) is absent in Matthew and Luke, including the possible disrespect Jesus had for his family (Mark 3:33–34; cf. Matt. 12:49; Luke 8:21). When Jesus was praying, Mark says the disciples fell asleep *three times* and Jesus rebuked them (14:37–41); Luke only mentions one time and says that they slept for sorrow, and Jesus only gave a mild reminder to be vigilant so as not to be overcome in the time of trial (Luke 22:45–46). Again, it is easier to say that Matthew and Luke removed potential embarrassments than that Mark substituted Jesus' more favorable comments about his disciples with less favorable ones.[48] The arguments against Markan priority do not adequately answer the arguments in favor of Markan priority.[49] While it has been argued earlier that Mark was written first and that Matthew and Luke made use of Mark, does it follow that they did not use a Q source as was argued earlier by Ferrar and Goodacre? I have shown that the many parallels, some word-for-word, between Matthew and Luke but not in Mark strongly suggest that they both used another source. Since they did not follow the same sequence as they did when they used Mark, it is likely that there may have been both written and oral traditions that they both used, and this fits well with the notion of a Q tradition or even document that was used by both. Likewise, since neither Matthew nor Luke used all of Mark, they likely did not use all of the source that they have in common, and perhaps some of the M and L material may be material that only one of the evangelists used from Q and the other did not. These are only suggestions, of course, but Markan priority appears much more certain.

What Gave Rise to the Gospels?

Since Jesus left no writings of his own behind and he did not occupy any sort of official position that would have caused an official record of his actions

48. See C. A. Evans, *Mark 8:27–16:20* (WBC 34B; Nashville: Nelson, 2001), xlv–lviii. See also his discussion of Q, including the agreements among the Synoptics, their sequences, divergences, and the material unique to Mark.

49. A collection of arguments against Markan priority is found in Farmer, *Synoptic Problem*, which calls into question not only the priority of Mark, but also the existence of any "Q" document. His work is commanding because of its extensive detail, but his arguments have had little influence on the majority of New Testament scholars today. J. A. Fitzmyer, in his article "The Priority of Mark and the 'Q' Source in Luke," in *Jesus and Man's Hope* (Pittsburgh: Pittsburgh Theological Seminary, 1970), 1:181–90, offers strong arguments against Farmer's work on the subject. In favor of Matthean priority, see also B. C. Butler, *The Originality of St. Matthew: A Critique of the Two-Document Hypothesis* (Cambridge: Cambridge University Press, 1951); A. M. Farrer, "On Dispensing with Q," in *Studies in the Gospels: Essays in Memory of R. H. Lightfoot* (ed. D. E. Nineham; Oxford: Blackwell, 1955), 55–86. More recently, David Laird Dungan is critical of Markan priority and is largely supportive of Farmer's position in his *A History of the Synoptic Problem: The Canon, the Text, the Composition, and the Interpretation of the Gospels* (New York: Doubleday, 1999).

or speeches to be kept, why would someone tell his story in a volume called a "gospel"? Jesus' life and teachings were remembered, of course, not simply out of historical interest, but because he had an overwhelming impact on those who followed him during his short ministry. However, since many in the earliest churches believed that Jesus was going to return soon, why were the Gospels written?

It is highly likely that the delay of the return of the risen Christ and the deaths of many of the original eyewitnesses prompted some in the church to produce a written record of the story that gave rise to their faith. Oral tradition had considerable influence in the early church, but in time it would become very difficult to continue the story of Jesus without it being written down. Likewise, the earliest churches had those eyewitnesses around who could tell the stories of Jesus and pass on his teachings to them, but as new churches were planted in lands far from Palestine, it became more difficult for the original eyewitnesses still in the church to be with them. It therefore was important to have a written record of what was at the heart of the faith that the early Christians could pass on to new followers of Jesus. The Gospels were likely born in such a context.

But since the earliest followers of Jesus were Jewish and spoke Aramaic, or some Hebrew, why were the Gospels not written in Hebrew or Aramaic, the languages current in Palestine? What historical events would have provided occasions for writing down this oral tradition about Jesus *in Greek*? Certainly the growth of the gentile mission probably had something to do with the emergence of the Greek New Testament writings, since the number of gentiles in the church (most of whom spoke Greek) was increasing, but it likely also had to do with the consequent decline in the number of Jews who were attracted to the message about Jesus. With the decline in the number of Jews who responded positively to the Christian message, it made sense to those who continued to make the Christian proclamation to write that story in Greek. Only the Greek texts of the story about Jesus have survived, although it is possible that the *Hebrew Gospel* (or *Gospel of the Hebrews*), which was adopted by many Jews, originally existed in Hebrew. As the church grew among both Jews and gentiles in the Diaspora, there was a need for the story of Jesus to be put in Greek, the most-used international language of the day, even for most Jews.

Again, the most probable catalyst for writing the Gospels was the death of the most prominent leaders in the early church—Peter, James, and Paul, but others in the apostolic community as well. The Roman persecutions in which these leading apostles died were likely a significant motivation for some to write down the story of Jesus that was circulating orally earlier. Following this line of reasoning, Gospel writing probably began around the year AD 60, when the apostles and original eyewitnesses were growing older and local persecutions were increasing. Earlier forms of the story of Jesus may have existed (Luke 1:1–4), but we do not have access to them, except perhaps Q.

In the process of passing on the story of Jesus in oral form, the actual historical sequence of most of the oral tradition about him was probably lost except for the broad outline of his ministry. That outline includes Jesus' baptism by John, his initial preaching and strong appeal to crowds of people in Galilee, the growing hostility from Jewish religious leaders, and finally his arrest, trial, crucifixion, and resurrection. Within this generally accepted outline of Jesus' ministry and fate, many of the events reported in the Gospels could have occurred either early or late in Jesus' ministry. The exact times and places of the events in Jesus' career were not of significant interest to the evangelists and were not given careful attention. Luke, however, may be the exception, as he did claim to offer an outline of the sequence of Jesus' activities (Luke 1:3). Again, the broad outline of Jesus' ministry was fairly well established in the traditions of the early church, but the specific sequence of his deeds and teachings was not at first considered important.

The Gospels selectively reflected the story of what took place in the story of Jesus, but also were no doubt welcomed and functioned as authoritative writings in the early churches, likely from the time they were first produced. This does not suggest that the Gospels were inventions of the early churches designed to meet their later developing needs, though some development in those traditions is discernible. The traditions about Jesus formed the instruction for early Christian churches. Early Christian interpretation and development of these traditions about Jesus does not mean that the early Christians significantly altered them by putting words in the mouth of Jesus or creating new actions in his story to help them advance their mission and life. From the beginning, what Jesus said and did was important to his followers, and the stories about him were continually applied to ever new and changing situations of the emerging churches. That has always been a characteristic of the stories about Jesus in the Gospels for the churches.[50] What was remembered was also relevant to the needs of the churches. Eventually the majority of the churches rejected the more sensational stories about Jesus that were circulating, especially in the second and third centuries, and they did not welcome any fabrication or expansion of the events reported in the Gospels. Metzger rightly

---

50. Richard Bauckham, in *Jesus and the Eyewitnesses: The Gospels as Eyewitness Testimony* (Grand Rapids: Eerdmans, 2006), makes a strong case for the authenticity and reliability of the Gospels as based on eyewitness reports.

maintains that what survived in the Gospels was completely "homogeneous with the original meaning, whose full vitality is thus unfolded for the benefit of the whole Church."[51]

The New Testament Gospels

The New Testament Gospels all contain many christological formulations about the person of Jesus and his special relationship with God that are well beyond the scope of a historian's inquiry, but they also locate Jesus in time and in a geographical location and tell us more about him than all other sources combined. We will briefly examine what we can say about their reliability as witnesses, but much of the information about their background is readily available in standard New Testament introductions listed in the bibliography and will not be discussed here. I will say something about the authorship of Mark as well as his reliability, since Mark is widely acknowledged to be the originator of the Gospel genre and was known and used by both Matthew and Luke and possibly known also to John.[52]

The Gospel of Mark

As we saw above, from ancient times until the last quarter of the nineteenth century, Mark was without question the most neglected of all four canonical Gospels. Despite this widespread neglect, the Gospel of Mark was nevertheless well known and used or cited by several early church writers and documents including Papias, Irenaeus, and Clement of Alexandria, as well the authors of the *Gospel of Peter*, the *Shepherd of Hermas*, Tatian's *Diatessaron*, and Tertullian, Origen, Eusebius, Epiphanius, Augustine, and Jerome. However, even after Irenaeus praised the Gospel of Mark in his description of the four-fold Gospel collection (*Against Heresies*, 1.10.5, 8; ca. AD 170–180), the use of Mark in the early churches decreased for several centuries.

Only after the modern quest for the historical Jesus emerged in the late nineteenth century, when most biblical scholars began to conclude that Mark wrote the first Gospel, did Mark gain significant attention. Today several major commentaries on Mark have appeared, and it is one of the most studied

---

51. B. M. Metzger, *The New Testament: Its Background, Growth, and Content* (New York: Abingdon, 1965), 87. See also Stanton, *Gospels and Jesus*, 163.

52. I have discussed issues of date, context, and substance in more detail in Lee Martin McDonald and Stanley E. Porter, *Early Christianity and Its Sacred Literature* (Peabody, MA: Hendrickson, 2000), 274–313.

Gospels because of its priority over Matthew and Luke. Mark's purpose seems straightforward—he aims to tell the story of Jesus who is the Son of God (1:1) in such a way that it calls forth faith in the reader or hearer.

Authorship

The Gospel of Mark, as is true of the other canonical Gospels, was produced as an anonymous work. The current superscription, "The Gospel according to Mark" (*euangelion kata Markon*), likely comes from the end of the second century. In the middle of the second century Bishop Papias of Hierapolis (ca. AD 140) attributed the work to John Mark, the companion of Peter. His comments are preserved by Eusebius, bishop at Caesarea and the first major church historian (ca. 325), in his *Ecclesiastical History*.

> In the same writing he [Papias] also quotes from interpretations of the words of the Lord given by the Aristion mentioned above and traditions of John the Presbyter. To them we may dismiss the studious; but we are now obliged to append to the words already quoted from him a tradition about the Mark who wrote the Gospel, which he expounds as follows. "And the Presbyter used to say this, 'Mark became Peter's interpreter and wrote accurately all that he remembered, not, indeed, in order, of the things said or done by the Lord. For he had not heard the Lord, nor had he followed him, but later on, as I said, followed Peter, who used to give teaching as necessity demanded but not making, as it were, an arrangement of the Lord's oracles, so that Mark did nothing wrong in thus writing down single points as he remembered them. For to one thing he gave attention, to leave out nothing of what he had heard and to make no false statements in them.'" This is related by Papias about Mark. (*Hist. eccl.* 3.39.14–16, LCL)

Eusebius himself says Mark, as Peter's follower, was asked by the Christians in Rome to compose his Gospel.

> But a great light of religion shone on the minds of the hearers of Peter, so that they were not satisfied with a single hearing or with the unwritten teaching of the divine proclamation, but with every kind of exhortation besought Mark, whose Gospel is extant, seeing that he was Peter's follower, to leave them a written statement of the teaching given them verbally, nor did they cease until they had persuaded him, and so became the cause of the Scripture called the Gospel according to Mark. And they say that the Apostle [Peter], knowing by the revelation of the spirit to him what had been done, was pleased at their zeal and ratified the scripture [Mark's Gospel] for study in the churches. Clement [of Alexandria] quotes the story in the sixth book of the Hypotyposes, and the bishop of Hierapolis, named Papias, confirms him. He also says that Peter mentions Mark in his first Epistle. (*Hist. eccl.* 2.15.2, LCL)

On the basis of ancient testimony from ancient times, John Mark, the companion of Paul and Barnabas (Acts 13:13; 15:36–39) and subsequently of Peter (1 Pet. 5:13), has been acknowledged as the author of the Gospel bearing his name. While not all scholars agree on Mark's authorship, based on Papias's comments, early church fathers have argued that Mark *adapted* the teaching of Peter in writing his Gospel. Since it was acknowledged early on that Mark did not have any firsthand knowledge of Jesus' teachings or deeds, most church fathers traced his report back to Peter.[53] This squares with Eusebius's earlier report (ca. 330) that Mark learned from Peter and without Peter's awareness prepared his Gospel, and that it was subsequently approved by Peter for reading in the churches (*Hist. eccl.* 2.15.1–2). Earlier still, Irenaeus (ca. AD 170–180) said that "after [Peter's and Paul's] death, Mark, the disciple and interpreter of Peter, transmitted to us in writing what was preached by Peter" (*Haer.* 3.1.1). If this is so, Mark was written after the death of Peter, who died during Nero's persecution of Christians in Rome (ca. AD 64–67). The earliest church testimony says that John Mark, a companion of Barnabas, Paul, and Peter, received eyewitness testimony and wrote it down.

Confidence in Mark's reliability is supported by use in Matthew and Luke. If John Mark wrote this gospel, it likely contains reliable information about Jesus that goes back to the beginning of the church. Mark's reference to the failure of the disciples, including Peter, in their fleeing the Roman guard when Jesus was arrested (Mark 14:50) may well have come from Peter himself. That story was subsequently downplayed in Matthew and Luke, but could the story have come from Peter, who was anxious to set forth the actual record about what happened?

If Mark had a connection with Peter and constructed the first gospel, then its value in reconstructing the story of Jesus cannot be minimized. Mark was obviously aware of oral tradition about Jesus circulating in the early churches and likely made use of it in his writing. In the post-Easter period, all who continued to follow Jesus most likely knew a considerable amount of teaching that was circulating orally in the churches (see Acts 2:42). Further, since this Gospel does not make a claim to be written by an apostle, and since all of the earliest testimony points to Mark, his authorship has substantial

---

53. Later, in his Prologue to Mark, Jerome (ca. AD 340–420) reflects early Christian perspectives as follows: "Mark, the interpreter of the Apostle Peter, and the first bishop of the church of Alexandria, who himself has not seen the Lord, the very Saviour, is the second [who published a Gospel], but he narrated those things, which he had heard [his] master preaching, more in accordance with the trustworthiness of the things performed than [in accordance with their] sequence" (*Evidence of Tradition* [trans. Daniel J. Theron; Grand Rapids: Baker, 1957; repr., 1980], 53).

support. Many gospels were produced pseudonymously in the second and third centuries under apostolic names, but Mark is different. Why would a pseudonymous writer have chosen Mark? If there had not been reliable traditions supporting Mark's authorship of the Gospel that bears his name, how would this tradition have survived? There is nothing special about Mark in the New Testament that would lend any credibility to him. Indeed, in the book of Acts, he is reported to have given up on Paul and Barnabas's first missionary endeavor (Acts 13:13), and Paul, no doubt as a result of Mark's weakness, subsequently rejected taking him on their second missionary journey (Acts 15:36–39). These are hardly credentials to commend the name of Mark to the early church, even in light of his recovery from his initial timidity and later profitable ministry (see 2 Tim. 4:11; 1 Pet. 5:13). The point here is obvious. It does not make sense for the ancients to fabricate Mark as the author of the Gospel bearing his name.

Date

It is not possible to be precise about the dating of Mark's Gospel, even if John Mark wrote it. If Irenaeus's testimony that Mark was written *after* the death of Peter is true, we may be able to date the Gospel in the middle to late 60s or even early 70s. Since Peter was likely executed during the Neronian persecution (ca. AD 64–67),[54] Mark may have been written anytime after AD 64–65 or as late as the early 70s. If it was written before the death of Peter and with Peter's approval, then it could even have been written in the early to middle 60s. There is debate among scholars over whether Mark refers to the destruction of Jerusalem (Mark 13:1–2), an event that had considerable impact on the early churches. Some scholars call this a *vaticinium ex eventu* (a prophecy after the event has taken place), in other words, a prophetic fabrication. On the other hand, Mark makes no reference to the relocation of Jerusalem Christians to Pella (east of the Jordan River) in the mid- to late 60s or even to Peter's death. This suggests an earlier date.[55] Evans claims that

54. The first document that speaks of Peter's and Paul's death is *1 Clem.* 5–6, but the details are not clear. The *Acts of Peter*, which was circulating in the last half of the second century, perhaps around AD 180–90, indicates that Peter died during the persecutions of Nero in Rome. The death of Paul is also described in a late second-century document that depends on the *Acts of Peter*. In *Acts of Paul* 11.1–7, the detailed description of the martyrdom of Paul is dated in the reign of Nero. Although the stories presented have numerous fabrications and some sensationalism, few scholars doubt the basic premise that both Peter and Paul were put to death during the Neronian persecutions of Christians around AD 64–65.

55. Marxsen believes that the references in Mark 13 to "signs" and "rumors of wars" indicate that the time of writing was during the period of the Jewish war (AD 66–70), but before the destruction of Jerusalem in AD 70. He suggests the date of its composition sometime between

scholarly pessimism is unwarranted and that before the fall of Jerusalem and the destruction of the temple there were many who had predicted that the temple would be destroyed. Jesus' prediction fits well within the context of the day when, because of the moral failure of the people and the leadership of the nation, others also were predicting the destruction of the temple.[56] While scholarly dating of Mark in the 70s is common, the evidence for this is slim. If the Gospel of Mark was written shortly before or after the death of Peter, but before the destruction of Jerusalem, it could have been written in AD 64–70. If it was written with Peter's approval, then sometime in the early 60s is likely.

Reliability

While it is unlikely that Mark himself composed all of the units of tradition in his Gospel and drew on a number of traditions circulating about Jesus in the early churches, he likely initiated the gospel genre that set the pattern and scope that subsequent gospel narratives followed—namely, focusing on Jesus' baptism, ministry, teaching, death, resurrection, and exaltation as Son of God and Lord. Matthew and Luke added a genealogy and birth story, but the rest of the pattern is the same. Mark's use by Matthew and Luke suggests Mark as a primary reliable source for information about Jesus. But was Mark faithful to his sources (Peter?), and does he present a reliable picture of Jesus? Evidence that Mark did not create vivid details in his Gospel if they were lacking in his sources can be seen in numerous places where he could have invented details in order to present a more vivid story (3:13–19; 6:6–16; 6:30–34; 6:53–56), such as we find in other reports where he seems to know more of the context (5:1–20; 9:14–29; 10:17–22), but he does not. When Mark did not have details, he chose not to invent them. We cannot conclude from this that Mark lacked imagination, but instead that he was a careful author and faithful transmitter, and not a fabricator in telling his story. It is noticeable that Mark often used sharp language that was softened in Matthew and Luke, as in the cases of Mark 4:38b ("Teacher, do you not care . . . ?") with Matthew 8:25 and Luke 8:24, but also compare Mark 6:5 with Matthew 13:58 or Mark 10:17–18 with Matthew 19:16–17. Mark also uses pre-Easter titles for Jesus such as "teacher" or "rabbi" (Mark 4:38; 10:17), but Matthew and

---

AD 67 and 69. See his *Introduction to the New Testament* (trans. G. Buswell; Philadelphia: Fortress Press, 1968), 113.

56. C. A. Evans, "Predictions of the Destruction of the Herodian Temple in the Pseudepigrapha, Qumran Scrolls, and Related Texts," *JSP* 10 (1992): 89–147. Evans argues that there was widespread peasant resentment of the Herodian temple's operation by the corrupt and non-Zadokite priestly families, and concludes that Jesus, like many others of his day and before, predicted the destruction of the temple, employing the classical prophets' predictions, especially Jeremiah's and Ezekiel's (146–47).

Luke often use post-Easter titles such as "Lord" or "Master" (Matt. 7:21; 8:25; and Luke 8:24). At times Mark used language that may have offended Christians or the disciples, as in the case of James and John requesting places of authority in Jesus' kingdom (Mark 10:35–37), but in Matthew 20:21 it is their mother. In Mark 14:33 Jesus is "greatly distressed and troubled," but this is softened in Matthew 26:37, and Luke omits it altogether. The failure of the disciples to stay awake in Gethsemane while Jesus was praying (Mark 14:71) is softened in Luke 22:45. In Mark 14:71 Peter cursed and denied knowing Jesus, but in Luke 22:60 Peter says, "I do not know what you are saying." It is easier to understand why Matthew and Luke would soften Mark's language than why Mark would harden Matthew's and Luke's language if he were using their works to construct his own. When Mark received a tradition in isolation without knowing its historical context, he did not supply the missing historical links. However, Matthew and Luke often supply such links in places where Mark has none. In Luke 5:33 Luke connects fasting with the supper in Levi's house, but Mark does not (2:18). Matthew connects Jesus' withdrawal in 14:13 with the execution of John the Baptist, but not Mark (6:30–31). These expansions are difficult to explain if Mark is dated after Matthew or Luke. It suggests that when his traditions did not have the connections, he did not invent them. Finally, Mark's inclusion of Jesus' ignorance of the date of the coming kingdom (Mark 13:32) is not found in Matthew or Luke, and also Jesus' cry of dereliction while on the cross (Mark 15:34) is softened in Luke (Luke 23:46). For these reasons, a case can be made for the basic reliability of Mark's handling of his sources. He was both frank and conservative in the materials that he handled and did not invent what he did not have or hide even the embarrassing things that are softened in Matthew and Luke.[57]

Although Mark's careful handling of his sources is generally recognized, this does not prove that his sources were historically reliable. What limits the level of expansion or even fabrication in Mark or the sources that he employed in writing his narrative about Jesus is that several eyewitnesses were still living when he constructed his Gospel, and his story of Jesus had already been circulating orally in churches long before he put his Gospel in writing. Since the main outline of Jesus' career and passion was regularly repeated in the early churches and thus kept alive in their memory (see Acts 2:22–36; 1 Tim. 3:16), any invention by Mark is highly unlikely and would likely have been easily detected in the churches. Also, Jesus' use of parables, aphorisms, and epigrams made it easy to pass along his teachings without significant loss of important detail.

---

57. A still-useful summary of these comparisons is in C. E. B. Cranfield, "The Gospel of Mark," *IDB* 3:267–77.

Again, Mark's inclusion of traditions that discredit Peter and the other apostles and those things that might be cause for embarrassment about Jesus, such as Jesus' ignorance about the time of his second coming (13:32) and his cry from the cross (15:34), point to his general reliability and reflect his faithfulness to his sources. Martin Hengel underscores the reliability of Mark because behind such a work as Mark "an authority must stand. Only thus is it explained that Luke and Matthew relied upon it massively and that it was not lost despite the existence of more comprehensive Gospels such as Luke and Matthew and the 'apostolic' authority of the latter, which reused 80 per cent of it."[58]

Message

Of considerable importance for Mark is what scholars have called his "messianic secret." This phenomenon was first introduced into scholarly discussions by William Wrede in 1901 and 1913. He noted that in Mark, Jesus wanted to keep his messianic identity a secret, and forbade the demons and even his disciples from disclosing his true identity (see 1:32–34; 3:12; 4:10–12, 33–34; 8:30; 9:9; see also 16:7).[59] Wrede dubbed this phenomenon the "messianic secret" (German, *Messiasgeheimnis*) and accounted for it as either coming from a pre-Markan tradition that Mark used or as invented by Mark himself to explain the differences between Jesus before and after his resurrection. Adela Yarbro Collins recognizes that Mark builds suspense in his narrative in his unfolding identity of Jesus when Jesus finally identifies himself as the "Son of the Blessed," which is the same as "Son of God" (14:62), and that that accounts for the "secret" in Mark.[60]

This secret, however, is a very poorly kept secret in Mark, and the people could not suppress Jesus' identity for long. For example, when Jesus commanded the people not to tell anyone, they often spoke even more about him (7:36–37; 8:36). Again, as we can see in the accusatory question of the high priest against Jesus when Jesus stood before the Sanhedrin, this advice was not well kept (14:61–62).

---

58. "Eyewitness Memory and the Writing of the Gospels: Form Criticism, Community Tradition and the Authority of the Authors," in *The Written Gospel* (ed. M. Bockmuehl and D. A. Hagner; Cambridge: Cambridge University Press, 2005), 92.

59. *Das Messiasgeheimnis in den Evangelien* (Göttingen: 1901; 2nd ed., 1913), translated by J. C. G. Grieg, *The Messianic Secret* (Cambridge: James Clarke & Co., 1971).

60. Adela Yarbro Collins, *Mark: A Commentary* (Hermeneia; ed. H. W. Attridge; Minneapolis: Fortress, 2007), 170–72, 214, and 704, offers a brief but useful summary of the arguments related to the messianic secret in Mark. In her discussion of 15:39, she also carefully summarizes the use of this designation in the ancient Jewish religious literature and in the Roman world, where the term was used of emperors (764–71).

Mark, of course, does not leave his *readers* in doubt about the identity of Jesus. From beginning to end, they are told in both word and deed that Jesus is the anticipated Messiah (1:1), and they learn that he must suffer and die (8:31; 10:45). However, it is only in the post-Easter period that the true identity and mission of Jesus could be understood. Wrede correctly concluded that Mark had theological motives for sharing his story the way he did and that he used these messianic secret stories *to let his readers know that the Messiah must die*. Mark makes it clear that even the disciples did not fully understand who Jesus was, what he said, or his role before his resurrection. Because the disciples had anticipated a ruling and reigning messiah and not a crucified victim of humiliation, injustice, and abuse, one can understand why there was considerable confusion on their part.

However, the historical and theological motives Wrede described need not be at odds with one another. Craig Keener, for instance, suggests instead that if Jesus had accepted such designations early in his ministry, he would have brought the wrath of Rome and the Jewish religious leadership upon himself. Consequently, he delayed making his identity known "until the appropriate time" when he would fulfill his role as Messiah and avoid the certain execution that did in fact come when he finally made his identity known![61] The secrecy issue in Mark largely has to do with what is apparent throughout—namely, that Mark is giving an apology (defense) for the death of Jesus.[62] In other words, for Mark the Messiah must suffer and die and nothing could interfere with that mission. Jesus, therefore, revealed his identity to the disciples, but commanded them not to tell the crowds or anyone else. Revealing his true identity too soon could interfere with the necessity of going to the cross before his earthly mission was accomplished.

Mark's primary concern is to present Jesus as the Son of God, and the significance of his message for readers facing an uncertain future and going through various trials for their faith and mission is obvious. Jesus has triumphed over all enemies, even the abandonment by his closest friends, and he endured a cruel death on a cross. This would surely have been significant for those believers facing an uncertain future. Jesus' story offered hope and was directly related to recognition of God's activity in him. Mark's identification of the presence of the kingdom of God in Jesus' life, ministry, suffering, and resurrection would have been a source of encouragement.

61. Craig S. Keener, *The Historical Jesus of the Gospels* (Grand Rapids: Eerdmans, 2009), 263–64.

62. For example, see Robert H. Gundry, *Mark: A Commentary on His Apology for the Cross* (Grand Rapids: Eerdmans, 1993), 1022–26, who argues that Mark intended to defend the shameful death of Jesus that was at the heart of the rejection of Jesus in Mark's time. He illustrates this position convincingly throughout his commentary.

Main Concerns

Mark has several major areas of interest in telling his story about Jesus: the kingdom of God, the identity of Jesus, what it means to be his disciple, the so-called messianic secret, and finally the importance of the cross in the story of Jesus. For Mark, Jesus' role as Messiah and Son of God never conflicted with his humanity. Jesus was in a special relationship with God, as we see in his baptism and transfiguration, but he was also human and could eat, tire, hunger, suffer, and die. Mark defends the necessity of the cross for Jesus, but acknowledges Jesus' identity from the beginning (1:1, 11; see also 9:7) as the Son of Man who has the power to forgive sin (2:10), suffers and is crucified (8:31), offers his life as a ransom (10:45), has a place of authority and will be "seated at the right hand of Power [God]," and will be "coming with the clouds of heaven" (14:62). "Son of Man" is the most frequent self-designation of Jesus in all four Gospels (some eighty-one times). It can be a reference to a king, as in Psalm 2:7, or simply to a human being, often translated as "mortal" in Ezekiel (2:1, 3, 6, passim), but the term takes on a special meaning in Daniel 7:13 and in the later *Parables of Enoch* (probably written ca. 40 BC), in which the Son of Man comes from God to accomplish the will of God on earth. It is unlikely that Mark invented this title for Jesus since the early church did not use it of him. Outside of Jesus' self-designation it is found in the New Testament only in Acts 13:33, when Paul cites Psalm 2:7 in reference to Jesus.

Another of Mark's chief concerns is to clarify the role of a disciple of Jesus. Those who follow Jesus must be willing to leave all worldly securities behind (1:16–18; 2:13–14) and even life itself (8:34–35).

For Mark, the Messiah must die as a ransom for the people (10:45), and nothing could interfere with Jesus' purpose of going to the cross, so his identity was withheld from the public domain (the messianic secret as in 1:25–26; see also 1:34; 3:11–12; 8:29–30; 9:7–9). Jesus' identity and passion predictions that he shared with his disciples were difficult for the disciples to comprehend when they were concerned more about who would have a prominent place of leadership in the coming kingdom. A crucified messiah was simply not clear to them (9:30–32). However, in defense of Mark, we should not expect Mark, who wrote after Easter, to have been less clear about the identity of Jesus than what he understood at the time he wrote. His readers surely understood more than the pre-Easter disciples.

Postscript: The Secondary Ending of Mark

Most New Testament scholars today recognize that Mark 16:9–20 is a late addition to Mark's Gospel, but they disagree on whether 16:8 was its original ending. It ends with the postpositive conjunction "for" ("*for* they were afraid"—Greek, *ephobounto gar*). It was unusual in ancient Greek to conclude a literary work with a conjunction as in 16:8, but an instance is found in the first-century Pseudo-Demetrius's *Formae Epistolicae*, which ends with *opheilō gar* ("*for* I owe" or "*for* I am indebted"). More importantly, since Mark contains no appearance stories in his Easter tradition, but does have a promise of them in 16:7, it seemed odd to some in the early church, so they added appearances to Mark's story. Having begun with the promise of "good news" (1:1), it does seem odd to end with the women leaving the tomb saying nothing to anyone, "for they were afraid" (16:8). Did Mark originally end with 16:8, or was there more?

In her commentary, Yarbro Collins summarizes well the arguments on both sides of the question. She rightly concludes that ending a book with a conjunction is rare, but not as strong an argument against ending at 16:8 as earlier supposed. She favors the Gospel concluding with the women leaving without saying anything, claiming that their actions were understandable given the phenomenon of the angelic being at the tomb and the event of the resurrection of Jesus itself. She cites parallel expressions of fear at remarkable events in Mark and concludes that Mark does not focus on the appearances, but rather the resurrection of Jesus itself. She adds that had there been no subsequent development in the Easter tradition that led Matthew, Luke, and John to include appearances, no one would have felt the need to add them in Mark. Mark is simply focusing on the "numinous and shocking character of the event of Jesus' resurrection from the dead."[63] She does not see a tension between verse 7, with the promise of an appearance, and verse 8, which concludes with the women fleeing from the tomb saying nothing to anyone.

N. C. Croy, on the other hand, lists a large number of scholars who argue for a lost or unfinished ending of Mark. He concludes that 16:8 is an unnatural ending of a Gospel that begins on a note of hope and ends on a note

---

63. Adela Yarbro Collins, *Mark*, 797–801, here 800. She also references a supporting article by Larry W. Hurtado, "The Women, the Tomb, and the Purposes of Mark," in *A Wandering Galilean: Essays in Honour of Sean Freyne* (ed. Zuleika Rogers with Margaret Daly-Denton, and Anne Fitzpatrick McKinley; Supplements to the Journal for the Study of Judaism; Leiden: Brill, 2009). Yarbro Collins concludes that a resurrection appearance in Mark was not necessary to fulfill Mark's narrative purposes (801). Several earlier commentators share her conclusion, e.g., E. P. Gould, *The Gospel according to Mark* (ICC; Edinburgh: T&T Clark, 1896; repr., 1969), 301–2; R. Fuller, *The Formation of the Resurrection Narratives* (London: SPCK, 1972), 64–67; R. H. Lightfoot, *The Gospel Message of St. Mark* (Oxford: Oxford University Press, 1950), 80–97; and Hugh Anderson, *The Gospel of Mark* (New Century Bible; London: Oliphants, 1976), 357–59.

of fear and silence.[64] He contends that 16:7 leads us to anticipate a forth-coming appearance of Jesus to the disciples. The fact that appearances are listed not only in Matthew, Luke, and John but also in Acts (1:3–9) and Paul (see 1 Cor. 15:3–8; 9:1) suggests an anticipated appearance in the original ending of Mark. Even though the women were no doubt filled with shock and fear at what they saw or experienced, 16:7 nevertheless seems to require that they *not* keep silence. Concluding with 16:8 likely assumes a more so-phisticated audience for Mark than was the case, and it is difficult to think that Mark would expect his readers to fill in the answer to the question that 16:8 raises. It is more likely that the original ending of Mark had the women report to the disciples, as we see in Matthew, Luke, and John. Supporting this, the most complete manuscript of Mark, Codex Vaticanus (ca. 350), has an interesting conclusion to Mark. Generally in Vaticanus when a book concludes, the copier(s) leaves blank the rest of the column on which the book or letter ends, but begins the next book at the top of the next column. In the case of Mark, however, after the ending of the Gospel in one col-umn, the next column is completely blank. This suggests doubt in the early churches about the ending of Mark at 16:8, and so extra space was left for a subsequent conclusion.[65]

Also, the damaged text at the beginning and ending of the Gospel (it begins with an incomplete sentence in 1:1)—the earliest surviving copies were in a codex or book form—suggests the possibility that the outer pages of this manuscript have been lost, perhaps because of extended use or some natural disaster that damaged the manuscript, or perhaps during a time of persecu-tion. It is difficult to imagine why Mark would leave an appearance story out of his Gospel if such stories were known, as they surely were (1 Cor. 15:3–8) by his time. Mark 16:9–20, though added late, nevertheless contains early traditions that parallel the other canonical Gospels.[66]

Luke-Acts

Because of the similarity in the introductions of Luke and Acts (Luke 1:1–4; Acts 1:1–2), as well as in their language patterns and theological congruity, quite early in church history it was concluded that Luke the companion of

---

64. N. Clayton Croy, *The Mutilation of Mark's Gospel* (Nashville: Abingdon, 2003). Croy offers a long and impressive list of both earlier and contemporary scholars who advocate a lost or unfinished ending of Mark (174–77).

65. The earliest copy of Mark in the Chester Beatty papyri (P[46]), dating at the beginning of the third century, is missing the beginning; it starts at 4:36 and ends at 12:16. It is too fragmented to be of help with this question.

66. These parallels are listed in Evans, *Mark 8:27–16:20*, 546–51.

Paul was the author of both books. However, it is difficult to prove author-ship or date since, as in the case of all of the Gospels, they were written anonymously. Authorship in this case is an important matter, as it is in the case of Mark. If the two volumes were written by Luke, the historical value of much of the material in the Gospel is greatly enhanced, since Paul had considerable contact with the early eyewitnesses in Jerusalem. Arguments about authorship of Luke must also deal with Acts. Both volumes were writ-ten by the same person, but separated early on, perhaps no later than AD 140, when Marcion included the Gospel of Luke in his collection of Christian Scriptures but not Acts. Luke-Acts[67] is commonly recognized as two volumes by the same author, who sought to trace Christianity from its origins to its spread throughout the Roman Empire, especially to Rome. All early church tradition attributes Luke-Acts to Luke the companion of Paul, but there are challenges to its reliability, and most of the challenges focus on Acts more than the Gospel. The author of Luke-Acts continues the same method developed by Mark because, according to Rudolf Bultmann, Luke was "interested in an historically continuous and connected presentation, whose demands . . . he realizes much more comprehensively than Mark."[68] The author sought to explain carefully the origins of Christianity in the life, death, and resurrec-tion of Jesus, as well as its growth and development from Jerusalem to Rome. The author is completely involved in the story of Jesus and the growth of the early church, and has a special concern to share the universal appeal of the Christian message for Jews and gentiles alike (Luke 2:32; 3:6; 4:14–27; 13:29; 15:11–32; and Acts 10:34–43). Like Mark, Luke is not interested solely in the "cold facts" of history, but rather in proclaiming the truth about Jesus the Christ that invites or encourages individuals to faith in him.

The date, authorship, purpose, view of history, and reliability of Luke-Acts have been at the center of many scholarly debates for almost two centu-ries. We will focus mostly on authorship and reliability here; the other issues

67. The designation "Luke-Acts" is usually attributed to H. J. Cadbury, *The Making of Luke-Acts* (London: Macmillan, 1927). For a discussion of this, see I. H. Marshall, "Acts and the 'Former Treatise,'" in *The Book of Acts in Its Ancient Literary Setting* (ed. B. W. Winter and A. J. Clarke; vol. 1 of *The Book of Acts in Its First Century Setting*; ed. B. W. Winter; Grand Rapids: Eerdmans, 1993), 163–84. For objections to the idea of "Luke-Acts," see Mikeal C. Parsons and Richard I. Pervo, *Rethinking the Unity of Luke and Acts* (Minneapolis: Fortress, 1993), and Andrew F. Gregory and C. Kavin Rowe, eds., *Rethinking the Unity and Reception of Luke and Acts* (Columbia: University of South Carolina Press, 2010). Their arguments, while quite interesting, are not compelling. The significant parallels between Luke and Acts in language and style as well as theological interest argue in favor of one author of the two volumes.

68. Rudolf Bultmann, *The History of the Synoptic Tradition* (trans. J. Marsh; 2nd ed.; Oxford: Blackwell, 1972), 363.

are discussed in considerably more detail in the standard New Testament introductions.

Authorship

From the second century, the "we" passages of Acts (16:8–17; 20:5–15; 21:1–18; 27:1–28:16) were used to argue that Luke the companion of Paul wrote both volumes. Irenaeus (ca. 180) referred to them as evidence that Luke wrote Luke-Acts.

> For he [Luke] says that when Barnabas, and John who was called Mark, had parted company from Paul, and sailed to Cyprus, "we came to Troas"; and when Paul had beheld in a dream a man of Macedonia, saying, "Come into Macedonia, Paul, and help us," "immediately," he says, "we endeavored to go, understanding that the Lord had called us to preach the Gospel unto them. Therefore, sailing from Troas, we directed our ship's course towards Samothracia." . . . As Luke was present at all these occurrences, he carefully noted them down in writing, so that he cannot be convicted of falsehood or boastfulness, because all these [particulars] proved both that he was senior to all those who now teach otherwise, and that he was not ignorant of the truth. That he was not merely a follower, but also a fellow-laborer of the apostles, but especially of Paul. (Irenaeus, *Haer.* 3.14.1, *ANF*; cf. 3.13.3)

In the list of Paul's missionary companions, only Luke and Jesus called Justus appear to be candidates for authorship of the Luke-Acts corpus, and all early church traditions name Luke as the author. Some scholars refer to the "we" and "us" passages in Acts to confirm that Luke was a participant in some of the journeys of Paul. For them, the "we" passages are not simply a literary convention but rather reflect Luke's personal experience with Paul. Other ancient historical writings make use of the first-person plural in narrations of journeys often, but not always, to indicate participation (see especially *Polyb.* 36.12, but also 12.27.1–6; Lucian, *Ver. hist.* 47; and Homer, *Od.* 12.402–25). More recently, arguments have been made that the author simply relied on an earlier continuous source that had been interpolated throughout the larger narrative and marked by the retention of the use of "we." This is more reasonable since the "we" passages have an outlook and theology that is distinctive when compared to the rest of the Acts narrative, and it does not seem to reflect awareness of some important aspects of Paul's theology, epistles, or even the title that Paul used of himself ("apostle").[69] Kümmel posits that

69. See S. E. Porter, "The 'We' Passages," in *The Book of Acts in Its Graeco-Roman Setting* (ed. D. W. J. Gill and C. Gempf; vol. 2 of Winter, *Book of Acts*; Grand Rapids: Eerdmans, 1994),

the compiler of Luke-Acts found the "we" passages in the sources he used to compile his work and simply left them in the final form of his work.[70]

Date and Occasion

F. C. Baur[71] questioned Lukan authorship of Acts, its early date, and its reliability as a source for early Christianity because he saw a tendency of the author to smooth out the differences in the early churches, especially by making Peter look like Paul in regard to gentile freedom from the law (see Acts 10:34–43; 15:7–11; Gal. 2:11–14) and Paul to look like Peter in regard to keeping the law (Acts 16:3; 18:18; 21:26–27). Because of these "catholicizing tendencies" in the book of Acts, Baur suggested a date of around 150 or later for the book. The "tendency" Baur spoke about led to a school called "Tendenz Criticism," which persisted well into the twentieth century.[72] Luke-Acts shares some characteristics of an ancient romance, such as its depiction of the adventures of heroes who travel and have various dangerous encounters, but there are also significant differences.[73]

The title "Acts of the Apostles" was later ascribed to Acts (ca. AD 150–180), and that suggests that it was about the apostles, but Luke shows little interest in *all* of the apostles. The title is nevertheless important evidence of the early church's quest to root its origins in apostolic activity, even though Acts concentrates its narrative around Peter (chaps. 1–12) and Paul (chaps. 9 and 13–28).

Clearly the author of Luke-Acts was a zealous advocate for the Christian faith and viewed the early Christians as models for conduct who showed how the Christian movement, which began as a Jewish sect in Palestine, grew to have universal appeal to both Jews and Gentiles. The author also makes it clear that the early followers of Jesus and the Roman government were not in conflict.

545–74. See also Hans Conzelmann, *Acts of the Apostles* (Hermeneia; Philadelphia: Fortress, 1987), xxxvi–xl.

70. Kümmel, *Introduction*, 131–32. One need not deny Lukan authorship of Acts to believe that the "we" passages derive from another source.

71. See summary of Baur in Lee Martin McDonald, "Baur, Ferdinand Christian (1792–1860)," in *Encyclopedia of Early Christianity* (ed. Everett Ferguson; 2nd ed.; New York: Garland, 1997), 177–78.

72. Baur is best known for his application of Hegelian dialectical philosophy of the development of history (thesis, antithesis, and synthesis) to the development of early Christianity and his use of it to date New Testament writings. He saw the conflict between the earliest strands of Jewish Christianity (thesis) represented by Peter and James, and gentile Christianity (antithesis) represented by Paul, and the book of Acts (synthesis) as an attempt to bring both elements together. Baur saw this synthesis as representing the catholicizing tendencies of the second-century church.

73. See R. I. Pervo, *Profit with Delight: The Literary Genre of the Acts of the Apostles* (Philadelphia: Fortress, 1987).

Dating the Gospel of Luke is always in conjunction with the book of Acts. Acts was written after Luke (see Acts 1:1–2), and there are verbal parallels to Acts in *1 Clement* (ca. 90), *Epistle of Barnabas* (ca. 130–140), *Martyrdom of Polycarp* (ca. 150–160), *Didache* (ca. 90), and *Shepherd of Hermas* (ca. 140), but this may only be evidence of a common vocabulary in early Christian writings. Justin Martyr (ca. 150–160) makes the first apparent citations from Acts (cf. Acts 1:8 with *1 Apol.* 50.12 and Acts 17:23 with *2 Apol.* 10.6). Irenaeus is the first writer to mention Acts by name and also ascribe it to Luke (see *Haer.* 3.1.1; 3.10.1; 3.12.1–5). Acts is also mentioned in the Anti-Marcionite prologue of Luke (ca. 180 or later), and it says that Luke was a Syrian from Antioch, a disciple of the apostles who later followed Paul and who served the Lord as a single man until his death in Boeotia (Bithynia?) at the age of eighty-four. Clement of Alexandria (ca. 180) frequently cites Acts in a Scripture-like manner (e.g., *Strom.* 3.6.49; 7.9.53). Origen makes use of several texts from Acts, but is vague about its scriptural status (*Or.* 12.2; 13.6). This is sufficient to establish that both the Gospel of Luke and Acts were well known in the second and third centuries.[74]

In more recent times, arguments in favor of Luke the companion of Paul as the author of Luke-Acts were focused on the so-called medical terms in Luke-Acts. Since Luke was called "the beloved physician" (Col. 4:14; cf. Philem. 24), W. K. Hobart (1882) argued that the medical terms in Luke-Acts were proof that the two volumes were written by Luke. Subsequently, Adolf von Harnack (1907) drew the same conclusions.[75] He reinforced Hobart's arguments, maintaining that "the evidence is of overwhelming force; so that it seems to me that the third gospel and the Acts of the Apostles were composed by a physician," namely Luke.[76] Subsequently, H. J. Cadbury and others rejected Hobart's and Harnack's arguments, observing that the medical terms were also used by other educated persons who were in no way connected with the medical profession.[77] The result is that most scholars now generally dismiss this argument.

74. For a more complete listing of early references to Luke-Acts, see L. M. McDonald, *The Biblical Canon* (Peabody, MA: Hendrickson, 2006; repr., Grand Rapids: Baker Academic, 2011), 385–87; and L. M. McDonald, "Canon," in *Dictionary of the Later New Testament and Its Developments* (ed. R. P. Martin and P. H. Davids; Downers Grove, IL: InterVarsity, 1997), 132–44, here 137.

75. W. K. Hobart, *The Medical Language of St. Luke* (London: Longmans Green, 1882).

76. A. von Harnack, *Luke the Physician* (New York: Putnam, 1907), 175–98 (p. 198 and similar comment on p. 223), originally published in German in 1906. His subsequent work on Acts supported the same conclusions. Cf. his *The Acts of the Apostles* (London: Williams & Norgate, 1909).

77. H. J. Cadbury, *The Style and Literary Method of Luke* (Cambridge, MA: Harvard University Press, 1920), 39–72; cf. H. J. Cadbury, "Lexical Notes on Luke-Acts. II. Recent Arguments for Medical Language," *JBL* 45 (1926): 290–309.

The ecclesiastical and sacramental matters in Acts are quite primitive in comparison to the more developed views in the later first and second centuries, as we see in Clement of Rome and Ignatius. The primitive picture of the early church in Acts also suggests a first-century dating of the work, and Lukan authorship is no longer completely out of the question.

As in the case of the Gospel of Mark, those who deny Lukan authorship and an early dating (before AD 70) of Luke-Acts must explain the attribution of the work to a little-known non-apostolic person (Luke) when many pseudonymous gospels were attributed to apostolic figures. Also, since Paul and Peter are the heroes of Acts, it is strange that their deaths during Nero's persecution are not mentioned; Paul even anticipates a favorable hearing before the emperor when he arrives in Rome and is treated well (Acts 28:23–31). Again, however, those who deny Lukan authorship note the differences in the theology of Luke-Acts and Paul, namely, Paul emphasized reconciliation, redemption, and justification by faith, but those are not features of Luke's theological perspective. Likewise, Luke's omission of Paul's favorite self-designation, "apostle," has given pause to many scholars in making Luke the author of the two-volume work. There is also no mention of Paul's letters. Nevertheless, if Luke the companion of Paul wrote the Luke-Acts corpus, then its date sometime before the mid-60s seems likely since there is no mention of the deaths of Peter and Paul, the two leading figures of Acts. Nevertheless, the majority of biblical scholars generally place the date of composition after AD 70, with authorship not by a companion of Paul. An early date for Luke-Acts also pushes the Gospel of Mark to an earlier date, possibly in the early 60s.

Long ago, F. F. Bruce commented that "the attitude to Roman power through-out Acts makes it difficult for some readers to believe that the Neronian persecution of c. AD 65 had taken place," and said that Paul's appeal to Rome (Acts 25:10–12; 26:32) anticipates a favorable hearing, noting that if Luke was written at a time during or after Nero had already begun his attack on Christians, it is doubtful whether the author would have portrayed such an optimistic picture at the end of Acts. Bruce adds that "prominence is given in Acts to subjects which were of urgent importance in the church before AD 70, but which were of less moment after that date. Such were the terms of Gentile admission to church fellowship, the coexistence of Jews and Gentiles in the church, [and] the food requirements of the apostolic decree [Ch. 15]."[78] For these reasons, an early dating of Luke-Acts, say between AD 64 and 67, seems possible, even

---

78. F. F. Bruce, *The Acts of the Apostles: The Greek Text with Introduction and Commentary* (3rd ed.; Grand Rapids: Eerdmans, 1990), 14, 17.

though the work may not generally have become known in the early churches until some twenty or twenty-five years later.[79]

Several scholars date Luke-Acts after or around AD 70 and do so on the basis of the prophecies of the Gospel of Luke, which speak of the fall of Jerusalem and the destruction of the temple, which strongly suggests images of the Jewish war (see Luke 17:22–36; 21:20–28; 23:28–31). However, there are no adequate grounds for assuming that all predictions must have occurred after the events to which they refer took place. Bruce contends that "it is, indeed, quite uncritical to assume that every prediction which comes true is a *vaticinium ex eventu* [a prediction after the fact], quite apart from the consideration that these were the predictions of the Messiah Himself. The prediction of wars and sieges and sacking of cities is a common place of history."[80] While our focus here has been on dating Acts, which is easier to do than the Gospel, most scholars agree that the same author wrote both books, beginning with the Gospel and concluding with Acts.

Consequences for Interpretation and Reliability

Lukan authorship is far more important than the dating of Luke-Acts. If Luke was a companion of Paul, that would add considerable credibility to his story, as he would have had firsthand access to the leaders of the churches in the first century, including Paul, Timothy, possibly Peter at Antioch, Barnabas, James, and many others. If the author was Luke the companion of Paul, it follows that his sources for the life of Jesus and his history of the spreading of the Gospel by the earliest community of Christians would have a more credible connection to early eyewitness accounts of the events he describes. This is also precisely what divides scholars—because of Luke's seeming lack of awareness of the major themes of Paul's preaching, Paul's letters, and the title he used of himself.

An early dating and Lukan authorship of Luke-Acts (ca. AD 64–67) support the idea that the tradition about Jesus in that corpus was not a late notion originating in the needs of a community of Christians in answer to problems that arose in the church. This is especially true of the Gospel, but also of Acts. Lukan authorship and an early dating of Luke-Acts obviously

79. In the first edition of Bruce's Acts commentary (1951), he uses these points to argue that the time of the writing of Luke-Acts was around AD 60–61. Subsequently he moderated his position and allows that Luke-Acts could have been written later. He explains: "If, then, a date in the late 70s or 80s of the first century (say, in the principate of Titus or early in that of Domitian) is assigned to Acts, most of the evidence will be satisfied." But Bruce prefers a date in the mid- to late 60s. See F. F. Bruce, *Acts of the Apostles* (Downers Grove, IL: InterVarsity Press; 3rd rev. ed., 1990), 18.

80. Bruce, *Acts*, 16.

do not *prove* that Paul was well acquainted with the teaching of the life and ministry of Jesus, but the establishment of this would argue strongly for Luke's awareness of a common early tradition about Jesus that circulated both in and outside Palestine.

These basic questions about the authorship and date of Luke-Acts have clearly not been resolved, and must at this point remain open for future study and more substantial argumentation. However, even those scholars who are more skeptical about the early dating and authorship of Luke-Acts regularly appeal to this corpus to identify the core teaching of Jesus and the dating of the New Testament writings and early church history. It is difficult if not impossible to formulate any coherent understanding of the early church, from whatever perspective or stance one has regarding authorship and date, without considerable dependence upon Luke-Acts.[81]

Purpose and Perspectives

Why did Luke see the need to write another gospel besides those already circulating among the early Christian communities (Luke 1:1–4)? Likewise, what theological concerns did he address in his two-volume work? This following summation of his aims and special concerns will address only the most important issues in Luke-Acts, and readers will be directed to some of the more detailed works on this subject for a more complete discussion. We will focus first on Luke's understanding of history and salvation, followed by his understanding of the identity of Jesus (Christology) and the Holy Spirit.

a. History and Salvation. For Luke, the salvation of God takes place in history, which for him is God's activity in world history—that is, in the time and space occupied by ancient rulers and leaders whether in the Roman Empire or in Judaism. He begins the story of Jesus by locating it during the reign of Herod the Great (Luke 1:5) and locating the beginning of Jesus' ministry during the ministry of John the Baptist, and he gives five historical reference points; namely, the fifteenth year of Tiberius's reign, Pontius Pilate was the governor of Judea, Herod (Antipas) was the tetrarch of Galilee, Philip Herod was tetrarch of Ituraea and Trachonitis, and Lysanias was tetrarch of Abilene during the high priesthood of Annas and Caiaphas (Luke 3:1–2). For Luke, faith in Jesus cannot be separated from God's activity in human history. Conzelmann has observed that Luke's story has three important connections to history, and all come in a sequence; namely, the time of the law and prophecy, the time of preaching the kingdom of God seen in the

81. Some portions of this section are a summary of L. M. McDonald, "Acts of the Apostles," in *Encyclopedia of Early Christianity*, 14–17.

activity of Jesus, and the time of the church.[82] However, Bovon points out that while Luke emphasizes the continuity of the Christian mission with its Jewish roots and that the apostles and early witnesses practiced the law of Moses, he claims that Luke does not believe that all Christians should follow that example of keeping the law.[83] Likewise, unlike in the Pauline tradition (Rom. 5:8–10; 6:10; 1 Cor. 15:3; Gal. 1:4; Eph. 1:7), Luke does not emphasize the significance of the cross or death of Jesus for salvation. He generally only says that the death of Jesus was in the plan of God (Acts 2:22–36), but he says little about its significance for the salvation that God has for his people. The two possible exceptions in the Luke-Acts corpus are in Luke 22:19–20, where the blood of Jesus seals the new covenant that God makes with his people expressed in the institution of the Last Supper, and in Acts 20:28, where the church of God was obtained or purchased with the blood of Jesus (literally "with the blood of his own"). Aside from these two texts, there is nothing else that speaks of the significance of the death of Jesus for the forgiveness of sins. As Luke concludes the first part of his story, Jesus cites the Scriptures to show to the disciples that repentance and forgiveness of sins are found only in Jesus' name, but Luke does not indicate that Jesus died for our sins as we see so prominently in Paul (1 Cor. 2:2; 15:3; Rom. 3:21–25).

Several commentators have urged that Luke's interest in history cannot be separated from his view of salvation and that the term "salvation-history" is the best way to describe Luke's enterprise. Oscar Cullmann especially is known for this position, and he claimed that it was true of the rest of early Christianity as well. Hans Conzelmann argued that Luke had "de-eschatologized" the Christ event in favor of a historical salvation; that is, he removed the future aspects of the coming kingdom. Reflecting on Luke 9:27, he saw in Luke that the future coming kingdom has given way to a "timeless" kingdom visible in Jesus.[84] Cullmann, on the other hand, claimed that Luke held both the present aspects of the kingdom of God and the future coming kingdom in tension and that both are important parts of Luke's message about Jesus,[85] but this may be an overstatement. For Luke, the salvation of God takes place now in the history of the world, not only in the future, and it is universal in scope; that is, salvation is a possibility not only for the Jews, but also for gentiles.

---

82. Conzelmann, *Acts of the Apostles*, xlv.

83. François Bovon, *Luke 1: A Commentary on the Gospel of Luke 1:1–9:50* (Hermeneia; Philadelphia: Fortress, 2002), 10.

84. See his *Die Mitte der Zeit*, 92–105.

85. Oscar Cullman, *Heil als Geschichte: Heilsgeschichtliche Existenz im Neuen Testament* (Tübingen: J. C. B. Mohr, 1965); English translation, 1967, *Salvation in History* (trans. S. G. Sowers; London: SCM, 1967), 46–64 and 204–9. He sees the Christ event both at the center of history and the beginning of the new age that is to come.

The salvation of God is rooted in the Jewish Scriptures, which focused on God's deliverance (Acts 13:47; cf. Isa. 49:6) and in which salvation was extended to the gentiles as well as the Jews (Isa. 45:22). Because God's final offer of salvation to the Jews was rejected, it now goes to the gentiles (Acts 28:28). Luke also emphasizes that the blessing of God's salvation that was promised to the Jews is the coming of the Holy Spirit, who is now also poured out on all flesh (humanity) (see Acts 2:17–21; cf. Joel 2:28–29).[86] This salvation of God is extended through Jesus—and only through Jesus—to the lost (Acts 4:12; see also Acts 7:25 and Luke 2:11; 7:25; 19:10), whether Jew or gentile, and it includes both positive and negative blessings from God. It always means a rescue from the judgment of God that is coming to the earth, but also positively it refers to the blessing of God that comes from being in a right relationship with God and living in obedience to him. Some of the parables of Luke significantly reflect this salvation of the lost, as in the cases of the lost sheep, the lost coin, and especially the lost son (Luke 15:11–32).[87] For Luke, the kingdom of God and the salvation that it brings comes to all humanity in Jesus, and it is both a present reality (Luke 10:9; 11:20–23; 17:20–21) and yet still future, with apocalyptic judgments that will come to those who are evil as well as blessings to those who are faithful (Luke 17:22–37; 21:5–38). Luke holds this "already but not yet" focus on the kingdom of God in a tension (17:20–24). The presence of the rule of God is available now to all who call upon the Lord, but there are future aspects of the kingdom that are not yet present (10:11–12; 21:31; 22:18).

b. Christology. In the Gospel of Luke, Jesus is both a prophet who is a leader of his people (7:16; 9:7–9, 19) and also the Messiah (2:26), the anointed one of God who will bring salvation to the people (9:20). He is the Son of God (2:32–33), whom Luke equates with the messianic role (4:41). Both Jesus' messianic role and his title as Son of God are brought together at Jesus' trial before the Sanhedrin (22:66–70). Jesus is the Messiah who delivers the righteous ("wheat") to God for salvation, but also the "chaff" for judgment (3:15–17). In this sense, the Messiah is an eschatological or end-time deliverer. These roles, Messiah, Son of God, and Son of Man, are discussed above in the Markan perspectives. Luke claims that Jesus the Christ is also Lord of all (Acts 2:36;

---

86. See I. H. Marshall, *Luke: Historian and Theologian* (Contemporary Evangelical Perspectives; Grand Rapids: Zondervan, 1971), 95–102, on the substance of salvation for Luke.

87. See Luke Timothy Johnson, *The Gospel of Luke* (SP 3; Collegeville, MN: Liturgical Press, 1991), 22–23, and Marshall, *Luke: Historian and Theologian*, 93–222. Marshall deals with the implications and meaning of salvation in Luke. While this is a dated treatment, it is still a valid and useful discussion that focuses on the main streams of Luke's perspective of salvation.

10:36; 16:31). Believing in Jesus as Lord is for Luke the same as believing in God (Luke 2:11; Acts 16:31–34).

c. The Holy Spirit. The book of Acts has often been called the book of the Holy Spirit, and so it is, since the Spirit is involved in telling the story of Jesus and the ongoing ministry of the early church in bringing others to acknowledge Jesus as Christ and Lord of all. There are five accounts of the outpouring of the Spirit on believers in Jesus (2:1–4; 4:28–31; 8:15–17; 10:44; 19:6). Luke Timothy Johnson rightly concludes that, "for Luke, all Christians manifestly 'have' the Holy Spirit."[88]

Central to Luke's understanding of the activity of God and the salvation that comes through Jesus is the promised Holy Spirit, who has now come to all who receive God's salvation through the risen Christ (Acts 2:14–21). The power of the Spirit comes from God mediated through Jesus (Luke 24:49; Acts 2:1–21, 32–33). Indeed the presence of Jesus continues among his followers through the Holy Spirit, and for Luke the presence of the Spirit is evidence of the resurrection of Jesus from the dead (Acts 10:37–40), and Jesus is present in the proclamation of the forgiveness of sins that occurs when faith is placed in him and the manifestation of the Holy Spirit is poured out on all, both Jews and gentiles (Acts 10:44–47; 11:15–16; 15:8).

The Gospel of Matthew

We have already argued above that Matthew made considerable use of Mark as his primary source, plus a written and/or oral tradition ("Q") also known and used by Luke, and probably also a third source only found in Matthew, commonly referred to as "M." The third source includes such items as Matthew's genealogy of Jesus, his birth tradition, his reference to the earthquakes at the death and resurrection of Jesus, and others. Matthew, more than any other evangelist, relates how his story of Jesus fulfilled the Old Testament Scriptures. He also focuses on issues in contemporary Judaism in the time of Jesus. For Matthew, Jesus was *more* radical in his obedience to the law than other religious leaders of his day, and he expected his disciples to go beyond what is required (see Matthew 5, "you have heard it said, but I say unto you . . ."). Matthew appears to have been written especially for teachers in the church addressing issues facing the early Jewish Christian communities following the destruction of the temple and their and his desire

---

88. Johnson, *Gospel of Luke*, 17. See also his commentary in the same series, *The Acts of the Apostles* (ed. Daniel J. Harrington; SP 5; Collegeville, MN: Liturgical Press, 1992), 14–18, for a brief but careful discussion of the role of the Holy Spirit in Acts and the implications of this for Christian faith.

to be faithful to the law. The widespread use of the Gospel of Matthew in the early churches—far more than any other Gospel—testifies to its reception in the early churches and widespread acceptance of Matthew's reliability in telling the story of Jesus.

Authorship

Matthew, the Epistle of James, Hebrews, and the *Didache* (ca. AD 90) are the most important expressions of Jewish Christianity in the first century. Like the other canonical Gospels, Matthew was written anonymously, and although Matthew is often called the "First Gospel," in contemporary scholarship this has more to do with its place in the New Testament canon than when it was written or by whom.[89] By circa 150–180, a tradition emerged in the church attributing authorship of this gospel to the apostle Matthew. However, Matthew's dependence on Mark suggests that the author was not an apostle. For almost two centuries now, most New Testament scholars have doubted the traditional view that Matthew the apostle wrote the Gospel that bears his name. It is more likely that the author was a Hellenistic Christian Jew, but some scholars have even asked if the author was a gentile.[90]

The arguments for authorship are both external and internal; that is, they come from the early church fathers and from the Gospel itself. The first *external* evidence commonly cited in favor of Matthean authorship comes from Papias, Bishop of Hierapolis (ca. AD 140), whose work is no longer available but is quoted by Eusebius in the fourth century. After making comments about Mark (Mark is mentioned first by Papias), Papias wrote: "Matthew collected the oracles/sayings [*ta logia*] [of Jesus] in the Hebrew language [which may mean Aramaic], and each [teacher?] interpreted [or "translated," *hermēneusen*] them as best he could" (*Hist. eccl.* 3.39.16, LCL). It has probably been a misunderstanding of what Papias intended that led Irenaeus, Tertullian, Origen, and Eusebius to conclude that *ta logia* (or "sayings") composed a gospel. It is questionable whether Papias himself drew this conclusion. Earlier in the same passage Papias refers to "Mark who wrote the Gospel," who had not heard or followed Jesus, but who followed Peter

---

89. I will refer to the "first Gospel" or simply "Matthew" from time to time in the following discussion without a specific reference to date or authorship. For convenience's sake I will continue to refer to this work by its traditional name.

90. For example, Davies and Allison have noted that in the last hundred years only seven scholars have accepted Matthew the apostle as the author of the work that bears his name. Most agree that the author was a Jewish Christian, although Davies and Allison refer to some eleven scholars who have concluded that a gentile writer produced the work. See W. D. Davies and D. C. Allison Jr., *A Critical and Exegetical Commentary on the Gospel according to Saint Matthew* (ICC; Edinburgh: T&T Clark, 1988–97), 1:10–11.

and later made "an arrangement of the Lord's oracles" (*Hist. eccl.* 3.39.15, LCL). Eusebius clearly introduces the Papias tradition with "Mark wrote the Gospel," but when Papias mentions Matthew collecting oracles or sayings of Jesus, does he have in mind a gospel with narrative connections that include both the sayings of Jesus and his deeds? The parallels between what Papias says about Mark and Matthew are not exact; the passage raises questions about whether he intended to say that the apostle Matthew wrote a gospel or simply collected sayings of Jesus that others interpreted or translated as they saw fit. If Papias's intention was to say that Matthew the apostle wrote the Gospel that now bears his name, this is the earliest witness to authorship of that Gospel, but it is possible that Papias intended to say only that Matthew collected *sayings* of Jesus and wrote them in Hebrew or Aramaic. Some of these may have been included in the Gospel of Matthew, but that is uncertain.

Later Irenaeus (ca. 180) claimed that Matthew wrote his gospel in the Hebrew dialect (Aramaic?) *while* Peter and Paul were preaching the gospel in Rome (*Haer.* 3.1.1; cf. Eusebius, *Hist. eccl.* 5.8.2). Eusebius reports a story from Pantaenus (ca. AD 170), the director of a Christian school in Alexandria, that Matthew wrote a gospel *in Hebrew* that was taken as far east as India by Bartholomew and left there in its Hebrew letters (*Hist. eccl.* 5.10.3). Jerome (Hieronymus, ca. 390–395) claimed to have seen and copied the Hebrew form of Matthew's Gospel (*Vir. ill.*, PL 23.643), but few scholars today believe that this testimony has credibility.

It is unlikely that the Gospel of Matthew, as it now stands, ever existed in Hebrew or Aramaic. It is a Greek document, and thus far all attempts at putting it back into Hebrew or Aramaic have not been successful or received approval from most Matthean scholars. Daniel Harrington more correctly claims that the Gospel of Matthew was written in Greek and always has been in Greek. He nevertheless adds that a complete copy of Matthew's Gospel in Hebrew appears in the body of a fourteenth-century Jewish polemical treatise called *Even Bohan* ("The Touchstone"). Study of this document is not complete, but Harrington notes that it makes Judaism and Christianity more compatible than does the canonical version, and offers a higher estimation of John the Baptist.[91]

Since most ancient external testimony about authorship depends on a reading or misreading of Papias, what value does it have? On the other hand, Clement of Alexandria, Irenaeus, Origen, and Eusebius were all Greek

---

91. D. J. Harrington, *The Gospel of Matthew* (SP 1; Collegeville, MN: Liturgical Press, 1991), 4.

speakers and wrote extensively in Greek, but believed that the Gospel of Matthew had been translated from Hebrew into Greek.[92] Their conclusions, however, may not be trustworthy. It is not clear how Matthew wrote in Hebrew but incorporated a Greek Gospel (Mark) into his work and allowed it to determine the material he presented. It is unlikely that Matthew was an apostle since it would be strange if an eyewitness borrowed the text of someone who was not an eyewitness to tell the story of his own calling to follow Jesus (cf. Matt. 9:9–11 with Mark 2:14)! Why would an eyewitness need to use another source (Mark) to articulate his own calling?[93] The external evidence points to a Palestinian Jew named Matthew, but the internal evidence points to one well versed in Hellenism who may have been a Jew, but not Matthew the apostle.[94]

Davies and Allison conclude that the author was a Jewish Christian familiar with the Hellenistic world, but whose Greek, though better than Mark's, was still far from the quality one can find in other treatises produced in Greek by Jewish authors whose native tongue was Aramaic (e.g., Josephus, who was a contemporary of the author of Matthew's Gospel). Perhaps all that can be said with assurance about the author of this Gospel is that he was a Christian and more familiar than Mark and Luke with the geography of Palestine. Because of this and his awareness of the Jewish context of early Christianity, it is likely that the author was a teacher in the church. Also, because of the overlapping of Judaism and Christianity in Matthew, it is likely that the Gospel was written to a Jewish Christian community.

Date and Location

There is no way to date or locate with precision the Gospel of Matthew, but there are a few parameters. Matthew's date is determined broadly on the one hand by its use of Mark—that is, it could not have been written before AD 64–67—and on the other by possible references to it in the book of Revelation (cf. Rev. 1:7 and Matt. 24:30; Rev. 3:3 and Matt. 24:43), so not later than AD 90–100. Besides this, there are also allusions to Matthew in *Didache* 7:1 (Matt. 28:16) and 8:1–2 (Matt. 6:16 and 6:5), dating around AD

92. Davies and Allison make this point in *Commentary on Matthew*, 1:12–13.

93. Only Matthew has the name "Matthew" for the tax collector who followed Jesus, while Mark and Luke only mention Levi (Mark 2:14; Luke 5:27). Also, they never refer to Matthew as a tax collector in their list of Jesus' disciples (Mark 3:18; Luke 6:15). Meier has suggested that the prime example of a sinner in the Gospels is the tax collector, and that Matthew may have made a play on the Greek words, since the Greek term for a disciple or learner is *mathētēs* (verb *mathēteuō*) and it sounds very much like Matthew. This would reflect a prime example of how a sinner could become a disciple. See J. P. Meier, "Matthew, Gospel of," *ABD* 4:627.

94. Davies and Allison, *Commentary on Matthew*, 1:9.

90. It is also cited in the letters of Ignatius (ca. AD 115–117; cf. Ign. *Smyrn.* 1.1 and Matt. 3:15, as well as Ign. *Pol.* 2.2 and Matt. 10:16). From the internal allusions to the destruction of Jerusalem in Matthew 22:7 (cf. 21:41; 27:25), a date of around AD 80–90 is possible, though this is uncertain. Also the mention in Matthew 24 of "signs" that come before the "end time" may reflect the experience of Matthew's readers during the early years of Emperor Domitian's reign (AD 81–96).

Since Matthew was produced in Greek, it is less likely that it would have been produced in Judea or anywhere in Palestine. This Gospel is Jewish in much of its focus, but it also appears to be open to a gentile mission (Matt. 8:5–11; 28:19). This may suggest that the Christians Matthew addressed had a large Jewish and gentile population that came to faith in Jesus without the requirements of the law and its traditions (21:43–46). Such a community might have been located in a Decapolis city in northern Palestine where both Greek and Aramaic were spoken and where there was also a considerable understanding of the Jewish traditions. Antioch of Syria is also a possible location since it had a significantly mixed community of Jewish and gentile believers who were welcomed into Christian fellowship without the requirement of circumcision and participating in other Jewish traditions. Supporting this is the fact that the first clear references to Matthew's Gospel come from Ignatius, the bishop of Antioch, AD 115–117.

Because of Matthew's negative language against Jewish leaders and eventually against the whole nation (see 21:4–43; 22:7), some scholars have asked whether the author of Matthew was a gentile, since his perspective contrasts significantly with that of Paul, who was abused by his fellow countrymen (1 Thess. 2:13–16) but who, nevertheless, desired their conversion (Rom. 9:1–5; 10:1–4; 11:1–5, 23–27). The context for Matthew's community changed considerably by the end of the first century, and many in that community no longer saw the conversion of Israel as viable. Matthew's language, however, is not so much anti-Semitic as it is anti-Judaic; namely, it focused on Jewish beliefs and practices, not Jewish ethnicity. By the end of the first century, Christians believed that there were three classes of people—namely, Jews, gentiles, and Christians. Matthew apparently opposed the Judaism that survived the destruction of Jerusalem and those Jews who had not accepted Jesus as their promised Messiah, including those who opposed Christianity.

Purpose and Message

Like the other evangelists, Matthew wrote his Gospel to tell the significance of Jesus for an audience in his own day. Also like the others, he did not write an unbiased historical report for subsequent generations. The most important issues for Matthew are the identity of Jesus as the Messiah, the kingdom of heaven, discipleship, and the church.

Matthew also maintained the continuity of ancient Judaism and its sacred Scriptures with the activity of Jesus and his followers. More than any other evangelist, he emphasizes the prophecy-and-fulfillment motif to show that in Jesus, from birth to death, the Scriptures foresaw and foretold this story. According to R. T. France, the most prominent word characterizing Matthew's perspective about Jesus is "fulfillment." See, for example, references such as, "this took place to fulfill what the Lord had spoken by the prophet" (see 1:22; 2:15, 17, 23; 4:14; 8:17; 12:17; 13:35; 21:4; 27:9; and cf. 13:14; 26:54).[95]

For Matthew, Jesus is the one who most clearly understood the law and came to fulfill its essential meaning (5:17), as we see in the series of antitheses in 5:21–48 ("you have heard it said, but I say unto you"), and he was the law's most capable interpreter (12:1–8).[96] Those who follow Jesus, Matthew says, are also connected to a long-standing Jewish tradition that has been turned over to the followers of Jesus because of the faithlessness of Israel's leaders (21:43–46). In Jesus' parable of the vineyard, for example, the vineyard is Israel (Isa. 5:1–7), and the murdered son is Jesus, but the new tenants are the followers of Jesus (21:33–46).

Matthew also has a significant interest in the theme of righteousness throughout his Gospel and expresses Jesus' interest in ethical behavior that conforms to the will of God in Scripture. Indeed, the righteousness of Jesus' followers must exceed the righteousness of the scribes and the Pharisees (5:20; 7:21–23). Why this is so surprising is that Mark never uses the noun "righteousness," and Luke only uses it once (1:75), but Matthew's frequent use of it shows Jesus teaching God's more strict ethical demands for his disciples (see 5:6, 10, 20; 6:1, 33; and by inference in 5:16, where "good works" is equivalent to "righteousness").[97]

Following the genealogy of Jesus in 1:1–17 there are five short narrative sections in Matthew 1 and 2 that focus on the Scriptures that are fulfilled in the story of Jesus; for example, he was baptized to "fulfill all righteousness" (3:15). The theme of fulfillment is also at the heart of the identity of Jesus and his mission in the world. In the case of the birth story, Matthew demonstrates that the Scriptures are fulfilled in Jesus who is the Messiah of the nation. Matthew is steeped in the Jewish Scriptures, citing them more frequently than the other evangelists, and he believes that they are fulfilled in the life of

95. Richard T. France, "Matthew, Mark, and Luke," in G. E. Ladd, *A Theology of the New Testament* (rev. ed.; Grand Rapids: Eerdmans, 1993), 212–45, here 218–19.

96. Harrington, *Gospel of Matthew*, 17.

97. Stanton, *Gospels and Jesus*, 70–71.

Jesus. Among the important theological issues for Matthew are those related to Christology (the identity of Jesus as the Messiah), the kingdom of heaven (= the same as Luke's kingdom of God), discipleship, and the church.

Jesus' Identity

For Matthew, Jesus has an exalted identity in which he is not only the long expected Messiah, but also the Lord of his church, the Son of God, and the Son of Man. We will look briefly at each of these titles in Matthew.

a. Messiah and Son of David. Matthew provides a high Christology for his readers, and that is one of the central themes of his Gospel. He begins in 1:1–17, stating openly the identity of Jesus as the Messiah (Christ) who is also the son of David and, consequently, the legitimate heir to the throne of David. At times, "son of David" appears to be another term for the long-awaited Messiah in Matthew, as in 9:27; 12:23; 15:22; 20:30–31; 21:9, 15. Notice that in the latter instances, the chief priests and scribes were angry because the crowds used this title in reference to Jesus. In several places, Jesus is acknowledged as the long-expected Messiah of Israel (1:1,16, 17, 18; 11:2; 16:16–20; 22:42–45), and Jesus himself claims this self-designation (23:10).

While there is an element of secrecy about his messianic role, it is more subdued in Matthew than in Mark. The disciples are more aware of the true identity of Jesus and are also portrayed much more positively in Matthew than they are in Mark. Matthew combines the notion of a Messiah who will free Israel from its bondage and establish the kingdom of God (heaven) with the image of royalty as we see in the birth narratives in which royalty (the Magi) come to see Jesus in a house to offer gifts fit for a king (see discussion of this below in chapter 4). The focus on the kingship of Jesus can also be seen in Herod's fear that a successor might replace him as king of Israel (2:1–18).

b. Son of God. Jesus is also acknowledged or recognized as the Son of God, that is, one in a special and unique relationship with God, by Satan and demoniacs (4:2–6 and 8:29) and by his disciples after Jesus calmed the storm (14:33). He is the final authority for all who follow him (28:19). Joseph and Mary flee to Egypt to fulfill the prophecy in Hosea, originally about Israel, that out of Egypt God would call his son (2:13–15). The Son of God motif is quite pronounced in Matthew, and speaks of Jesus' special relationship with the heavenly father. He is identified as the Son of God at his baptism (3:17) as well as at his transfiguration (17:5).

c. Son of Man. One of the most common designations for Jesus in Matthew is Son of Man. This is Jesus' most common description of himself, and most instances have a divine flavor about them. Although in a few cases the designation may only be a reference to his humanity, the overwhelming majority of references to the "Son of Man" function as divine titles that speak of more than a human being, for example, 9:6; 12:8; 13:37–41; 19:28; 25:31; and even 26:24. In Matthew, these designations have the flavor of one about whom the Scriptures speak, such as we see in Daniel 7:13–14, and many instances refer to the apocalyptic one who will come at the end of the ages to establish God's kingdom (10:23; 16:27–28; 17:9; 19:28; 24:27, 30, 37–39, 44; 25:31; 26:64).

d. Lord. Matthew's use of "Lord" in reference to Jesus may be nothing more than "sir" in some places, but several instances may also reflect the church's most common title for Jesus after his resurrection—namely, "Lord" in the sense of his divine nature. This is often apparent where there is a combination of this designation with other messianic titles such as "son of David," but also elsewhere (3:3; 7:21–22; 8:2, 6, 8, 21, 25; 9:28; 12:8; 14:28–30; 15:22, 25–27; 16:22; 17:4, 15; 18:21; 21:3, 9; 22:43; 23:39; 24:42).

When these titles are combined with the opening comments to Joseph about who Jesus is—namely, that he will be "God with us" (1:23)—and with the closing words of the Gospel when Jesus says, "I am with you always, to the end of the age" (28:20), there is little doubt in Matthew about the identity of Jesus. He is the very presence of God among humanity.

Major Themes

a. Scripture. Matthew was interested in the continuity of ancient Judaism and its sacred Scriptures with the activity of Jesus and his followers. More than any other evangelist, he emphasizes the prophecy and fulfillment motif, seeking to show that, from Jesus' birth to his betrayal, the Scriptures foresaw and foretold the story of Jesus.

b. Righteousness. As we saw above, Matthew has a significant interest in the theme of righteousness, and throughout his Gospel he expresses Jesus' interest in ethical behavior that conforms to the will of God in Scripture. Matthew uses it several times in reference to God's more strict ethical demands placed on the disciples of Jesus (see 5:6, 10, 20; 6:1, 33; and by inference in 5:16 where "good works" is equivalent to "righteousness").[98]

It is probable that Matthew introduces this motif into the story of Jesus in order to deal with a particular problem in the community of faith for which he wrote; namely, the problem of unethical behavior, especially among the new gentile converts to his church. This is not to say that Jesus did not teach about ethical behavior, but rather that Matthew probably heightened this teaching, stressing those aspects of it that were most relevant to his situation (*Sitz im Leben*). Meier, who claims that the Gospel of Matthew originated

---

98. Ibid.

in Antioch, observes that there were many Jewish Christians there, but also a large number of gentile Christians who had little background or experience in ethical behavior.[99] Their conduct, he suggests, may stand behind the inclusion of much of the material on morality and ethical behavior in Matthew's Gospel. For Matthew, appropriate ethical behavior involves the keeping of the law. Meier states that in 5:17, in Matthew's perspective Jesus did not come to destroy or abandon the law, but to fulfill it. Matthew says that all Christians should obey the law, even exceeding all others (scribes and Pharisees) in their obedience to it (5:19–20).

c. Discipleship. Harrington has shown that, whereas in Mark the disciples frequently misunderstand Jesus, in Matthew they generally understand him and often serve as models for the Matthean community (see 13:52; 16:12; but, like Mark, he also highlights their weakness at times, as in 6:30; 8:26; 14:31; 16:8; 17:19–20). The disciples are empowered by the continuing presence and power of the risen Lord in order to make disciples and faithfully convey the teaching of Jesus to all who follow Jesus (28:19–20).[100] For Matthew, the disciples' mission in the world in the post-Easter season is to make even more disciples for Jesus in all the nations (28:19–20).

d. Church (Ecclesiology). Matthew is the only Gospel writer to mention the church (Greek = *ekklēsia*, 16:18; 18:17). For him, Israel, by participating in the death of Jesus (27:25), has taken on itself the judgment of God and rejected its place in the coming kingdom, which has now been transferred to the church (21:43–46). There is no reference in Matthew as to how the church should be ordered, organized, or led, but some of the early leaders in it were "prophets" (10:40–41), "wise men," and "scribes" (13:52; 23:34), with Peter as the foundational leader (16:18–19) who had the power of the risen Christ as his strength to lead it. The members of this church are also involved in matters of discipline with the goal of reconciliation, but also with the same authority to excommunicate those who have offended others if the discipline is not accepted (18:15–18).[101]

Reliability

The reliability of Matthew's witness to the Jesus tradition is more important than the question of authorship or the time of its composition. This question can only be settled by a careful look at the sources Matthew used in writing his Gospel. We have already shown that Matthew used Mark, Q, and M (and

---

99. Meier, "Matthew, Gospel of," 624.

100. Harrington, *Gospel of Matthew*, 19.

101. Meier, "Matthew, Gospel of," 639. See his more complete discussion of these matters on 637–40.

possibly a list of Old Testament Scriptures he believed Jesus had fulfilled). The last may have originated with the apostle Matthew or even with Jesus, who, according to Luke, revealed himself to the disciples from the Old Testament Scriptures (24:44–48). The so-called M portions of Matthew may have been written down as early as AD 50, but more likely in the 60s or 70s. More importantly, many of the traditions in Matthew's Gospel likely circulated in oral form for years *before* being incorporated into the Gospel.[102] If there is any plausibility to this, then Matthew relied heavily on earlier traditions about Jesus that were circulating in the primitive churches, and therefore his Gospel is worthy of serious consideration in telling the story of Jesus. Like the other evangelists, Matthew mingles what can reliably be argued as history by all fair-minded historians with remarkable theological statements about Jesus' identity that are beyond the historian's craft to investigate. In this combination of history and theology (or faith), Matthew presents his story of Jesus in a way that calls people to faith in him as Lord and Messiah in whom all authority resides (28:19).

The Gospel of John

From the second century on, many Christians identified the Gospel of John as "the spiritual Gospel," and the Synoptic Gospels were often seen as providing more of the "outward facts" about Jesus. For example, when describing the four Gospels, Clement of Alexandria (ca. 180) said: "John . . . conscious that the outward facts had been set forth in the Gospels [Synoptics], was urged on by his disciples, and, divinely moved by the Spirit, composed a spiritual Gospel" (reported by Eusebius, *Hist. eccl.* 6.14.7, LCL). Such descriptions led many church leaders and subsequent biblical scholars to view John's Gospel not so much as history, but rather as a theological treatise that focused more on Jesus' divinity than on matters of historical substance. It was widely accepted even in modern times that John was more involved in interpretation than in sharing a historical narrative.

Modern New Testament scholarship has also tended to ignore the Gospel of John as a useful source on the history of the life and ministry of Jesus. This was due not only to the significant differences between John and the

---

102. Filson, *A New Testament History* (London: SCM, 1971), 364, and T. W. Manson, *The Teaching of Jesus* (Cambridge: Cambridge University Press, 1937), 27–28, held that Matthew could have been the author of the Q document, or Sayings Source, which may account for his name being attached to this Gospel quite early by the church fathers. See also in the previous section Dunn's discussion in *Jesus Remembered* of the origin of the sayings of Jesus prior to his death.

Synoptics, but also to the widely accepted notion that John reflects *theological* rather than historical interests. For several generations it has been common to say that the Gospel of John has more Hellenistic and Gnostic tendencies than scholars believed were present in the actual historical context of Jesus in Palestine.[103]

Paul Anderson has shown that while John's Gospel was welcomed and employed in the early churches as a means of establishing the important christological framework of early Christianity, in modern critical studies the Gospel was all but eliminated from consideration in the quest for the historical Jesus and has been "exiled from the canons of historicity by critical scholars."[104] He notes that even today in some historical investigations of Jesus, later extracanonical gospels have supplanted John in this historical quest.

Many contemporary scholars are now beginning to reconsider the long-held prejudice against the historical value of the Fourth Gospel. Instead of a strictly Hellenistic context, some scholars are now interpreting John in terms of a first-century Jewish context that was also influenced by Hellenism. They are examining John in fresh ways and appropriating important historical data that John alone provides for understanding the context of first-century Judaism and early Christianity and also for knowledge about Jesus himself. Several scholars have challenged the earlier disregard of John and are more impressed with its knowledge of the life and ministry of Jesus than was acknowledged earlier.[105] No one suggests that John's portrait of Jesus is the only one that should be considered, but rather that his story of Jesus should be considered along with the Synoptics as a separate and valuable historical resource that deserves more consideration than it was given earlier. John was probably aware of the Synoptic Gospels or the tradition that they reflect, but produced a differ-

---

103. H. K. McArthur, introduction to *In Search of the Historical Jesus* (ed. H. K. McArthur; London: SPCK, 1970), 3–20, here 9.

104. Paul N. Anderson, *The Fourth Gospel and the Quest for Jesus: Modern Foundations Reconsidered* (Library of New Testament Studies Series 321; London: T&T Clark, 2006; paperback printing, 2007), 191.

105. See, for example, Paul N. Anderson, "Aspects of Historicity in the Gospel of John: Implications for Investigations of Jesus and Archaeology," in *Jesus and Archaeology* (ed. James H. Charlesworth; Grand Rapids: Eerdmans, 2006), 587–618; Paul N. Anderson, Felix Just, SJ, and Tom Thatcher, eds., *Critical Appraisals of Critical Views* (vol. 1 of *John, Jesus, and History*; Symposium Series 44; Atlanta: SBL Press, 2007); and more recently Paul N. Anderson, Felix Just, SJ, and Tom Thatcher, eds., *Aspects of Historicity in the Fourth Gospel* (vol. 2 of *John, Jesus, and History*; Symposium Series 49; Atlanta: SBL Press, 2009). Also helpful in this regard as well as in his careful interpretation of this Gospel is Craig S. Keener's *The Gospel of John: A Commentary* (Peabody, MA: Hendrickson, 2003); and J. Ramsey Michaels, *The Gospel of John* (NICNT; Grand Rapids: Eerdmans, 2010), a recent and well-informed study on the interpretation of John.

ent portrait of Jesus. Despite the differences, several scholars are now pointing to the overlap in several important traditions reflected in all four Gospels.[106]

There are many perplexing questions about John, including its authorship, date, provenance, theological stance, historical value, and relationships with the Synoptic Gospels. Indeed, some biblical scholars see John as one of the most perplexing and intriguing books of the New Testament, but some of them have begun to view John as an important resource for understanding Jesus in history. Others continue to be cautious.

Distinctive Features

John's peculiarities in vocabulary and style are worth recounting here. He has the only examples of a double "amen" on the lips of Jesus (1:51; 10:1; 12:24), and he frequently includes Jesus' use of the "I am" formula (e.g., 6:35, 41, 48, 51; 8:12, 24–28, 58; 9:5; 15:5) to speak of his special relationship with God and his authority over his mission. Unlike the Synoptic Gospels, John *seldom* uses the terms "kingdom" (of God or of heaven), "Sadducees," "scribes," "forgive," "demons," and "tax collectors."[107] In the Synoptics there are few long discourses by Jesus. Matthew's Sermon on the Mount (Matt. 5–7), for example, is made up of short sayings only some of which are complete in themselves, but in John there are several long discourses that are at times repetitious (see John 14–16). Some terms are found more frequently in John than in the Synoptics, for example, "love." John prefers the verb *agapaō* (noun, *agapē*) for "love," but not exclusively so, and he also uses *phileō* interchangeably for the same idea.[108] Other words used with frequency are "truth," "I am," "life," "Jews," "world," "witness," "remain," and "father."[109] However, the most distinctive features of John are his high Christology, which acknowledges the divinity of Jesus throughout his ministry, and also his emphasis on eternal life that comes from God through Jesus the Christ (e.g., 3:16; 10:10).

106. This is especially true of D. Moody Smith, *John among the Gospels: The Relationship in the Twentieth-Century Research* (Minneapolis: Fortress, 1992); and C. K. Barrett, who argues that the Gospel of Mark influenced the author of the Gospel of John. See Barrett's *Gospel according to St. John: An Introduction with Commentary and Notes on the Greek Text* (2nd ed.; Philadelphia: Westminster, 1978). More recently, Paul Anderson has argued against a one-way relationship, namely that John depends on the Synoptic Gospels and not the other way around. See his *Fourth Gospel*, 101–25. At any rate, the distinction between these sources is not as clear as it once was thought to be, and scholars are taking more notice of some of the parallels than was the case earlier.

107. These observations come from R. Kysar, "The Gospel of John," *ABD* 3:912–31, here 914.

108. See, e.g., 3:35 and 5:20, where both terms are used for the Father's love for the Son.

109. See Barrett, *Gospel according to St. John*, 5–6, for a complete listing of these terms in Greek and also for common Synoptic expressions that are rare or missing in John.

John and the Synoptics

John certainly has a different tone and substance than the Synoptics, although they overlap in the broad outline of Jesus' ministry, death, and resurrection. Some scholars have also found more parallels in some of the sayings of and about Jesus, as well as in some of his activities.[110] They have also found that many of John's claims are historically credible. For instance, there is no need to say that the Gospel of John is wrong when it asserts that Jesus did not baptize, but that only his disciples did (John 4:2).

John also shows a willingness to use more laudatory and postresurrection designations of Jesus *during his lifetime* such as "Word," "Lord," "Son of God," and "Lamb of God." Bultmann earlier indicated that one of the significant differences between John and the Synoptics has to do with the faith and general picture of the earliest church—that is, its *Sitz im Leben*, or social setting—which can be detected more clearly in the Synoptics than in John. He notes that "while in the Synoptics the vicissitudes, the problems, and the faith of the earliest Church are reflected, scarcely anything of the sort can any longer be discovered in John."[111] Besides this, one also sees that John has a different chronology of events than that found in the Synoptics, as in the earlier placements of Jesus' cleansing of the temple and the so-called Last Supper with his disciples. John also makes the length of Jesus' ministry about three years rather than the one or two years implied in the Synoptics.[112] It is also apparent that the scene of most of Jesus' activity in John is shifted from Galilee to Judea, especially Jerusalem.

There remain many questions about John, however. Why does he not mention that Jesus was baptized by John, tempted in the wilderness, or transfigured? Why does he fail to include the parables of Jesus, especially when he records several extended discourses by him? Why is the cleansing of the temple early in John's Gospel (2:13–21), but late in the Synoptics, where it is introduced as a factor in Jesus' arrest and trial? In John, why are "signs" or indicators of the identity of Jesus (e.g., 2:11; 4:54; 9:16; 10:41; 11:47; 12:18, 37; 20:30) different than in the Synoptics, where the signs or wonders are more indicators

---

110. Anderson, *Fourth Gospel*, 74–75. He appropriately asks whether the later embellishments about the historical record of a battle prove that the battle never occurred or that "symbolized expansions upon traumatic experiences prove that they never happened" (73). His point is certainly justifiable in Johannine studies, and because John shares more than the Synoptics do about the significance of the events he describes, this does not thereby disprove their authenticity!

111. Rudolf Bultmann, *Theology of the New Testament* (New York: Scribner, 1955), 2:5.

112. T. W. Manson notes here that the order of events in John's Gospel could have been written as a corrective to Mark's order of events, which Papias said was incorrect. See Manson, *Teaching of Jesus*, 23.

of the arrival of the reign of God that Jesus announced?[113] Most importantly, why do Mark and John appear to disagree on a key factor that led to Jesus' arrest (cf. Mark 11:18 and 13:1–2 on the driving of the money changers and criticism of the temple with John 11:45–53)?[114]

All of these factors raise the question of whether John knew of the other Gospels. If so, did he reject them, try to correct, modify, or interpret their presentation of Jesus, or did he simply want to supplement them?[115] Martin Hengel insists that John knew and presupposed the Synoptic Gospels, making use of Mark and Luke while largely ignoring Matthew, when he set out to write a more accurate Gospel.[116] Barrett agrees that John was familiar with Mark and to a lesser extent with Luke, as we will see later in several parallels between John and Luke. He suggests that John's passion story is an edited version of Mark into which John introduced fresh material.[117] Moody Smith reminds us that at the beginning of the twentieth century, scholars regularly assumed John's knowledge of the Synoptics, but from 1955 to 1980 they began to argue that John was both ignorant and independent of the Synoptics. He concludes that "we have now reached a point at which neither assumption is safe, that is, neither can be taken for granted. Any exegete must argue the case afresh on its merits. . . . Apart from its ancient canonical setting, John's independence is obvious enough. The problem is how to understand and articulate it."[118]

The similarities between John and the Synoptics are fewer and not as striking as some have supposed, but they also present a puzzle. For example, John generally agrees chronologically with the Synoptics in the broad outline of Jesus' life and ministry, including his coming to John the Baptist while John was baptizing (John 1:29–34), the beginning of his ministry in Galilee (1:43–2:1), and his arrest, crucifixion, burial, and resurrection. There is also an interesting parallel between Luke's sequence of resurrection, appearance, ascension, and the giving of the Spirit in John and Luke, though in Luke—unlike in John—the ascension is a last appearance. Some parallels may have come from a common oral tradition circulating in the churches when the Gospels were written, and that tradition may have been incorporated by all of the evangelists, including the broad outline of the ministry of Jesus. John and Luke also agree on the

---

113. These observations are made by Kysar, "The Gospel of John," *ABD* 3:914–15.

114. Barrett, *Gospel according to St. John*, 47, discusses this issue.

115. See the discussion of R. A. Spivey and D. M. Smith, *Anatomy of the New Testament* (4th ed.; New York: Macmillan, 1989), 159–61.

116. M. Hengel, *The Johannine Question* (trans. J. Bowden; Philadelphia: Trinity Press, 1989), 75–76, 194n8.

117. Barrett, *Gospel according to St. John*, 15–21.

118. Smith, *John among the Gospels*, 189.

general location of Jesus' resurrection appearances (Jerusalem), the number of angels at Jesus' tomb (two), and that Jesus ascended to the Father, albeit in a somewhat different sequence, as we noted above.

There are several important similarities in all four evangelists, especially in Jesus' self-testimony as the Son of God and the Son of Man, the presentation of the passion story, and the importance given to the gentiles. Smith highlights six striking verbatim agreements between John and Mark (Mark 6:37 = John 6:7; Mark 14:3, 5 = John 12:3, 5; Mark 14:42 = John 14:31; Mark 14:54 = John 18:18; Mark 15:9 = John 18:39; Mark 2:11–12 = John 5:8–9). He points out that when John agrees with the Synoptics, he tends to agree with Mark's order.[119] Barrett concludes from this that "where Mark and John agree closely together, as occasionally they do, there is no simpler or better hypothesis than that John drew his material from Mark, not in slavish imitation, but with the frequent recollections which a well-known and authoritative source would inspire."[120] Whether or not John made use of the Synoptics as sources, the important question is whether he had them in mind when he produced his Gospel. Beasley-Murray does not think that the evidence is strong enough to draw firm conclusions on the matter,[121] but from the above parallels this possibility may need to be reconsidered.

Authorship, Date, and Location

Early church testimony about the authorship of the Fourth Gospel is mixed, but it is predominantly in favor of John the apostle and son of Zebedee. For example, Theophilus of Antioch (ca. 180) quotes from the Fourth Gospel, calling it Scripture, and ascribes it to John the apostle, who he claims published the work from Ephesus (*Autol.* 2.2). Irenaeus says John was the "Beloved Disciple" ("the disciple whom Jesus loved"; see John 13:23–26; 19:25–27; 20:2; 21:7, 20–24) or the "other disciple" (18:15–16; 20:3–4) who wrote the Gospel (see *Haer.* 3.1.1). From the third century, starting with Origen, no one seems to have doubted that the apostle John was the Beloved Disciple who also wrote the Fourth Gospel.[122]

Some of the external traditions, however, are not favorable to Johannine authorship of the Fourth Gospel. The "Alogi," a second-century Christian group in Asia Minor who rejected the divinity of Christ, attributed the Gospel

119. Smith, *John among the Gospels*, 3; cf. B. H. Streeter, *The Four Gospels: A Study of Origins* (London: Macmillan, 1936), 397–99.

120. Barrett, *Gospel according to St. John*, 15–16.

121. G. R. Beasley-Murray, *John* (WBC 36; Waco: Word, 1987), xxxv–xxxvii.

122. The Valentinian Gnostic teacher Heracleon (ca. 160) wrote the first known commentary on the Gospel of John, but it is not certain whether he attributed it to John the apostle.

to Cerinthus, a Gnostic writer. They also said that he wrote the book of Revelation. Their rejection of Jesus as the divine Word (*logos*) is what earned for them the name "Alogi," perhaps first attributed to them by Epiphanius (*Pan.* 51) in the late fourth century AD. The Alogi's rejection of Johannine authorship of the Fourth Gospel may have been more for theological rather than other considerations, since John affirms Jesus' divinity, origins, and relationship to God. Their rejection of John as the author, however, is supported by the lack of any reference to John in the famous letter of Ignatius (ca. AD 115) to the Ephesian church. Since he mentioned Paul's connection with the church at Ephesus, it is strange that the apostle John was not mentioned, especially if other church traditions are true that he lived and died there (see Eusebius, *Hist. eccl.* 3.23.5–6). Since John the apostle reportedly lived there longer than Paul did, if Eusebius is correct, one would expect Ignatius to say something about the apostle John, but he does not. Also, Polycarp, a contemporary of Ignatius who died around AD 155 and lived in the nearby city of Smyrna, never quotes the Gospel of John, even though he does quote 1 John, and says nothing about the apostle John in Ephesus. Also, Justin Martyr (ca. AD 150) speaks of the "memoirs of the apostles" (the canonical Gospels) but never attributes the Fourth Gospel to John the apostle or even mentions John in connection with a Gospel. Whether much can be made from these "arguments from silence" is debatable, but the external evidence that attributes the Gospel to John the apostle comes from the latter part of the second century and is not overwhelming. The Gospel itself, like the others, was written anonymously.

Writing in the fourth century, Eusebius reflects early church tradition about John the apostle, saying that he wrote the Gospel and that it was being read in all of the churches. He notes it is placed after the Synoptics because the other evangelists had finished their Gospels before John wrote his. He states that the first three Gospels were bold in what they did and said, and that "they neither had the knowledge nor the desire to represent the teachings of the Master in persuasive or artistic language" (*Hist. eccl.* 3.24.1–3). Eusebius goes on to say that John knew and welcomed the Synoptic Gospels.

> The three gospels which had been written down before were distributed to all including himself [John]; it is said that he welcomed them and testified to their truth but said that there was only lacking to the narrative the account of what was done by Christ at first and at the beginning of the preaching. (3.24.7, LCL)

Eusebius adds that John did not include a genealogy of Jesus because Matthew and Luke already did, so he began with a description of Jesus' divinity since this role "had been reserved for him by the Divine Spirit" (*Hist. eccl.* 3.24.13, LCL).

Although the author of John does not identify himself as John the son of Zebedee, some contend that the Gospel points in that direction, since internally it features the "disciple whom Jesus loved" (13:23; 20:2), who is also believed by some scholars to be the "other disciple" (see John 20:2; cf. 19:35 and 21:24). That may not be the case since the Gospel does not identify the "Beloved Disciple." James Charlesworth has reopened the question of the identity of the Beloved Disciple and the author of the Gospel of John.[123] He lists twenty-four reasons against John the apostle being the author of John,[124] and offers eight additional reasons for reopening the question of the search for the identity of the Beloved Disciple.[125] Charlesworth points out that the majority of New Testament scholars today do not believe that the apostle John wrote the Gospel of John, but rather that it was written by someone else who was well acquainted with Jerusalem in the first century. As a result of a detailed and careful interpretation of John, he challenges a lot of traditional scholarship by concluding that the Beloved Disciple is Thomas, whose portrait reflects the ideal disciple, who anchors Jesus in history and who contends for the "*continuity between the crucified one and the resurrected Lord.*"[126] The problem, of course, is the identity of this Beloved Disciple, since his name is nowhere given in the Gospel itself, unless that person is Lazarus (11:3).

It is possible that the apostle John was martyred quite early, as one may surmise from Mark 10:38–39. Is it possible that he was put to death with James in Acts 12:2, since he is not mentioned by name after that? Whether in fact John, the son of Zebedee and disciple of Jesus, or some other disciple of Jesus actually wrote this Gospel cannot be settled here, even though the testimony of late second-century teachers points to John the apostle.[127] Martin Hengel suggests that the corpus of writings attributed to John the apostle in the New

123. See J. H. Charlesworth, *The Beloved Disciple: Whose Witness Validates the Gospel of John?* (Valley Forge, PA: Trinity Press, 1995).

124. Ibid., x–xii.

125. Ibid., 14–21.

126. Ibid., 428–37 (italics his). He offers here eight criteria to support his conclusion.

127. Irenaeus, who became bishop of Lyons in AD 177, says that he heard Polycarp (who was martyred in AD 155) relate what he had heard from John and the other disciples about Jesus. Irenaeus also says that John composed the Gospel in Ephesus. He writes: "Afterwards [he has just mentioned the other three Gospels], John, the disciple of the Lord, who also leaned upon His breast, did himself publish a Gospel during his residence at Ephesus in Asia" (*Haer.* 3.1.1). Eusebius, on the authority of Irenaeus, adds that Papias, bishop of Hierapolis (ca. AD 140), was a hearer of both John and Polycarp (*Hist. eccl.* 3.39).

Testament instead goes back to a contemporary named John the Elder who was likely an eyewitness of the events he reports.[128]

Most scholars today recognize that the vocabulary, style of writing, and even the theology of the three epistles attributed to John are similar to that of the author of the Fourth Gospel. Since the author of 2 and 3 John calls himself an elder (*presbyteros*) in the opening verse of each letter, it is possible that the author of the Fourth Gospel and 1 John was an elder and not an apostle. It is unlikely that an apostle would refer to himself as an elder instead of the more prestigious title of apostle (2 John 1:1; 3 John 1:1) if an apostle wrote it.[129] Hengel discusses the frequency of the name "John" in the ancient Jewish world and suggests that the author of the Gospel of John was John the Elder, a likely contemporary with Jesus and the apostles who in his older years was highly regarded by the community he addressed in Asia Minor as "the disciple whom Jesus loved." Only *later* did the ancient church fathers identify John the son of Zebedee as this disciple.[130]

In regard to dating John's Gospel, the consensus is that it was written sometime during the last decade of the first century. The evidence of its early use comes from Egypt, where a small fragment of the Gospel of John from around AD 125 has been found.[131] The fragment offers evidence that John was written not much later than the early decades of the second century, but more likely it was written several years earlier. John's Gospel was known among Gnostic Christians no later than AD 130.

Although it is still possible that John was written in or near Ephesus near the end of the first century, it is also possible that it was written somewhere in Palestine, since the Hellenistic flavor found in the Gospel may have been

128. Hengel, *Johannine Question*, 132–34.

129. Kümmel, *Introduction*, 165–74, offers several arguments against Johannine authorship of the Gospel, not unlike those in Charlesworth. Kümmel contends that the author of the Gospel is simply unknown.

130. Hengel, *Johannine Question*, 102–35. See also J. L. Price, *Interpreting the New Testament* (2nd ed.; New York: Holt, Rinehart & Winston, 1971), 579–80. I should note that the John who authored the Apocalypse (the book of Revelation) does not identify himself as an apostle, and it is probably the case that there were many others who had the name of John in the early church, not all of whom were apostles. According to Rev. 1:1, John identifies himself as a "servant" of God and not as an apostle or an elder. As a comparison of the language, style, content, and vocabulary of Revelation shows, it is not likely that the author of Revelation is the same as the author of John and 1, 2, and 3 John.

131. It is now housed in the John Rylands Library of the University of Manchester, England, and identified as P. Ryl. Greek 457, but also known as P[52], and contains a few lines from John 18:37–38. The next oldest papyrus manuscript known is also from the Gospel of John, and its fragmentary text is of John 18:36–19:7, commonly known as P[90], and it dates ca. AD 150. It was found at Oxyrhynchus (P.Oxy. 3523) in Egypt and is now at Oxford, England. Recent textual critics have begun to date these texts later, but the debate is not yet settled.

found among the Essene writings at Qumran.[132] Antioch of Syria has been suggested as an alternative location by the early fourth-century church father Ephraem of Syria, who in an Armenian version of his commentary on Tatian's *Diatessaron* claimed that "John [presumably the apostle] wrote that [Gospel] in Greek at Antioch, for he remained in the country until the time of Trajan [c. 112]."[133] Because second-century Gnostic Christians relied heavily on John's Gospel, and because Heracleon, a late second-century Gnostic teacher from Alexandria, Egypt, produced a commentary on John, some suggest that the Fourth Gospel was written in Alexandria. For the most part, however, by the third century most early Christian writers attributed the Fourth Gospel to John the apostle, who, they claim, wrote it in or near Ephesus.[134] Again, there is no consensus among biblical scholars on the authorship or the location of the writing of the Fourth Gospel, but most agree that it was written in the last decade of the first century.

Recent studies of the Essene community at Qumran have shown several parallels with John's Gospel, and today it is not uncommon to hear contemporary biblical scholars speak of John as "the gospel most clearly engaged with Judaism."[135] Although no one suggests that the author of John had any direct connection or affiliation with the Dead Sea Scrolls community, it is not uncommon to hear that the author of the Gospel had a Palestinian origin and reflects a Palestinian Jewish perspective. Charlesworth argues that the Gospel of John is the most Jewish of the canonical Gospels.[136] The features in John that were earlier considered typical of later Gnostic dualism—namely, the focus on ethical and eschatological dualism and the contrasts between light and darkness as well as truth and falsehood—are more consistent with the Dead Sea Scrolls than with Philonic Judaism of Alexandria or the later

132. Spivey and Smith (*Anatomy*, 161) raise this possibility.

133. Beasley-Murray (*John*, lxxix) notes that this tradition is attributed to the Armenian version of Ephraem's commentary, but few scholars give that tradition much credibility. The tradition of an Antioch origin of the Gospel continues to have considerable approval in the scholarly community because of its parallels with the *Odes of Solomon,* which possibly originated in Antioch of Syria, but also because of the close affinities with Syrian Gnosticism and the writings of Ignatius of Syrian Antioch. Kümmel, *Introduction*, 246–47, supports this conclusion. Beasley-Murray, *John*, lxxix–lxxxi, raises the possibility that the Gospel arose in Palestine because of the author's familiarity with the Jewish social and religious environment of the first century. He suggests that it was at least written by one who was at home in Palestine even if the Gospel was later taken to Antioch and from there to Ephesus.

134. For a defense of this position, see S. van Tilborg, *Reading John in Ephesus* (NovTSup 83; Leiden: Brill, 1996).

135. J. H. Charlesworth, ed., *John and the Dead Sea Scrolls* (New York: Crossroad, 1990), xiii, xv.

136. Ibid.

Christian Gnostic (Mandaean) documents. Raymond Brown concludes that "one can no longer insist that the abstract language spoken by Jesus in the Fourth Gospel *must* have been composed in the Greek world of the early second century AD."[137]

If the Gospel of John had a non-Palestinian origin, it is quite likely that it was written in either Alexandria, where there was a large Essene population, or possibly Ephesus because it may also have had a first-century Essene community.[138] Because of the significant familiarity of the author with Palestine, and Jerusalem in particular, it is likely that the Gospel of John originated in Palestine, although Ephesus may be a good alternative.

Purpose and Historical Origins

The author's purpose in writing John's Gospel is clearly stated in 20:30–31; namely, to convince readers to believe in Jesus as the Christ and Son of God. From the beginning, readers are presented with an opportunity to have eternal life or the light of God in their lives through Jesus, who has a special relationship with the Father (e.g., John 1:4, 7–9; 3:15–21, 36; 4:14, 36; 5:21–24; 6:40; 10:10; etc.). In John, gifts from God and eternal life, while yet future, are nevertheless available now (3:16–18; 5:24; 10:10; 11:25–26). The giving of the Spirit suggests the realization of the future divine blessings in one's present experience (7:38–39; 16:7; 20:22–23). In John, the future is not totally realized in the present, but will come in a final *eschaton*, or end-time climax, that awaits those who believe in Jesus (5:25). It may be that John wanted to correct a heavy emphasis on the future at the expense of a pressing concern for the present.

It is also possible that the context for the writing of John lies in a time of crisis, such as during the Domitian persecutions of Christians at the end of the first century. Perhaps John reflects a time when some Christians were discouraged over the delay of the return of the risen Christ. It is difficult to determine the context in which the book was produced. No suggestions have gained unanimous approval. Interpreters of John have recognized that many

137. R. E. Brown, "The Dead Sea Scrolls and the New Testament," in Charlesworth, *John and the Dead Sea Scrolls*, 8.

138. For the arguments for an Alexandrian origin, see W. H. Brownlee, "Whence the Gospel of John?," in Charlesworth, *John and the Dead Sea Scrolls*, 188–89; or those for Ephesus, see M.-E. Boismard, "The First Epistle of John and the Writings of Qumran," in Charlesworth, *John and the Dead Sea Scrolls*, 156–65, who argues only for 1 John, but his comments are also relevant to the origins of the Gospel. Boismard draws attention to the parallels between John the Baptist and Qumran and argues that John the apostle was a follower of John the Baptist and also that John the Baptist had disciples doing missionary work in Ephesus during the time of Paul's ministry (Acts 19:1–7).

concerns were pressing the community that John addressed, including the threat of persecution and the Docetic heresy, which denied that Jesus had come in the flesh, claiming he only "appeared" to have a physical body.

A recent perspective on John that has received some support is that John was written to encourage Christians who had been recently expelled from the Jewish synagogues. There are three references to expulsion from synagogues in 9:22; 12:42; and 16:1–2. Do these reflect the circumstance of the historical Jesus or the author of the Gospel of John and his community—or both? Could the author have used such references to offer encouragement to the community he was addressing? Jesus' high claims about his relationship with God (3:16; 5:18; 6:41–65; and especially 10:7–18 and 22–34) may have contributed to the expulsion of Christians from the synagogues.[139] The fact that John uses the term "Jews" (*Ioudaioi*) more often than any other Gospel writer (sixty-six or sixty-seven times, compared to sixteen in the Synoptics combined), and contains several pejorative passages about them (6:41–50; 9:18; 10:31; 18:12, 36–38; 19:12), lends credibility to this view. Kysar draws attention to John's reference to the superiority of the Christian revelation over the Hebraic revelation (1:17–18; 6:49–51; 8:58; cf. 2:13–22) and concludes that John is writing from a polemical context in which Jewish Christians were being excluded from the synagogue. He suggests that the most appropriate context for that expulsion was following the destruction of the temple in AD 70, when the dominant surviving Jewish sect (Pharisaism) was seeking to establish its identity in light of that event.[140]

Aims and Historical Reliability

John had no doubt that what he reported about Jesus actually happened, and that the conclusions he drew about Jesus' identity were true. While he packs his narratives full of symbolic and theological meaning (e.g., Jesus' words to the woman at the well in Samaria in 4:10–14), there is nothing to suggest that he had little or no interest in the truthfulness of the stories he presented in his Gospel. In other words, while John adds considerable theological interpretation to the events he reports, nothing leads one to suppose that he doubted that the events he described actually happened. Likewise, John's chronology of the story of Jesus, although often different from that of the Synoptic Gospels, is not necessarily wrong.

Despite the traditional description of John as the "spiritual Gospel," one cannot conclude that John was uninterested in presenting a story about Jesus

---

139. Kysar, "John, The Gospel of," *ABD* 3:918.
140. Ibid.

in history as well as in faith. More scholars are now suggesting that behind John's interpretation of his stories about Jesus are credible historical events that cannot be ignored. The usual scholarly skepticism about the historical reliability of John appears to be changing in favor of a more balanced approach that looks for more history in John's Gospel. There is general agreement that the Synoptics and John were all heavily influenced by theological concerns, but also that they made sure that God's activity in Jesus was inextricably bound to history. Kysar lists three features of John that are now widely considered to be more historical than earlier believed: (1) the three-year length of Jesus' ministry, (2) the unique (to John) focus on Jesus' ministry to the Samaritans in 4:1–42, and (3) the authentic words of Jesus in the Gospel's discourses, even if filtered through the community's concerns. He concludes that John's value for understanding the historical Jesus, as with the other Gospels, must be "critically mined for what might be historical, and each individual saying and each feature of every narrative must be evaluated."[141]

John likely preserves a reliable account of Jesus' early ministry in and around Jerusalem that parallels the ministry of John the Baptist and is omitted in the Synoptic Gospels, except for a possible allusion to that ministry in Matthew 4:12. Today there is considerable interest in the sources that influenced the author of John who used a Passion Narrative, a signs or miracle tradition, and possibly also a discourse tradition.

In recent years this emerging "paradigm shift" in historical Jesus research has led to a reconsideration of the historical credibility of John's Gospel. In presenting the evidence for this shift, Charlesworth highlights what contemporary archaeologists have confirmed about John's familiarity with Palestine and the culture of Jerusalem in particular.[142] All of the evangelists include a high Christology, that is, Jesus' special relationship with God and the essential need to follow him in order to have forgiveness of sins and peace with God. John's *interpretation* of Jesus is shared by all of the evangelists, but this does not mean there is no credibility in them. Hengel acknowledges that there is much in John that gives historians pause, but says that just because something is not historically verifiable it does not mean that it did not happen! He concludes: "An inability to prove the historicity

141. Ibid., 3:930.
142. See "The Historical Jesus in the Fourth Gospel: A Paradigm Shift?," *JSHJ* 8 (2010): 3–46. See also his "From Old to New: Paradigm Shifts concerning Judaism, the Gospel of John, Jesus, and the Advent of 'Christianity,'" in *Jesus Research: An International Perspective* (ed. James H. Charlesworth and Petr Pokorný; Grand Rapids: Eerdmans, 2009), 56–72. See also Anderson, *Fourth Gospel* (see his other references cited above) for a similar positive assessment of John's historical credibility and several other examples.

of something does not mean that it is pure unhistorical fiction. Certainly the evangelist is not narrating historical, banal recollections of the past but the rigorously interpretive spirit paraclete leading into truth, which has the last word throughout the work."[143]

The lack of smooth transitions between several of the passages in John suggests that the author of the Gospel used several sources and remained loyal to them by not inventing transitional phrases where they did not exist. For example, the sequence of events in John 5 and 6 should probably be reversed since they reflect a rather clumsy way that Jesus traveled to and from Jerusalem. From the end of John 4 (specifically after 4:43) to the end of chapter 8, it is difficult to bring together in a coherent sequence the travels of Jesus between Galilee and Jerusalem. The same difficulty arises in John 20:1–18, which meshes the visits of Mary and the disciples to the empty tomb. Whatever the cause, many scholars today agree that some chapters are out of order and that a final editing of John likely took place after its initial writing (see 4:2; 19:35; 21:24 as possible evidence of this).

Many scholars also agree that chapter 21 is an "appendix" to the Gospel, which originally concluded at 20:31.[144] Chapter 21 not only brings the resurrection appearances into harmony with those in Matthew and Mark, but also deals with Peter's restitution and the tradition about the death of the "other disciple." Whatever the case, the change from the first-person singular "I" to the first-person plural "we" in 21:24 demonstrates an addition to the

143. Hengel, *Johannine Question*, 132. See also his *Studies in Early Christology* (Edinburgh: T&T Clark, 1995), 333–57.

144. The continuation of the story in John 21 appears contradictory to the preceding chapter since Jesus had already appeared to the disciples in Jerusalem and commissioned them in 20:19–29, but in 21:1–12 the disciples are not evangelizing but fishing in Galilee. They do not recognize him when he comes to them *again*, and they are not involved in the mission that he gave to them in 20:22–23. John 20:30–31 appears to be a summary closing of the whole Gospel and why it was written. On the other hand, 21:1–25 appears to be a harmonization of the location of the appearances of Jesus with Matthew and Mark, as well as an attempt to reconcile Peter with Jesus after his earlier threefold denial of knowing him and to explain the death of the "other disciple." This harmonization both is clumsy and reflects other editorial activity involved in this harmonization (see 21:24–25). Chapter 21 therefore is not likely an original part of John's Gospel, but was added to the original document shortly after the Gospel was written or even in the early second century. Stanley E. Porter disagrees in his contribution to my Festschrift volume, "The Ending of John's Gospel," in *From Biblical Criticism to Biblical Faith: Essays in Honor of Lee Martin McDonald* (ed. W. H. Brackney and Craig A. Evans; Macon, GA: Mercer University Press, 2007), 55–73. He has made a clear and consistent argument for John 21 being an original part of the Gospel, but his strongest argument hinges on the presence of John 21 in the earliest surviving New Testament manuscripts. However, the oldest surviving complete copy of John was produced in the late second or early third century. I agree that one cannot argue against John 21 on the basis of linguistic or verbal parallels, but Porter has not adequately answered the arguments above or dealt adequately with the inconsistencies.

text of John. The original writer may have been an eyewitness or a likely secondary editor (19:35).

John's motivation for writing is not so much to record the historical details of Jesus' life, or to correct the Synoptic portrait of Jesus, but rather to present the theological concerns that the Jesus story addressed. These concerns were also pressing issues for his anticipated readers. John is also uniquely interested in the subject of eternal life and how this can be found in Jesus (20:30–31); but even though John has theological interests, there is no reason to suppose that he denied the historicity of the events he described. History does not yield to theological interpretation in John, but instead becomes a vehicle for conveying it. This is especially true in his account of the death of Jesus, which C. H. Dodd long ago argued is worthy of serious historical consideration. He concluded that John's passion narratives should be accepted as representing a separate and important line of tradition, with the possibility that John may be inferior to Mark in some respects but superior in others.[145]

The historical reliability of John continues to be debated, and although many scholars acknowledge this possibility, few appear to rely upon it. If the current interest in the Gospel of John is any guide, then future studies will undoubtedly give more credibility to John as a separate historical source for understanding the story of Jesus.

Many years ago Rudolf Bultmann argued that John's Gospel presented a fully realized eschatology; that is, the future promise of the kingdom has been completely inaugurated here and now in and through Jesus' ministry and sacrifice. For Bultmann, the essence of Jesus' mission and thought in John is wrapped up in his cross, a theme that he also found prominently in the letters of the apostle Paul.[146] He concluded that the future elements in the Gospel (5:27–29; cf. 1 John 2:18, 28) are the work of a later editor and not an original part of John's Gospel.[147] Bultmann's interpretation of John is no longer as popular and convincing as it once was. Subsequent scholars recognize that while John largely replaces the focus on the future coming kingdom of God so dominant in the Synoptic Gospels with an emphasis on present "eternal life" inaugurated in the life, ministry, and fate of Jesus (1:12; 3:17–21; cf. 1 John 2:25; 4:16; 5:20), still in John there is a final consummation that awaits a future realization. John emphasizes the preexistent Jesus who is the Word

---

145. C. H. Dodd, "Some Considerations upon the Historical Aspect of the Fourth Gospel," in McArthur, *In Search of the Historical Jesus*, 89. See also pp. 82–92 for more support for Dodd's point.

146. Rudolf Bultmann, *Theology of the New Testament* (2 vols.; trans. Kendrick Grobel; New York: Scribner, 1951, 1955), 2:75–92.

147. Ibid., 2:39.

of God and who not only descended to the earth, but also will ascend to be with the Father who sent him (John 3:13; 20:17–18). For John, the future has descended to earth in the ministry of Jesus, but the future is still to come when the complete blessing of God will be consummated. The passages that most challenge Bultmann's interpretation of John are 5:28–29; 11:23–26; and 14:2–7. See also John's reference to the "last day" that is yet to come in 6:39–40, 44, 54; and 12:48.[148] John's Gospel has not forsaken the future in favor of the present, but the present experience of eternal life is clearly an important part of the focus in the Fourth Gospel.

Assessment of the Gospels as Historical Sources

In the foregoing discussion, I have highlighted some of the primary characteristics in the canonical Gospels that are critical for an investigation of the historical Jesus that combines historical and faith perspectives. All of the evangelists underscore that God's activity in Jesus takes place in human history, and each gives specific historical details that enable the reader to say that Jesus was fully human, but also that he had a special relationship with God. They all acknowledge that Jesus' story is both historical and theological. He was born in human flesh, lived, hungered, thirsted, knew the limitations of humanity, and died at the hands of Roman soldiers in Jerusalem during the Roman occupation of the Jewish homeland. On the other hand, he had a special relationship with God, who acted uniquely in Jesus to bring salvation and hope to humanity. While biblical scholars have attempted many times to separate the historical from the theological, the evangelists did not. Both dimensions were uniquely bound together in the story that they tell about Jesus.

It is understandable that historians examining the story of Jesus cannot affirm *as historians* the unique and remarkable stories about Jesus in the Gospels, but this does not mean that they did not happen or that they are untrue. The credibility of the Gospels is that they were written when some of the eyewitnesses of events described in them were still alive. Had the evangelists reported something far afield from what had been circulating orally about

148. Andreas J. Köstenberger, *A Theology of John's Gospel and Letters: The Word, the Christ, the Son of God* (Biblical Theology of the New Testament; Grand Rapids: Zondervan, 2009), 295–97. See Also Craig S. Keener's discussion of this topic in his *The Gospel of John: A Commentary* (2 vols.; Peabody, MA: Hendrickson, 2003), 323. He points out also that realized and future eschatology coexist among the residents at Qumran in the time of Jesus without substantial observable tension.

Jesus in the churches, the churches would surely have rejected it as they did other unreliable portraits of Jesus. Perhaps because the stories about Jesus and his teachings had been circulating in the church from its beginning by those who were close to Jesus, it is understandable why Christians welcomed written traditions that reflected this early oral tradition about Jesus. Churches early on used them in their teaching, preaching, and mission activities. The Gospels themselves also display evidence of dependence on earlier sources about Jesus, some of which may well have been produced *before* the death of Jesus and were included in the post-Easter stories about Jesus that were taught in the churches and informed the evangelists in writing their Gospels.

The canonical Gospels contain no major departures from the received traditions about Jesus that were circulating in the churches in the first century; at least, scholars have not been able to show that. Those traditions, both written and oral,[149] that informed the evangelists no doubt included stories about Jesus that were relevant to the emerging churches in the first century, but there is no evidence that the evangelists invented stories about Jesus' life and teachings to satisfy the needs of a later generation of his followers. Many New Testament scholars acknowledge that there was some growth and development in the oral and even written traditions about Jesus circulating in the churches, but this does not deny their essential reliability in telling the story of Jesus. It does not seem possible, for example, that anything could have been introduced that would call into question either the teaching of Jesus or the historical facts about his life, ministry, death, and early belief in his resurrection. Some have suggested that the story in Matthew 27:51–53 about the rending of the temple curtain and the return to life of those who were buried outside of Jerusalem and their walking through the streets of the city following the death of Jesus is evidence of expansion. These verses suddenly appear without adequate interpretation and have no parallel in the other Gospel traditions. This is the type of "expansion" that may have been introduced into the Gospels for the purpose of clarifying the significance of the death of Jesus; namely, with his death the "end times" came that were proclaimed by the prophets of old. Such examples clarify the meaning of the events the evangelists describe. They often use language that seems odd to us,

149. More than any others, Birger Gerhardsson has devoted much of his career to establishing the general reliability of the oral traditions about Jesus that were circulating in the early churches. His best-known contributions to this subject include *The Reliability of the Gospel Tradition* (Peabody, MA: Hendrickson, 2001), a collection of some of his earlier publications on the subject, and *Memory and Manuscript: Oral Tradition and Written Transmission in Rabbinic Judaism and Early Christianity with Tradition and Transmission in Early Christianity* (a combined edition with a new preface; Biblical Resource Series; Grand Rapids: Eerdmans, 1998).

but must be understood in terms of the story they were trying to tell. This will become more obvious as we focus on the life of Jesus. Regardless, this does not seriously alter the essential message of Matthew or the other evangelists. In fact, this example may help us to understand how, for Matthew, history is at times used as a vehicle for communicating theological truth. It is worth noting also, as we will see later in the story of Jesus, that only Matthew has a story of the earthquakes at the death and resurrection of Jesus. Just prior to those events in the Gospel (Matt. 24:7–14), Jesus speaks of earthquakes at the beginning of the last days. Could it be that Matthew was trying to communicate with this story that in the death and resurrection of Jesus the kingdom of God had arrived? Such stories are an aid in interpreting Matthew's story rather than a distraction.

When does history give way to theological interpretation, or when does it become a vehicle for conveying it? The answer may be found in our use of the principles of multiple attestation and coherence, mentioned earlier, or in the worldview of the early Christians, which was open to the activity of God in history, as well as in a careful interpretation of the traditions themselves. If a story is repeated in other traditions and if it coheres with other facts that we have been able to establish about Jesus, then from a historical perspective we can make a case for its authenticity as a genuine part of the earliest traditions about Jesus. We can say further that, in the case of Christianity's most important events—the death and resurrection of Jesus—though many of the details surrounding them in the Gospels differ, their essential message is the same; namely, that Jesus of Nazareth, who died, is now alive and worthy of our faith, and that this has great significance for all who will receive it. According to Stanton, the canonical Gospels contain three basic layers of tradition: the level of the life of Jesus himself, the level of the early church that transmitted the traditions both orally and in written form, and the level of the teaching of the evangelists.[150] Through careful sifting of the evidence in each of these levels, it is possible to present a credible and reliable story of Jesus.

The question of authorship of the Gospels is less significant in the cases of Matthew and John and more so in the cases of Mark and Luke-Acts. There is no consensus among scholars on authorship of any of the Gospels, but the arguments in favor of Mark's authorship of his Gospel are not insignificant, even if not conclusive. In the case of Luke, scholars are quite divided, as we have seen; nevertheless, Luke's lack of mentioning either the death of Peter or Paul or the destruction of the temple in Jerusalem suggests a pre-AD 70

---

150. In this conclusion, I have simply reversed the sequence of Stanton's assessment of what is in the Gospel tradition. See his *Gospels and Jesus*, 152.

date of composition of the Luke-Acts corpus. The case for the authorship of either Matthew or John, on the other hand, is not compelling nor as important since both were written anonymously and both were written later than Mark or Luke, but both authors depend on earlier sources and offer valuable information regarding the story of Jesus. All evangelists reflect the commonly accepted primary tradition about Jesus that was circulating in the earliest churches. Agreement from multiple sources speaks strongly in favor of the reliability of the broad outline and content of Jesus' ministry, and all of the Gospels affirm that Jesus both died and was raised from the dead. When applied to the Gospel tradition, this criterion of multiple attestation suggests that the evangelists offer a reliable story of the ministry and message of Jesus.

As we have seen earlier, one's understanding of history often influences how the New Testament is interpreted and what conclusions are drawn. The mixture of historical and theological features in the Gospels is not an impediment to their interpretation, but this combination must be acknowledged. We cannot expect a historian, who examines history with a different set of criteria, to be open to the unique activity of God in history that is central to Christian faith. It is possible, as we will see, to examine the Gospels and determine from them several historically authentic features about Jesus. These alone, however, cannot account for the impact that Jesus had on his followers, or for the emergence of the early churches.

What happened in the story of Jesus has historical roots in the sense that there was a string of events that led to the death of Jesus and the understandable devastation of his disciples; but the story does not end there in the Gospels. The convergence of history and theology in the story of Jesus offers an explanation for the transformation of the disciples after Jesus' execution and the emergence of the early churches.

Dunn contends that the traditions about Jesus that are preserved in the Synoptic Gospels are just the sort that we would expect to be preserved. In this limited sense, the Gospels are biographies, even though not the kind that we are used to today.[151] As the traditions about Jesus were put in written form, some modifications were made to meet the needs of the church. How much "modification" was made is, of course, at the heart of considerable scholarly debate.

The earliest Christians were concerned to preserve the memory of Jesus in the churches and to pass it on to their new converts and community. They were more concerned with the substance and meaning of what Jesus had said and done than with the meticulous level of verbal precision that is common

151. J. D. G. Dunn, *The Living Word* (Philadelphia: Fortress, 1988), 30–31.

in contemporary scholarship. The substance of the Gospels was undoubtedly a "living tradition" in the earliest churches before it was eventually put in written form. Finally, it is also critically important that we understand the evangelists' interest in historicity *on their own terms*, not with ones that we impose on them.[152] At times their stories overlap, but at times they also have differences. They all have different emphases, but in the broadest outlines they tell the same story.

152. Ibid., 43.

3

Other Sources for Studying the Historical Jesus

||||||||||||||||||||||||||||||||||||||||||||||||||||||||||||

Several other ancient nonbiblical sources refer to Jesus or reflect the context in which he ministered, and some of them confirm historical elements about Jesus that are in the canonical Gospels. Many of these sources are of limited value, some are both absurd and mythological, but a few are helpful. Understandably, those sources that came from the opponents of Jesus and early Christianity are often pejorative. Most of the nonbiblical or noncanonical sources have very little reliable historical information about Jesus except that he lived and died. On a positive note, these sources often show that the story of Jesus did not take place in a historical vacuum and that knowledge of him and his followers was common in antiquity.

For our purposes, the most important question is whether these other ancient sources advance our knowledge of Jesus. The short answer is no, but again they often do confirm what we learn about him in the canonical Gospels. The surviving sources are essentially in three categories, namely Christian, Greco-Roman, and Jewish. I have also added a section on the value of archaeology for this inquiry. Several scholars are beginning to acknowledge the value of archaeological inquiry, which often clarifies the context in which Jesus lived and sometimes some of the comments that he made. Not infrequently several of these sources offer a skewed portrait of Jesus and his followers, but students of the historical Jesus are well served by having an awareness of them. We begin with the ancient Christian sources.

||||||||||||||||||||||||||||||||||||||||||||||||||||||||||||||||||||||||||||||||||||||||||||||||||||||||||||||||||||||||||||||||||||||||||||||||||||||||||||||||||

Apocryphal Gospels

The most commonly referenced apocryphal gospels employed in recent historical Jesus research include the following:

Apocryphon of James (preserved in Nag Hammadi Codex I)

Dialogue of the Savior (preserved in Nag Hammadi Codex III)

Gospel of the Ebionites (preserved in quotations by Epiphanius)

Gospel of the Egyptians (preserved in quotations by Clement of Alexandria)

Gospel of the Hebrews (preserved in quotations by various fathers)

Gospel of the Nazarenes (preserved in quotations by various fathers)

Gospel of Peter (preserved in a large fragment from Akhmim and Papyrus Oxyrhynchus 2949)

Gospel of Thomas (preserved in Nag Hammadi Codex II and Papyrus Oxyrhynchus 1, 654, and 655)

Protevangelium of James (preserved in a supposed letter of Clement of Alexandria)

Oxyrhynchus Papyrus 840

Oxyrhynchus Papyrus 1224

Papyrus Egerton (+ Papyrus Köln 255)

Fayyum Fragment (= Papyrus Vindobonensis Greek 2325)[a]

a. James H. Charlesworth and Craig A. Evans, "Jesus in the Agrapha and Apocryphal Gospels," in *Studying the Historical Jesus: Evaluations of the State of Current Research* (ed. B. Chilton and C. A. Evans; Leiden: Brill, 1998), 479–533, here 480, have supplied this list. They also list parallels between canonical Gospels and the apocryphal gospels reflecting the considerable dependence of the latter on the former (491–95).

||||||||||||||||||||||||||||||||||||||||||||||||||||||||||||||||||||||||||||||||||||||||||||||||||||||||||||||||||||||||||||||||||||||||||||||||||||||||||||||||||

Apocryphal Gospels

The so-called apocryphal gospels present various stories about the words and/ or deeds of Jesus that were not included in the church's New Testament. Many of these come from the second and third centuries and reflect both legendary and even fanciful stories about Jesus. There were perhaps as many as forty of these ancient gospels,[1] and it is generally acknowledged that the majority of them are strange in their details and often fill in the gaps in the story of

1. Christopher Tuckett, "Forty Other Gospels," in *The Written Gospel* (ed. Markus Bockmuehl and Donald A. Hagner; Cambridge: Cambridge University Press, 2005), 238–53, makes this claim. See also Hans-Josef Klauck, *Apocryphal Gospels: An Introduction* (London: T&T Clark, 2003), who offers an important introduction to this literature and its impact in early Christianity and its value for today.

Jesus in the canonical Gospels. They tell stories about Jesus' birth, childhood, family, ministry, death, and resurrection, but also something about prominent New Testament figures such as Peter, Paul, and James. They sometimes offer special knowledge that Jesus supposedly imparted to his disciples. Again, they do not appreciably add to our knowledge of Jesus nor offer independent and reliable testimony about him.

The Value of the Noncanonical Gospels

Scholars disagree considerably on the value of these sources, and some, as we will see below, even prefer the portrait of Jesus in a few of them instead of the canonical sources. Whether Jesus actually said or did any of the things attributed to him in these sources is highly debatable. Charlesworth and Evans,[2] as well as Meier,[3] argue that these noncanonical Christian sources do not constitute an important or even independent source for the teachings or deeds of Jesus, but rather that most of them are dependent on one or more of the New Testament Gospels. Meier also concludes that the rabbinic material, the agrapha, and the apocryphal gospels do not "offer us reliable new information or authentic sayings that are independent of the NT."[4] His conclusion is worth repeating:

> For better or for worse, in our quest for the historical Jesus, we are largely confined to the canonical Gospels; the genuine "corpus" is infuriating in its restrictions. For the historian it is a galling limitation. But to call upon the *Gospel of Peter* or the *Gospel of Thomas* to supplement our Four Gospels is to broaden out our pool of sources from the difficult to the incredible.[5]

Other scholars disagree and place far more confidence in several of the noncanonical sources. Helmut Koester, for instance, argues that the canonical Gospels were dependent upon noncanonical sources such as the *Sayings*

2. Charlesworth and Evans, "Agrapha and Apocryphal Gospels." See also C. A. Evans, "Jesus in Non-Canonical Sources," in Chilton and Evans, *Studying the Historical Jesus*, 443–78. Evans identifies the rabbinic and other noncanonical sources as "dubious sources" that at best only provide "a modicum of helpful information about the historical Jesus" and only confirm some of the historical aspects of Jesus' life—namely, he lived in Palestine and died there. Only Josephus has anything substantial to say that confirms the existence of Jesus (477–78).

3. John P. Meier, *A Marginal Jew: Rethinking the Historical Jesus* (ABRL; New York: Doubleday, 1991), 1:112–66, draws similar conclusions to Charlesworth and Evans (above) on the value of the noncanonical sources for historical Jesus research.

4. Meier, *Marginal Jew*, 1:140.

5. Ibid., 140–41.

Source ("Q"), the *Gospel of Thomas*, the *Dialogue of the Savior*, the *Unknown Gospel of Papyrus Egerton 2*, the *Apocryphon of James*, and the *Gospel of Peter*.[6] J. D. Crossan also depends heavily on extracanonical literature for his portrait of Jesus as a Jewish peasant Cynic philosopher, and he believes that some of this literature predates the canonical literature and offers authentic sayings of Jesus.[7] He even dates the *Gospel of Peter* before the Synoptics and the Gospel of John, namely in the 50s of the first century AD. The dating of these sources varies widely among scholars who study them, but the strong differences in the scholarly community suggest that final answers to questions raised about the earliest and most authentic sources for the study of Jesus and his teachings, as well as the dependencies and relationships of these sources, have not yet been settled by biblical scholars.

Papias's comments (ca. AD 140) cited earlier about the circulation of the oral teachings of Jesus—namely, "For I did not suppose that information from books would help me so much as the word of a living and surviving voice" (Eusebius, *Hist. eccl.* 3.39.4, LCL)—confirm that oral traditions were passed on in the churches and that they had more meaning or value for him than those written in books. This witness informs us of the significance that many oral sayings of Jesus had in the early churches; but again, of those that have survived, there is little in them that warrants significant attention.

Three Commonly Cited Gospels

To illustrate, I will only briefly mention three of the more commonly cited noncanonical gospels. More complete discussions of these and other sources can be found in the sources listed in the footnotes.

The Gospel of Thomas (*Gos. Thom.*)

The Gospel of Thomas is an esoteric document that simply lists sayings of Jesus with almost no historical narrative. Its focus is on a special secret knowledge that Jesus revealed to his disciples and that was written for the spiritually

6. For a complete discussion, see Helmut Koester, *Ancient Christian Gospels: Their History and Development* (Philadelphia: Trinity Press, 1990). For his arguments and conclusions, see also his "Apocryphal and Canonical Gospels," *HTR* 73 (1980): 105–30, and *"Überlieferung und Geschichte der früchristlichen Evangelienliteratur,"* ANRW 2.25.2 (1984): 1:463–542.

7. See for example John Dominic Crossan, *The Historical Jesus: The Life of a Mediterranean Jewish Peasant* (San Francisco: HarperSanFrancisco, 1991), xi–xiii, xxvii–xxxiv, 332–40, and 427–34. See also his *Four Other Gospels: Shadows on the Contours of Canon* (Minneapolis: Seabury, 1985), 144, and *The Cross That Spoke: The Origins of the Passion Narrative* (San Francisco: Harper & Row, 1988), 404, in which he argues that the *Cross Gospel*, which is a source of the *Gospel of Peter*, lies behind the passion narrative in all four canonical Gospels.

elite in churches; salvation is assumed to be attained through this knowledge rather than through an act of faith or dependence on the acts of Jesus in his death and resurrection. This gospel does not deal with the question of sin, but rather seeks an escape from the physical body and the physical world. It has 114 sayings of Jesus and has a clear orientation of male superiority, especially in its concluding verse.[8]

A number of its sayings have obvious parallels with the canonical Gospels, and the question for scholars has been which came first, *Gos. Thom.* or the canonical Gospels. The majority of New Testament scholars have taken the latter option, noting that there are parallels in *Gos. Thom.* to all four of the canonical Gospels, including the special material in both Matthew ("M") and Luke ("L") and even John.[9] It is much easier to explain the use by *Gos. Thom.* of the canonical Gospels than the other way around. None of the material that is special to *Gos. Thom.* is found in the canonical Gospels, and if they depended on *Gos. Thom.*, one would expect to see some of that material in them. The following list of parallels between *Gos. Thom.* and the canonical Gospels illustrates this point.

The Parallels between the Gospel of Matthew ("M" material) and *Gos. Thom.*	
5:10—*Gos. Thom.* §69a	13:24–30—*Gos. Thom.* §57
5:14—*Gos. Thom.* §32 (= P.Oxy. 1 §7)	13:44—*Gos. Thom.* §109
6:2–4—*Gos. Thom.* §6, §14	13:45–46—*Gos. Thom.* §76
(= POxy 654 §6)	13:47–50—*Gos. Thom.* §8
6:3—*Gos. Thom.* §62	15:13—*Gos. Thom.* §40
7:6—*Gos. Thom.* §93	18:20—*Gos. Thom.* §30 (= P.Oxy. 1 §85)
10:16—*Gos. Thom.* §39	23:13—*Gos. Thom.* §39, §102
11:30—*Gos. Thom.* §90	(= P.Oxy. 655 §2)

The Parallels between the Gospel of Luke ("L" material) and *Gos. Thom.*	
11:27–28 + 23:29—*Gos. Thom.* §79	12:49—*Gos. Thom.* §10
12:13–14—*Gos. Thom.* §72	17:20–21—*Gos. Thom.* §3 (= P.Oxy. 654
12:16–21—*Gos. Thom.* §63	§3), §113

8. Its controversial conclusion is as follows: "Simon Peter said to them: Let Mariham [Mary Magdalene] go out from among us, for women are not worthy of the life. Jesus said: Look, I will lead her that I may make her male, in order that she too may become a living spirit resembling you males. For every woman who makes herself male will enter into the kingdom of heaven" (trans. from Beate Blatz, "The Coptic Gospel of Thomas," in *New Testament Apocrypha* [ed. W. Schneemelcher; trans. R. McL. Wilson; 2nd ed; Louisville: Westminster John Knox, 1991], 1:129).

9. A helpful discussion of the arguments for a late date of *Gos. Thom.* and its dependence on the canonical Gospels is in Craig A. Evans, *Fabricating Jesus: How Modern Scholars Distort the Gospels* (Downers Grove, IL: InterVarsity, 2006), 67–77. See also a helpful summary of *Gos. Thom.* in Paul Foster, *The Apocryphal Gospels: A Very Short Introduction* (Oxford: Oxford University Press, 2009), 31–41.

The Parallels between the Gospel of John and *Gos. Thom.*	
1:9—*Gos. Thom.* §24 (= P.Oxy. 655 §24)	7:32–36—*Gos. Thom.* §38 (= P.Oxy. 655 §38)
1:14—*Gos. Thom.* §28 (= P.Oxy. 1 §28)	
4:13–15—*Gos. Thom.* §13	8:12; 9:5—*Gos. Thom.* §77

The More Obvious Parallels between the Gospel of Mark and *Gos. Thom.*	
2:18–20—*Gos. Thom.* §104	4:30–32—*Gos. Thom.* §20
3:31–34—*Gos. Thom.* §99	6:4–5—*Gos. Thom.* §31
4:3–9—*Gos. Thom.* §9	7:15—*Gos. Thom.* §14c

Besides the above parallels, Nicholas Perrin has shown that many of the Syriac "catchwords" in *Gos. Thom.* are also in the Syrian *Diatessaron* (Greek = "through four," or the same work by another title, *The Gospel of the Mixed*), Tatian's gospel harmony that he produced by combining the four canonical Gospels (ca. AD 160–170).[10] The parallels between *Gos. Thom.* and the *Diatessaron* suggest that *Gos. Thom.* depended on the canonical Gospels presented in the *Diatessaron* and that *Gos. Thom.* was written sometime after Tatian's production in the last half of the second century, rather than during the middle of the first century as some scholars have argued.[11]

The Gospel of Peter (*Gos. Pet.*)

For several centuries, *Gos. Pet.* was cited by various church fathers and clearly influenced the thinking of several early church teachers, possibly including Origen in his *Commentary on Matthew* 10.17. Eusebius clearly (see *Hist. eccl.* 3.25.6 and especially 6.12.3–6) refers to its initial use at the end of the second century in churches overseen by Bishop Serapion. Many other attempts have been made to show a broader use of it in early Christianity, but without

10. Concerning this work, Eusebius writes: "Their former leader Tatian composed in some way a combination and collection of the Gospels, and gave this the name of *The Diatessaron*, and it is still extant in some places. And they say that he ventured to paraphrase some of the words of the apostle, as though correcting their style" (*Hist. eccl.* 4.29.6, LCL).

11. See Perrin's complete argument in Nicholas Perrin, *Thomas and Tatian* (Academia Biblica 5; Atlanta: Society of Biblical Literature, 2002). Scholars who argue for a first-century date for *Gos. Thom.* and its independence from the canonical Gospels include James M. Robinson, "LOGOI SOPHŌN: On the Gattung of Q," in *Trajectories through Early Christianity* (by James M. Robinson and Helmut Koester; Philadelphia: Fortress, 1971), 71–113; and J. D. Crossan, *The Historical Jesus: Life of a Mediterranean Jewish Peasant* (San Francisco: HarperSanFrancisco, 1991), 427–30. For another discussion of the parallels between *Gos. Thom.* and the canonical Gospels, see Koester, *Ancient Christian Gospels*, 75–128. Those scholars who reject an early date for *Gos. Thom.* and contend that it depends on the canonical Gospels include Robert M. Grant, *The Secret Sayings of Jesus* (Garden City, NY: Doubleday, 1960), 113; Harvey K. McArthur, "The Dependence of the Gospel of Thomas on the Synoptics," *ExpTim* 71 (1959–60): 286–87; Klyne Snodgrass, "The Gospel of Thomas: A Secondary Gospel," *SecCent* 7 (1989–90): 19–38; Christopher Tuckett, "Thomas and the Synoptics," *NovT* 30 (1988): 132–57; and Meier, *Marginal Jew*, 1:130–39.

convincing evidence. A fragment of *Gos. Pet.* that dates from the eighth or ninth century was found at Akhmim in Upper Egypt, showing that it was in use in some churches at least until that time, but it is not clear how widespread its use was. Its likely use in Western Syria also suggests its composition in that region. The surviving text from Akhmim begins with Pilate's washing of his hands followed by the condemnation, death, and resurrection of Jesus, and it ends with Peter, Andrew, and Levi departing for the Sea of Galilee/Tiberias. Only some sixty verses of it remain, and it is likely a Jewish-Christian document written sometime between AD 100 and 130.[12]

What remains in the fragmented *Gos. Pet.* has little that warrants confidence in its integrity and reliability and nothing that justifies its use by the canonical Gospel writers, contrary to what Crossan has claimed.[13] Rather, it weaves together portions of the canonical Gospels, having in view a later generation of Christians facing a different set of circumstances than those we see in the first century.

The Gospel of the Hebrews (*Gos. Heb.*)

This gospel may be the same as the *Gospel of the Nazarenes*, and it is an early Jewish-Christian gospel. Until recently its value has been largely ignored, but owing to the work of James Edwards it is receiving renewed interest as an ancient source that may shed some light on Jesus and early Christianity.[14] Its text is first referred to or cited in Ignatius's *Letter to the Smyrnaeans* 3:1–2. See also Jerome, *Illustrious Men* 16, who ties Ignatius's quote to *Gos. Heb.* Edwards has shown a strong agreement between Luke and *Gos. Heb.* He contends that Luke depended on *Gos. Heb.*, and makes a case that the early church fathers concluded the same (see Luke 1:1–4).[15] This gospel likely stands closer to the canonical Gospels than any other noncanonical gospel and is not as sensational

---

12. For a more complete discussion of the background and contents of *Gos. Pet.*, see Christian Maurer and Wilhelm Schneemelcher, "The Gospel of Peter," in Schneemelcher, *New Testament Apocrypha*, 1:216–22, followed by their translation of the document on 223–27. See also the brief description by Foster, *Apocryphal Gospels*, 87–101. He includes photographs of the document showing its ending in the middle of a sentence.

13. J. D. Crossan suggests that *Gos. Pet.* lies behind the passion narratives in the New Testament. See his *Cross That Spoke*, 404. Evans, *Fabricating Jesus*, 80, 256–57n5 and 6 has explained Crossan's view and noted its weakness. He also notes Helmut Koester's view that the basis for *Gos. Pet.* reflects an older text under the authority of Peter that is independent of the canonical Gospels (80).

14. See James R. Edwards's recent examination of this Jewish-Christian document in his "The Hebrew Gospel in Early Christianity," in *"Non-Canonical" Religious Texts in Early Judaism and Early Christianity* (ed. Lee Martin McDonald and James H. Charlesworth; Jewish and Christian Texts in Contexts and Related Studies Series; London: T&T Clark, 2012), 116–52; see also his more complete discussion of the possible influence of *Gos. Heb.* on the Synoptic tradition in *The Hebrew Gospel and the Formation of the Synoptic Tradition* (Grand Rapids: Eerdmans, 2009).

15. Edwards, "The Hebrew Gospel in Early Christianity," 151–52.

as the non-Jewish noncanonical gospels. There are some similarities with the remnants of the other Jewish gospels, namely the *Gospel of the Nazarenes* and the *Gospel of the Ebionites*, but what remains of each is insufficient to allow many definitive comparisons or conclusions. What is currently known of *Gos. Heb.* is that it is at times at odds with the canonical Gospels in that the Holy Spirit is female (a Jewish characteristic) and James the Just participates at the Last Supper and is the first witness to the resurrection. At times it appears to support the Synoptic tradition at the baptism of Jesus, though there is not complete agreement here. The Spirit waits until the coming of the Son, with whom the Spirit has union (it "rests in," not "on," Jesus), and is called Jesus' "mother." The gospel's date is difficult to establish, but the suggested dates range from the 50s to approximately AD 140. According to the *Stichometry of Nicephorus* (ca. AD 850), there were some 2,200 lines in this gospel.

Minimal Value for Jesus Research

The divide among New Testament scholars over the value of the noncanonical gospels is considerable, but after reading through them, one is struck by their generally fanciful interpretations and/or expansions of the canonical Gospels, reflecting the interests and concerns of later generations that followed the formation of the New Testament Gospels. Meier's assessment of the known noncanonical gospels seems justified and worthy of repeating here. He writes, "Contrary to some scholars, I do not think that the rabbinic material, the agrapha, the apocryphal gospels, and the Nag Hammadi codices [which contain the Gnostic documents] (in particular the *Gospel of Thomas*) offer us reliable information or authentic sayings [of Jesus] that are independent of the NT."[16] Similarly, Elliott argues that the historical value of the apocryphal descriptions of Jesus has to do with their revealing the theological motives and social conditions that gave rise to this literature. He concludes that the church chose the New Testament corpora of writings that come from the first century over the later, apocryphal Christian writings, distinguishing the "less extravagant, terse, more 'spiritual,' complex, profound—from the apocrypha, with its verbosity, sensationalism, and occasional deviation from standard teachings." Elliott concludes that, in his judgment, the church's rejected texts "were legitimately branded as 'apocryphal,' in the sense of 'secondary,' 'of dubious quality,' and 'inferior' in all sorts of ways." Their greatest value, he claims, is in their ability to showcase the thoughts and insights of post-biblical Christianity.[17] I agree

16. Meier, *Marginal Jew*, 1:140.
17. J. K. Elliott, *The Apocryphal Jesus: Legends of the Early Church* (Oxford: Oxford University Press, 1996), 210–11. Tuckett, "Forty Other Gospels," agrees and concludes that although

with Meier's and Elliott's assessments and also add that nothing in the agrapha or apocryphal gospels offers anything that could be considered an advance in the story of Jesus over what we see in the canonical Gospels. With the possible exception of *Gos. Heb.*, they all appear to postdate the canonical gospel traditions; but even in the instance of *Gos. Heb.*, most of what we find is compatible with the story in the New Testament Gospels.

Greco-Roman Sources

Within a few years after the death of Jesus, knowledge of him and his followers had reached Rome and other major cities in the Roman Empire. Many of the initial reports about him and those who followed him were unsettling to the Romans, especially those among the educated classes, and led to suspicion and pockets of persecution in various locations. In his letter to the Corinthian Christians Paul reflected the reality of those perceptions, stating that *not many* mighty or noble or persons known for their wisdom were among the followers of Jesus (1 Cor. 1:26). The Christians' willingness to welcome the poor, lowly, and despised was considered distasteful by some, especially to the elite in society. Many false rumors circulated about the Christians that led to misunderstandings of who they were, of what they were about and practiced, and even about Jesus himself. For example, Christians were sometimes accused of cannibalism when they partook of the bread and cup that symbolized the body and blood of Christ in the communion meal. They were even accused of eating children.[18] Also, their love for one another and others was occasionally misunderstood, especially when they broke bread together and referred to this act as a "love feast." This led to accusations of Christians practicing incest and immorality, sometimes called "Oedipodean intercourse," based upon the classical story of Oedipus of Thebes marrying his own mother. Finally, the Christians' rejection of the state divinities, including their refusal to worship the Roman emperor, led to accusations of atheism (Athenagoras, *Leg.* 3; Minucius Felix, *Oct.* 9).

These and other charges were brought against the Christians, and resentment against them was considerable, leading to negative and hostile comments and actions against them and their founder, Jesus. Isolated persecutions against Christians continued with greater and lesser intensity in their first three

---

these noncanonical gospels offer little that sheds light on the historical Jesus, they "may be far more interesting and fascinating for the light they throw on later periods of Christian history, in some cases (e.g., in the second century) when other sources are sadly lacking" (253).

18. On this and related issues, see S. Benko, *Pagan Rome and the Early Christians* (Bloomington: Indiana University Press, 1984), esp. 54–78.

centuries. The following collection of quotations from antiquity, though not exhaustive, offers some sense of how the Christians and their founder were perceived by state officials, prominent philosophers, and competing propagandists.[19] Generally speaking, Christians were not trusted, understood, or appreciated by the educated and leadership classes in the Greco-Roman world of the first two centuries. This suspicion made them easy targets of false accusations, and eventually they were the recipients of cruel and torturous persecutions empire-wide in the third and fourth centuries. In the surviving testimony, there are also occasional reflections about Jesus, depicted as the leader of an early band of followers called Christians. There is nothing new about Jesus in these various descriptions, and what is historical is dependent either on Christian sources or non-Christian traditions circulating in the Greco-Roman world. The latter are generally negative and often have a misperception and misrepresentation of Jesus and his followers. Their historical value is not negligible, however, because they let us know that Jesus of Nazareth lived in Palestine in the first part of the first century AD and that he led a band of followers. They also let us know that he was known by several titles, especially "Christ," but also "king" and "wise man." These ancient sources often offer independent evidence for the existence of Jesus and provide statements about his death and those who followed him.

Tacitus

Tacitus (Cornelius Tacitus, ca. AD 55–120) was a member of the senatorial aristocracy and a major Roman historian. His best-known writings are *Histories* (ca. 105–110) and the *Annals* (ca. 116–117), and to a lesser degree *Agricola* and *Germania*. For our purposes, his significance lies in his telling the story of the great fire at Rome in AD 64 and Nero's blaming the fire on the Christians. Although Tacitus claims that the Christians perpetuate a "hideous and shameful" religion and constitute a "deadly superstition," he does not believe that the Christians were guilty of starting the fire. He writes:

> But all human efforts, all the lavish gifts of the emperor, and the propitiations of the gods, did not banish the sinister belief that the conflagration [the burning of Rome] was the result of an order. Consequently, to get rid of the report, *Nero fastened the guilt and inflicted the most exquisite tortures on a class hated for their abominations [flagitia], called Christians by the populace. Christus, from whom the name had its origin, suffered the extreme penalty during the reign of Tiberius at the hands of one of our procurators, Pontius Pilate, and a deadly*

---

19. For a more detailed study of such responses, see R. L. Wilken, *The Christians as the Romans Saw Them* (New Haven: Yale University Press, 1984).

superstition, thus checked for the moment, again broke out not only in Judea, the source of the evil, but also in Rome, where all things hideous and shameful from every part of the world meet and become popular. Accordingly, an arrest was first made of all who confessed; then, upon their information, an immense multitude was convicted, not so much of the crime of arson, as of hatred of the human race. Mockery of every sort was added to their deaths. Covered with the skins of beasts, they were torn by dogs and perished, or were nailed to crosses, or were doomed to the flames. These served to illuminate the night when daylight failed. Nero had thrown open his gardens for the spectacle, and was exhibiting a show in the circus, while he mingled with the people in the dress of a charioteer or drove about in a chariot. Hence, even for criminals who deserved extreme and exemplary punishment, there arose a feeling of compassion; for it was not, as it seemed, for the public good, but to glut one man's cruelty, that they [Christians] were being destroyed. (*Ann.* 15.44.2–8)[20]

Tacitus makes clear that Jesus was a Jew, that his name had now become "Christus," that he had begun this new religion, and that he was executed at the hands of Pontius Pilate. He obviously believes that what the Christians teach and do is inappropriate and suspicious, but that they do not deserve to pay for the crime (the burning of Rome) committed by Nero.

Suetonius

Suetonius (Gaius Suetonius Tranquillus, ca. AD 69–130) was a friend of Pliny the Younger and a government official under the emperor Hadrian. He wrote *Lives of Illustrious Men* and also *Lives of the Caesars*. In the latter he tells the story of the Caesars from Julius to Domitian. Suetonius describes the expulsion of Jews from Rome (mentioned in Acts 18:2) as follows: "Claudius expelled the Jews [Jewish Christians only?] from Rome who, instigated by Chrestus [Christ?], never ceased to cause unrest" (*Claud.* 25.4). The name "Chrestus" is most likely an error by Suetonius, who was unfamiliar with the emerging Christian movement. The word *chrestus* was actually an early designation for a servant or slave, but mistakenly used here in reference to the popular Christian designation for Jesus.[21] Suetonius also seems to assume that Chrestus (Christ) was present in Rome and caused the unrest that led to the expulsion of the Jews (Jewish Christians?). In his description of the life of Nero, he speaks of the persecution of Christians as follows: "Punishment

20. This translation is from J. Stevenson, ed., *A New Eusebius: Documents Illustrative of the History of the Church to AD 337* (London: SPCK, 1957), 2–3, italics added.
21. C. A. Evans, *Ancient Texts for New Testament Studies: A Guide to the Background Literature* (Peabody, MA: Hendrickson, 2005), 298–99.

was inflicted on the Christians, a class of men given to a new and wicked superstition" (*Nero* 16.2).[22]

Mara bar Serapion

Following the Jewish revolt in Palestine, a Syrian Stoic, Mara bar Serapion from Samosata, wrote a letter from an unknown Roman prison to his son, in which he refers to the murder of three "wise" persons (Socrates, Pythagoras, and *likely* Jesus) by their countrymen and the consequent divine judgment against those nations. His letter offers the earliest pagan testimony to Jesus (perhaps AD 73–74). Mara provides what has been called a "benevolent" report[23] about Jesus, even though Jesus is not referred to by name. He speaks instead about a wise "king," a designation several times associated with Jesus in the Gospels when he was crucified under the Roman accusation "King of the Jews" (Matt. 27:11, 29, 37; Mark 15:2, 9, 12, 18, 26; Luke 23:3, 37–38; and John 18:33, 39; 19:3, 14–15, 19, 21). He is called "King of Israel" in Matthew and Mark (Matt. 27:42; Mark 15:32) and in the *Gospel of Peter* (3:2; 4:2). Jesus' role as a king is inferred in Matthew's genealogy, where he is referred to as the son of David and where subsequently wise men from the east come bearing gifts fit for the king of the Jews (Matt. 1:1–17; 2:1–2), and also in the angelic announcement to Mary (Luke 1:32–33).

Scholars generally agree that Mara is describing Jesus' fate at the hands of his fellow Jews (cf. Acts 4:10 and 1 Thess. 2:14–15). Mara bar Serapion has no specific references to Pilate or to Jesus' execution, perhaps out of fear for his own safety, nor does he mention Jesus' resurrection or his messianic claims, but the letter offers independent evidence of Jesus' activity and execution in Palestine in the first century and places the blame for it on the Jews. Mara was neither a Jew nor a Christian. His letter is as follows:

> For what advantage did the Athenians gain by the murder of Socrates, the recompense of which they received in famine and pestilence? Or the people of Samos by the burning of Pythagoras, because in one hour their country was entirely covered with sand? Or the Jews *by the death* of their wise king, because from that same time their kingdom was taken away? For with justice did God make recompense to the wisdom of these three: for the Athenians died of famine; and the Samians were overwhelmed by the sea without remedy; and the Jews,

22. New Testament scholars often take "Chrestus" to be a reference to Jesus, but some classical scholars are less certain about the meaning of the name.

23. Gerd Theissen and Annette Merz, *The Historical Jesus: A Comprehensive Guide* (Minneapolis: Fortress, 1998; German ed., *Der historische Jesus: Ein Lehrbuch* [Göttingen: Vandenhoeck & Ruprecht, 1996]), 76–79.

desolate and driven from their own kingdom, are scattered through every country. Socrates is not dead, because of Plato; neither Pythagoras, because of the statue of Juno; nor the Wise King, because of the laws which he promulgated.[24]

According to Theissen and Merz, Mara probably got his information from early Syrian Christians, but that is not certain. If so, we do not have independent data here.[25] Mara was not a Christian, but offers the first favorable report about Jesus outside of the Christian community.

Pliny the Younger

Pliny (Gaius Plinius Caecilius Secundus, AD 61–120) was an educated member of the Roman aristocracy (he was a senator) and governor of Bithynia. He produced a ten-volume collection of letters (ca. AD 111) that are invaluable historical documents covering the period of Trajan's reign as Roman emperor (AD 98–117) and include early reflections of attitudes toward the Christians by Emperor Trajan. Evidently, being a new governor, he had not yet experienced any trials of the Christians, and wrote to Trajan in his tenth letter seeking advice on how to deal with them. He told the emperor what his practice had been in regard to the Christians, noting that some informants had reported to him that certain individuals were Christians, and, upon investigating the matter, he found out that there were three kinds of persons coming before him: (1) those who freely confessed that they were Christians and refused to deny their faith, and were consequently executed; (2) those who denied that they ever were Christians and were given the opportunity to perform a pagan religious act (probably pouring out a libation to the gods and/or the emperor) and to curse Christ, after which they were released with no recriminations; and (3) those who had actually been Christians, but turned away from the Christian faith and returned to pagan practices, confirming this by worshiping the pagan images of the gods and cursing Christ. These persons were also released. The relevant part of his letter is as follows:

Pliny's Letter to Trajan

It is my custom, lord emperor, to refer to you all questions whereof I am in doubt. Who can better guide me when I am at a stand, or enlighten me if I am in ignorance? In

---

24. William Cureton, ed., *Spicilegium Syriacum: Containing Remains of Bardesan, Meliton, Ambrose and Mara Bar Serapion* (1885; repr., Lexington: American Theological Library Association, 1965), 73–74 (italics his).

25. Theissen and Merz, *Historical Jesus*, 78.

investigations of Christians I have never taken part; hence I do not know how the crime is usually punished or investigated or what allowances are made. So I have had no little uncertainty whether there is any distinction of age, or whether the very weakest offenders are treated exactly like the stronger; whether pardon is given to those who repent, or whether a man who has once been a Christian gains nothing by having ceased to be such; whether punishment attaches to the mere name apart from secret crimes [*flagitia*], or to the secret crimes connected with the name. Meanwhile this is the course I have taken with those who were accused before me as Christians. I asked them whether they were Christians, and if they confessed, I asked them a second and third time with threats of punishment. If they kept to it, I ordered them for execution; for I held no question that whatever it was that they admitted, in any case obstinacy and unbending perversity deserve to be punished. There were others of the like insanity; but as these were Roman citizens, I noted them down to be sent to Rome.

Before long, as is often the case, the mere fact that the charge was taken notice of made it commoner, and several distinct cases arose. An unsigned paper was presented, which gave the names of many. As for those who said that they neither were nor ever had been Christians, I thought it right to let them go, since they recited a prayer to the gods at my dictation, made supplication with incense and wine to your statue, which I had ordered to be brought into court for the purpose together with the images of the gods, and moreover cursed Christ—things which (so it is said) those who are really Christians cannot be made to do. Others who were named by the informer said that they were Christians and then denied it, explaining that they had been, but had ceased to be such, some three years ago, some a good many years, and a few even twenty. All these too both worshipped your statue and the images of the gods, and cursed Christ.

They maintained, however, that the amount of their fault or error had been this, that it was their habit on a fixed day to assemble before daylight and *recite by turns a form of words to Christ as a god*; and that they bound themselves with an oath, not for any crime, but not to commit theft or robbery or adultery, not to break their word, and not to deny a deposit when demanded. After this was done, their custom was to depart, and to meet again to take food, but ordinary and harmless food; and even this (they said) they had given up doing after the issue of my edict, by which in accordance with your commands I had forbidden the existence of clubs. On this I considered it the more necessary to find out from two maid-servants who were called deaconesses, and that by torments, how far this was true; but I discovered nothing else than a perverse and extravagant superstition. I therefore adjourned the case and hastened to consult you. The matter seemed to me worth deliberation, especially on account of the number of those in danger; for many of all ages and every rank, and also of both sexes are brought into present or future danger. The contagion of that superstition has penetrated not the cities only, but the villages and country; yet it seems possible to stop it and set it right. At any rate it is certain enough that the almost deserted temples begin to be restored, and that fodder for victims finds a market, whereas buyers till now were very few. From this it may easily be supposed, what a multitude of men can be reclaimed, if there be a place for repentance. (*Ep.* 10.96)[26]

---

26. This translation is from Stevenson, *New Eusebius*, 13–14.

Pliny's information appears to be from widespread secondhand rumors about the Christians, but he is aware of the reverence of the Christians for "Christ as a god." For those willing to curse Christ and honor the pagan gods, personal safety could be achieved, but not for those who did not repent of their honoring Christ. Pliny viewed any honoring or giving reverence to Christ as an affront to the Roman gods. It is also important to note that by the early second century, the title "Christ" had also come to be a part of Jesus' name, as in "Jesus Christ."

Trajan

Trajan (Roman emperor, AD 98–117) replied to Pliny the Younger in Bithynia and in so doing gave a timely report on the legal status of Christians in the Roman Empire around AD 111–112:

> You have adopted the proper course, my dear Secundus, in your examination of the cases of those who were accused to you as Christians, for indeed nothing can be laid down as a general ruling involving something like a set form of procedure. They are not to be sought out; but if they are accused and convicted, they must be punished—yet on this condition, that whoso denies being a Christian, and makes the fact plain by his action, that is by worshipping our gods, shall obtain pardon on his repentance, however suspicious his past conduct may be. Papers, however, which are presented unsigned ought not to be admitted in any charge, for they are a very bad example and unworthy of our time. (Pliny, *Ep.* 10.97)[27]

Graffiti

That Christianity was held up to ridicule and slander is seen in graffiti on a stone in a guardroom on Palatine Hill in Rome. Its precise date is difficult to establish, though it is probably from the middle to late second century. The etching depicts a figure of a man with the head of an ass hanging on a cross. Next to the figure is a man, of whom nothing is known, standing by the cross with his head raised in a gesture of adoration. The inscription reads: "Alexamenos worships his god."[28]

Lucian of Samosata

Lucian (ca. AD 120–180), a man who wrote satires about religious and philosophical individuals and their thought, did not hesitate to make biting comments

---

27. Ibid., 16.
28. See Everett Ferguson, *Backgrounds of Early Christianity* (3rd ed.; Grand Rapids: Eerdmans, 2003), 561.

about people with whom he had differences. Among his many writings is the story *On the Death of Peregrinus*, a satirical depiction of the life and death of a charlatan named Proteus Peregrinus, who lived in the early to middle second century AD and promoted himself as a prophet. He deceived, among others, a group of Christians and took them for considerable sums of money. Some scholars conclude that Lucian was writing about the life of Polycarp, who was martyred about the same time that Peregrinus died. That is difficult to substantiate, although they point to some parallels in *The Martyrdom of Polycarp*. Besides the interesting though not exact parallels, there is little support for that conclusion. Of special interest, however, is Lucian's detailed description of a wandering charismatic taking advantage of the early Christians and finally their response. Lucian had no respect for the Christians and speaks of them as simple and gullible people. Concerning the charlatan Proteus Peregrinus, he writes:

> It was then that [Proteus] learned the wondrous lore of the Christians, by associating with their priests and scribes in Palestine.[29] And—how else could it be?—in a trice he made them all look like children; for he was prophet, cult-leader, head of the synagogue, and everything, all by himself. He interpreted and explained some of their books and even composed many, and they revered him as a god, made use of him as a lawgiver, and set him down as a protector, next after that other, to be sure, whom they still worship, *the man who was crucified in Palestine because he introduced this new cult into the world.*

Lucian then tells how Peregrinus was arrested and imprisoned as a charlatan, upon which Christians came from far and near to offer aid and comfort, so that he continued to profit from their gullibility. Lucian continues:

> The poor wretches have convinced themselves, first and foremost, that they are going to be immortal and live for all time, in consequence of which they despise death and even willingly give themselves into custody, most of them.
>
> *Furthermore, their first lawgiver* [Jesus] *persuaded them that they are all brothers of one another after they have transgressed once for all by denying the Greek gods and by worshipping that crucified sophist himself and living under his laws.* Therefore they despise all things indiscriminately and consider them common property, receiving such doctrines traditionally without any definite evidence. So if any charlatan and trickster, able to profit by occasions, comes among them, he quickly acquires sudden wealth by imposing upon simple folk. (*On the Death of Peregrinus* 11–14, LCL. Italics added.)

---

29. This is a probable confusion of Christianity with Judaism since Christians did not have office holders called priests or scribes in their churches. The term "priest" was not adopted by the church until much later, after the time of Lucian.

These passages show, among other things, that the early Christians were often persecuted for their faith, that by and large they did not draw on the wealthy and learned classes, that they worshiped Jesus as a divine being, and that they cared for those of their number who were imprisoned by reason of their witness. Further, there was a perception on the part of the non-Christian world that many of the Christians were not afraid to face the consequences for being Christians (confiscation of property, imprisonment, or death), and that their eschatological hope was a primary source of encouragement to them. This supports the New Testament witness in these matters. The above source also notes that the interpretation of their Scriptures by a prophet inspired by the Spirit was commonplace, and that they were generous in their giving.

Celsus

Compared to the other critics of Christianity, Celsus (fl. ca. AD 178–180) shows more understanding of what the Christians believed, taught, and practiced than do his contemporaries. He seems to have read a number of Christian writings besides merely listening to the rumors being spread about them. His arguments against the Christians, which were the most serious of the second century and even later, were examined in detail and answered some fifty years later by Origen in his *Contra Celsum*. Celsus, like Lucian, objected to the simplicity of the Christians and criticized their choice of faith over reason (*Cels.* 1.9, LCL). He also objected to their God becoming a human being and to their drawing their followers from slaves, women, little children, and sinners (3.44, 59, 64).

Celsus's attitude toward Jesus was no better than what he had to say about Jesus' followers. He writes: "He [Jesus] was brought up in secret and hired himself out as a workman in Egypt, and after having tried his hand at certain magical powers he returned from there, and on account of those powers gave himself the title of God" (1.38). Celsus also accused Jesus of practicing sorcery (1.6, 68). He showed an obvious lack of knowledge about Jesus in these texts, but he generally had a good understanding of the low economic and educational status of the Christians and the simple outline of their faith. Concerning the resurrection of Jesus, he wrote:

> We must examine this question whether anyone who really died ever rose again with the same body. Or do you think that the stories of these others really are the legends which they appear to be, and yet that the ending of your tragedy is to be regarded as noble and convincing—his cry from the cross when he expired, and the earthquake and the darkness? While he was alive he did not help himself,

but after death he rose again and showed the marks of his punishment and how his hands had been pierced. But who saw this? A hysterical female, as you say, and perhaps some other one of those who were deluded by the same sorcery, who either dreamt in a certain state of mind and through wishful thinking had a hallucination due to some mistaken notion (an experience which has happened to thousands), or, which is more likely, wanted to impress the others by telling this fantastic tale, and so by this cock-and-bull story to provide a chance for other beggars. (2.55)[30]

Celsus clearly had some familiarity with the church's teaching about the resurrection of Jesus either from oral or written traditions and showed his disdain for the story that was central to the church's proclamation. Origen's later response to him shows how serious Celsus's arguments against Christianity were and also the influence that Christians had gained before the triumph of Christianity in the fourth century.

Marcus Aurelius

Writing around AD 170, Marcus Aurelius (Roman emperor AD 161–180) alludes in his *Meditations* to the Christians' obstinacy in choosing death over conformity. At that time Christians were known as those who were willing to face death for their religious convictions, and to do so with dignity and resolve rather than making public displays for self-glorification. Aurelius, however, only mentions the Christians once by name in a passage that may contain a later Christian interpolation:

How admirable is the soul which is ready and resolved, if it must this moment be released from the body, to be either extinguished or scattered or to persist. This resolve, too, must arise from a specific decision, not out of sheer opposition *like the Christians*, but after reflection and with dignity, and so as to convince others, without histrionic display. (*Med.* 11.3, italics added)[31]

Galen

Galen was a Greek from Pergamum (ca. AD 129–199) who rose from being a physician to gladiators to become the physician of Marcus Aurelius's court.

---

30. This is Henry Chadwick's translation of Origen, *Cels.*, preserved in Stevenson, *A New Eusebius*, 137.

31. This translation is from A. S. L. Farquharson, *Marcus Aurelius, Meditations* (Oxford: Clarendon, 1944). See the index to the LCL edition for references to Christians in Aurelius, and note that there is only one explicit mention.

He wrote not only about human anatomy and physiology, but also philosophical treatises. He was an ardent monotheist, and so it is not surprising that he wrote about both Jews and Christians, the leading monotheists of the day. His comments about the Christians—disparaging their intellectual ability but praising their moral achievements—are among the most favorable non-Christian comments about the Christians in the second century AD. He writes:

> One might more easily teach novelties to the followers of Moses and Christ than to the physicians and philosophers who cling fast to their schools.
>
> . . . in order that one should not at the very beginning, as if one had come into the school of Moses and Christ, hear talk of undemonstrated laws, and in that where it is least appropriate.
>
> . . . If I had in mind people who taught their pupils in the same way the followers of Moses and Christ teach theirs—for they order them to accept everything on faith—I should not have given you a definition.
>
> . . . Most people are unable to follow any demonstrative argument consecutively; hence they need parables, and benefit from them—and he [Galen—adds the editor who preserved this extract from a lost work] understands by parables tales of rewards and punishments in a future life—just as now we see the people called Christians drawing their faith from parables (and miracles) and yet sometimes acting in the same way as those who philosophize. For their contempt of death (and of its sequel) is patent to us every day, and likewise their restraint in cohabitation. For they include not only men but also women who refrain from cohabitating all through their lives; and they also number individuals who have reached such a point in their control regarding their daily conduct and in their intense desire for rectitude that they have in fact become not inferior to those who are true philosophers.[32]

Thallus

Not much is known about Thallus, a first-century Roman or Samaritan historian, but some scholars claim that he refers to the darkness that covered the land when Jesus was crucified (Matt. 27:45; Mark 15:33; Luke 23:44–45). Much later, the famed Christian teacher Julius Africanus (ca. AD 170–240) noted that in Thallus's third book of the histories of the then-known world, the darkness that came over the land was a datable, natural event that was caused by an eclipse. Theissen and Merz note that this date is also reported by Phlegon of Tralles from the early second century, who claims to have received

32. This translation is taken from R. Walzer, *Galen on Jews and Christians* (London: Oxford University Press, 1949), supplied by R. M. MacMullen and E. N. Lane, eds., *Paganism and Christianity, 100–425 CE: A Sourcebook* (Minneapolis: Fortress, 1992), 168.

this knowledge from Thallus himself and who placed this eclipse of the sun on November 24 of AD 29. They also note that this information may have been Thallus's attempt to dispel Christian claims about events at the death of Jesus.[33] There is not likely any reliable historical information here about the darkness over the land, but it is worth noting that the timing for the death of Jesus may be a useful piece of information derived from this source.

Jewish Traditions about Jesus

Jesus and his earliest followers were Jews, and they began a religious movement or sect *within* first-century Judaism. The earliest Christians claimed that they were the successors of the Jewish traditions, hopes, and blessings, including their sacred Scriptures. They eventually welcomed gentiles as a part of their community of faith (Acts 15) and claimed that salvation was found only in Jesus their Messiah/Christ (Acts 4:12), and that his followers were the "true Israel" (Gal. 6:16; Rom. 2:25–29).

The early followers of Jesus regularly gathered for worship and prayer in the temple in Jerusalem and even in the various Jewish synagogues as late as AD 100–135. Jewish Christians were still living in Sepphoris (Zippori), the capital of Galilee, and having regular contact with fellow Jews (*Abodah Zarah* 16b) at the end of the second century. The initial separation of Jews and Christians took place in AD 62 when James, the brother of Jesus, was executed in Jerusalem and many Jewish Christians fled to Pella, southeast of the Sea of Galilee and east of the Jordan River. The final separation of Christians from the Jews followed the Bar Kochba rebellion against Rome, a messianic movement in Palestine (AD 132–135). Christians did not support that movement led by the self-proclaimed messianic figure Simon Bar Kozibah (Kochba) because that would have implied a rejection of Jesus as their Messiah.

Biblical scholars have long recognized that Jesus and the early Christians are closer in perspective to the Pharisees mentioned in the New Testament than to any other first-century sect of Judaism. This can be seen in their commitment to keeping the law (Matt. 5:17–20; Acts 21:17–26), table fellowship (Acts 10:9–29; 11:2–12; Gal. 2:11–14), acceptance of the same sacred Scriptures (Luke 24:44; John 5:39), affirmation of the resurrection of the dead (Rom. 8:11, 18–23; 10:9; 1 Cor. 15:3–11), and eschatological beliefs about a coming kingdom of God (Acts 1:6). In the Gospels, Jesus and his followers often disagreed with the Pharisees over their commitment to the Jewish oral traditions (Mark 2:13–3:6; 7:1–13;

---

33. Theissen and Merz, *Historical Jesus*, 84–85.

Luke 11:37–52), including how the Sabbath was to be observed. The Pharisees are mentioned ninety-nine times in the New Testament, eighty-six of which are in the Gospels. Some of their views and practices can be seen in Josephus's description of them (*Ant.* 13.12–15; 18.171–72; *Life* 10–12). The Pharisees held to observance of the law, the tradition of the elders, divine providence with human accountability, a future resurrection, and the coming of a messianic figure.[34]

Since Jesus and his first followers emerged in Jewish settings, we may well ask what evidence regarding Jesus survives from non-Christian Jewish sources. The main evidence for noncanonical Jewish traditions about Jesus comes from Josephus and from rabbinic writings.

Josephus

Flavius Josephus (ca. AD 37–120), the Jewish general and historian, was born of royal descent from the Hasmonean line and was also a priest who supported the Pharisees. As an educated member of the aristocracy, he was in charge of the defense of Galilee at the outbreak of the Jewish revolt in AD 66–73. After surrendering to Vespasian, he prophesied that Vespasian would become the Roman emperor. When that in fact happened, he was treated well by Vespasian. He took the name Flavius from his Roman patrons and wrote a number of literary works to defend the Jewish people. He is the principal historian of the Jewish people in the first century AD and an essential source for the study of the context and history of early Christianity in Palestine. Scholars generally recognize that Christians, who were the primary preservers of Josephus's works after the eleventh century, probably inserted some of the comments about Jesus and the early Christians into Josephus's writings. But with care, some of Josephus's comments about Jesus can still be discerned. There are three primary texts in Josephus that have bearing on Jesus, his time, and his followers. We start with his comments about John the Baptist, which are similar to New Testament references to John:

> He [John the Baptist] was a good man and exhorted the Jews to lead righteous lives, practice justice towards one another and piety towards God, and so to join in baptism. In his view this was a necessary preliminary if baptism was to be acceptable to God. They must not use it to gain pardon for whatever sins they committed, but as a consecration of the body, implying that the soul was thoroughly purified beforehand by the right behavior. When many others joined the crowds about him, for they were greatly moved on hearing his words, Herod

34. Eckard J. Schnabel, "Pharisees," in *New Interpreter's Dictionary of the Bible* (Nashville: Abingdon, 2009), 4:485–96.

feared that John's great influence over the people would lead to a rebellion (for they seemed ready to do anything he might advise). Herod decided therefore that it would be much better to strike first and be rid of him before his work led to an uprising, than to wait for an upheaval, become involved in a difficult situation and see his mistake. Accordingly John was sent as a prisoner to Machaerus, the fortress mentioned before, because of Herod's suspicious temper, and was there put to death. (*Ant.* 18.117–19, LCL)

Josephus also provides important information about the death of James, the brother of Jesus, and mentions in a noncommittal fashion that Jesus was called the Christ.

Possessed of such a character, Ananus thought that he had a favorable opportunity because Festus was dead and Albinus was still on the way. And so he convened the judges of the Sanhedrin and brought before them a man named James, the brother of Jesus who was called the Christ, and certain others. He accused them of having transgressed the law and delivered them up to be stoned. Those of the inhabitants of the city who were considered the most fair-minded and who were strict in observance of the law were offended at this. (*Ant.* 20.200–203, LCL)

The third passage from Josephus speaks about Jesus but appears to have been altered or interpolated by Christians. In his *Commentary on Matthew* (10:17) Origen states that Josephus did not become a Christian, but in the following passage it appears that he did. It is highly doubtful that the statements "he was the Messiah," "he appeared to them on the third day," and "holy prophets had foretold this" are genuine. Nevertheless, Josephus could well have written the rest of this passage, which does refer to Jesus. The questionable parts are in italics.

At about this time lived Jesus, a wise man, *if indeed one might call him a man. For he was one who accomplished surprising feats and was a teacher of such people as accept the truth with pleasure.* He won over many Jews and many of the Greeks. *He was the Messiah.* When Pilate, upon an indictment brought by the principal men among us, condemned him to the cross, those who had loved him from the very first did not cease to be attached to him. *On the third day he appeared to them restored to life, for the holy prophets had foretold this and myriads of other marvels concerning him.* And the tribe of the Christians so called after him has to this day still not disappeared. (*Ant.* 18.63–64, LCL)

The Rabbinic Tradition and Jesus

Josephus, who wrote in Greek, calls himself a Pharisee. After the destruction of the temple in AD 70, the Pharisees took the lead in establishing a center of

Jewish religious life in matters of law and purity at Jamnia (Yavneh). Rome recognized the Pharisaic teachers as the governing body for the internal life of the Jewish people in Palestine.[35] The *primary* expressions of Judaism that survived the first century in Palestine and in Babylon are reflected in rabbinic Judaism, whose roots go back mostly to the first-century Pharisaic rabbis, especially Hillel, Gamaliel, and Simon. Not all references to the Pharisees in the Mishnah are clear, but the reference to them in *m. Yadayim* 4.6–8 is. Some scholars debate whether Pharisaic Judaism is the only surviving voice of first-century expressions of Judaism, but there are several traits among them that appear to establish a close relationship.[36] The rabbinic writings evidence affinities to first-century Pharisees, especially in terms of their teachings about agricultural law, Sabbath keeping, festival observance, and purity regulations.

Rabbinic Reference to Jesus and His Followers

Rabbinic literature from the second to the sixth century AD also contains references to Jesus, but they are infrequent and generally show a significant bias against Jesus. This hostility is to be understood as a consequence of both closeness and difference. Jews and Christians have long appealed to a similar collection of sacred Scriptures, namely the Hebrew Bible (*Tanakh*), that is, the Christian Old Testament. Most early followers of Jesus were Jews who continued to be actively involved in religious activities related to the Jewish temple and synagogue. But Jewish religious opposition to the teachings of Jesus and his followers was present from the beginning (Mark 2:23–3:6; 14:1–2, 53–65; Acts 4:1–6; 5:17–42, passim), and the opposition became more intense over emerging Christian views regarding the law, observance of purity rituals, Sabbath keeping, and welcoming uncircumcised gentiles into their fellowship. Perhaps most significantly, Christians had a very different view of the identity of Jesus. As Christians claimed that they were the heirs of Jewish blessings through faith in Christ (Gal. 3:6–9; Rom. 4:1–15), including the promised outpouring of the Holy Spirit at the end of the ages (Acts 2:16–33; see also Dan. 12:2; Joel 2:28–32; Ezek. 36:26–27), Jewish opposition to followers of Jesus grew. Early Christian literature is also frequently negative in its assessment of the Jews, but most of it is not so much anti-Semitic as anti-Judaic; namely, it is not a racial attack as much as a religious one, though it was every bit as vitriolic.[37]

---

35. Ferguson, *Backgrounds of Early Christianity*, 414–15.

36. Jacob Neusner, *Judaism in the Beginning of Christianity* (Philadelphia: Fortress, 1984), 45–61.

37. Lee Martin McDonald, "Anti-Judaism in Early Christianity," in *Anti-Semitism and Early Christianity: Issues of Polemic and Faith* (ed. C. A. Evans and D. A. Hagner; Minneapolis: Fortress, 1993), 215–52.

The paucity of direct references in rabbinic writings to Jesus, the Christians, and their literature may be due to the fact that the Mishnah and the two Talmuds are largely focused on *halakah*, law, rather than on *haggadah*, or history (story). History as such is not a *primary* interest in rabbinic literature, and the few references to the time in which Jesus lived are generally considered unreliable along with many rabbinic statements about Jesus.[38] Some initial negative references to Jesus and the Christians were later modified in manuscripts after the Christians gained political influence and power in the Roman Empire following the conversion of Constantine to the Christian faith.[39]

Parallels

The New Testament writers reflect several views similar to those of later rabbinic sages, especially in the teaching of Jesus. These parallels include:

a. Some Teachings of Jesus. When Jesus said the whole law depends (Greek, *krematai*: "hangs"; Heb., *tala*) on two commandments—namely, to love God with all one's self and one's neighbor as oneself (Matt. 22:37–40)—he was reflecting a long-standing Jewish and later rabbinic understanding that many commandments depend or "hang" on one or a few of them. This can be seen in *Sifra* of Leviticus 19:2, where the command to be holy underlies the rest of the commands. According to Bar Kappara (*b. Ber.* 63a, 18), "what short text is there upon which all the essential principles of the Torah depend? In all thy ways acknowledge Him and He will direct thy paths" (a reference to Prov. 3:6; see *b. Ber.* 63a, 18, Soncino trans.). Here and in the Matthew text the law depends on a single command.

This same principle is found elsewhere in rabbinic writings, namely in *m. Ḥag.* 1.8, *t. Ḥag.* 1.9, and *t. 'Erub.* 8.23, where other laws, even large ones, are considered like mountains hanging by a hair (a smaller command with an important principle). It is reported that Hillel once received a pagan man on the basis of the principle "what is hateful to you, do not [do] to your neighbor: that is the commentary thereof; go and learn it: that is the whole Torah, while the rest is the commentary" (*b. Šabb.* 31a, 12–13, Soncino). Matthew's description of all of the law "hanging" on loving God and one's neighbor is the same principle of a single or smaller command containing the essence of

---

38. See Robert E. Van Voorst, *Jesus outside the New Testament: An Introduction to the Ancient Evidence* (Grand Rapids: Eerdmans, 2000), 75–134 and 104; Jacob Neusner, *Judaism and Christianity in the Age of Constantine* (Chicago: University of Chicago Press, 1987), and Neusner, *Judaism in the Beginning of Christianity*, 54–57; Shaye J. D. Cohen, *Josephus in Galilee and Rome: His Vita and Development as a Historian* (Columbia Studies in the Classical Tradition 8; Leiden: Brill, 1979), 253.

39. Raymond Brown, "The Babylonian Talmud on the Execution of Jesus," *NTS* 43 (1997): 158–59; and Van Voorst, *Jesus outside the New Testament*, 100–132.

all of the commandments. This does not mean, however, that the other parts could be ignored, as we see in Matthew 5:18, where Jesus says, "Not one letter, not one stroke of a letter will pass from the law until all is accomplished."[40]

b. Rabbinic Parables. Several parables of Jesus are similar to parables in later rabbinic writing. Since there are no New Testament parables outside of those attributed to Jesus, the rabbinic parallels are especially notable. Evans, MacArthur, and Johnston have listed some thirty-two parables and similarities with forty others that come from the Tannaitic era (roughly the first and second centuries AD). Jesus' parables reflect a common Jewish means of communicating sacred truth and sometimes have parallels in later rabbinic tradition. See, for example, the Sower and the Four Soils (Mark 4:3–8; Matt. 13:3–8; Luke 8:5–8; cf. *m. 'Abot* 5.15); the Wicked Tenants (Mark 12:1–11; Matt. 21:33–44; Luke 20:9–19; cf. *Sipre Deut.* §312 [on Deut. 32:9]); the Lost Sheep (Matt. 18:10–14; Luke 15:3–7; cf. *Midr. Pss.* 119.3 [on Ps. 119:1]; *Exod. Rab.* 2.2 [on Exod. 3:1]; *Gen. Rab.* 84.6 [on Gen. 39:2]); the Wise and Foolish Maidens (Matt. 25:1–13; cf. *b. Šabb.* 153a and *Qoh. Rab.* 9.8 §1); the Pearl of Great Price (Matt. 13:45–46; cf. *Midr. Pss.* 28.6 [on 28:7]; cf. Luke 11:5–8; 18:1–8).[41]

Other similarities include several parallels located in the Mishnah (*m.*), Tosefta (*t.*), the two Talmudim (*y.* and *b.*), various *Midrashim* (*Midr.*), and the Targumim (*Tg.*). Several of these have Old Testament parallels as well. I will simply list these parallels in the New Testament Gospels, Old Testament books, and rabbinic literature as follows:

1. **Matthew**: Matt. 2:2, cf. Jer. 23:5, Num. 24:17 and *Tg. Num.* 24:17, *Tg. Mic.* 5:1–3; Matt. 2:23, cf. Isa. 11:1, 4:2 and *Tg. Isa.* 11:1, *Tg. Zech.* 3:8, 6:12; Matt. 3:12, cf. *Tg. Isa.* 33:11–12; Matt. 5:4, cf. Isa 61:2 and *y. Ber.* 2.4, *Lam. Rab.* 1.16; Matt. 5:9, cf. *m. Pe'ah* 1.1, *m. 'Abot* 1.12; Matt. 6:13, cf. *b. Ber.* 60b; Matt. 7:4–5, cf. *b. Qidd.* 70a, *b. 'Arak.* 16b, and *b. B. Bat.* 15b; Matt. 9:13, cf. Hos. 6:6, *'Abot R. Nat.* 4, *b. Šabb.* 31a, *Num. Rab.* 8.4 (on Num. 5:6); Matt. 26:73, cf. *b. Ber.* 32a, *b. Meg.* 24b, *b. 'Erub.* 53b; Matt. 27:62–66, cf. *m. Sanh.* 6.5. 2. **Mark**: Mark 1:11, cf. *b. Sukkah* 52a, *Midr. Pss.* 2.9 (on Ps. 2:7), *Tg. Isa.* 41:8–9, 42:10; Mark 1:30, cf. *b. Ned.* 41a; Mark 3:3, cf. *m. Yoma* 8.6, *b. Šabb.* 132a; Mark 4:24, cf. *m. Soṭah* 1.7, *Tg. Isa.* 27:8 (cf. also *b. Šabb.* 127b, *b. Meg.* 28a, *b. Roš Haš.* 16b.); Mark 9:4, cf. *Deut. Rab.* 3.17 (on Deut. 10:1); *Pesiq. Rab.* 4.2; Mark 9:50, cf. *m. Soṭah* 9.15; Mark 10:14, cf. *b. Sanh.* 110b, *b. Yoma* 22b, *b. Nid.* 30b, *Kallah Rab.* 2.9; Mark 12:29–30, cf. Deut. 6:4–5 and *m. Ber.* 2.2 and 9.5, *m. Soṭah* 7.8, *t. Roš*

---

40. David Daube, *The New Testament and Rabbinic Judaism* (London: Oxford University Press, 1956), 250–53.

41. See Evans, *Ancient Texts for New Testament Studies*, 418–23; and H. K. McArthur and R. M. Johnston, *They Also Taught in Parables: Rabbinic Parables from the First Centuries of the Christian Era* (Grand Rapids: Zondervan, 1990).

Haš. 2.13 and *t. Soṭah* 7.17; Mark 14:22, cf. *m. Ber.* 6.1; Mark 14:62, cf. *Midr. Pss.* 2.9. **3. Luke:** Luke 1:15, cf. Num. 6:3, Judg. 13:4, and *m. Naz.* 9.5; Luke 2:22, cf. Lev. 12:6, *m. Ker.* 6.9; Luke 3:17, cf. *Tg. Isa.* 33:11–12; Luke 6:1, cf. *m. Šabb.* 7.2, *b. Šabb.* 73a–b; Luke 6:38, cf. *m. Soṭah* 1.7, *t. Soṭah* 3.1, 2; Luke 7:39, 41, 48, cf. *Tg. Neof.* Exod. 32:31; Luke 10:42, cf. *'Abot* 2.8, 3.2; Luke 13:32, cf. *'Abot* 4.15, *b. Ber.* 61b; Luke 13:34–35, cf. *Tg. Isa.* 28:11–12 and 32:14; Luke 17:20, cf. *b. Sanh.* 98a; Luke 18:11–12, cf. *b. Ber.* 28b; Luke 19:39–40, cf. Hab. 2:11, *Tg. Hab.* 2:11, *b. Ta'an* 11a, *b. Ḥag.* 16a, *Midr. Pss.* 73.4 (on Ps. 73:10); Luke 24:46, cf. Isa. 53, Hos. 6:2, Joel 2:32, and *b. Sanh.* 97b. **4. John:** John 1:1–2, cf. Gen. 1:1, *Tg. Neof.* Gen. 1:1; John 1:3, cf. *Tg. Neof.* Gen. 1:26–27, *Tg. Isa.* 44:24; John 1:18, cf. Exod. 33:20, *'Abot R. Nat.* (A) 31.3, *Gen. Rab.* 8.2 (on Gen. 1:26), *Tg. Onq.* Exod. 33:20–23; John 3:3–5, cf. *b. Yebam.* 48b; John 4:12–13, cf. *Tg. Neof.* Gen 28:10; *Frg. Tg.* Gen. 28:10; John 6:31, cf. Ps. 78:24, *t. Soṭah* 4.3; John 7:53–8:11, cf. *m. Sanh.* 6.1–4; John 8:12, cf. *Sipre Num.* § 41 (on Num. 6:25), *b. B. Bat.* 4a, *Deut. Rab.* 7.3 (on Deut. 28:1), *Exod. Rab.* 36.3 (on Exod. 27:20); John 9:22, cf. *b. Ber.* 28b–29a, *Amidah* § 12; John 12:41, cf. *Tg. Isa.* 6:1, 5; John 19:36, cf. Exod. 12:46, *m. Pesaḥ.* 7.10–11. (See Evans, *Ancient Texts*, 342–409.)

References to Jesus

Rabbinic sages appear to know very little of pre-70 Jewish history and the emergence of Christianity. Following Christianity's fourth-century triumph, the rabbis made several modifications in their references to Jesus or the Christians in some editions of the Babylonian Talmud, but some references remained.

a. Yeshu. Scholars often debate whether some rabbinic texts actually refer to Jesus. Some contend that a number of such references do exist, and they cite a rabbinic Babylonian *baraita* (an earlier tradition, probably second or third century AD) as a reference to Jesus (Yeshu) and his death.[42] The disputed passage is as follows:

> On the Eve of the Passover Yeshu was hanged [a common term for crucifixion; see Gal. 3:13]. For forty days before the execution took place, a herald went forth and cried, "He is going forth to be stoned because he has practiced sorcery and enticed Israel to apostasy. Anyone who can say anything in his favour, let him come forward and plead on his behalf." But since nothing was brought forward in his favour he was hanged on the eve of Passover. (*b. Sanh.* 43a, Soncino)

If Yeshu here is a reference to Jesus, as some scholars contend, it appears that some Jews took responsibility for the death of Jesus. Later, following the Christian triumph in the Roman Empire, some rabbis, perhaps out of fear of

---

42. Raymond Brown, *The Death of the Messiah: From Gethsemane to the Grave; A Commentary on the Passion Narrative of the Gospels* (2 vols.; ABRL; New York: Doubleday, 1994), 1:376–77.

reprisals, changed the text in subsequent editions of the Talmud. Van Voorst has shown in several examples that the Jews viewed Christianity as a heretical movement. He claims that the *Toledoth Yeshu* (Hebrew, "generations of Jesus"), first attested in AD 826 but compiled from earlier sources, contains negative interpretations of Jesus' life, especially claiming that he was the illegitimate son of Mary and a Roman guard named Panthera, a charge that first came from Celsus in the second century, and that Jesus' powers came from black magic or from stealing a holy name from the temple. *Toledoth* contains one of the most negative arguments against Jesus and the Christian movement in the late rabbinic era or early Middle Ages.[43] How could this *Yeshu* document have emerged without a widespread negative assessment of Jesus within the rabbinic community? This text likely points to Jesus since this Yeshu was executed on the eve of the Passover by hanging (crucifixion), accused of being a sorcerer, and given a trial. There are no other known candidates who fit these details.

Because this text was later censored in several editions of the Talmud, it is more likely that it does refer to Jesus of Nazareth. Brown argues that this conclusion is supported by a Munich manuscript that enlarged "*Yeshu*" to "*Yeshu ha-Nosri*" (or "Yeshu the stoned," which is likely generic for "executed").[44] If the reference to Yeshu in *b. Sanhedrin* 43 is a reference to someone other than Jesus of Nazareth, there would be no reason to censor it in later Talmudic times when Christians had more influence in the Roman Empire. This conclusion is also supported by Celsus, who, according to Origen, cites a Jew (perhaps imaginary) saying: "We punished this fellow [Jesus] who was a cheater," and "we had convicted him, condemned him, and decided that he should be punished" (*Cels.* 2.4; 2.9). Celsus's Jew raises objections to belief in Jesus and claims that his followers invented tales about his life after the fact (1.28; 2.12–16, 25) and that his disciples were "infamous rabble and lowlife" (1.62–65; 2.46). Finally, he claims that Jesus' followers abandoned the law (1.1–4; 3.5; 5.33).[45] Origen also noted that Jesus was charged with being a sorcerer (*Cels.* 1.28.71), as we see in the passage above. Because of the specificity of Celsus's charges, it appears possible that *b. Sanhedrin* 43a is about Jesus of Nazareth.

b. Other Names for Jesus. There were several names given to Jesus in the Talmudic literature, and scholars continue to debate whether all of them refer to Jesus, though some may be possible. See, for example, references to Jesus as "Ben Stada," including some parallels to aspects of his story in the Gospels

---

43. Van Voorst, *Jesus outside the New Testament*, 104–6 and 122–25.
44. Brown, *Death of the Messiah*, 1:376–77 and n114.
45. Ibid., and Claudia Setzer, *Jewish Responses to Early Christians: History and Polemics, 30–50 C.E.* (Minneapolis: Fortress, 1994), 147–51.

(see *m. 'Abot* 5.19, *b. Giṭ.* 56b–57a, *b. Sanh.* 106b, *b. Sanh.* 107b, *b. Soṭah* 47a). Jesus is also sometimes referred to negatively as "Balaam," the corrupt Old Testament prophet (Num. 31:16; cf. 2 Pet. 2:15; Jude 11; Rev. 2:14). Occasionally, in order to avoid the use of a particular name, the rabbis spoke about "a certain person," which may be a reference to Jesus of Nazareth. For example, "Said R. Simeon b. Azzai, 'I discovered a family register in Jerusalem, in which was written: "Mr. So-and-so is a *mamzer* [having been born of an illicit union], of a married woman and someone other than her husband" (*m. Yebam.* 4.13 [trans. Neusner, p. 348]. See also *b. Yoma* 66d and *t. Yebam.* 3.3–4). Some rabbinic texts refer to Jesus' mother (*b. Sanh.* 106a, *b. Ḥag.* 4b), and others to Jesus by a different name (Ben Stada or Ben Satara), as in *b. Sanhedrin* 43a; compare with *t. Šabbat* 11.15; *b. Šabbat* 104b, *b. Sanhedrin* 103a; *b. Berakhot* 17b. In one place Jesus' disciples appear to be named, as in the case of Matthew or "Mattai" (*b. Sanh.* 43a). Elsewhere there is a possible reference to the resurrection of Jesus that condemns one who "made himself alive by the name of God" (*b. Sanh.* 106a). While there is some doubt that all or any of these references are about Jesus, his disciples, or his mother, it is possible that some are. The references in question suggest an awareness of several aspects of Jesus' story from an uninformed historical perspective in the Talmudic literature.

c. *The Eighteen Benedictions.* These Jewish "benedictions," repeated in rabbinic literature, are sometimes called the *Shemoneh 'Esreh* and contain a curse on heretics (the *Birkat Ha Minim*). Originally they probably referred to Sadducees (*birkat ha-seduqim*), perhaps because of their denial of the resurrection. The *Benedictions* date in their current form from the first century BC to around AD 70–100. The twelfth benediction (or curse) was initially against all heretics, but eventually it appears that it was applied specifically to Jewish Christians along with others thought to be heretics. These *Benedictions* were prayed three times a day by Jews (male or female and young or old) and comprise the most important of Jewish prayers. The twelfth benediction in the Palestinian recension reads: "And for apostates let there be no hope; and may the insolent kingdom be quickly uprooted, in our days. And may the Nazarenes [followers of Jesus?] and the heretics perish quickly; and may they be erased from the Book of Life; and may they not be inscribed with the righteous. Blessed art thou, Lord, who humblest the insolent." Although disputed, the twelfth benediction likely refers to Jewish Christians, as we see in its reference to "Nazoreans," or "Nazarenes" (Hebrew, *noserim*).[46]

---

46. Emil Schürer, *The History of the Jewish People in the Age of Jesus Christ, 175 BC–AD 135* (revised by Geza Vermes, Fergus Millar, and Martin Goodman; Edinburgh: T&T Clark, 1987), 2:461 and also 455–63. See also Hyam Maccoby, *Early Rabbinic Writings* (Cambridge Commentaries on the Writings of the Jewish and Christian World, 200 BC to AD 200; Cambridge:

When it became more and more difficult to ignore Christians as they grew in number after the fourth century, vituperative language was more present in both Jewish and Christian communities, with more references to each community and with little historical accuracy.[47] When rabbinic comments were made about Jesus or Christians, or when Christians made references to the Jews, they were generally quite negative and pejorative. Given that they were the two surviving expressions (sects) of Judaism from the first century, and are, in a real sense, siblings, one can expect a certain familiarity with each other's traditions.

Jesus, Archaeology, and the Dead Sea Scrolls

Two relatively recent fields of inquiry for those involved in life of Jesus studies are biblical archaeology and the Dead Sea Scrolls. A generation ago there was very little that most New Testament scholars knew about either of these fields of inquiry, and their works showed little interest in them. There was a common view that archaeology only had importance for Old Testament studies, and the full range of the Dead Sea Scrolls had not yet been published. As more advances in archaeology were made in Israel and surrounding areas that focused on the late Second Temple period (essentially up to the time of the destruction of the temple in Jerusalem in AD 70), New Testament scholars began to see considerable relevance in these finds for their particular disciplines. Discoveries in Israel, Greece, Turkey, and elsewhere led to significant new investigations of biblical passages, and biblical inquiry was considerably enhanced. Some scholars began again to read ancient inscriptions and lesser-known documents that had earlier only received scant attention in the academic world.[48] Because of recent archaeological discoveries, especially in Israel, Jordan, Greece, and Turkey, New Testament scholars began to recognize archaeology's relevance for understanding the world of the New Testament and often the context, life, and ministry of Jesus. Similarly, as more information became known about the Dead Sea Scrolls, especially after their full publication in the 1990s, many important parallels between the teaching of Jesus and his followers and that

---

Cambridge University Press, 1988), 208–9, who offers a useful discussion of the *Eighteen Benedictions,* arguing that they eventually, not initially, reflected an anti-Christian sentiment.

47. McDonald, "Anti-Judaism in Early Christianity," 215–52.

48. A highly valuable collection of documents that have come to light in recent years showing the relevance of archaeological discoveries has been published in a multiple-volume series by Macquarie University in Australia and now by Eerdmans, titled *New Documents Illustrating Early Christianity* (Grand Rapids: Eerdmans, 1987–2002). Many other such studies have followed and led to considerable advances in our understanding of the context of early Christianity and New Testament studies.

of the Essenes at Qumran became obvious to New Testament scholars. I was initially quite skeptical of the value of learning anything useful from the Dead Sea Scrolls except for taking us much closer to the original texts of the Old Testament books. However, several colleagues brought to my attention their considerable value for understanding the New Testament, including some of the teachings of Jesus. These scrolls are the closest Jewish sources that we have to the New Testament writings, and several biblical scholars have shown their considerable relevance for knowing more about Jesus than was previously known.

Scholars now are significantly more aware of how both of these fields of inquiry have improved our understanding not only of the context of the story of Jesus but also of some of his teachings. Students who are involved in life of Jesus research will be considerably rewarded by examining the relevance of recent archaeological discoveries and the Dead Sea Scroll texts in their pursuit of knowing Jesus in history. Jesus is best understood in his own Jewish context of the first century in Palestine.

Archaeology and the Story of Jesus

As noted above, biblical archaeology has advanced our understanding of the world of the New Testament and often the story of Jesus. Below I will list several important advances that have been made in our understanding of Jesus in his context as a result of significant cooperation between archaeologists and biblical scholars. Historically archaeologists have been generally unfamiliar with biblical inquiry, and biblical scholars have been generally unfamiliar with the results of archaeological research. Happily, this has begun to change, due in part to Hershel Shanks's pivotally significant popular publication, *Biblical Archaeology Review*. It has aided considerably in bringing biblical and archaeological scholarship together in fruitful ways that advance our understanding of biblical literature and the ancient Jewish and Greco-Roman context of early Christianity. Several other recent publications have contributed to a greater understanding of the time of Jesus and our knowledge of and about Jesus himself.[49]

49. Helpful contributions to this field of inquiry include James H. Charlesworth, ed., *Jesus and Archaeology* (Grand Rapids: Eerdmans, 2006); James H. Charlesworth and Walter P. Weaver, eds., *What Has Archaeology to Do with Faith? Faith and Scholarship Colloquies* (Philadelphia: Trinity Press, 1992); James H. Charlesworth, "Jesus Research and Archaeology," in *The World of the New Testament: Cultural, Social, and Historical Contexts* (ed. Joel B. Green and Lee Martin McDonald; Grand Rapids: Baker Academic, 2013); John McRay, *Archaeology and the New Testament* (1991; repr., Grand Rapids: Baker Academic, 2008); John Dominic Crossan and Jonathan L. Reed, *Excavating Jesus: Beneath the Stones, behind the Texts* (revised and updated; San Francisco: HarperSanFrancisco, 2001); Craig A. Evans, *Jesus and His World: The Archaeological Evidence* (Louisville: Westminster John Knox, 2012). A very helpful volume by the late leading archaeologist

Survey of Archaeological Findings

A few of the many important archaeological finds that aid in our understanding of Jesus include the following:

1. Discovery of the village of Nazareth, where Jesus was raised
2. Likely discovery of the house where Jesus met with Peter and his disciples in Capernaum
3. A synagogue in Magdala beside the Sea of Galilee where Jesus met Mary and taught
4. Discovery of Chorazin and Bethsaida
5. Greater knowledge of Roman crucifixions and Jewish burial practices in antiquity
6. Discovery of the likely site of Jesus' crucifixion and death
7. Pools of Siloam and Bethesda
8. Steps entering the southern entrance to the Temple Mount, on which Jesus likely walked

Charlesworth lists some of the many significant finds related to first-century Palestinian Judaism that enable scholars to reconstruct life in Palestine during that era that was also familiar to Jesus. These artifacts include the following:

- Hair, mirrors, necklaces, perfume bottles, mirrors, earrings, rings, bracelets, glass ungentaria, wooden combs, tweezers, gold pendants, numismatics (esp. "widow's mites" and Tyrian shekels)
- Leather sandals and wool clothing

Ehud Netzer, *The Architecture of Herod the Great Builder* (Grand Rapids: Baker Academic, 2006), shows the personal involvement of Herod the Great in many remarkable building projects and allows us to understand more the grandeur of the Herodian buildings that Jesus and his contemporaries were able to view. Subsequently, Netzer also discovered the burial place of Herod the Great at the Herodium in Palestine. His burial site is reported in Josephus's *Antiquities*, but its exact location eluded biblical scholars until Netzer's many years of excavating the Herodium site led to the discovery of its location. See also Richard A. Horsley, *Archaeology, History, and Society in Galilee: The Social Context of Jesus and the Rabbis* (Valley Forge, PA: Trinity Press, 1996); William H. C. Frend, *The Archaeology of Early Christianity: A History* (Minneapolis: Fortress, 1996); Raymond E. Brown, *Recent Discoveries and the Biblical World* (Wilmington, DE: Michael Glazier, 1983); and a very useful dictionary by John J. Rousseau and Rami Arav, *Jesus and His World: An Archaeological and Cultural Dictionary* (Minneapolis: Fortress, 1995). The archaeological encyclopedic resources that should be consulted on places and artifacts relevant to New Testament studies include Ephraim Stern, ed., *The New Encyclopedia of Archaeological Excavations in the Holy Land* (4 vols.; New York: Simon & Schuster, 1993); Eric M. Meyers, ed., *The Oxford Encyclopedia of Archaeology in the Near East* (5 vols.; New York: Oxford University Press, 1997); and Avraham Negev and Shimon Gibson, eds., *Archaeological Encyclopedia of the Holy Land* (London: Continuum, 2005). Other discoveries are continually coming to light, and the list of contributions to this field continues to grow.

- Weapons, including helmets, shields, swords, spears, knives, ballista stones, catapult arrowheads, and arrowheads
- Bronze and iron vessels, rings, and phallic images worn by many
- Glass and bronze serpents that are clearly Herodian
- Ceramic lamps, inkwells, oil fillers, plates, bowls, jars, metal plates, spoons, and wine dippers, glass spoons, ungentaria, gold and silver earrings worn by women in Jerusalem and its environs, stone vessels, tables used by Jews—all used in Judea and Galilee during Jesus' time
- Marble, ceramic, and bronze statuettes of Aphrodite and Hermes
- Stone gates, walkways, tunnels, and sewers in Jerusalem
- Ornamental plaster in Yodefat, Migdal, Jerusalem, Masada, and elsewhere
- Liquefied bones (human?) on columns from Herod's Royal Stoa in the temple
- Frescoed walls in many mansions in Jerusalem
- A palace south of the temple, a boat, anchors, net sinkers, and fish hooks used in Galilee of Jesus' time (Wachsmann, *Excavations of an Ancient Boat*)
- Anchors and docks in the Dead Sea
- Ossuaries (bone boxes) dating from Jesus' time
- Baths, bathtubs, cisterns, and *mikva'ot* (ritualistic cleansing pools)
- Scrolls found in several places on the western and eastern sides of the Dead Sea
- A lighthouse on the northwestern edge of the Dead Sea
- Cities built by Herod the Great in Judea and Samaria
- Theaters, especially in Jerusalem and Sepphoris
- Aqueducts, valleys, rivers, hills, mountains, and a lake familiar to Jesus
- Villages, like Yodefat and Gamla, that have lain in ruins since the Roman conquest of AD 67
- The amphitheaters, gates, and monumental buildings in pre-70 Tiberias
- The Herodium and Herod's tomb
- Herod's desert retreats and palaces
- Caesarea Maritima and architecture seen by Peter and Paul as they went to Rome
- The site of the monumental Augusteum on the way to Caesarea Philippi
- A synagogue in which Jesus sat and taught, according to the Gospels

- Inscriptions from ordinary people on shards, ossuaries, and monuments
- Tombs from Jesus' time in Galilee and Judea (some with rolling stones)[50]

Among some of the more significant finds from the Dead Sea Scrolls for Jesus research, Charlesworth lists the following:

- Proof that pre-70 Jews were fascinated by and believed in angels, God the King, kingdom, the Messiah, the Son of God, resurrection, and other technical terms used by Jesus but never defined by him
- The evidence that some of Jesus' most difficult sayings are clarified by the study of the Dead Sea Scrolls, especially the *Damascus Document.*
- The evidence that John the Baptizer was connected in some ways to Qumran and may have left that community[51]
- A better comprehension of Jesus' deeds, especially the exorcisms
- Criteria for discerning the Messiah (4Q521)
- The source of some of the dualism in the Gospel of John, especially the focus on the sons of light and darkness (see John 3:19–21)[52]

Thousands of coins used in the temple, including the so-called widow's mite and the silver coin for paying the temple tax, have now been discovered. Because scholars have now been able to establish the significant role of the temple in Jewish life in the first century, Jesus' comments about the temple (Mark 13:1–2; John 2:19–20; cf. Mark 14:57–58; 15:29; cf. Acts 6:13) likely contributed significantly to his arrest and execution. The passages just noted also suggest the Jesus did not have as high a view of the importance of the temple as some have supposed. Was it because he saw it was corrupted, and was that the reason for his "cleansing" of the temple?

Also, because of archaeological research to the west and south of the Temple Mount, we have a much better picture today of the ancient temple than was possible earlier. Charlesworth notes that among the many discoveries related to the temple that pre-date AD 70 are remains of the balustrade warning non-Jews not to continue farther, and massive stones in the temple foundation that are heavier than those in the Egyptian pyramids, some of which weigh about 470 tons. There were also shops, streets, sewers, numerous *mikva'ot* (ritual baths), monumental steps especially on the south end of the Temple Mount, and gates leading up and into the temple. He further notes that the Pool of

50. Charlesworth, "Jesus Research and Archaeology."
51. See Charlesworth, ed., *The Scrolls and Christian Origins* (vol. 3 of *The Bible and the Dead Sea Scrolls*; ed. James H. Charlesworth; Waco: Baylor University Press, 2006).
52. J. H. Charlesworth, ed., *John and the Dead Sea Scrolls* (New York: Crossroad, 1990), 76–106.

Bethesda (variant: Bethzatha) and the Pool of Siloam, mentioned in the New Testament, have also been recovered.[53]

As a result of recent archaeological research, it is now known that the author of John's Gospel was quite familiar with pre-70 Jerusalem, including the place of houses and the pools mentioned above. It is likely that the palaces of Herod and Caiaphas have also been excavated. Likewise, the elevated stone within the Church of the Holy Sepulcher (or nearby) may well be the place where Jesus was crucified, though according to J. E. Taylor the site of Golgotha (Mark 15:22; Matt. 27:33; Luke 23:33; John 19:17) may be south of the present traditional site on the junction of two roads.[54] The traditional site, however, was clearly visible for the pubic to see on a road, and outside Jerusalem walls in AD 30 but not AD 44. Charlesworth has noted rightly that according to Quintilian (*Decl.* 274), crucifixions were organized on busy highways so that many people would see the crucifixions and fear Roman power. Shimon Gibson has reported that executions took place just outside Jaffa Gate in Jerusalem and that according to Tacitus (*Ann.* 2.32.2) all crucifixions must be outside a city.[55] This, of course, fits well with what the author of Hebrews said about Jesus' suffering "outside the city gate" (13:12).

In terms of the act of Roman crucifixion, a heel bone with a spike in it and portions of a cross were found in an ossuary (bone box) of a certain person named Yehohanan who was crucified around the time of Jesus' death. It was discovered at Giv'at ha Mivtar within northern Jerusalem. The victim was between twenty-four and twenty-eight years old. Outside the present walls of the old city are several first-century tombs. Some have rolling stones before the door, as in the case of the traditional burial site of the Herodian family behind the modern King David Hotel (cf. Mark 15:46; John 20:1; Luke 23:50–53; Matt. 27:60).

In the first centuries BC and AD, there was a practice of placing a body in a tomb for about a year, and when the body had decomposed, the bones were placed in stone boxes called ossuaries. Generally, some family member would etch on the ossuary the name of the person whose bones had been interred. Not long ago, an ossuary discovered in Israel made international news because the etching on the side reads, "James the son of Joseph, brother of Jesus." An international debate has ensued over its authenticity, but the arguments in favor of it referring to James the brother of Jesus are considerable.[56] Hundreds of

---

53. Ibid.

54. J. E. Taylor, *Christians and Holy Places* (Oxford: Clarendon Press, 1993).

55. S. Gibson, *The Final Days of Jesus: The Archaeological Evidence* (Oxford: Lion, 2009), 116–17.

56. For a careful examination of this ossuary and its inscription, see Craig A. Evans, *Jesus and the Ossuaries: What Jewish Burial Practices Reveal about the Beginning of Christianity*

ossuaries have been recovered that date almost always from Herod the Great (40 BC to 4 BC) to the destruction of the temple in AD 70, after which the practice of using ossuaries largely ceased. It is not clear why this practice ceased, but it was carried on for about a hundred years, mostly in and around Jerusalem. Charlesworth also notes that the names on the ossuaries, like "Jesus the son of Joseph," "Mary," "Jude," along with incised images that look like crosses, do not indicate that the remains are related to the Palestinian Jesus Movement,[57] but they do indicate the kinds of burial practices in and around Jerusalem in the time of Jesus.[58] Most likely the tombs and ossuaries of Herod, Caiaphas, Annas, and (possibly) Simon of Cyrene have been recovered. Debates rage regarding the recently discovered Talpiot Tomb and its connection, if any, with Jesus of Nazareth or his family.[59]

Details from Some Key Discoveries

There are many other important archaeological discoveries that are relevant for historical Jesus research, including the following four examples:[60]

1. Migdal, home of Mary Magdalene. In 2011, excavations in Migdal revealed an area for docking ships. It has stones with circular holes for tying small flat-bottom boats. Migdal was an ideal site for ships and boats since the current went counterclockwise from Migdal to Capernaum, Hippus, and Tiberias, and finally back to Migdal. Also a wide road was uncovered in the western part of Migdal that is possibly the famous *Via Maris*, the main artery from Egypt to the East. Migdal was burned by Titus's troops at the beginning of the Roman war with the Jews in AD 67. A synagogue in Migdal was destroyed in that battle, likely an event that Josephus referred to as "sanctuaries (*hiera*) set on fire" by the Roman soldiers (*J.W.* 7.144).[61] Archaeologists have found remains

---

(Waco: Baylor University Press, 2003). He discusses many ossuaries that date to the first century, including the Yehohanan Ossuary mentioned above and Caiaphas (John 18:24), as well as others (see pp. 91–122).

57. The "cross" is one of the oldest symbols. It can denote the dot, the circle, and the square—and also the cross. Images that look like crosses antedate Christianity by at least one thousand years. See J. F. Strange's sane advice in "Archaeological Evidence of Jewish Believers?," in *Jewish Believers in Jesus* (ed. O. Skarsaune and R. Hvalvik; Peabody, MA: Hendrickson, 2007), 710–41.

58. Charlesworth, "Jesus Research and Archaeology."

59. See the forthcoming James H. Charlesworth, ed., *The Tomb of Jesus and His Family? Exploring Ancient Jewish Tombs near Jerusalem's Walls* (Grand Rapids: Eerdmans, 2013), which has biblical scholars, archaeologists, forensic scientists, and other scholars examining these topics and the possibility of Jesus being buried in the Talpiot Tomb.

60. Much of the following discussion is partially selected and summarized from Charlesworth, "Jesus Research and Archaeology."

61. Ibid. He adds that a correct perspective on Galilee is now provided by five main publications: M. Aviam, *Jews, Pagans and Christians*; M. A. Chancey, *The Myth of a Gentile Galilee*;

of a synagogue in which, according to the Gospels, Jesus could have worshiped and taught. All evangelists report that Jesus taught in the synagogues in Galilee. Migdal is only one hour by boat from Capernaum, Jesus' headquarters for his itineraries and the place where he likely met Mary Magdalene.

2. Capernaum. The headquarters for Jesus' ministry in Galilee was Capernaum, a small village that was a Jewish fishing center with perhaps one to two thousand people. The excavators have found no *mikva'ot* at Capernaum, but the people may have immersed themselves in the Kinneret (Sea of Galilee), which was filled with "living water" pouring from the northern mountains. A home has been found at Capernaum that some scholars think was the home of Peter and the place where Jesus stayed in this village (see Mark 1:21–34; Matt. 8:14–16). The size of homes and bedrooms are now clarified. By modern standards, they were quite small, and all family members likely slept in one bed. The white marble synagogue at Capernaum was likely built in the late fifth century, since a coin from the late fifth century was found under the floor. More importantly, in the center of the foundation of this synagogue are the remains of another building. Several scholars have indicated that this may have been the foundation of a synagogue from the time of Jesus where Jesus reportedly taught (Mark 1:29). We may not have found the precise home where Jesus stayed during his Galilean ministry, but the village was small; a number of first-century ruins of homes have been found there, and one of them is likely the place where Jesus stayed. Today a modern octagonal church has been built over the site that some have argued is Peter's house. It is not clear why this location would have been selected unless a strong tradition was associated with it.

3. Bethsaida. Bethsaida is mentioned by Pliny the Elder (*Nat.* 5.15.71), Josephus (*Ant.* 18.4–6, 28, 106–8; *J.W.* 2.168; 3.57, 515; *Life* 398–406), Ptolemy (*Geog.* 5.16.4), and the New Testament Gospels (Mark 6:45; 8:22; Luke 9:10; John 1:44; 12:21). Archaeologists believe that they have discovered; the location of Bethsaida. This is likely the hometown of Philip, Andrew, and Simon, and perhaps James and John, the sons of Zebedee. Jesus visited Bethsaida. Coins of Herod Philip, the ruler of this area from 4 BC to AD 34, have been discovered here, and in one locus a lance, a dagger, and a gold coin of Antoninus Pius were found dating from AD 138.

4. Synagogues. How and in what ways does archaeology help in assessing the evangelists' report that Jesus taught in synagogues throughout Galilee, as

M. H. Jensen, *Herod Antipas in Galilee* (2nd ed.; WUNT 2/215; Tübingen: Mohr Siebeck, 2010); J. Zangenberg, H. W. Attridge, and D. B. Martin, eds., *Religion, Ethnicity and Identity in Ancient Galilee*; U. Leibner, *Settlement and History*.

in Mark 1:39? What evidence exists that there were synagogues as the term implies—not buildings, but public gathering places for Jews?

Evidence of first-century synagogue buildings has likely been found at Masada, Herodium, Jerusalem, Qiryat Sefer, Modiin, Jericho, and also at Capernaum, Khirbet Qana, Gamla, and Migdal.[62] Jesus likely visited one or possibly two of these synagogues (Capernaum and Migdal), but because the evangelists do not mention his visiting other synagogues in Jerusalem or Jericho, we cannot be sure of the others. The synagogues at Masada and the Herodium date some thirty-six years after Jesus' death and were not typical synagogues of the early first century. The Zealots probably built both structures. The Capernaum synagogue of Jesus' time has not survived, and it may have been demolished when a later one was constructed on its site. The synagogue at Migdal meets all the criteria for Jesus to have taught there. It is within his main area of work and was operating during the 20s when he preached to crowds and in synagogues. It is certain now that the building in Migdal is a synagogue, and it clearly antedates not only 67, but also the first century AD. Although small, it is an elaborate edifice and may have had a scriptorium, or place for depositing sacred scrolls, to its west. As noted above, the newly uncovered synagogue at Migdal ceased to exist after AD 67 when Titus burned Migdal. Archaeologists now suggest that Jesus most likely taught in that synagogue.

Clearly Jesus research has been impacted by archaeological advancements. Archaeologists have recently produced foundational data that cannot be ignored in future Jesus research. There is abundant evidence of Jewish life in first-century-AD Palestine.

The Dead Sea Scrolls

Since the discovery of the famous Dead Sea Scrolls in 1947–1956, biblical scholars have recognized their considerable value for biblical research, not only in the text of the Old Testament (Hebrew Bible) books, but also in regard to the scope of the Jewish Scriptures in the time of Jesus. Several scholars have drawn our attention to the significant parallels between Jesus and his followers and the Essenes, who resided at Qumran and copied and/or produced the religious literature found in eleven caves in or near Qumran. Although many volumes have been produced on the importance of the Dead Sea Scrolls over the last fifty years, those that highlight the relevance of this discovery

---

62. See, e.g., D. D. Binder, *Into the Temple Courts: The Place of the Synagogue in the Second Temple Period* (SBLDS 169; Atlanta: Society of Biblical Literature, 1999); L. I. Levine, "Evidence for Ancient Synagogues: Geography and Chronology," in *NEAEHL* 4:1421–24.

for New Testament studies have been produced especially in the last twenty years.[63] When scholars first began comparing the Dead Sea Scrolls and the New Testament writings focusing on Jesus in particular, many sensational claims initially emerged, such as that Jesus was an Essene and had direct contact with those at Qumran.[64] Such claims have been answered carefully and generally disregarded as sensational nonsense.[65]

The Essenes and the Jesus Movement

In his survey of parallels between the Dead Sea Scrolls and the story of Jesus, Richard Horsley reminds us that both the Essenes and Jesus and his followers are the only two *known* renewal movements in the first-century Jewish context, and that "knowledge of a contemporary Judean protest-and-renewal (of Israel) movement parallel to the early communities of Jesus' followers is the primary significance of the DSS [Dead Sea Scrolls] for our understanding of the historical Jesus."[66] He also shows how both groups (Essenes and Jesus and his followers) had similar views on living in a world that is dominated by the demonic and evil spirits (cf. 1QS 3–4 and 1QM with the exorcisms in Mark 1:21–28; 9:14–29, 38–41). For the Essenes, the *Kittim* (Romans) were the embodiment of an evil spirit. Horsley reminds us that while there were other Judean apocalypses that offered similar symbolism, only the Essenes

63. Notable among these are Charlesworth, *Jesus and the Dead Sea Scrolls,* and his three volumes of scholarly essays, *The Bible and the Dead Sea Scrolls* (Waco: Baylor University Press, 2006), especially vol. 3, *The Scrolls and Christian Origins.* Other books on the Dead Sea Scrolls that include their significant parallels with Jesus and their relevance for New Testament studies are George Brooke, *The Dead Sea Scrolls and the New Testament* (Minneapolis: Fortress, 2005); Geza Vermes, *The Dead Sea Scrolls: Qumran in Perspective* (Philadelphia: Fortress, 1977); Peter W. Flint, *The Bible at Qumran: Text, Shape, and Interpretation* (Studies in the Dead Sea Scrolls and Related Literature; Grand Rapids: Eerdmans, 2001); Casey D. Elledge, *The Bible and the Dead Sea Scrolls* (Boston: Society of Biblical Literature, 2005). For an attractively illustrated and popularly written volume that identifies, among other things, the importance of the Dead Sea Scrolls for understanding Jesus and early Christianity, see Craig A. Evans, *Guide to the Dead Sea Scrolls* (Holman Quick Source; Nashville: B&H Publishing, 2010). There are many other volumes on this subject that have emerged in recent years, and more are forthcoming.

64. See, for example, Barbara Thiering, *Jesus and the Riddle of the Scrolls: Unlocking the Secrets of His Life Story* (San Francisco: HarperSanFrancisco, 1992); and her *Jesus the Man: A New Interpretation of the Dead Sea Scrolls* (New York: Doubleday, 1992). She also claimed that Jesus was betrothed to Mary Magdalene at precisely 10:00 p.m. on Tuesday, June 6, AD 30!

65. See especially Otto Betz and R. Riesner, *Jesus, Qumran and the Vatican* (London: SCM, 1994), 99–113; and H. Stegemann, *The Library of Qumran: On the Essenes, Qumran, John the Baptist, and Jesus* (Grand Rapids: Eerdmans, 1998), 28–30.

66. Richard A. Horsley, "The Dead Sea Scrolls and the Historical Jesus," in Charlesworth, *Bible and the Dead Sea Scrolls,* 3:39–40.

and Jesus and his followers were "actively engaged in the struggle, on the side of what they saw as the final divine initiative."[67]

The story of Jesus in Mark begins with a quote from Isaiah 40:3 about "preparing the way of the Lord" (Mark 1:3; Matt. 3:3), and those at Qumran cite this very text with similar views that it was being fulfilled in their own community (1QS 8:13–14). Horsley also points out that both communities had similar views about divorce, rejecting the specific permission for divorce in Deuteronomy 24:1–4 that was articulated by the Pharisees and high priesthood in Jerusalem (cf. 11QT 57 and CD 4:13–21 with Luke 16:18 and Mark 10:2–9).[68] Both groups also apparently rejected the high priesthood and the temple in Jerusalem. Horsley suggests that it is not clear on what basis the Jews from Galilee (home of Jesus and his early followers) would have had any attachments to the temple in Jerusalem, but notes the parallel conflict that the Essenes and Jesus and his followers had with the high priesthood (see Mark 14:53–65; Matt. 26:57–68; Luke 22:66–71; John 18:19–24; and Acts 4:1–10; 5:17–33; 23:1–5; cf. 1QpHab 1:3; 8:9–11; 9:5–12; 11:4). Neither the Essenes nor the early followers of Jesus offered sacrifices in the temple, and neither community practiced such sacrifices. For the Christians, Jesus was their sacrifice for sins (see 1 Cor. 15:3; Rom. 5:8–9; Heb. 10:1–18). For those at Qumran, their community was the true temple and their lives were a sacrifice as they sent up like incense their works of the law (1QS 8:10; 9:3–5; 4Q174 1:2–7).

Jesus was accused of criticizing the temple and may in fact have spoken against it (Mark 13:1–2; 14:58; 15:29–30; Acts 6:13–14; John 2:19; see also Stephen's speech in Acts 7:48–54), since it was a part of the accusations against him. All four evangelists report the story of his cleansing of the temple (Matt. 21:12–17; Mark 11:15–19; Luke 19:45–48; John 2:13–20). Resistance against the temple is also found among the Essenes at Qumran, who refused to pay the yearly temple tax (it was not so prescribed in the Torah, or Law) and paid the temple tax only once in a lifetime (4Q159 2:6–8). Horsley concludes that both Jesus and the Essenes at Qumran were dedicated to the renewal of Israel over against the temple and the high priesthood.[69] He also finds parallels between Jesus and the Righteous Teacher at Qumran, both of whom served in the role of a new Moses or prophet (see Jesus' use of "you have heard it said, but I say unto you" in Matt. 5:21–22, 27–28, 31–32, 38–39, 43–44). Neither community was organized like the high priesthood in Jerusalem (see 1QS 8:1–4). On the other hand, he adds that while the Righteous Teacher

---

67. Ibid., 41–42.
68. Ibid., 44–45.
69. Ibid., 49–50.

of Qumran revealed all of the mysteries to the wise scribes and priests at Qumran, Jesus hid them from the wise and intelligent and revealed them to infants (Luke 10:21).[70]

Brooke reflects on several parallels between Jesus and the Dead Sea Scrolls, including their concept of God, the Hebrew Scriptures as their guiding force, their fondness for the same scriptural books (Genesis, Deuteronomy, Isaiah and the Twelve, and the Psalms). He also mentions the parallels in the pneumatic, eschatological, and messianic exegesis, the citation of Isaiah 40:3, the focus on the new covenant, and the continuation of prophecy in both groups.[71] He adds to this their similar views on a cosmic-shaped chronology, including two ages and two worlds, a cosmos full of demons and angels, an eschatological redemption for the poor, a messianology, similar attitudes toward Jerusalem, the temple and cultus, the sinfulness of all human beings, the recognition of a God of forgiveness and grace, salvation and justification as a gift from God, the significant stress on the importance of prayer, a heightened notion of inward holiness, the symbolic use of water (baptisms), shared possessions, condemnation of divorce, emphasis on the "sons of light," one prophetic and charismatic person (Righteous Teacher/Jesus), celibacy as being married to God, and an emphasis on the Holy Spirit. There are some twenty-seven differences, but there are parallels that one cannot easily ignore.

Most of these similarities can be accounted for as shared views among the various Jewish sects in the first century AD, but some scholars have asked whether there may have been a more direct contact between Jesus and the Essenes.[72] A commonly held view is that John the Baptist may have grown up among the Essenes and may have shared much of what he learned there with those who followed him—including Jesus, who accepted his baptism. Elledge has drawn attention to some of the commonly held views of John the Baptist and the Essenes at Qumran, both of whom were active near the Jordan River (Matt. 3:1; Luke 1:80). Josephus places John's execution at Machaerus, located on the east side of the Dead Sea and east of Qumran (see Josephus, *Ant.* 18.116–19). Both John and the Essenes practiced ritualistic immersions (baptisms), and both required that repentance accompany that act of purification (Mark 1:4; cf. *Ant.* 18.117 and 1QS 3:8–9). Both John and the Essenes referred to the Holy Spirit as the agent of cleansing of sinful human beings

---

70. Ibid., 57–60.

71. For a discussion of this preference for the same sacred texts at Qumran and in the teachings of Jesus and in the rest of the New Testament, see Brooke, *Dead Sea Scrolls and the New Testament*, 27–51. See also James H. Charlesworth, "The Dead Sea Scrolls and the Historical Jesus," in *Jesus and the Dead Sea Scrolls*, 1–74, here 35–37, on this same topic.

72. Brooke, *Dead Sea Scrolls and the New Testament*, 20–25.

(Mark 1:8 and 1QS 4:21), both had strong views about the coming end of the current age and the beginning of a new age when God will be in control (Matt. 3:2; Luke 3:3–17 and compare 1QS 3:13–4:26), and both had very strict rules about marriage (Mark 6:14–29 and 11QT 57; CD 4:20), including the importance of self-denial (Mark 1:6; Luke 3:10–14). Finally, both in John's announcement of the coming kingdom and in the eschatological views of the Essenes, Isaiah 40:3 played an important role (Mark 1:3; Matt. 3:3; Luke 3:4–6; 1QS 8:13–16). Along with the above, Jesus' ministry began in conjunction with John's preaching, and he had high praise for John (Luke 7:28–29), was baptized by him (Mark 1:9), and preached a similar message about repentance as preparation for the coming kingdom of God (Mark 1:15).[73] These parallels suggest Jesus' familiarity with some of the Essene teaching at Qumran, but this does not necessarily mean that he had direct contact with the Essenes. Rather, he was familiar with the teachings of John the Baptist, who either had direct contact with the community of Essenes at Qumran or at least held a similar worldview current in Palestine in the time of Jesus.[74] While it is possible that Jesus had direct contact with the Essenes (perhaps in Jerusalem), the evidence is not as compelling. It is more likely that the parallels between Jesus and the Essenes were popular or common notions held in various Jewish sects of the first century.

Key Passages from the Scrolls

Several passages in the Dead Sea Scrolls have particular relevance for understanding the teaching of Jesus, and three of these parallels are particularly significant for our purposes.

1. 4Q521. In Luke 7:18–22 (see parallel in Matt. 11:2–5), Jesus meets with John the Baptist's disciples, who ask him whether he is the one who is to come or whether they should wait for another (v. 20). Jesus responds by referring to Isaiah 61:2–3 and its parallel in 35:5–6, but he adds something not in either of those texts—namely, that the dead are raised (Luke 7:22; Matt. 11:5). In the parallel passage in the Dead Sea Scrolls, which also appeals to the Isaiah passages, the passage begins with "the heavens and earth will obey His Messiah" and a reference to the Isaiah passage, but, like Jesus, the writer adds: "then he will heal the slain, resurrect the dead, and announce glad tidings to the poor." The Qumran writer saw the Isaiah text as a reference to the coming Messiah and, like Jesus, also added that the dead would be raised. Jesus' response to John's disciples was a clear yes, and the Qumran text makes this clear. Jesus

---

73. Casey D. Elledge, *The Bible and the Dead Sea Scrolls* (Leiden: Brill, 2005), 118.
74. Evans, *Guide to the Dead Sea Scrolls*, 304–6.

announced to John's disciples that he was the Messiah. This Qumran text, 4Q521, remarkably coincides with what Jesus said to them.

2. 4Q246 and "Son of God" and "Son of the Most High." It has become common for some scholars to take the many references to Jesus as "Son of God" or "Son of the Most High" in the New Testament (e.g., Mark 1:1; 5:7; 14:62; Luke 1:32–35; 8:28) as lacking a high Christology. That is, they suggest that any who were faithful followers of God were viewed as sons of God (John 1:12). This designation was common also in the Greco-Roman world for emperors; for example, Caesar Augustus (Octavian) was called both "god" and "son of God" (P.Oxy. 257; P.Oxy. 1266), and Tiberius his son called himself both "Son of God" and "Son of Zeus the Liberator" (SB 8317; P.Oxy. 240).[75] It has been commonly thought that Christians borrowed the term from pagan sources to describe their understanding of Jesus; however, as Evans has shown, similar designations were well known both in the Old Testament and among the Jews at Qumran (e.g., Gen. 14:18–20; Num. 24:16; Isa. 14:14, passim; as well as in the Dead Sea Scrolls, in 1QapGen 12:17; 20:12; 1QH 4:31; 6:33; 1QS 4:22; and elsewhere).[76] In particular, 4Q246 1:7b–2:1 speaks about the coming of a king who will conquer the nations and rule with justice and will be called "Son of God, and they shall call him Son of the Most High." This is remarkably similar to Gabriel's announcement to Mary in Luke 1:32–35 (see also Mark 15:39). Evans concludes that this passage was "right at home in first-century Palestine."[77]

3. 4Q525 2:1–7 and Jesus' Beatitudes. Some of the Beatitudes of Jesus in Matthew 5:1–11 and Luke 6:20–23 have parallels in the Qumran literature. For example, Jesus' reference to the blessedness of those who are "pure in heart" in Matthew 5:8 is quite similar to "[Blessed is he who walks] with a pure heart" in 4Q525 2:1. There are several other parallels between Jesus' Beatitudes and those in this Qumran text. Those in the Jesus Seminar who argue that Jesus' teaching is best understood in terms of Greco-Roman philosophy, and Cynicism in particular, fail to appreciate that Jesus' teachings were at home in a first-century Palestinian Jewish context. Evans notes that the difference between the Qumran text and Jesus is that the former is rooted in Jewish wisdom teaching, but Jesus "gave it his own eschatological spin."[78]

---

75. More examples of this are in Craig A. Evans, "Jesus and the Dead Sea Scrolls from Qumran Cave 4," in C. A. Evans and Peter Flint, eds., *Eschatology, Messianism, and the Dead Sea Scrolls* (Studies in the Dead Sea Scrolls and Related Literature; Grand Rapids: Eerdmans, 1997), 91–100, here 92–94.

76. Ibid.

77. Ibid., 94.

78. Ibid., 95–96. These and other examples of parallels between Jesus' teaching and texts discovered at Qumran are discussed in Evans, "Jesus and the Dead Sea Scrolls," and in Brooke,

Dead Sea Scrolls and the New Testament, 217–97. There are also several articles that reflect parallels between Jesus or his disciples and the Dead Sea Scrolls in Charlesworth, *Jesus and the Dead Sea Scrolls*, especially in regard to Jesus' attitude toward the temple and his views about table fellowship.

169

PART THREE

The Story of Jesus in History

(Events and Teachings)

4

The Story of Jesus in History

From His Birth to His Scriptures

|||||||||||||||||||||||||||||||||||||||||||||||||||||

The following examination of the life of Jesus will focus on the events of Jesus' life, ministry, and teaching from the perspective of the canonical Gospel writers, but also will be using the historical-critical methodology described earlier. Some of these events are not historically quantifiable (as discussed in chap. 2), since they are reported as divine activity and are surrounded with theological implications. This does not necessarily mean that they did not happen, but only that historians as historians have no adequate way to assess them. Nevertheless, they are reported in the Gospels as events in the life of Jesus, and will be examined from both a historical and theological framework. In other words, we will ask what was reported and what the evangelists meant to say in their telling of their stories about Jesus. Much of the theological focus was covered in the previous discussion of the sources for studying the story of Jesus, but additional material will be added where it is appropriate in each of the following sections.

The following discussion is in no way exhaustive either in the stories and activities of Jesus reported in the Gospels or in the massive collection of contemporary literature that examines the story of Jesus in remarkable detail. It is more of a survey of what are generally considered the most important, or at least best-known, events in Jesus' life. Indeed, since the available research on the life of Jesus is so vast and constantly growing, I can only reasonably touch upon those works that I think are illustrative of the best of biblical scholarship. Readers interested in pursuing further and more detailed research than is possible here may consult the resources referred to in the footnotes and listed in the bibliography.[1]

Events in the Life of Jesus

Although the evangelists report a number of events in the life of Jesus, there are only a few that are in all four canonical Gospels, and those stories in more than one Gospel are not always in the same sequence. Scholars generally agree on the sequence of major events or stories about Jesus in the Synoptic Gospels, but not many others. Among the stories about Jesus and his teachings, those marked with an asterisk are in at least three of the four Gospels and in *roughly* the same order.

(1) Birth. This is found only in Matthew 1:18–25 and Luke 1:26–38 and 2:1–20, and these accounts are clearly independent of each other and significantly different in their focus except on the nature of the birth of Jesus. On the other hand, Mark and John start their story at the beginning of Jesus' ministry with the story of John the Baptist's ministry and Jesus' contact with him.

(2) Childhood. Only Luke (2:21–52) records anything about the so-called hidden years of Jesus, those from his birth to his baptism. Even then he speaks only about the time of Jesus' dedication in the temple and later of Jesus' journey to Jerusalem to celebrate the Passover at age twelve. Although Luke portrays Jesus as a remarkable child (2:46–47), he is nonetheless described as a child who grew in a natural manner (2:52).

*(3) Baptism. All three Synoptic evangelists agree that John the Baptist baptized Jesus in the Jordan River prior to Jesus beginning his ministry. Only the Fourth Gospel, however, has John recognize and announce Jesus while he was baptizing others (1:28). The author does not say that John baptized Jesus (1:29–34), even though he reports that John the Baptist saw the Spirit descend upon Jesus (John 1:32).

(4) Temptation. This story is mentioned in all three Synoptic Gospels, but it is only described in Matthew and Luke. It is also reported in Hebrews, but not in detail (Matt. 4:1–11; Mark 1:12–13; Luke 4:1–13; see also Heb. 2:18; 4:15).

*(5) Early Galilean Ministry. All four evangelists agree that Jesus' earlier ministry was in the region of Galilee (Matt. 4:12; Mark 1:14; Luke 4:14; John

---

1. A further resource is Craig A. Evans, *Life of Jesus Research: An Annotated Bibliography* (NTTS 24; rev. ed.; Leiden: Brill, 1996), but, because of the pace at which new books in this field appear, it was dated by the time it was published, and even his own more recent and substantial works are not included in it.

1:43), although they do not agree on which villages Jesus visited or the order in which they were visited. For John, Jesus' ministry begins in Galilee shortly after the scene at the Jordan River when John acclaims Jesus and Jesus calls his disciples (see John 1:43–2:12).

*(6) Transfiguration. The story of the transfiguration of Jesus is found in roughly the same place in the Synoptic Gospels (Matt. 17:1–8; Mark 9:2–8; Luke 9:28–36)—namely, just prior to Jesus' journey south to Jerusalem, where he was arrested and crucified. The significance of the event evidently is that it was intended to give assurances to the disciples regarding the coming of Jesus into his kingdom in the relatively near future. The transfiguration story is not mentioned in John's Gospel, but there is an apparent reference to it in 2 Peter 1:16–18. Similarities between the appearance of Jesus in the transfiguration and his resurrection appearances have prompted some form critics to hypothesize that the story is a transposed resurrection narrative put back into the earthly life of Jesus.

*(7) Triumphal Entry into Jerusalem. All four evangelists agree that when Jesus came to Jerusalem, he was well received by the common people and rejected only later by the religious leaders (Matt. 21:1–11; Mark 11:1–10; Luke 19:28–38; John 12:12–19). The Old Testament references in each of the Gospels indicate that Jesus was being hailed as the coming Messiah in Jerusalem by the crowds of people just days before he was arrested and crucified.

*(8) The Last Supper. The first three evangelists report that just prior to his arrest in the Garden of Gethsemane, Jesus shared a final meal, the Passover, with his disciples (Matt. 26:26–29; Mark 14:22–25; Luke 22:14–23). It is not clear if this was the same Passover meal mentioned in John (13:1–17:25), but see also John 6:41–59, where Jesus, in the region of Galilee, describes bread and the cup as his body and blood.

*(9) Arrest and Trial. All of the evangelists agree essentially on the time of the arrest and trial, or hearing, of Jesus before the high priest and Sanhedrin—namely, some time after a final meal with his disciples while Jesus was praying in the Garden of Gethsemane. There are, however, some differences in the details of the various accounts (Matt. 26:36–56; Mark 14:32–50; Luke 22:39–54; John 18:1–11).

*(10) Crucifixion and Resurrection. All four Gospels have these events at the conclusion of Jesus' arrest and trial (Matt. 27:32–28:20; Mark 15:21–16:8; Luke 23:26–24:49; John 19:16b–20:31). However, the details associated with these events vary in accordance with the theological motifs of each evangelist.

(11) Ascension. Only Luke and John have an ascension story, but the time of this event is different in their narratives. John has an ascension between the first and second appearance of Jesus (John 20:17), but Luke has it at the

end of all of Jesus' appearances to the disciples (Luke 24:50–51; Acts 1:1–11). However, both writers have it in the same *broad* sequence of death, resurrection, and the giving of the Spirit.

The Life of Jesus: From Birth to His Scriptures

The following discussion is a brief survey of the life of Jesus. As noted above, I will not restrict my discussion to what a historical-critical approach can deduce, although I will make use of that approach throughout this study. I will also focus on some of the evangelists' theological motives as they tell the story of Jesus (or *Yeshua*[2]).

The Birth of Jesus

Matthew and Luke use the story of Jesus' birth to communicate their understanding of the good news about him. There is no other reference in the New Testament to this event and no theology outside of Matthew and Luke is built upon it. Matthew and Luke present remarkably different stories about Jesus' birth, and we will focus on the significance they have attached to this event.

Location

In the New Testament, only Matthew and Luke discuss the birth of Jesus. Although they have quite different stories about the birth and genealogy of Jesus, it is important to note that both agree that the birth of Jesus took place in Bethlehem. It is reasonable to conclude that Bethlehem is the location of his birth, even though both evangelists also agree that Jesus grew up in Nazareth. The information elsewhere in the New Testament says that he came from Nazareth or was raised there (see, for example, Mark 1:9; 6:1–3; 10:47; Luke 4:16, 34; 18:37; 24:19; Acts 2:22; 3:6; 4:10; and elsewhere). The location of Bethlehem for Jesus' birth was also in keeping with a Jewish tradition about the place where the coming messiah was to be born (Mic. 5:2–4). The shepherd king who would come to rescue Israel was, like David (1 Sam. 17:12), not to be from the capital city, Jerusalem, but instead from the city of promise, Bethlehem. Matthew and John see Bethlehem as the divinely ordained place

---

2. The name "Jesus" is the Greek form of the Hebrew *Yeshua*, or Joshua. It was a common name in the first century AD and has numerous parallels in the century before and after the time of Jesus. After him the Jews, because of the rise of Christianity, reverted to using the earlier form, Joshua. Josephus mentions some ten persons by the name of Jesus. See, for example, in *Ant.* 20.223 a reference to Jesus, the son of Gamaliel.

of the birth of the Messiah (Matt. 2:5–6; John 7:41–42). Some scholars reject this view and focus only on Nazareth, even though both Matthew and Luke place Joseph and Mary in Bethlehem during the birth of Jesus for different reasons and departing to Nazareth also for different reasons (cf. Matt. 2:1–23 with Luke 2:1–20, 39–40). John elsewhere only mentions that Jesus is from Nazareth (18:5, 7); his text seems to question whether a messianic figure could come out of Nazareth. He reports Nathaniel's response when he hears that Jesus came from Nazareth (John 1:45–46). Did John or Mark know where Jesus was born?

If we did not have the infancy narratives of Matthew and Luke, we might well conclude from the Gospels that Jesus was born in Nazareth. Outside of Matthew, there is nothing in the rest of the New Testament that refers to the place of Jesus' birth *as a fulfillment of prophecy*. Luke does not draw attention to the fulfillment of Scripture, but like Matthew does claim that Jesus was born in Bethlehem. In the Gospel of John there is a reference to the belief that the Messiah will come from Bethlehem (7:42), but the author of John does not himself connect Jesus with that place and appears to assume that he came from Nazareth. As in the cases of the genealogy, which we will examine below, and the nature of the birth itself, the question here is whether to assume that the reference to Bethlehem is a *theological* statement in Matthew and Luke rather than a *historical* one. The question that some scholars raise is whether Matthew and Luke knew the accepted location of the birth of the coming Messiah and inserted the reference to Bethlehem into their texts. Apart from Matthew and Luke, Jesus' primary significance in the rest of the New Testament has to do with his teachings (e.g., 1 Cor. 7:10–11; 11:23–25), his death and resurrection (1 Cor. 15:3–8; 1 Pet. 2:23–24; Heb. 10:1–18; 1 John 2:1–2), or hope for his coming (1 Thess. 1:9–10; 1 John 2:28; Rev. 22:20; passim).

Interestingly, Bethlehem is found some fifty times in the Old Testament and Nazareth not once. In the New Testament, Bethlehem is only found in the infancy narratives in Matthew and Luke and in John 7:42. It has been suggested that John is using irony on the part of the objectors to Jesus; that is, they wanted to disprove his identity as Messiah based on his origin in Nazareth instead of Bethlehem, but John's readers knew of the tradition about Jesus' birth in Bethlehem. However, this motif is highly unlikely in the Gospel of John, which only emphasizes the place of Jesus' origin as Nazareth (1:45–46) and does not focus on Davidic Christology, but rather that he came from above (3:13; 8:23).[3] While the New Testament and early church emphasis is certainly

3. John P. Meier makes this argument in his *A Marginal Jew: Rethinking the Historical Jesus* (ABRL; New York: Doubleday, 1991), 1:214–16.

on Jesus' teachings and his fate, it may not be necessary to choose between history and faith in this matter. Accepting the difficulty of harmonizing Matthew and Luke in the details each shares about the birth of Jesus, we can nonetheless affirm both agree on the location; only Matthew cites the Micah 5:2–4 passage, and Luke simply states the location as necessary for Joseph to comply with a Roman tax law. Jerome Murphy-O'Connor, however, concludes that it is both. In his debate with Steve Mason on the location of Jesus' birth, he points to historical traditions from the second century that point to Bethlehem. O'Connor notes references from Justin Martyr (ca. 100–165), who argues with Trypho that Jesus was the Messiah proclaimed in the Jewish Scriptures (Old Testament). O'Connor claims evidence from archaeological discoveries from the church built over the traditional birth site, and cites Origen (185–254), who mentions the cave in Bethlehem where Jesus was born, which attracted visitors as early as AD 231–246 (*Cels.* 1.51). O'Connor also cites Jerome (AD 342–420), who in his *Epistle* 58 says Jesus was born in Bethlehem. Jerome likely produced his Latin Vulgate translation of the Scriptures in a cave adjacent to the cave where Jesus reportedly was born. Jerome reports that the cave had been dedicated to Adonis (or Thammuz) from the time of Hadrian (AD 135), but was recovered in the time of Constantine and is the cave "where the infant Messiah once cried."[4] Another early church tradition from the second century also states that Jesus was born in a cave. When Mary's time of delivery had arrived, she asked Joseph to take her down from the donkey, as they were traveling to Bethlehem, and "he found a cave there and brought her into it, and left her in the care of his sons, and went out to seek for a Hebrew midwife in the region of Bethlehem" (*Prot. Jas.* 18.1).[5]

Another matter related to location is Matthew's account of the flight into Egypt, which appears to be incompatible with the account given by Luke, who has Joseph and Mary simply return to Nazareth after they completed all that was appropriate following the birth of their child. Does the story of Joseph and Mary's flight to Egypt have another motive—namely, the recognition of Jesus as the Son of God? Matthew's reference in 2:15 suggests this when he cites Hosea 11:1 from the Hebrew (Masoretic Text), "Out of Egypt I have called my son," rather than using the Septuagint or Greek version of Hosea, which reads: "Out of Egypt I called his children." It may also be, as

4. Justin, *Dial.* 78.6; Origen, *Cels.* 1.51; and Jerome, *Epistle* 58. See the Steve Mason and Jerome Murphy-O'Connor debate in *The First Christmas: The Story of Jesus' Birth in History and Tradition* (Washington, DC: Biblical Archaeological Society, 2009), 33–63, here 49–57.

5. Translation from J. K. Elliott, *The Apocryphal New Testament: A Collection of Apocryphal Christian Literature in an English Translation based on M. R. James* (Oxford: Clarendon, 1993), 64. See also the whole context in sections 17–21 on pp. 63–65.

Brown suggests, that the quotation of the Hosea passage in Matthew has an exodus motif, that is, the reference to an exodus that precedes the exile.[6] In the Septuagint version of Exodus 4:19–20, Moses is told to return to Egypt since those seeking to kill him are dead. This may be a part of what Matthew has in mind in his narrative about Jesus, who is the new Moses who gives an intensified and clarified version of the law in Matthew 5–7. It may also be possible that Bock's notion is correct, that Matthew cites the Hosea text to show the recapitulation or repetition of God's saving activity in history.[7] Whatever we can say about the various differences in these two birth narratives, it is clear that neither evangelist depended on the other and that both evangelists appear to have exercised considerable freedom with the traditions about Jesus' birth. In an interview not long ago, Sean Freyne concluded that the birth narratives were simply trying to fill in the gaps in the story of Jesus that was circulating among the followers of Jesus in the first century. They were perhaps following a well-known tradition of acknowledging the remarkable births of those who were remarkable individuals. It is difficult to establish where they got their information about the birth of Jesus since it is unlikely to have come from eyewitness sources. He also acknowledges that Jesus' family may have come from Bethlehem in Judea and after his birth moved to the region of Galilee (Nazareth).[8]

Date

The traditional date of the birth of Jesus in the year AD 1 is based on a miscalculation of some four to five years by Dionysius Exiguus, a Roman abbot (ca. AD 525), whose calculations were later taken up into the calculations of the archbishop and biblical scholar James Ussher (1581–1656). In his two-volume work *Annales Veteris et Novi Testamenti* (1650–1654),[9] which was

6. R. E. Brown, *The Birth of the Messiah: A Commentary on the Infancy Narratives in Matthew and Luke* (ABRL; Garden City, NY: Doubleday, 1977; rev. ed., 1993), 219–21. Brown's commentary is the classic text on the birth of Jesus and without question the most detailed investigation of the biblical and nonbiblical traditions related to the birth of Jesus.

7. See Darrell L. Bock, *Jesus according to Scripture: Restoring the Portrait from the Gospels* (Grand Rapids: Baker Academic, 2002), 71–72. He also has a careful discussion of the birth and childhood of Jesus in pp. 51–76. Given his abundant citations of the Jewish Scriptures, it is hard to believe that Matthew was unaware of the original context of Hos. 11:1, namely, that God is speaking about rescuing his people, that is, the Israelites' deliverance from Egypt.

8. See his interview with Hershel Shanks in "Jesus of History vs. Jesus of Tradition," *BAR* 36, no. 6 (Nov./Dec. 2010): 36–47, especially 45. Freyne does not choose between history and theology, but adds that the Bible gives us "theologically interpreted history" (p. 46), and includes several features in the birth stories that he believes are historically reliable.

9. This historic volume has been attractively republished in modern times as James Ussher, *The Annals of the World* (revised and updated by Larry and Marion Pierce; Green Forest, AR:

used for centuries in various editions of the King James Bible, including the well-known *Scofield Reference Bible* notes, Ussher argues for a date of 4004 BC as the time of the creation of the world and for the traditional date of AD 1 that we now refer to as the year of Jesus' birth. Ussher pointed to the birth of Jesus as the center of history and dated all events as happening before the birth of Christ or after (BC/AD).[10] The revision of Ussher's work dates the birth of Jesus at 5 BC and explains two taxations as follows:

> Luke would rather mention him [Quirinius] than the governor Saturninus, because he would compare this taxing with another that was made ten years later by the same Quirinius, after Archelaus was sent into banishment. He stated that, of the two taxings, this was the first taxing and this was the time of the birth of Christ. When this first taxing was enacted, Joseph went up from Galilee, from the city of Nazareth into Judea, to the city of David, called Bethlehem. He was of the house and lineage of David and would be taxed there with his wife Mary, who was due to deliver. (Ussher, *Annals of the World*, §§ 6057–6058)

Recent support for an earlier dating of Jesus' birth is all but universally accepted. The primary arguments for changing the traditional date from AD 1 to around 6–4 BC are based on the following factors.

(a) The Evidence from Matthew. According to Matthew 2:1–16, Jesus was born during the reign of Herod the Great. Our best available evidence on the death of Herod comes from Josephus, who says that Herod's death occurred after he had reigned for thirty-four years, which began three years after he was appointed as king by Rome (*Ant.* 17.191; *J.W.* 1.665). In other words, his death is more likely around March or April of 4 BC, although it may have been as early as December of 5 BC.

If Matthew's reference to Jesus' birth during the reign of Herod is reliable, then the traditional reference to the time of the birth has to be pushed back to somewhere around 7–4 BC, but no later than 4 BC, the latest year likely for the death of Herod the Great. Also, since Herod reportedly put to death a large number of children under the age of two, evidently the oldest that he thought the child might be (Matt. 2:16, 20), this supports the 6–4 BC dating. Matthew implies that Herod wanted to ensure that he had

---

Master Books, 2003). It is still a very valuable resource and cites a number of ancient sources that would otherwise have been lost to biblical scholarship.

10. The more recent scholarly practice of dating history as BCE = Before the Common Era, and CE = in the Common Era instead of BC (Before Christ, or Before the Christian era) and AD (*Anno Domini*, Latin, "in the year of our Lord") continues to date historical events on the basis of Ussher's dating method, even though the best available evidence for dating shows that the traditional time of Jesus' birth (Ussher's dating) is a few years later than the actual date.

destroyed the child described by the Magi, who he thought might threaten his rule (2:16–20).

(b) The Evidence from Luke. Luke also affirms that since John the Baptist was born during Herod's rule (Luke 1:5), and Jesus was born about six months later (see Luke 1:24–57), it is reasonable to suggest that Jesus also was born in the days of Herod the Great. Some factors about the date of Jesus' birth should be noted: (1) Luke dates the baptism of Jesus and the beginning of his ministry during the time of John the Baptist's ministry, which he places in the fifteenth year of the reign of Tiberius Caesar (Luke 3:1), whose reign as emperor began in AD 14 after the death of Augustus (Octavian). The first two years of his reign (AD 12–14) was likely a co-regency with Augustus, but none of the ancients date Tiberius's reign before the death of Augustus. If we add fifteen years to that time, then Jesus' baptism and the beginning of his ministry may have begun sometime around AD 29. If Luke intends to start the reign of Tiberius at the beginning of his co-regency with Augustus, then AD 26–27 is possible.

(2) Luke claims that Jesus was *about* thirty years old when John baptized him (3:23), which suggests that Jesus was born around 3–1 BC or even earlier. Luke, however, was not precise in 3:23, and the "about thirty" could be more or less than thirty by a few years. Since Luke indicates that the birth of John the Baptist, and by inference that of Jesus, was during the reign of Herod the Great (1:5–25), then a birth time around 6–4 BC is plausible.

Interestingly, the author of the apocryphal book *The Protevangelium of James* not only says that Herod the Great sought to kill Jesus and that Mary hid him in a manger, but also that Herod tried to have John the Baptist executed as well! "But Elizabeth, when she heard that John [the Baptist] was sought for, took him and went up into the hill-country. And she looked around to see where she could hide him" (22.2–3).

(3) The Problem of Quirinius (2:1–2). Luke says that Quirinius was governor of Syria when Jesus was born, but Tacitus the Roman historian states that Quirinius began as governor only *after* Archelaus (son of Herod the Great) was expelled from office by Rome in AD 6 (*Ann.* 6.41). Josephus claims that Quirinius ordered a census in AD 6–7 that caused a significant rebellion among the Jews. He writes:

> Quirinius, a Roman senator who had proceeded through all the magistracies to the consulship and a man who was extremely distinguished in other respects, arrived in Syria, to be governor of the nation and to make an assessment of their property. Coponius, a man of equestrian rank, was sent along with him to rule over the Jews with full authority. Quirinius also visited Judaea, which had been

181

annexed to Syria, in order to make an assessment of the property of the Jews and liquidate the estate of Archelaus [son of Herod the Great, cf. Matt. 2:22]. Although the Jews were at first shocked to hear of the registration of property, they gradually condescended, yielding to the arguments of the high priest Joazar . . . to go no further in opposition. (*Ant.* 18.1–2, LCL; see also *J.W.* 2.117; 7.253.)

If Tacitus and Josephus are correct about the date of Quirinius, then by Luke's accounting, the birth of Jesus comes too late (AD 6) and Luke is out of step with historians of the time. To resolve the problem, Geldenhuys long ago argued that Quirinius had a dual reign and ordered a dual enrollment or registration as Luke 2:2 indicates, the first of these in the first decade BC and the second in the first decade AD. The latter is probably referred to in Acts 5:37 and in Josephus, *Antiquities* 20.97–105.[11] Josephus, however, does not mention that Quirinius served as magistrate in Syria on more than one occasion, and this has some importance since he specifically refers to Quirinius's rule (*Ant.* 17.353 and 18.1–4). A marble slab from Tivoli (Tibur) currently in the Vatican Museum that dates to sometime after AD 14 mentions an unnamed official who served as legate of Syria on two occasions, but there is nothing in the inscription that specifically identifies the official with Quirinius. A second inscription, found in Pisidian Antioch in 1912, is dedicated to G. Caristanius Fronto, a colonist of Antioch who served as a prefect for two magistrates. It reads: "prefect of P. Sulpicius Quirinius, chief magistrate (*duumvir*), prefect of M. Servilius."

A third inscription reads similarly, although specifying that Fronto is now the prefect of a third magistrate as well.[12] From these inscriptions it is not possible to prove conclusively that Quirinius had a dual reign in Syria. It is possible that Publius Sulpicius Quirinius became consul in Syria in 12 BC and died in AD 21 (see Tacitus, *Ann.* 3.48 and Strabo, *Geogr.* 12.6.5), but arguing from this that there was a dual reign and a dual census is conjecture. What is even more difficult to deal with is the reason for calling a census for the taxation of the people by Augustus when Herod the Great was king and he himself had his own taxes and tax collectors. The client king paid tributes to Rome, but was free to collect his own taxes from the Jews. However, in other examples Rome did levy taxes directly upon the people. For instance, after Herod the Great died and his ruthless son Archelaus was deposed by the

---

11. Norval Geldenhuys, *The Gospel of Luke* (NICNT; Grand Rapids: Eerdmans, 1951), 100.

12. The first inscription can be read in W. M. Ramsay, *Was Christ Born in Bethlehem?* (New York: Putnam, 1898), 273; the second and third can be read in W. M. Ramsay, *The Bearing of Recent Discovery on the Trustworthiness of the New Testament* (London: Hodder & Stoughton, 1915), 285 and 291.

emperor in AD 6, significant changes had occurred. After that, Judea was no longer a Herodian tetrarchy but was a Roman province under the governance of Syria (Josephus, *Ant.* 18.1–5), and it was directly taxed by Rome, not the Herodians. As a result there was widespread rebellion in the land, and Judas the Galilean led a revolt against Rome (Josephus, *Ant.* 18.3–4). Does Luke confuse this time with the time of the birth of Jesus? He certainly uses the taking of a census for tax purposes to indicate why Joseph and Mary left Nazareth and arrived in the town of Bethlehem. A papyrus dating around AD 104 indicates that for Egyptian censuses, those making declarations were to go to their areas of origin.[13] Luke uses the same word for census (*apographē*) as that which is widely used in the abundant Egyptian papyri, in which almost continuous records indicate that censuses were taken at regular intervals from 11/10 BC to AD 257/258. These censuses took place every fourteen years from AD 33/34 on, but were probably at seven-year intervals before that. If censuses were held at the same times outside of Egypt, and this is far from certain, the census Luke refers to could be the one held in 4/3 BC. There is apparently no simple answer available to this difficult issue of correlating Luke's story of the birth of Jesus with available historical data, and questions remain about Luke's understanding of the historical context of the birth of Jesus.[14] Perhaps the way to reconcile this issue is to note that according to Josephus, Herod the Great himself conducted a census at roughly 7 to 6 BC that also decreed a loyalty to Augustus (*Ant.* 15.368 and 17.42). This took place when P. Quinctilius Varus was governor of Syria in 7/6 BC. Meier points to the confusion here by noting the difficulty of reconciling Luke's dating with other known histories of that period and also that given her condition, Mary would not have been required to make the trip with Joseph. Likewise, there is no reference to the flight to Egypt or Herod's seeking to kill children, as in Matthew. Jesus is even presented in the temple, which was not far from Herod the Great's palace.[15]

(c) The Evidence from John. During the cleansing of the temple incident that is placed near the beginning of Jesus' ministry in Jerusalem in John (earlier than in the Synoptic Gospels, which place it in the last week of Jesus' ministry before his crucifixion), Jesus responds to his antagonists who ask for evidence of his authority to do what he has done, saying: "Destroy this temple, and in

---

13. *Sel.Pap.* 2.220.18–27 (= P.Lond. III 904), in A. S. Hunt and C. C. Edgar, *Select Papyri* (LCL; London: Heinemann, 1934).

14. For a more detailed analysis of this problem, see Brown, *Birth of the Messiah*, 551–55. On the Egyptian census, see R. S. Bagnall and B. W. Frier, *The Demography of Roman Egypt* (Cambridge: Cambridge University Press, 1994), esp. 1–5; cf. 14–16.

15. Meier, *Marginal Jew*, 1:211–13.

three days I will raise it up." His critics responded that the temple had been in the making some forty-six years (2:19–20), and they clearly doubted that Jesus could raise it up in three days. According to Josephus, Herod began the rebuilding of the temple in the eighteenth year of his reign (*Ant.* 15.380). This refers either to 20/19 BC, eighteen years after he was made king by the Romans in 37 BC, or to 23/22 BC, eighteen years after he in fact began to rule in 40 BC. This could account for the difference in Josephus's reference to the building of the temple in the fifteenth year of Herod's reign (*J.W.* 1.401). Most scholars argue from the date of the conferral of Herod's kingship by the Romans in 37 BC, and they follow Josephus's reference (*Ant.* 15.380) in the matter.

The historical significance of this is that if the temple was begun in 20/19 BC, then forty-six years later would put the beginning of Jesus' ministry around AD 26. The fact that the temple was unfinished during the time of Jesus is supported by the fact that building was still going on both in and around the temple in the early AD 60s during the time of the high priesthood of Albinus (see Josephus, *Ant.* 20.219).

The difficulty with using this passage to date Jesus' ministry or to correlate the date of his birth is that the cleansing of the temple is reported in the Synoptic Gospels at the Passover just prior to Jesus' death, but in John at the beginning of Jesus' ministry some two or three years before his death. There is considerable difficulty in being more precise in our dating than saying that Jesus' ministry began somewhere around AD 26 or 27 at the earliest and concluded around AD 30. An approximate age of thirty years old when Jesus was baptized by John (Luke 3:23) still allows his birth to be sometime before the death of Herod in 4 BC.

That Jesus may have been older than thirty, and perhaps in his forties, has been suggested based on the debate between Jesus and the "Jews" in John 8:52–59. After Jesus responds to the question of whether he is greater than Abraham, he says, "Your ancestor Abraham rejoiced that he would see my day; he saw it and was glad" (v. 56). Then the Jews respond, "You are not yet fifty years old, and have you seen Abraham?" (v. 57). This reference to "not yet fifty years old" is too imprecise to be used in calculating Jesus' exact age. All that can be said from this polemical passage is that Jesus appeared to the Jews on that occasion to be younger than fifty, perhaps in his forties or less. This text is not necessarily contrary to the view that Jesus was ministering in his thirties and possibly middle to late thirties. If he had been born some two or more years before the death of Herod (4 BC), then the passage in John *overlaps* somewhat with the data presented in Matthew and Luke, but from the available data, we simply cannot establish a firm date for Jesus' birth, the start of his ministry, or his death.

John's Gospel, however, is helpful regarding the length of Jesus' ministry and the likely time of his death. According to all the Gospels, the time of Jesus' death is fixed with the Jewish Passover after either the period of one year of ministry (as Matthew, Mark, and Luke suggest by mentioning only one Passover) or after a two-and-a-half- or three-year period, which John suggests based on the number of Passover meals that Jesus celebrated in Jerusalem. If this is so, the beginning of Jesus' ministry would be around AD 26/27 and his death around 29/30. If he began his ministry around thirty years of age, we still have a probable date for Jesus' birth that precedes the traditional dating offered by Ussher's chronology. Meier is no doubt right in concluding that, for a marginal figure of Greco-Roman history, "these figures are remarkably good, and perhaps they are the best we can hope for."[16]

Questions about Jesus' Miraculous Conception

What is the point of the miraculous birth stories in Matthew and Luke? Why do only Luke and Matthew have stories of Jesus' birth, and why are their stories so different? Why is no theology in the rest of the New Testament built on the so-called virgin birth (better referred to as the virginal conception)? Why are there no explicit or even implicit references to Jesus' phenomenal birth mentioned elsewhere in the New Testament, not even in Galatians 4:4–5, Mark 6:3 ("son of Mary"), John 1:13, and John 7:41–42? Do Matthew and Luke say more with the virgin birth story than Mark, John, and Paul do without it? How should Isaiah 7:14 be understood in Matthew 1:23 and in the book of Isaiah? Do the virgin birth stories presume too much about Mary's and Joseph's understanding of Jesus, since in subsequent reports Mary has concern for Jesus' behavior and appears to have a lack of understanding about his mission (Mark 3:21, 31–35)? Is it possible that Mary did not fully grasp the significance of Jesus after all that had happened to her? She seems puzzled in her understanding of his role (Luke 2:19, 50–51). How credible then is this story of Jesus' birth in Matthew and Luke?

The ancients were quite familiar with remarkable births, both in the Old Testament (Samuel) and in the New (John the Baptist), but even in pagan lore (the pharaohs, Alexander the Great, Augustus [Octavian[17]], and even Apollonius

---

16. Meier, *Marginal Jew*, 1:382.

17. See this important reference in Suetonius, *Aug.* 94.4, which says: "When Atia had come in the middle of the night to the solemn service of Apollo, she had her litter set down in the temple and fell asleep, while the rest of the matrons also slept. On a sudden a serpent glided up to her [note: serpents often represented a familiar "spirit"] and shortly went away. When she awoke, she purified herself, as if after the embraces of her husband, and at once there appeared on her body a mark in colours like a serpent, and she could never get rid of it; so that presently she ceased ever to go to the public baths. In the tenth month after that Augustus [Octavius] was born and therefore regarded as the son of Apollo" (LCL).

of Tyana),[18] although these parallels are not precise and have few similarities with the virgin birth stories of Matthew and Luke. In other stories, the focus seems to be that remarkable (great) people had remarkable births. In regard to wicked rulers wanting to kill the hero whose birth had been foretold, Brown mentions several examples, including Gilgamesh, Sargon, Cyrus, Perseus, and Romulus.[19] Does Herod's fear and jealousy over a potential replacement that led to his anger and execution of children under two years of age come from this? Casey concludes that the event did not happen since the population would not have tolerated it and Josephus never reports it, but suggests that the story, may reflect dependence on the Moses story in which Pharaoh determined to kill the children of the Israelites (see Exodus and Josephus, *Ant.* 2.205–6, 215, 235). He also seems to assume that there were a large number of children involved.[20] Bock suggests instead that since Bethlehem was a small community in the first century, it was not a large number of children who were killed and that Herod's willingness to kill his own family members contributes to the likelihood that he performed this activity.[21]

What is the origin of the notion of a virginal conception in Matthew and Luke? In support of the remarkable conception, Matthew appeals to Isaiah 7:14 in the Septuagint (or Greek) version, which refers to a virgin (Greek, *parthenos*) rather than the Hebrew text of Isaiah 7:14, which speaks only of a "young" woman (Heb., *'almah*) and appears to be fulfilled *in that day* by Maher-shalal-hash-baz (Isa. 8:1–3). Luke does not mention that passage, but like Matthew includes the tradition of Jesus' remarkable birth. Where does this story originate? It may have been a logical inference drawn from the early church's affirmation of Jesus as the Son of God, or, perhaps, as Brown has suggested, from a theology of the sinlessness of Jesus. However, as Brown correctly insists, the surviving evidence of that period does not allow one to make assertions about the relationship between the sinlessness of Jesus and the virgin birth.[22] On the other hand,

18. See Philostratus, *Vit. Apoll.* 1.4–6, in which the origins of the first-century itinerant philosopher Apollonius were considered divine; that is, the child bears the image of the divine Proteus, the mother has a remarkable birth, and the child is called a "son of Zeus."

19. Brown, *Birth of the Messiah*, 227n39.

20. Maurice Casey, *Jesus of Nazareth* (New York: T&T Clark, 2010), 148–49. He adds that when human beings were "sufficiently highly thought of," secondary traditions emerged about their birth in Judaism.

21. Bock, *Jesus*, 71n21. He refers to Josephus's comments about Herod's willingness to destroy even his own family members in order to defend his role as king (see *Ant.* 15.218–31, but also 16.151): "When one looks on the punishments and the wrongs which he inflicted upon his subjects and his closest relatives . . . one is forced to regard him as bestial and lacking all feeling of moderation."

22. Brown, *Birth of the Messiah*, 527–28. He also suggests that the whole miraculous conception story in Matthew and Luke may not be historical so much as the evangelists' exercising their

this does not suggest that Jesus was sinful. The author of Hebrews reflects the view of early Christianity, namely that Jesus was tempted in all ways such as we are, yet without sin (Heb. 4:15). Both evangelists in their own individual manner say that Jesus was born without the agency of a human father. Whatever one concludes about the historical basis of the virgin birth, it is clear that at the least the authors were making a christological statement about the person of Jesus—namely, that he is the Christ, or Messiah, of God, who is in a peculiar relationship with God reserved for no other, and in the case of Matthew, he is the rightful heir to the throne of David (but see also a similar comment in Luke 1:33). Again, remarkable births in antiquity were well known, and it was not uncommon to portray the conceptions of remarkable people with remarkable stories. Can this be the background for the virgin birth stories? Christian use of well-known practices in antiquity is not uncommon. The point appears to be that Matthew and Luke wanted to affirm the uniqueness of Jesus from the time of his birth through his life and finally his triumph over death itself.

Comparing Matthew and Luke

In comparing the birth stories of Matthew and Luke, we see that Matthew focuses on royalty—after the birth, Jesus and his parents are in a house, not a stable or cave, and he is presented the special gifts of the Magi[23] from the east (2:11).[24] On the other hand, Luke mentions the placing of Jesus in an animal-feeding trough, a manger, and says that there was no room for the couple in the inn and has nothing to say about the rich gifts presented to him by the Magi. Rather, Luke focuses on the poor shepherds who come to the manger scene to witness the birth of their anticipated messianic figure. According to Matthew,

---

freedom to "use various types of literature to guide God's people" (608n103). See his extended discussion on pp. 165–201.

23. The Greek term here is *magoi* and possibly refers to priests that are engaged in astrology and/or fortune telling. See also Dan. 1:20; 2:2; 4:6–7; 5:7, where the reference is to magicians or diviners of dreams. An interesting volume on the Magi is Brent Landau, *Revelation of the Magi: The Lost Tale of the Wise Men's Journey to Jerusalem* (New York: HarperCollins, 2010). Landau has published an apocryphal manuscript that has more about the Magi written from the Magi's perspective and reflects more about them than any other known source. He includes a helpful introduction and comment about the manuscript.

24. Nothing for certain is known about the Magi, and they are never mentioned again in the New Testament. Traditionally their number has been three, but since Matthew does not mention their number, it appears that tradition has related the number of Magi to the gifts they brought (gold; frankincense, perhaps for medicinal use; and myrrh, an anointing oil). Ancient inscriptions indicate that King Seleucus II Callinicus offered these same gifts to the god Apollo at the temple in Miletus in 243 BC. According to Isaiah, when God gathers his people back in their homeland, nations and kings will come to Zion bringing "gold and frankincense" (Isa. 60:3, 6). Brown, *Birth of the Messiah*, 608–10, suggests that the roots of the story of the Magi are likely in the Balaam narrative in Num. 22–24.

Joseph and Mary evidently lived in Bethlehem, and only after the threat to the life of their newborn child did they first go to Egypt and subsequently consider not returning to Bethlehem, but rather going to Nazareth to protect their child. Luke says nothing about the threat to Jesus' life and indicates that Joseph and Mary originally came from Nazareth and went to Bethlehem only because of the census and then returned to Nazareth after all that was necessary regarding the dedication of the child in the temple had taken place.[25]

Matthew says that an angel appears to Joseph in a dream warning him to take Jesus and Mary to Egypt because of Herod's threat to the child (2:13–14). Luke apparently does not know this story, and simply says that Joseph and Mary *returned* to Nazareth with their child after the time of his circumcision, purification, and presentation to the Lord, and after they offered a sacrifice in the temple (2:21–25). Matthew says nothing about Mary or Joseph living in Nazareth prior to the birth of Jesus, which apparently suggests that Joseph and Mary had been living in Bethlehem. There is no reference in Matthew to Luke's story about the registration (a census for tax purposes) or about there being no room for them in the inn when they came to Bethlehem from Nazareth (Luke 2:1–7) or about the visit from the shepherds or their angelic announcement (Luke 2:8–20), but only the reference to their being in a house when the Magi, following the leading of "his star," come to see the child and present their gifts (Matt. 2:1–12). Also, only in Matthew is Joseph warned in a dream to go to Egypt to save the child from Herod (2:13–15) and after the death of Herod not to return to Bethlehem, but to go to Nazareth to avoid dealing with Herod the Great's son Archelaus. Matthew indicates that only then did Joseph make his home in Nazareth (2:16–23). Nothing of this threat is found in Luke, who says nothing of the massacre of the children in Matthew 2 or the danger from either Herod or Archelaus.

Why are these birth and infancy narratives so different? This question is not easily answered, but it is probable that the construction of each of these accounts was based on a different *theological* agenda. Matthew clearly wants to show the importance of scriptural fulfillment, citing the Isaiah 7:14 passage in regard to Jesus being born of a virgin, Micah 5:2–5 in reference to his being born in Bethlehem, and Hosea 11:1 in regard to his coming out of Egypt. Matthew also has a focus on Jesus as the son of David and his legitimate right to the throne of David (see discussion of the genealogy below), and the gifts fit for a king coming from the Magi. Luke emphasizes Jesus' common heritage

---

25. Casey, *Jesus of Nazareth*, 143–69, has a useful if challenging discussion of the birth narratives and also presents Jesus living as a Jew in the first century AD and what that means. While he rejects the notion of a virgin birth, he usefully clarifies the Jewish and Greco-Roman contexts in which such notions emerge.

with the people in the visit by the lowly shepherds (2:8–20), in his poverty ("no room in the inn," 2:7), in a poor family's sacrifice in the temple (2:24), and in the genealogy, which emphasizes not the Davidic heritage (though David is mentioned in 3:31), but his connection with all of humanity. Meier says that the point of these widely differing stories is that the church, not Mary or Jesus, wished to make the major theological point that "what Jesus Christ was fully revealed to be at the resurrection (Son of David, Son of God by the Power of the Holy Spirit) he really was from his conception onward."[26] The differences are accounted for by the theological purposes each evangelist had, but are those differences incompatible? As we will see, the various attempts to harmonize differences in the Gospels often lead to innovative and often bizarre interpretations. The evangelists clearly made use of a variety of stories to craft their message that Jesus is the Messiah and worthy of our trust, confidence, and obedience.[27]

Because of the considerable differences in these narratives, and because they appear to serve early church apologetics, many if not most critical scholars do not see much historical evidence for the life of Jesus in the birth stories of Matthew and Luke. However, if the criterion of multiple attestation described earlier is taken seriously, in light of the fact that the birth stories of Matthew and Luke appear to represent independent traditions, more historical credibility should be given to those parts of the story of Jesus' birth that are in agreement, especially the time of Jesus' birth and the location. The theological value of the rest of those stories in Matthew and Luke, however, should not be ignored. These stories have an important message that all evangelists advance in their overall story about Jesus. There are basic facts, such as the agreement that Jesus was born in Bethlehem during the reign of Herod the Great (Matt. 2:1; Luke 1:5), who died around 5/4 BC. There are other significant factors involved in this story, such as the angelic visitations, the special circumstances of conception, and the visitors coming to see the child, that attest to his special qualities and divine origin. Such factors should not be ignored since they all contribute to the story the evangelists were trying to present.

The Genealogy of Jesus

Matthew and Luke have the only two genealogies of Jesus in the Gospels, and they are significantly different. There is silence about them in the rest of the New Testament, although in several places the New Testament writers

26. Meier, *Marginal Jew*, 1:213.
27. Brown, *Birth of the Messiah*, 608, makes this point as he tries to sort out the differences in the birth stories.

emphasize that Jesus is from the line of David.[28] This point is made in both genealogies (Matt. 1:1, 6, 17; Luke 2:4; 3:32–33), but Matthew clearly makes more of this connection than does Luke (see David referred to in Matt. 1:1, 6, and 17). Both genealogies emphasize that Jesus was born in a Jewish family. He was a Jew and his unfolding story in all of the Gospels cannot be understood apart from this fact.

Theologians have tried for centuries to harmonize these two genealogies, but always in brittle and unconvincing ways. Both Matthew and Luke offer the genealogy of Joseph and not Mary. The view that each focuses on a different parent, widely held even today, was first proposed in 1490 by Annius, the bishop of Viterbo in central Italy. This view, though obviously intended to account for the clear differences between Matthew and Luke, still fails to deal adequately with the fact that both genealogies focus on Joseph and not Mary. While it is true that Joseph is given priority in Matthew's story of the birth of Jesus and Mary is given priority in Luke's account, both genealogies refer to Joseph as the father of Jesus and neither refers to Mary. Awkwardly, in Matthew the grandfather and father of Joseph are Matthan and Jacob (1:15–16), but in Luke they are listed as Matthat (the same?) and Heli (3:23–24). We will see below how these are often brought together.

The Purposes of the Genealogies

Unlike in modern genealogies, which simply identify everyone known in a family tree, ancient genealogies often are drawn up with a purpose, such as to identify who is the legitimate successor to rulership over a nation or the rightful heir to an inheritance. It is not uncommon for unfavorable individuals to be left out of them! Matthew, for instance, omits mentioning three bad kings in Jesus' genealogy (Ahaziah, Joash, and Amaziah, who should come after Joram). Matthew apparently depends *largely* on the genealogy in 1 Chronicles 1–2 and Ruth 4:18–22 for much of his information on the genealogy of Jesus. Also, we should note that Matthew has forty-two generations covering the same time that Luke does, but Luke has fifty-five or fifty-six generations for that period. Matthew presents three periods of fourteen generations in his genealogy, and each period mentions David. Matthew starts with Abraham and descends to Jesus, but Luke starts with Jesus and goes back to Adam and even to God ("son of God," Luke 3:38).

---

28. Matthew and Luke both state that Jesus descended from the line of David (Matt. 1:1, 6, 17; Luke 2:4; 3:32–33), and this is supported elsewhere in the New Testament, as in Mark 10:47; 12:35–37; Rom. 1:3, and in the creedal formulation of 2 Tim. 2:8, but it is especially clear in Matthew and Luke-Acts (Matt. 9:27; 12:23; 15:22; 20:30; 21:9, 15; 22:42–45; Luke 3:31; 18:38–39; 20:41–44; Acts 2:25–31; 13:22–23).

Although Jesus' line of descent has a theological context in the Gospels, nevertheless, because of the multiple attestation of his Davidic descent in the Gospels and elsewhere in the New Testament, it is not likely that this part was simply invented and inserted into the traditions of the church. His Davidic descent appears to have been well known, and Matthew makes considerable use of it in his genealogy to say that Jesus is the legitimate heir to the throne of David. It is unlikely that the superscription "King of the Jews" over the head of Jesus on the cross is the source for this designation, since the title of king of the Jews was given to many non-Davidic persons from the time of the Hasmoneans, including the Idumeans from whom Herod descended.[29]

However, as one examines the two significantly different genealogies of Jesus listed in Matthew 1:2–17 and Luke 3:23–38, it is clear that there are apparent points of conflict. Some scholars have argued that both Matthew and Luke took over existing lists and modified them to suit their own purposes. Most current scholars, however, have rightly seen in the genealogies an attempt on the part of each evangelist to make a statement about Jesus and his mission.

Before analyzing these genealogies and their importance for each evangelist, we should note that in the ancient world biblical genealogies often had several different forms and characteristics employed for a variety of reasons. They sometimes ran from parent to child (1 Chron. 9:39–44), but they could also begin with the child and go back to the parent (1 Chron. 9:14–16). They are generally characterized by fluidity, in that some names could be deliberately deleted because certain family members had fallen into disgrace or were considered unimportant, or the differences may have reflected changes in social relationships. On occasion, simple error may be the cause for changes in a genealogy (see possibly 1 Chron. 4:39), that is, the writer may have accidently omitted (or included) names by error. However, social structures may also have been at the root of some of the changes (Gen. 36:9–14, 15–19; 1 Chron. 1:35–36). Some changes in genealogies may reflect political and geographical realignments (e.g., Gen. 46:9, 12, 17; and 1 Chron. 7:23). Linear genealogies were also used to legitimize one's rightful authority to rule as king of a people.[30] Again, this is apparently Matthew's intention as seen in his repeated focus on David. This is supported by the visit of the Magi to see Jesus and their presentation of royal gifts to him.

With this in mind, we should not be surprised if the genealogies of Jesus are different from each other and serve different purposes. The fact that Matthew has three evenly divided sections in his genealogy of Jesus, each consisting of

---

29. Meier, *Marginal Jew*, 1:219, 241–42.
30. R. R. Wilson, "Genealogy, Genealogies," *ABD* 2:929–32.

fourteen generations (but note that although in v. 17 he says there are fourteen generations in his third section [1:12–16], there are only thirteen listed), should cause us to ask whether Matthew intended his genealogy to be taken literally or if he rather intended it to serve a different purpose and to initiate his particular message about Jesus throughout his Gospel. On the other hand, is there a reason why Luke has the reverse order in his genealogy, and has so many more generations (seventy-seven to seventy-eight, compared to the forty-one in Matthew)? Also, why does Luke's genealogy come at the end of chapter 3 rather than at the beginning of his Gospel as in the case of Matthew? What is Luke's purpose for introducing this genealogy? We will now look at some of these issues to see how Matthew and Luke made use of their genealogies.

Matthew's Genealogy

Matthew's genealogy serves several important functions in his Gospel that can be seen most clearly by his placing it at the beginning of his Gospel. His intent is to show that Jesus is the legitimate heir to the Davidic throne and that he is the anticipated messiah and king, who many Jews of his day were hoping would liberate them from foreign domination and bring judgment to the nations. This fits with his reference to David, who is mentioned once in verse 1, twice in verse 6, and twice in verse 17. The three major divisions of fourteen generations identify the premonarchical period, the monarchical period, and the time from the exile to Jesus.

Matthew himself appears to be a relatively sophisticated Jewish sage, if not a highly trained Pharisee. He was steeped in the Judaism of his day and was also aware of the various interpretive skills of his fellow Jews.[31] He seems also familiar with the Hellenistic mentality and language of his age, but he could also appeal to both the Hebrew Scripture and its Greek translation, the Septuagint, or LXX. Knowing this about Matthew helps us to understand his use of symbolic language to convey his message about Jesus. For our purposes, this allows us to understand the meaning of what may be a symbolic rather than literal genealogy. Many scholars have looked for explanations for Matthew's highly rigid structure in his genealogy, but what is most likely is that he is using the genealogy to focus on the identity of Jesus as the rightful heir to the throne of David. Notice, for example, in the *gematria*[32] of the passage

31. See D. E. Orton, *The Understanding Scribe: Matthew and the Apocalyptic Ideal* (JSNT-Sup 25; Sheffield: JSOT Press, 1989).

32. Gematria is a method of interpreting the Scriptures by calculating the numerical value of words. It focuses on discovering a hidden meaning within a passage by adding up or studying the numerical value of words and numbers in the text. See, for example, the highly charged number 666 in Rev. 13:18, and elsewhere in that book when the number seven is used.

there is a focus on fourteen. This number likely also is intended to represent the numerical equivalent of David's name. In the Hebrew numerical system, the three consonants of David's name, d-w-d (or, d + v + d), are 4 + 6 + 4, totaling 14. The strong emphasis on David's name (five times), and the fact that his name can account for the presence of the three (consonants in his name) and the fourteen (numerical equivalent of his name), all suggest that this is where the solution to the meaning of Matthew's genealogy is to be found. It is probably also important that David's name is the fourteenth name listed. There is precedence elsewhere for the use of gematria in genealogies. For instance, the genealogy in Genesis 46:8–27 has a strong focus on the number seven. Gad is the seventh in the list and has seven sons, and his name has the numerical equivalent of seven. In the same passage, Rachel had fourteen sons, and Bilhah bore seven sons to Jacob, and the number of Jacob's family who went with him to Egypt was seventy. Although there are other numbers in this list, the number seven or numbers divisible by seven are quite pronounced. That numbers are important to Matthew can be seen in his preference for reporting activities or teachings in sets of three.[33]

Also in Matthew, Jesus' ancestry is traced through the line of kings, though, as noted above, three kings (Ahaziah, Joash, and Amaziah) are omitted after Joram in verse 18, and the actual number of names in verses 12–16 is not fourteen, but thirteen, in spite of the statement in verse 17. This may be due simply to an oversight in Matthew's calculations. Matthew mentions four women in Jesus' genealogy (Tamar, Rahab, Ruth, Bathsheba)—perhaps as a means of selecting women who could in some sense identify with Mary, who is listed as the mother of Jesus at the end of the genealogy (see 1:16, unlike other genealogies that do not mention the mother).

Brown suggests that these four women were chosen not only because there was something irregular, if not scandalous, about their union with their husbands, but also because each of the women played an important part in the plan of God. Consequently, each could be identified as one through whom the Holy Spirit worked, just as Matthew suggests has happened with Mary.[34]

---

33. For example, Matthew records the following threesomes: incidents in Jesus' childhood (chap. 2), incidents prior to Jesus' ministry (chaps. 3–4), temptations of Jesus (4:1–11), interpretations of "do not commit murder" (5:22), illustrations of righteousness (6:1–18), prohibitions (6:19–7:6), injunctions (7:7–27), miracles of power (8:23–9:8), complaints of Jesus' adversaries (9:1–17), responses to the question of fasting (9:14–17), examples of hostilities of the Pharisees (chap. 12), parables of sowing (13:1–32), sayings about "little ones" (chap. 18), parables of prophecy (21:38–22:14), parables of warning (24:32–25:30). A more complete listing of this phenomenon in Matthew is in W. D. Davies and D. C. Allison, *A Critical and Exegetical Commentary on the Gospel according to Matthew* (3 vols.; ICC; Edinburgh: T&T Clark, 1988–97), 1:85–87.

34. Brown, *Birth of the Messiah*, 71–74.

Matthew's genealogy focuses upon Jesus as the Messiah, that is, the Anointed One, or the Christ, and his right to be the heir of David's throne. We should finally note that all of the names after Zerubbabel from Abiud to Jacob are unknown.

Luke's Genealogy

Luke's genealogy (3:23–38) follows the beginning of Jesus' ministry, *after* Jesus has been anointed by the Spirit and identified as God's Son (3:22). There is a possible allusion here to Moses, whose genealogy is not given when he is first introduced in relation to his parents in Exodus 2:1–2, but only later after he had received his call from God in the wilderness (Exod. 6:14–27). In Exodus 2:1–2, not even Moses' parents' names are listed. Whether this identification with Moses was Luke's intention, there are parallels.

Several features of Luke's genealogy merit our further attention. For instance, he begins his genealogy with Jesus and proceeds backward to Adam and ultimately to God (3:38), a possible means of identifying Jesus as the Son of God and the Son of Man. In Hebrew, *adam* is the word for "man," as in "mankind " or "human." Also, since Jesus is acclaimed the "Son of God" in his baptism (3:22), genealogy (3:38), and temptation (4:3), this appears to be his major motif in telling the story of Jesus.

The genealogy in Luke's Gospel may serve the universalistic focus of his Gospel by showing that Jesus is related to the whole of the human race. Perhaps also Luke is emphasizing Jesus' role as Son of Man, a representative suffering servant in the tradition of Isaiah 53:10–12. It is likely that through the means of his genealogy Luke intends to identify Jesus with the whole human race and with God himself.

As noted above, Luke includes seventy-seven generations whereas Matthew only has forty-one. The period from Abraham to Jesus has fifty-six names in Luke, and even here, only half of the names are the same as those in Matthew's list, except for those after the time of the captivity. Many of the names after the exile in Luke's and Matthew's lists are not found anywhere else. There may be a pattern of eleven sevens in Luke's list, but that is not as evident with Luke as the fourteens are in Matthew.

The Early Childhood of Jesus

Not much is known about the childhood of Jesus, apart from the one passage in Luke 2:39–52, which speaks of Jesus' childhood visit to Jerusalem and his engagement with teachers in the temple (2:46). The following information about his early years, however, may be gleaned and inferred from the Gospels.

Social Setting

We can infer from Luke 2:24 that Joseph and Mary's offering in the temple was that of a poor family and that Jesus was probably brought up in relatively poor surroundings. Although the vast majority of the population would have been considered poor, the fact that Jesus had the trade of carpenter or stonemason probably put him at a higher socioeconomic level. Being a carpenter meant that Jesus would have been a member of the artisan class or a tradesman. From what we know of the growth of cities in the Decapolis region in the vicinity of Galilee, especially Sepphoris (today known as Zippori), although this city is not mentioned in the New Testament, people with various skills and subtrades such as Jesus' skills were in high demand. The city of Sepphoris was being rebuilt by Herod Antipas during Jesus' early years, and it may be that he was employed there since Sepphoris is only about four miles north of Nazareth. As a carpenter, Jesus was likely to have been physically strong, since in antiquity a carpenter normally cut his own timber and hauled it to his workshop. Also, the term "carpenter" or "wood-craftsman" (Greek, *tektōn*) was also used of stonemasons, who often cut, carried, and moved huge rocks. Jesus' ability to chase the money changers out of the temple, whether it was a few such persons or all of them, as all four Gospel writers report, is not out of step with a man of considerable strength such as we might expect from a carpenter in the prime of life.

From Mark 6:3, where Jesus is described as the son of Mary, perhaps a way of describing a son whose father had died, we might also infer that he had important responsibilities in his family early on, since he was the oldest male child in his home. It may be that the early death of Joseph resulted in poverty for the family as Jesus was growing up; but this is, of course, merely supposition. Joseph is *largely* unknown in the rest of the New Testament after the birth stories, aside from brief references to him, as in Matthew 13:55, the incident of Jesus' visit to Jerusalem as a child in Luke 2:39–52, his baptism in Luke's genealogy (3:23), and when he began his ministry in Luke 4:22. In Luke 4:22, John 1:45, and John 6:42 we may have a suggestion that Joseph was still alive when Jesus began his ministry, but that is not clear from those texts. Mary's *name* also seldom occurs outside of the infancy narratives (see Mark 6:3; Matt. 13:55; John 19:25; Acts 1:14). Mary was the mother of Jesus, and Joseph was the reputed father, but we cannot be certain that Joseph was still living as Jesus approached adulthood.

What seems likely is his apparent rejection of his family ties and social contacts (Mark 3:21, 31–35; 6:1–6; and especially Luke 14:25–26 and John 7:3–9). Jesus was from a fairly large family that included four brothers and at least two sisters (Mark 6:3). From Mark, it appears that Jesus' family did not follow him or believe in him during the days of his ministry, nor were even concerned about him (especially 3:21, 31–35), although John 2:1–5 may suggest otherwise. That seems to change at his death (John 19:26–27) and after the resurrection, as we see in his mother's participation in the post-Easter community of Jesus' followers (Acts 1:14) and in Jesus' brother James' leadership in the early church (1 Cor. 15:7; Gal. 1:19; 2:9; Acts 15:13).

Jesus' references to common things reveal his familiarity with a poor agrarian community. For example, he uses illustrations of sewing patches on a garment (Mark 2:21), the growth of a farmer's crop (Mark 4:26–29), the growth of the lilies of the field and the grass of the field (Matt. 6:28–30), a farmer with two barns (Luke 12:16–21), the sower who sowed seed (Mark 4:1–9), the price of small birds (Matt. 10:29–31; Luke 12:6–7), and the amount of a common worker's daily wages (Matt. 20:1–2).

Education and Literacy

A typical Jewish boy in Palestine in the first century would have been educated in the synagogue, taken annually to the temple in Jerusalem (if the family had the means), and given religious training in the home. Jesus' attendance at the synagogue and his visits to the temple, as well as his references to the law and its practice, all suggest that he had such training. This training, however, was not the same as that received by trained clergy. Jesus was a layperson in his theological education.

Some scholars, following Crossan, have suggested that Jesus probably could not read or write; that is, he was not literate, and, moreover, any peasant from a peasant town in Galilee in the first century could not read! Crossan concludes, given the high illiteracy rate at the time, that since "Jesus was a peasant from a peasant village," therefore, "Jesus was illiterate until the opposite is proven."[35] Casey challenges Crossan's conclusions and the numbers on which he bases his views, arguing that they are wholly unsustainable. Casey does not have Crossan's low confidence in what the evangelists regularly show about Jesus' literacy. Indeed, Crossan, without sufficient reason, cannot explain how such a person (a Jewish illiterate peasant) could be so familiar with the Jewish Scriptures and attract a following such as we can see in his recruiting disciples and other followers.[36] The Gospels make clear that Jesus was well informed by

35. John Dominic Crossan, *The Birth of Christianity: Discovering What Happened in the Years Immediately after the Execution of Jesus* (San Francisco: HarperSanFrancisco, 1998), 234–35. Crossan bases his argument on inexact numbers of literacy *outside* of Palestine and assumes they are appropriate for the time of Jesus.

36. Casey, *Jesus of Nazareth*, 159–63. See also Craig A. Evans, *Fabricating Jesus: How Modern Scholars Distort the Gospels* (Downers Grove, IL: InterVarsity, 2006), 35–38, who

the Jewish Scriptures and that he could read (Luke 4:16–17), and Casey notes how Jewish boys were educated in the Torah and taught how to read (even in Galilee). He also points out that Jesus' exegesis, or interpretation, of the Jewish Scriptures was advanced for his time (cf. Mark 12:10 quoting Ps. 118:22, and his interpretation of Exod. 3:6 in Mark 12:26–27) and certainly not the work of one who was an illiterate peasant. It is also unlikely that Jesus could challenge or chide religious leaders on their understanding of Scripture with the words "have you not *read*" if he himself could not read (see Mark 2:25; 12:10, 26; Matt. 12:3–5; 19:4; 21:16, 42; 22:31; Luke 6:3, or "is it not *written?*" in Mark 11:17, quoting Isa. 56:7)![37] As we will see later, Jesus was not only well informed in the Scriptures that now compose the Hebrew Bible, but also familiar with several other so-called noncanonical books.

Meier may be right to understand the well-known parable of the Good Samaritan (Luke 10:30–37) with its reference to the priest and the Levite as an "anticlerical joke" shared by Galileans who were distrustful of the clergy of their day.[38] It certainly was not a word from one who had joined their ranks.

The region where Jesus grew up had a large gentile population, and it is likely that he also learned enough Greek for the purpose of doing business with the gentiles of Galilee, as well as possibly even teaching others in Greek occasionally. Even so, his usual language was probably Aramaic, and, because of his synagogue training, he probably also had some knowledge of Hebrew. His contact with gentiles and his ability to communicate with them are well attested in the Gospels. For instance, Jesus almost certainly spoke Greek with the Syrophoenician woman in Mark 7:24–30, and with Pilate in Mark 15:2. In fact, it is probable that we have recorded the actual words of Jesus in Mark 15:2 (and parallels in Matt. 27:11; Luke 23:3; cf. John 18:28–37) in the dialogue between Pilate and Jesus, when he affirms that he is the king of the Jews. It may even be the case that Jesus' words in Matthew 16:13–20, delivered in the region of Caesarea Philippi, a Greek-speaking area, are a record of his actual conversation with his disciples.[39]

---

concludes after his summary of the known facts about Jesus' literacy, "The upshot of all of this is that whatever the literacy rates were in late antiquity, it is more than likely that Jesus himself could read" (p. 38).

37. Casey, *Jesus of Nazareth*, 159–63. Another recent resource that makes this same argument about the literacy of Jesus, as well as literacy in the time and location of Jesus, is Chris Keith, *Jesus' Literacy: Education and the Teacher from Galilee* (Library of New Testament Studies; New York: T&T Clark, 2011).

38. J. P. Meier, "Reflections on Jesus-of-History Research Today," in *Jesus' Jewishness: Exploring the Place of Jesus in Early Judaism* (ed. J. H. Charlesworth; New York: Crossroad, 1991), 89.

39. See S. E. Porter, "Did Jesus Ever Teach in Greek?" *TynBul* 44 (1993): 199–235.

John the Baptist, Jesus, and His Baptism

All four Gospels indicate that Jesus began his ministry during the time of John the Baptist's preaching. Jesus' message was closely tied to that of John, and, like him, Jesus called for true repentance as the preparation for the coming kingdom of God (see Mark 1:4, 15) and for baptism as the sign or seal of the reception of his preaching (see Mark 1:4; John 3:22–27). The popularity of John is attested not only in all four canonical Gospels and the book of Acts, where John's disciples were preaching as far away as Ephesus (Acts 19:1–7), but also in Josephus, whose comments about John merit attention:

> But to some of the Jews the destruction of Herod's army seemed to be divine vengeance, and certainly a just vengeance, for his treatment of John, surnamed the Baptist. For Herod had put him to death, though he was a good man and had exhorted the Jews to lead righteous lives, to practice justice towards their fellows and piety towards God, and so doing to join in baptism. In his view this was a necessary preliminary if baptism was to be acceptable to God. They must not employ it to gain pardon for whatever sins they committed, but as a consecration of the body implying that the soul was already thoroughly cleansed by right behaviour. When others too joined the crowds about him, because they were aroused to the highest degree by his sermons, Herod became alarmed. Eloquence that had so great an effect on mankind might lead to some form of sedition, for it looked as if they would be guided by John in everything that they did. Herod decided therefore that it would be much better to strike first and be rid of him before his work led to an uprising, than to wait for an upheaval, get involved in a difficult situation and see his mistake. Though John, because of Herod's suspicions, was brought in chains to Machaerus, the stronghold that we have previously mentioned, and there put to death, yet the verdict of the Jews was that the destruction visited upon Herod's army was a vindication of John, since God saw fit to inflict such a blow on Herod. (*Ant.* 18.116–19, LCL)

John's Significance in Israel

Much has been made of the dress and diet of John the Baptist (Mark 1:6), his practice of baptism in the Jordan, and the origin of his ministry in the Judean wilderness. Could there be a connection of John with the Essene community at Qumran or a similar community in that area? Is it improbable that such a connection existed, at least *before* the beginning of his ministry? It is interesting that John evidently rejected his priestly heritage (he was the son of Zechariah the priest, according to Luke 1:5, and because of that, he was in line to become a priest). It is even possible that, perhaps as a result of being born to parents who were already getting old (Luke 1:7), John was orphaned as a child and may have grown up in a community like Qumran, if not Qumran itself, that was known for taking in orphans. These are interesting possibilities, but connection with such a community is not mentioned either in the New Testament or in Josephus, and there are clear distinctions in the one-time baptism of repentance that John practiced and the daily ablutions at Qumran.

John was the first recognized prophet in Israel in more than three hundred years, and his influence upon his nation was considerable. His effect upon the region of Galilee is obvious, in that Jesus himself came from Nazareth in Galilee to be baptized by him in the Jordan River (Mark 1:9–11; Matt. 3:13–17; Luke 3:21–22). Later, Jesus' disciples practiced baptism as the sign and seal of the reception of their message about Jesus, just as John had done. There is general agreement among scholars that Jesus identified himself with the preaching of John the Baptist, and was soon thereafter baptized by John in the Jordan shortly before he began his own ministry around AD 27–28. There is little doubt that Jesus was baptized by John, as the Synoptics clearly state (Mark 1:9–11; Matt. 3:13–17; Luke 3:21–22; cf. Acts 10:37–38). John, however, who recounts the same story of the Spirit descending upon Jesus (1:29–34), does not mention Jesus' baptism as the agency of that descending Spirit, or the occasion for the divine approval ("This is my Son, the Beloved"). John does not mention that Jesus was baptized by John the Baptist or anyone else. This appears to be a conscious decision on John's part to deal with an obvious embarrassment for the church—that Jesus the Christ received a baptism *of repentance*. There appears to be no reason why the church would invent such a story or pass it along in their traditions if there was not some basis in reality for it.

The Meaning of Jesus' Baptism

If the tradition is authentic, why was Jesus baptized? If Jesus was sinless, as many early Christians proclaimed (2 Cor. 5:21; Heb. 4:15), why would he have submitted to John's baptism of repentance (Mark 1:4; Matt. 3:2–6, 11; Luke 3:3, 7–8, 10–14)? Meier suggests that it was because Jesus identified with John's message regarding the "imminent disaster that was threatening Israel in the last days of its history, a disaster to be avoided only by national repentance."[40] Jesus also continued several themes of John's preaching throughout his ministry, including God's care for those who are dispossessed and unfortunate (Matt. 25:31–46; cf. Luke 3:7–14; Matt. 3:7–10). To be sure, Jesus had a more "realized eschatology" than did John the Baptist; that is, to some extent the kingdom of God was present in Jesus' ministry, and he had less of a focus on the observance of holy days (Mark 2:18–22; Luke 5:33–39). However, both

---

40. Meier, "Reflections," 89.

John and Jesus emphasized the imminent coming kingdom, concern for the physically impaired (Luke 14:1–6) and the poor (Luke 14:12–14, 21–24), a changed life (repentance) as a prerequisite for entering into that kingdom, and baptism as the sign and seal under which that kingdom is accepted.

Perhaps we should differentiate between what the baptism by John meant to Jesus and what it meant for the evangelists. For them, it is obvious that they connected it with the identity of Jesus as the Son of God ("This is my Son, the Beloved"), the fulfillment of Psalm 2:7 and the servant of the Lord in Isaiah 42:1, cited in the declaration at his baptism (see Mark 1:11; Matt. 3:17; Luke 3:21–22) and also in the Gospel of John at the time that John was baptizing (John 1:34). For the evangelists, the beginning of Jesus' public ministry, initiated at his baptism, indicates that the fulfillment of prophecy is at hand and "the Son of God, the royal Davidic messiah, is anointed with God's spirit to be the final prophet and servant of the Lord sent to a sinful people."[41] Meier contends that both Jesus' and John's acceptance of the practice of baptism shows that they were centering their lives around a new ritual or rite that lacked the sanction of tradition and of the temple authorities. They thereby were calling into question the sufficiency of the temple and synagogue worship as the Jews practiced it at that time.[42]

But did the reception of John's baptism mean more for Jesus than just that? Did Jesus consider himself a *sinner* before God? The mere raising of that question takes us well beyond the available data in our sources and is beyond the scope of the historian to respond. Meier concludes that the texts do "not yield sufficient data to form a judgment in the matter" and reminds us that the acknowledgment of sin in antiquity was not like the experience we often think of today in which one confesses a list of personal sins.[43] It included rather an awareness that one was part of the history of sin because one was part of a sinful people. He finds examples of this in the prayers of confession of Ezra, who identified with his people and confessed their sin as a people to God (see Ezra 9:6–7, 10–11, 15). See also the corporate perspective of sin among the Essenes at Qumran:

> The priests shall recite the just deeds of God in his mighty works, and they shall proclaim all his merciful favours towards Israel. And the Levites shall recite the iniquities of the children of Israel, all their blameworthy offences and their sins during the dominion of Belial. And all those who enter the covenant shall confess after them and they shall say: "We have acted sinfully, we have transgressed,

41. Meier, *Marginal Jew*, 2:106.
42. Ibid., 110.
43. Ibid., 113.

we have sinned, we have committed evil, his judgment upon us and upon our fathers." (1QS 1:21–26 [trans. Martínez and Tigchlaar])

Meier concludes that we cannot know with certainty what was going on in Jesus' mind at his baptism, but we can at least assume that he acknowledged John as an eschatological prophet of God,[44] that Jesus agreed with John on the imminent judgment of God on a sinful Israel, and that he submitted to John's baptism "as a seal of his own resolve to change his life and as a pledge of salvation as part of a purified Israel."[45] Borg understands the meaning of "eschatological prophet" when applied to Jesus as follows: "To say that Jesus was the eschatological prophet is to say that he saw himself as the prophet of the end who proclaimed the end of the world in his own time and the urgency of repentance before it was too late. That was the core of his message and mission."[46] Although Borg, with others, does not believe that this picture was true of the historical Jesus—that is, that Jesus understood himself as an eschatological prophet—it is difficult to argue historically that Jesus was not drawn to the message of John the Baptist, who himself announced the coming of the end times. Jesus identified his ministry with John the Baptist, who proclaimed the near arrival of the end times and called upon the Israelites to prepare themselves for it (Matt. 3:2; Mark 1:2–4; Luke 3:2–9; John 1:19–23, as the quotation from Isa. 40:3 indicates).

The Synoptic Gospels portray the baptism of Jesus as an announcement of his being the Son of God, but there were other messages as well. For Mark, it was God showing his approval of Jesus' mission (cf. Mark 1:11 with Ps. 2:7 and Isa. 42:1). For Matthew, it was understood as necessary for Jesus' consecration to ministry to fulfill the demands of righteousness (Matt. 3:14–15). According to Acts 10:37–38, the baptism was evidently viewed as God's anointing of Jesus with the Spirit as he began his ministry. It may be that Jesus was baptized to identify with the people he came to save (Heb. 2:14–18; 4:15), but this is not clear in the New Testament. Nevertheless, this motif is evident in Luke; hence, after Jesus was born, he was dedicated in the temple, baptized along with the others coming to John, identified with the human race in his genealogy (Luke 3:23–38), and, like all humanity, was tempted but in his case did not sin (Luke 4:1–13).[47]

---

44. Eschatology (Greek, eschatos, "last") has to do with the end times or last things. Generally it refers to the study of the end times of history and the divine judgment of God. An eschatological prophet is one who announces that the end of time or history and God's intervention into human affairs has come or is about to happen.

45. Meier, Marginal Jew, 2:116.

46. M. Borg, Jesus: A New Vision; Spirit, Culture, and the Life of Discipleship (San Francisco: Harper, 1987), 11; cf. 14–16 and 20n25.

47. See also Bock, Jesus, 81–82, 86–88.

Jesus and John's Disciples

Before leaving our discussion of John, it is worth noting that there was a time when John sent his own disciples to Jesus to ask whether he was the Messiah of God or whether John should continue seeking another (Luke 7:18–19). Jesus' response to John's disciples is interesting, especially in the light of the documents from Qumran. Luke 7:21, with its parallel in Matthew 11:2–6, states that "Jesus had just then cured many people of diseases, plagues, and evil spirits, and had given sight to many who were blind." Jesus then tells them of his activity, saying, "Go and tell John what you have seen and heard: the blind receive their sight, the lame walk, the lepers are cleansed, the deaf hear, *the dead are raised*, the poor have good news brought to them. And blessed is anyone who takes no offense at me" (Luke 7:22–23, italics added; cf. Isa. 29:18–19; 35:5–6; 61:1). As we saw earlier in a text from Qumran (4QMessAp, also called 4Q521), there is a similar interpretation of the Isaiah passages from the Essenes. This Dead Sea Scroll text indicates that several Jewish groups of the early first century had similar understandings of what phenomena would accompany the coming of the messiah. The text in question reads:

> [For the heav]ens and the earth will listen *to his Messiah*, [and all] that is in them will not turn away from the holy precepts. Be encouraged, you who are seeking the Lord in his service! . . . Will you not, perhaps, encounter the Lord in it, all those who hope in their heart? For the Lord will observe the devout, and call the just by name, and upon the poor he will place his spirit, and the faithful he will renew with his strength. For he will honour the devout upon the throne of eternal royalty, freeing prisoners, *giving sight to the blind*, straightening out the twisted. Ever shall I cling to those who hope. In his mercy he will jud[ge] for *he will heal the badly wounded and will make the dead live, he will proclaim good news to the meek* [and] give lavishly [to the need]y, lead the exiled and enrich the hungry. [. . .] and all [. . .] (4Q521 2 II, 1–13).[48]

The exchange between Jesus and John's disciples is very important because it is an early reference to Jesus' understanding of his messianic role. This is a so-called Q passage in Luke that is quite similar to the wording in Matthew, and both show that Jesus answered John's disciples in the affirmative indicating that he was the Messiah, as the Qumran messianic text shows. The reference to making the dead live is not found in Isaiah, but is found in Matthew and Luke. Members of the Jesus Seminar have voted against the authenticity of

---

48. F. García Martínez, trans., *The Dead Sea Scrolls Translated: The Qumran Texts in English* (Leiden: Brill, 1994), 394. Square brackets [ ] represent gaps in the manuscript where the translator has supplied the words inside. The italics are added.

this passage,[49] apparently without sufficient cause, except for their prior assumption about what Jesus could or could not have said about himself. They regularly reject anything that identifies Jesus as an apocalyptic figure who sought to establish an apocalyptic kingdom of God. However, not only is this passage well attested in the New Testament, but the notion of a coming eschatological prophet is found at Qumran. There is every reason to believe that this passage came from Jesus himself and that he held an eschatological messianic perspective about the end of the age. That other contemporary first-century Jewish voices also believed the coming messiah would be accompanied by remarkable phenomena confirms this perspective.

The Temptation of Jesus

Matthew and Luke, following Mark and Q, indicate that Jesus was tempted in the wilderness after his baptism, before the beginning of his ministry. The story is not mentioned in John, and the only other references to this temptation story are found in the book of Hebrews (2:18; 4:15), where the author claims that Jesus was tempted so that he could identify with humanity and understand what humans face in their temptations. The purpose of the temptations is not clearly stated in the Synoptics, but several motives may be suggested. In Luke, the temptations appear to be related to the theme of Jesus' identification with humanity: his birth in lowly circumstances, his baptism with the people of Israel, his genealogy connecting him to all of humanity (through Adam) as well as God, and his temptations such as others face. When combined, these stories all present a vivid picture of Jesus' interest in and identification with humanity in all of its frailty and vulnerability. It may also be that in the temptations in Luke (4:1–13) and Matthew (4:1–11), the evangelists viewed the manner in which Jesus faced his temptations as a model for believers to follow. It is instructive that in Luke the Spirit descended upon Jesus at his baptism (3:22) and empowered him during his temptations (4:1) and in his ministry (4:14).

In his opening ministry at the synagogue in Nazareth, Jesus is invited to read from Isaiah 61:1–2 (cf. 58:6), which begins, "The Spirit of the Lord God is upon me" (Luke 4:16–21). Luke may have tried to show the church how to overcome temptation as Jesus did by showing that the ability to overcome is available to all those who rely upon the power of the Spirit when they face trials and who depend upon the sacred Scriptures. This was undoubtedly an important message for the early church, and, indeed, is so for the church of any age.

49. See R. W. Funk et al., *The Five Gospels: The Search for the Authentic Words of Jesus* (New York: Macmillan, 1993), 301–2.

Finally, it is difficult not to see the parallels and contrasts between the temptation of Jesus and the temptations of Israel in the wilderness. The number forty is prominent in both temptations, and the location of these temptations or trials is in the wilderness. Physical hunger was a part of both sets of temptations (Luke 4:3; cf. Num. 11:1–15). The contrasts, of course, are also clear. Jesus was obedient to God, and the Israelites, save Joshua and Caleb, were not (Num. 13:25–38). For the forty days of spying there were forty years of wandering in the wilderness. Jesus' temptations were for forty days in which he was obedient to God and dependent upon God (the Holy Spirit) for strength.

The Early Galilean Ministry

Jesus grew up in the region of Galilee, which, as we have mentioned, had a large gentile population and seems to have been a place where the Jews were strongly nationalistic. The region itself, the most fertile and agriculturally productive land in the nation, yielded many kinds of fruit, and the Sea of Galilee, also called Gennesaret, was well known for its plentiful fish. One of the earliest descriptions of the area near the time of Jesus comes from Josephus:

> Skirting the lake of Gennesar [Galilee], and also bearing that name, lies a region whose natural properties and beauty are very remarkable. There is not a plant which its fertile soil refuses to produce, and its cultivators in fact grow every species; the air is so well-tempered that it suits the most opposite varieties. The walnut, a tree which delights in the most wintry climate, here grows luxuriantly, beside palm-trees, which thrive on heat, and figs and olives, which require a milder atmosphere. One might say that nature had taken pride in thus assembling, by a *tour de force*, the most discordant species in a single spot, and that, by a happy rivalry, each of the seasons wished to claim this region for her own. For not only has the country this surprising merit of producing such diverse fruits, but it also preserves them: for ten months without intermission it supplies those kings of fruits, the grape and the fig; the rest mature on the trees the whole year round. Besides being favoured by its genial air, the country is watered by a highly fertilizing spring, called by the inhabitants Capharnaum [Capernaum]; some have imagined this to be a branch of the Nile, from its producing a fish resembling *corcacin* found in the lake of Alexandria. This region extends along the border of the lake which bears its name for a length of thirty furlongs and inland to a depth of twenty. Such is the nature of this district. (*J.W.* 3.516–21, LCL)

This is the region where Jesus began his ministry following his contacts with John the Baptist. After the arrest of John, Jesus returned to the Galilee region and began his ministry in villages near the Sea (or Lake) of Galilee. The Sea of Galilee, also known as the Sea of Tiberias (John 21:1) or the Lake of Gennesaret (Luke 5:1)—its modern Hebrew name is Yam Kinneret—is thirteen miles long and eight miles wide at its widest point. On its north shore in the first century was the little village of Capernaum, which had a population of some one thousand to fifteen hundred residents, possibly less.

Jesus and Galilean Hearers

It was at Capernaum that Jesus established the headquarters for his ministry in Galilee. On the east side of Galilee, and on the eastern side of the Jordan River to the south, there was the league of gentile cities called the Decapolis, where Jesus made two brief visits during his ministry (Mark 5:1–20; 7:31–37). From there he also went north and west to the region of Tyre and Sidon on the Phoenician seacoast (Mark 7:24–30), but the Gospels do not record that he went into the cities in either area. One might wonder whether Jesus went into the larger cities of the region such as Sepphoris, Tiberias, or Scythopolis, and if he did not, why not. There is no certain evidence that Jesus ever visited these places during his ministry. The only known large community that he visited was Jerusalem. For whatever reasons, he apparently went instead to the small towns, villages, and countryside in Galilee for most of his ministry.

The inhabitants of Galilee included low- to moderate-income farmers or fishermen (Mark 1:16–17), as well as many rootless peasants and itinerant craftsmen who were day workers, that is, paid at the end of the day (Matt. 20:1–16). The Jewish aristocracy of the region lived mostly in Scythopolis, Tiberias, and Sepphoris. Most of the lesser officials in the region—judges, civil administrators, tax collectors, stewards for absentee landlords—came from Jerusalem, and were resented by the residents of Galilee. Jesus' parable of the absentee landlord sending his servants to collect payment from wicked tenants for the use of his land (Mark 12:1–12)[50] is stinging in its indictment, since he told it to members of the Sanhedrin—chief priests, scribes, and elders (see the context in Mark 11:27). It appears that many of the citizens of Galilee were not as well schooled as those in Jerusalem or the big cities, and even ridiculed by other Jews. Notice, for instance, that two of Jesus' disciples were viewed as uneducated (Acts 4:13) when they stood before the Sanhedrin, and the question in John 1:46 as to whether anything good could come out

---

50. Although some members of the Jesus Seminar do not believe this parable comes from Jesus (R. Funk, B. B. Scott, and J. R. Butts, *The Parables of Jesus: Red Letter Edition; A Report of the Jesus Seminar* [Sonoma, CA: Polebridge, 1988], 50–51), it is most likely authentic, and nothing is in it that would not be familiar to a resident of Galilee of the first century, such as one who was raised in Nazareth.

of Nazareth reflected views about the region.[51] Not all who came from the region were uneducated or illiterate, as we have noted earlier, but it appears that this was a common perspective concerning those from the Galilee region.

Sepphoris, the capital of Galilee and the location of Herod Antipas's "ornament of all Galilee" (see Josephus, *Ant.* 18.27), was resented by the majority of the Jews in the region, especially during the rebellion of AD 66–70, when the citizens of that community remained loyal to Rome. In AD 25, Herod Antipas built Tiberias as a new capital city of the region, but Sepphoris continued to serve as a home for the wealthy and educated Jews of the region. Sepphoris, some four miles from Nazareth, was well within the view of its residents, since both cities were elevated on opposite sides of a valley. The finding of a Greek inscription from a Roman-period synagogue at Sepphoris may indicate that there was a Jewish-Christian synagogue there in the late first or second century, since the inscription has the typical Christian Chi-Rho monogram at its end.[52] By the fifth century, there was clearly a strong Christian presence in the city, as evidenced by reference to a bishop from Sepphoris at the Council of Chalcedon in AD 451, but there are also second-century reports of a Jewish Christian named Jacob who talked about Jesus at Sepphoris and gained permission to start a church.[53]

Jesus' Teaching and His Followers

In the region of Galilee, Jesus proclaimed a new order of reality that would come in the near future. He argued that the kingdom of God would reverse the social order and bring equality, liberation, and justice. This was Jesus' message in the synagogue in Nazareth (Luke 4:16–19; cf. also the Magnificat in Luke 1:46–55), and he commented on at least three occasions that the first would be last and the last, first (Matt. 20:16; Mark 10:31; Luke 13:30). It is clear from the Gospels that Jesus led a movement of disciples whom he had personally called to a radical change of lifestyle. He called them to renounce their home (Mark 1:16–20; 10:28–31; Matt. 8:20) or families (Luke 14:26–27), to give up their possessions (Matt. 10:1–10; Mark 10:25), to reject

51. It is interesting, as Crossan has observed, that Josephus gives the names of forty-five towns in the region of Galilee but never mentions Nazareth, and the Talmud refers to sixty-three towns from the region and never mentions Nazareth. See J. D. Crossan, *The Historical Jesus: The Life of a Mediterranean Jewish Peasant* (San Francisco: HarperSanFrancisco, 1991), 15, citing J. Finegan's research. Nazareth was obviously not a very significant village in the first few centuries AD.

52. For a reconstruction of the inscription, see E. Meyers, E. Netzer, and C. Meyers, *Sepphoris* (Winona Lake, IN: Eisenbrauns, 1992), 15.

53. Ibid., 16–17. They also recall the strong tradition supported in patristic literature and still upheld in the Roman Catholic Church that Joakim and Anna, the parents of Mary the mother of Jesus, were residents of Sepphoris.

self-protection (Matt. 5:38–39), and to live a life of self-denial (Mark 8:34–37; Luke 9:23–27; Matt. 16:24–26).

All four Gospels portray Jesus as an itinerant preacher who was essentially homeless and without a source of income. His disciples accompanied him on his journeys in Galilee, and it appears that on occasion women also accompanied him, especially on his journey to Jerusalem. Jesus said to a would-be disciple in Matthew 8:20 that "foxes have holes and birds of the air have nests, but the Son of Man has nowhere to lay his head." All the evangelists agree on this picture, and we find that Jesus frequently ate at the homes of others and was cared for by his followers (Mark 2:15–17; Luke 7:36–50; 11:37–44; 19:1–10), especially by the women (Luke 8:1–3). It may be that the main source of his daily care came from women who became his followers (see also Matt. 27:55–56; Mark 15:40–41).

Jesus' earliest followers essentially became wandering vagabonds who could be asked to endure such hardships of deprivation and trials because the kingdom of God was imminent and the call to men and women to repent and follow Jesus was urgent (Matt. 9:35–38). He asked for a radical decision from all who would follow him (Matt. 8:18–22; Luke 9:57–62). He seemed to reject wealth on the part of his followers, and he is recorded to have said that it would be easier for a camel to go through the eye of a needle than for a rich man to enter the kingdom of God (Mark 10:25).

Those persons who were most likely to hear Jesus' message and to be especially drawn to such a movement were the disenfranchised, who had everything to gain and nothing to lose by such a significant change in the social order. Jesus' call for justice, love of the poor, and the giving of mercy to the least in society (Luke 4:16–21; Matt. 5:3; 25:31–46) would especially have appealed to those who were deprived of justice, love, and mercy. Galilee was an area with many dispossessed and oppressed persons (Matt. 9:35–38). Paul's comments about the makeup of the church in Corinth (1 Cor. 1:26–27) shows that initially the gospel appealed to a similar kind of people outside Palestine, as we saw earlier in the criticisms made by Celsus in the second century (see also below).

However, not all that were attracted to Jesus in Galilee were "down-and-outers." For example, Zebedee had hired laborers (Mark 1:20; those who were able to hire laborers had a certain status in village communities). Also, one of Jesus' disciples was a tax collector, who would have been a person of means as well as educated (Matthew, or Levi). Further south in Jericho, Zacchaeus, a wealthy "chief" tax collector, became a follower of Jesus (Luke 19:1–10). One of Jesus' followers was a Zealot (Simon); one was a rich member of the town council, Joseph of Arimathea (Matt. 27:57; Luke 23:50–51); and even a Roman military officer came to Jesus seeking his help (Luke 7:2–10).

Jesus apparently could move freely among all groups of people, whether educated, powerful, rich, simple, or poor, but still those most likely to listen to him and most open to a radical change were those who were the most vulnerable in society and had nothing to lose in following him—the poor. The large numbers of poor and uneducated members of the church even in the second century prompted Celsus to write: "Let no one educated, no one wise, no one sensible draw near [to the Christians]. For those abilities are thought by us to be evils. But as for anyone ignorant, anyone stupid, anyone uneducated, anyone who is a child, let him come boldly" (Origen, *Cels.* 3.44, LCL).

Evidently some, but not many, educated and prosperous persons joined the Christian community in the early development of the church, which is no doubt behind Paul's comments in 1 Corinthians 1:26–29: "Consider your own call, brothers and sisters: *not many* of you were wise by human standards, not many were powerful, not many were of noble birth. But God chose what is foolish in the world to shame the wise; God chose what is weak in the world to shame the strong; God chose what is low and despised in the world, things that are not, to reduce to nothing things that are, so that no one might boast in the presence of God" (italics addded). We should note, however, that "not many" does not mean "not any," since we see people of means drawn to Paul's message (Acts 16:14; 17:4, 12). Also see how Paul chides those of means who eat before the poor can arrive for the community meal in 1 Corinthians 11:17–22.

Well into the second century, Christians were laughed at and mocked because of their uneducated and uncultured adherents. Only after the mid-second century AD did the church begin to have a respectable number of philosophers and scholars advocating the Christian faith, such as Justin Martyr, Irenaeus, Clement of Alexandria, Origen, and others. One of them, Aristides, originally from Pella in the region of Galilee south of the Sea of Galilee and east of the Jordan, taught in Athens and gave a defense of the Christian message before Hadrian the Roman emperor, and another named Quadratus gave a defense of the Christian faith (see Eusebius, *Hist. eccl.* 4.3.1–3).

A New Community

Considerable discussion has emerged about whether Jesus intended to found a religious community, that is, a new or renewed Israel. In the Gospels it is obvious from the very selection of the Twelve[54] that he had decided to

54. The exact identity of the Twelve is not clear from the accounts in the Gospels. All four Gospels mention Peter (called Simon and, in Paul's writings, Cephas), Andrew his brother, James and John (called the Sons of Thunder, or sons of Zebedee), Philip, Thomas, and Judas Iscariot. Matthew, Mark, Luke, and Acts also mention Bartholomew, Matthew, James the son of Alphaeus, and Simon the Zealot or Cananaean. Matthew and Mark add Thaddaeus. Luke,

establish some kind of community that was faithful to the Lord. The number twelve, the number of the tribes of Israel, would certainly lead some to that conclusion. Even his disciples were convinced that they would have authority in that community and were debating among themselves over who would be greatest in that impending kingdom (Mark 9:33–37). It is not likely that the early followers of Jesus would have invented the notion of the Twelve and later inserted it into the story of Jesus, especially since one of the Twelve, Judas Iscariot, is identified as the one who betrayed him. Meier is no doubt correct when he concludes that this could hardly be an invention of Christian propaganda. He observes the lesson from Qumran that some scholars have ignored, that Jesus' view on the imminent judgment of God and the coming of the eschatological kingdom did not mean that he was uninterested in organization. Qumran, an eschatological community with similar views about the coming kingdom of God, was also a very well-organized community.[55]

The Johannine Contribution

Thanks to John's Gospel, we learn that Jesus ministered frequently in Jerusalem, which helps us to understand why a strong church developed there after his death. Also from John we get a different idea of the length of Jesus' ministry. The Synoptic Gospels mention only one Passover and appear to reduce the ministry of Jesus to a period of about one year. The Passover meal was the occasion for the Last Supper of Jesus with his disciples (Mark 14:12–16; Matt. 26:17–19; Luke 22:7–13), and this is supported by Paul's reference to Jesus as "our paschal lamb" (1 Cor. 5:7). John, however, mentions three or possibly four such occasions during the career of Jesus (2:13; possibly 5:1; 6:4; 11:55; 12:1), and his record may well be more specific in this regard than the synoptic tradition, which follows Mark.

Healings, Exorcisms, and other Miracles[56]

Among the many features of Jesus' ministry are reports about his remarkable activity in healing persons from illnesses and physical ailments such as

---

Acts, and John add Judas the son of James (or in the case of John, "Judas, not Iscariot"), and John adds Nathaniel. This totals fourteen names. Clearly the number twelve was intended, but there is often confusion about who makes up the Twelve, including uncertainty whether Matthew and Levi, both called tax collectors, are the same. See E. P. Sanders, *The Historical Figure of Jesus* (London: Allen Lane / Penguin, 1993), 291.

55. Meier, "Reflections," 1:90–91.

56. Those wanting to do a more detailed study of the miracles of Jesus and others described in the New Testament will be well advised to read the two volumes on this subject by Craig S. Keener, *Miracles: The Credibility of the New Testament Accounts* (Grand Rapids: Baker Academic, 2011).

blindness, as well as engaging in such phenomena as exorcising demons, calming a storm, or walking on the water. One of the purposes or functions of such miraculous activity in Judaism was to authenticate claims of individuals. For instance, when Jesus offered forgiveness to a paralytic man, his authority to do this act was questioned by religious leaders. Jesus therefore healed the man from his infirmity in order to affirm his authority to forgive sins (Mark 2:1–12, especially v. 10; see also Luke 5:17–26, especially v. 24). According to the Gospel of John, the purpose of the many signs of Jesus was to convince observers and readers that Jesus is worthy of one's faith, which leads to life (John 20:30–31).

Known for His Miracles

Unlike John the Baptist, who did not perform miraculous deeds, Jesus was known for them. Some opponents of the early Christians pejoratively accused Jesus of being a magician, as we saw earlier in Celsus's criticisms of Jesus and the Christian movement (see Origen, *Cels.* 1.38; see also 1.9; 3.44, 59, and 64). Celsus accused Jesus of going to Egypt, learning magic, and returning to deceive the people, not unlike what was said about Simon in Samaria by the early Christians (Acts 8:9–11). What such accusations report is the widely acknowledged view that Jesus was involved in remarkable activities such as we see in the Gospels. His miracles were threefold: nature miracles, such as walking on the water, calming a storm, turning water into wine; healing miracles, such as raising Lazarus from the dead (John 11:38–44), healing (cleansing) the leper (Mark 1:40–45), giving sight to the blind (Mark 10:46–52), and many others; and exorcisms, that is, casting out demons from those who had been inhabited by them (Mark 1:21–28; 5:1–20). Again, the intention of Jesus in performing miraculous deeds was to bring people to faith and obedience to the call of God. Three cities where he did the majority of his miracles (Capernaum, Chorazin, and Bethsaida, near the northern part of the Sea of Galilee) were not convinced, and Jesus pronounced a curse on them for their hardness of heart and failure to repent after they had seen his mighty deeds (Matt. 11:20–24; Luke 10:13). The purpose of the miracles was to support and accredit the mission of Jesus (Luke 4:16–21). The anticipated messiah was expected to do such things (Matt. 11:2–6; Luke 7:18–23; see above discussion of the passage and its parallel in the Qumran document 4Q521), and many were convinced by such activities (John 7:31).

There are many other works on this topic, but nothing else compares with the completeness and carefulness of Keener's work. Readers will also still find Gerd Theissen's *Miracle Stories of the Early Christian Tradition: Studies of the New Testament and Its World* (trans. F. McDonagh; Edinburgh: T&T Clark, 1983), a very useful volume to consult on the structure and function of the miracle stories in the New Testament and especially in the story of Jesus.

According to the Gospels, Jesus was frequently involved in casting out demons (exorcisms), as we see in a variety of passages in the Gospels (Mark 1:21–27; 5:1–13; 9:14–29 and parallels).[57] At his temptation, after Jesus was tempted to do the remarkable in order to obtain physical sustenance (bread), and to seek God's rescue after putting him to the test, the devil (or Satan) promised worldly power and provision of wealth if Jesus would bow down and worship him (Matt. 4:1–11; Luke 4:1–13). It is interesting that Jesus did not respond that they were not the devil's to give. It was widely believed that evil had invaded this age and that Satan, as the "god of this age" or "ruler of this world," had power to inflict evil in the world (John 12:31; 14:30; 16:11) and cause humans to turn away from God. Satan's power over the world is assumed in Matthew 12:26 and Luke 11:17–18 (see also 2 Cor. 4:4), but in the exorcisms performed by Jesus, the rule of God overcomes the power or authority of evil in the world. The demons, or evil spirits, had the ability to inhabit individuals; this power was reversed by Jesus, who exorcised the demons from them, though Jesus states that they could once again inhabit a person from whom they had been exorcised (Matt. 12:43–45; Luke 11:24–26). Jesus' authority over the demons and his ability to withstand the temptation of the devil demonstrate that through him the rule of God overcame the power of evil and that God is present in the world through Jesus' activity, both in his miracles and in his ability to overcome evil in the world (Luke 11:20 and Matt. 12:28).[58] The miracles of Jesus functioned as an eschatological sign that the coming kingdom of God had broken into the present. This is further demonstrated in that by dependence upon the Spirit of God and the Scriptures, not only could Jesus overcome temptation and the devil (Luke 4:1–12), but so could those who followed him.

While many maladies were not well understood in antiquity and often were considered a form of demon possession or demonic activity, Jesus' healing activity and the exorcisms that he performed in the power of God could overcome the evil that had befallen individuals and demonstrate that Satan's power in the world could be overcome.

57. A helpful discussion of Jesus' activity in regard to demons and exorcisms is Loren T. Stuckenbruck, "Satan and Demons," in *Jesus among Friends and Enemies: A Historical and Literary Introduction to Jesus in the Gospels* (ed. Chris Keith and Larry W. Hurtado; Grand Rapids: Baker Academic, 2011), 173–97, esp. 183–93.

58. Stuckenbruck makes this point in "Satan and Demons," 183–87. He also supplies references to Jesus exorcising demons or evil spirits as well as to demons or evil spirits entering human beings; see Mark 1:34, 39; 3:15, 22–23; 6:13; 9:18, 28; Matt. 7:22; 8:16, 31; 9:33–34; 10:8; 12:24, 26–28; 17:19; Luke 9:40, 49; 11:14–15, 18–20; 13:32. For references to evil spirits entering human beings, see Mark 3:27; 5:12–13; 9:25; Matt. 12:29; Luke 8:30, 32–33; 22:3. See also Mark 5:13; 7:29–30; Matt. 12:43; Luke 8:2, 33; 11:14, 24. I am depending here on the research of Loren Stuckenbruck, "Satan and Demons," 181–85.

Modern Evaluation of the Miracles

Since the time of the Enlightenment, when David Hume and his contemporaries questioned the authenticity of all miracles, many theologians have tried to anchor their Christian faith in a Jesus of history, that is, in a Jesus without the so-called mythological reports about miracles attributed to him. All such stories about remarkable healings, walking on the water, and the like were summarily dismissed without distinction and removed from what were believed to be authentic stories about Jesus in the Gospels. Rudolf Bultmann, who acknowledged that Jesus was recognized as a miracle worker—that is, that he was known to have performed a number of healings—accepted this aspect of Jesus' activity, but he attributed it not to the supernatural miracle-working power of God, but rather to the often dimly understood realm of religious and psychological phenomena. Jesus' miracles were not viewed as extramundane phenomena (from God), but rather were explained on the basis of common or natural religious and/or psychosomatic experiences.

For more than a century, critical biblical scholars have been willing to acknowledge that the historical Jesus had an ability to do remarkable healings among people. This comes perhaps as a result of a greater awareness of the association of the mind with healing of the physical body, but skepticism remains in regard to the nature miracles such as walking on the water and especially the resurrection of the dead. This recognition of healing miracles and a rejection of the others is quite common today. For example, in a survey of New Testament scholarship on the matter, Craig Evans has applied the traditional criteria for authenticity to the miracles of Jesus and concludes that the older notion of myth can no longer be applied to the Gospel stories. He claims the notion "that miracles played a role in Jesus' ministry is no longer seriously contested," adding that "we are in what I think should be understood as a post-mythological era in life-of-Jesus research."[59] This does not mean, of course, that all historical-critical scholars now affirm all of the miracles of Jesus, nor that the source of his ability to do them came from "a bolt from the blue" (or God), but only that such phenomena actually did occur and that they are to be explained in intramundane, closed causal-nexus categories.[60]

Meier, rather than getting bogged down in a philosophical discussion on the possibility of miracles, argues that it is appropriate simply to recognize

---

59. C. A. Evans, "Life-of-Jesus Research and the Eclipse of Mythology," *TS* 54 (1993): 3–36, here 34 and 36.

60. See Keener, *Miracles*, 1:83–208, for a helpful discussion of antisupernaturalism in the scholarly world.

that faith healers and miracle workers are common phenomena not only in the ancient world, but in the present age as well.[61]

Although parallels to Jesus' miracles are sometimes sought in the examples of Onias (or Honi the Circle-Drawer), who lived in Palestine in the first century BC, and Rabbi Hanina ben Dosa, who lived perhaps before AD 70, these parallels are not that impressive and are not at all similar to the stories about the miracles of Jesus in the Gospels.[62] Others have tried to show parallels with the first-century itinerant philosopher Apollonius of Tyana, but, again, the parallels are not as impressive as the significant contrasts.

I conclude this brief look at the miracles of Jesus and commend again Keener's important and groundbreaking work on this subject noted above, as well as the reasonable conclusion offered by Dale Allison. After discussing the miracles attributed to Jesus in the Gospels, he writes:

> What we can confidently infer about the miracles of Jesus on the basis of modern historical criticism is that he was reputed to be and thought himself to be a successful exorcist, healer, and wonder-worker and that some who knew him believed that they had witnessed truly extraordinary events. It is also reasonable to surmise that the Synoptic stories give us a fair idea of how he went about casting out demons and healing the sick. But we cannot venture much further.[63]

Jesus' Message and His Appeal

Jesus' preaching and teaching brought a message of hope for the hopeless, and a warning to those who were comfortable with their securities in this world (Luke 12:16–21). He called for the abandonment of worldly securities and obedience to the call of God (Mark 8:34–37), and spoke of alertness and preparation for the coming kingdom of God and day of judgment that would test every person's preparation and vigilance (Mark 13:32–37; Matt. 24:36–51). He warned that all people would be judged on how they treated the hungry, thirsty, poor, naked, sick, and imprisoned (Matt. 25:31–46).

61. Meier, "Reflections," 1:93.
62. For discussion of these individuals and of miracles in the story of Jesus, see Meier, *Marginal Jew*, 2:581–88; also the miracles of Jesus and his understanding of miracles in general, 2:509–1038. Cf. G. Theissen, *Miracle Stories of the Early Christian Tradition* (trans. F. McDonagh; Edinburgh: T&T Clark, 1983), who offers a valuable historical and sociological context for interpreting the significance of the miracle stories. Keener also discusses these individuals and shows the differences in those activities and the miracles of Jesus and also the function of Jesus' miracles in *Miracles*, 1:61–65.
63. Dale C. Allison, *The Historical Christ and the Theological Jesus* (Grand Rapids: Eerdmans, 2009), 77.

The Kingdom

For Jesus, the kingdom was yet to come, but in some sense it was already present in his ministry. While many scholars interpret Jesus as an eschatological prophet focused on the future and imminent coming of God to establish his kingdom on the earth, the present aspects of the kingdom that were emphasized in the ministry of Jesus should not be ignored. Indeed, several scholars have interpreted Jewish apocalyptic in terms of the present and the future.[64] This certainly seems true in the case of Jesus. As noted above, this was seen in his authority over demons and miraculous activity.[65] This is also implied in Jesus' response to John the Baptist's question issued through his disciples, "Are you the one who is to come, or are we to wait for another?" (Luke 7:19), when he replied that the blind see, the lame walk, and the dead are raised—in other words, the answer could be seen in his miraculous activity, which was understood as a feature of the coming messiah and was now occurring in the present. Schuyler Brown rightly concludes that Jesus believed that in his mission of preaching, exorcisms, and healing, the kingdom of God was not only at hand, that is, soon to happen, but also present to some extent (see Matt. 12:28; Luke 17:21).[66] In the ministry of Jesus, the "not yet" of the kingdom of God was already present, *although not completely*. For Jesus the coming kingdom was still forthcoming (e.g., Mark 13; Matt. 6:10; 24:3–14; John 5:25–28). Although many scholars choose either the imminent apocalyptic understanding of the kingdom of God (it is near, but not yet here) in the teaching of Jesus, *or* the so-called realized eschatology, in which the kingdom is fulfilled in his ministry, it is more probable that both were always in view. The future has broken into the present in Jesus, but its fullness is yet future—again, the "already, but not yet."

The Law

In regard to the law, Jesus was not as strict in its observance as were those at Qumran or those in the strict Pharisaic tradition. He did not allow the keeping of the law to take priority over human need, whether in healing on the Sabbath or gathering food on the Sabbath. He associated freely with those whom "the righteous" considered unclean and of low esteem (Mark 2:15–17), was not concerned with keeping the traditional fasting days (Mark 2:18–22), and even felt free to violate traditions about working or healing on the Sabbath (Mark

64. John J. Collins, *The Apocalyptic Imagination* (2nd ed.; Grand Rapids: Eerdmans, 1998), 4–9; and his *Apocalypticism in the Dead Sea Scrolls* (New York: Routledge, 1997).

65. See Stuckenbruck, "Satan and Demons," 183.

66. S. Brown, *The Origins of Christianity: A Historical Introduction to the New Testament* (OBS; Oxford: Oxford University Press, 1984), 57.

2:23–27; 3:1–6). It was regarding the violation of traditional views about the Sabbath that the Pharisees took offense, and they began to look for ways to destroy him (Mark 3:6). On the other hand, it was Jesus' motivation to keep what the Scriptures said about the purity of the temple that caused him to overturn the money changers' tables there, a story found in all four Gospels (Mark 11:15–18; Matt. 21:12–13; Luke 19:45–48; John 2:13–17).

Jesus appears to announce a new morality, a new standard by which people are to be evaluated and judged by God. This is seen in his "you have heard it said" messages in Matthew's Sermon on the Mount (see especially 5:21–48), in which he intensifies the meaning and application of the law to levels not heard of before. Although there is considerable opposition to the idea that Jesus actually said these words, in part because they fit with Matthew's apologetic in showing Jesus was more faithful in keeping the law than were the Pharisees, still each of these "you have heard it said, but I say unto you" references fits the picture of Jesus that is portrayed in the Gospels. He did not abandon the law, but interpreted its higher sense primarily in caring for human need as more important than religious ritual. This is clear in his teaching of the greatest commandments—namely, loving God and one's neighbor—which has parallels to the teachings of Hillel before him (see also Mark 12:28–34; Luke 10:25–28; Matt. 22:37–40). Luke supplies a further parable that illustrates this very point, and isolates Jesus' understanding of the meaning of the law from that of the religious people of his day. On one occasion (Luke 10:25–37), Jesus stated that the end of the law was to love God and one's neighbor. On being challenged by a scribe of the law on who his neighbor was, Jesus told him not only who his neighbor was—anybody in need—but also how to be a neighbor—to care for the human in need, even one's enemies. In the parable of the Good Samaritan he contrasted the actions of a traditional enemy, the Samaritan, with those of traditional religious people, namely, the priest and the Levite.

The Temple

The long-standing Jewish view of the temple was that it was a house of prayer and worship. It was also a place where the gentiles could go and worship in the larger courtyard; but, in the time of Jesus, this part of the temple was a noisy place with animals and money changers. When Jesus saw the money changers in the outer courtyard of the temple and the noise that such an activity caused, he was apparently so incensed that he upset the tables of the money changers and drove them out of the temple (Mark 11:15–19; Matt. 21:12–16; Luke 19:45–48; John 2:13–22). The multiple attestation of this event strongly witnesses to its authenticity, even though we are not certain how

215

many were involved in the incident. Jesus' verbal response to the situation includes references to (or alludes to) Isaiah, who said that the temple was to be a place of prayer (Isa. 56:7), and focused on the place of the gentiles in such worship (Isa. 56:6–8). Also mentioned in the telling of this story are references to Jeremiah 7:2–14 (v. 11 in particular) and 26:8, which focus on holiness in God's house and persecution of the prophets. John, who places this event in the beginning of Jesus' ministry (2:13–22), appeals to Psalm 69:9 for justification of Jesus' actions. It may be that what stands behind this passage is an understanding of Zechariah 14:21, which focuses on holiness and the absence of a trader in the house of the Lord (which Jesus may have taken to be the same as money changers). The significance of this event is that it was one of Jesus' primary activities during his last week of ministry in Jerusalem that led to his arrest and was mentioned at his trial (Mark 11:15–19; 14:57–58; Luke 19:45–48; John 2:19).[67] It also shows Jesus' concern for true worship, and possibly even a concern for the gentiles, who had no other place to go. At the heart of Jesus' teaching and preaching was the message of the kingdom of God, and how one should prepare for its coming. Jesus, in some sense, saw the kingdom of God and God himself present in his own ministry and person. As we will see below, this was also a factor that led to his arrest and crucifixion. His message of warning was also tempered by a new commandment to love one's neighbor (Luke 10:25–37; Matt. 5:43–48; 22:36–40; John 13:31–35) and also to forgive those who offend or sin against us (Matt. 6:12; 18:21–35; Luke 17:3–4).

The Scriptures of Jesus

Considerable discussion has taken place among biblical scholars about the scope of the Scriptures that Jesus recognized. While a complete discussion of that cannot be undertaken here, we can say that the formation of the Bible, both Old and New Testaments, was still a future development for the early Christian church at the time when Jesus was ministering. The older view, that Jesus gave to his disciples a closed collection of sacred Scriptures that looks much like the current Hebrew Bible or the Protestant Old Testament, while appealing to many, cannot be reasonably established. We can say with assurance that many of the books that we now recognize as part of the Old Testament were certainly highly prized among various sects of Judaism in the time of Jesus, but there is no evidence that such a collection was *closed*

67. Other events included Jesus' willingness to violate Sabbath laws, his triumphal entry (which demonstrated his awareness of his role as Messiah), and his negative comments about the temple, all of which were factors that led to Jesus' crucifixion. See discussion in the next chapter.

in the time of Jesus. I have discussed this topic at length elsewhere,[68] but I can summarize here Jesus' familiarity with and use of many sacred or religious books that he cited in his teaching, including books that were not eventually included in the Protestant Old Testament or even in most Christian Bibles (Catholic or Orthodox). The books that Jesus cited the most were Deuteronomy, Isaiah, and the Psalms, but he also cited about two thirds of the books in the Old Testament. There are also several parallels in his teaching to some books that are now called apocryphal and even pseudepigraphal books. As we will see presently, these parallels in language and ideas suggest Jesus' knowledge of them or the oral traditions stemming from them in his generation.

Jesus and the Old Testament Canon

The full parameters of the Old Testament had not yet been decided during the time of Jesus, even though there is little doubt that the Pentateuch and most of the books that we identify as the Prophets had long been recognized as Scripture in Jesus' time. However, there is more variety in his citations than what we find in the later church fathers. We should note that the sacred texts that Jesus cites the most are similar to those most frequently cited by the Essenes at Qumran, as well as by the New Testament writers and the early church fathers.

So, what Scripture texts did Jesus cite? In the Synoptic Gospels, he appealed mostly to those texts that are now in the Hebrew Bible or the Protestant Old Testament. While he cited Isaiah, Psalms, Deuteronomy, and Exodus more frequently than the other Hebrew Bible books, he also showed considerable familiarity with other Jewish Scriptures, including those that we now call canonical, as well as some that scholars frequently call noncanonical (or apocryphal and pseudepigraphal) writings. The Synoptic Gospels indicate that Jesus frequently cited or alluded to four of the pentateuchal books, but he only referred to Numbers one time (Matt. 12:5; see Num. 28:9–10). In John, Jesus also cited the Psalms, Isaiah, Deuteronomy, and Exodus most frequently, but other Hebrew Bible books to a lesser extent (see listings below). According to John, Jesus cited all five Torah books but especially Deuteronomy. According to all of the evangelists, Jesus was also quite familiar with the Prophets, and especially Isaiah. Likewise in all four Gospels, Jesus cited the book of Psalms frequently, as we see in his reference to Psalm 22:1, and probably all of that

---

68. Lee Martin McDonald, *The Biblical Canon: Its Origin, Transmission, and Authority* (Grand Rapids: Baker Academic, 2011), 73–223; also in *Forgotten Scriptures: The Selection and Rejection of Early Religious Writings* (Louisville: Westminster John Knox, 2009), 35–150; and in *The Origin of the Bible: A Guide for the Perplexed* (New York: T&T Clark, 2011), 52–120.

Psalm (see Mark 15:34),[69] as well as in the reference to Psalm 69:4–9 cited in reference to Jesus' cleansing of the temple court in John 2:17.

While he referred to Daniel and Zechariah on several occasions, he did not cite all of the books in the Prophets or many other Old Testament books; namely, Joshua, Judges, Ruth, 2 Samuel, 1 Chronicles, Ezra, Nehemiah, Esther, Job, Ecclesiastes, Song of Songs, Lamentations, Obadiah, Nahum, Habakkuk, or Haggai. Nothing in the Gospels suggests that Jesus was either aware of them *or that he rejected them*; they are simply not mentioned, alluded to, or cited in the Gospels. On the other hand, there is nothing in the canonical Gospels or in early Christianity that suggests that Jesus restricted his understanding of Scripture to any collection that eventually became fixed in early Judaism and subsequently in early Christianity.

The question here is not so much whether Jesus or his earliest followers, or even the various Jewish sects of the first century AD, recognized the books in the current Hebrew Bible canon as sacred literature, but rather whether they cited or utilized *all* of the books in the current Hebrew Bible in the first century AD. More specifically, did Jesus accept as Scripture fewer or more than the books that are now in the Hebrew Bible or Protestant Old Testament? Interestingly, there are indications that some later rabbinic Jews were still questioning the sacredness of several Hebrew Bible books more than two centuries after the time of Jesus. For example, some rabbis excluded from public reading the following books: Song of Songs (*m. Yad.* 3.5; *b. Meg.* 7a); Ecclesiastes (*m. Yad.* 3.5; *b. Šabb.* 100a; see also Jerome on Eccles. 12:14); Ruth (*b. Meg.* 7a); Esther (*b. Sanh.* 100a; *b. Meg.* 7a); Proverbs (*b. Šabb.* 30b); and Ezekiel (*b. Šabb.* 13b; *b. Ḥag.* 13a; *b. Menaḥ.* 45a). On the other hand, some rabbis accepted Sirach as Scripture (*b. Ḥag.* 13a; *y. Ḥag.* 77c; *b. Yebam.* 63b; *Gen. Rab.* 8.2b; *b. B. Qam.* 92b).[70]

Jesus and Diverse Texts

While it is clear that Jesus supported his proclamation and mission with a variety of Hebrew Bible Scriptures, he was also informed by other religious literature. While the Law—especially Deuteronomy—the Psalms, and Isaiah formed the core of the sacred texts that Jesus cited, he also made frequent

---

69. There is little room for doubt that Jesus made use of this psalm at his crucifixion. It is not the kind of text the early church would have placed in the mouth of Jesus without some historical basis, since it appears to report Jesus' loss of faith. For an old but still interesting interpretation of the meaning of the passage, however, see Martin Dibelius, *From Tradition to Gospel* (Cambridge: James Clarke, 1982), 193–94, who claims that the reference to the first verse of this psalm was in fact a reference to the whole of it.

70. Alan Segal, *Sefer Ben-Sirah ha-Shalem* (Jerusalem: Bialik, 1953), cites eighty-five citations of Sirach in rabbinic literature through the tenth century AD.

use of Jeremiah, Ezekiel, and Daniel, and it is clear that he also knew and made use of several other writings that are now identified as noncanonical books. These allusions, citations, and verbal parallels let us know that Jesus was informed and influenced to some extent by that literature. While some of the following examples may simply reflect common religious and theological motifs circulating in Palestine in the time of Jesus and later, the multiplicity of the parallels at times also suggests direct knowledge and dependence.

It appears that in Matthew, Jesus made use of the language of Wisdom of Solomon. For example, in Wisdom 2:13 we read: "He professes to have knowledge of God, and calls himself a child of the Lord." There is some coincidence of language in Matthew 27:43, where we read: "He trusts in God; let God deliver him now, if he wants to; for he said, 'I am God's Son'" (see also parallels in thought in Wis. 2:18–20). Likewise, in Wisdom 3:7, the words, "*In the time of their visitation* they will shine forth, and will run like sparks through the stubble," have some parallel with the words in Luke 19:44, where Jesus says: "because you did not recognize *the time of your visitation from God.*" In both Wisdom 5:22 ("The water of the sea will rage against them, and rivers will relentlessly overwhelm them") and Luke 21:25 ("distress among nations confused by the roaring of the sea and waves"), the judgment of God comes upon the disobedient through raging waters.[71]

There are also a number of parallels between the *Book of Parables* in *1 Enoch* (chaps. 37–71, ca. 50–40 BC) and the teaching of Jesus in the canonical Gospels, especially in regard to references to the apocalyptic Son of Man. These are listed at the end of this chapter. What makes it unlikely that the *Book of Parables* in *1 Enoch* is a Christian document, as some have argued, is that it concludes by identifying Enoch, and not Jesus, as the Son of Man (71:5–17). Given the fact that the title "Son of Man" was one of Jesus' most frequent self-designations, it is unlikely that any Christian group would have created this book and given that title to another hero.[72] It is worth noting that those who deposited the scrolls at Qumran also had a high regard for the Enoch tradition. The recent interest in the books that make up the Enochic

---

71. See my forthcoming paper, "The Scriptures of Jesus" in James H. Charlesworth and Petr Pokorný (Grand Rapids: Eerdmans, 2013), and also a paper prepared for a forthcoming volume edited by Darrell L. Bock and James H. Charlesworth, *Parables of Enoch: A Paradigm Shift* (London; New York: T&T Clark, 2013). In both papers I have listed twenty-three of the most significant parallels between Jesus' teaching and noncanonical writings, along with a much longer list of parallels. I will list only a few of the more significant ones here.

72. See J. H. Charlesworth, "The Books of Enoch or 1 Enoch Matters: New Paradigms for Understanding Pre-70 Judaism," in *Enoch and Qumran Origins: New Light on a Forgotten Connection* (ed. Gabrielle Boccaccini; Grand Rapids: Eerdmans, 2005), 436–54.

collection, probably written over the period between the late fourth century BC and the first century BC or early first century AD, has resulted in a number of critical works examining the influence of these texts in early Christianity.[73] There are also several significant word parallels between the pseudepigraphal *Joseph and Aseneth* and the canonical Gospels, especially in Matthew.[74] It is difficult to date this book before the beginning of the Christian era, but is unlikely that Christians wrote it since Christian theological issues are not obvious in the document, even though New Testament writers drew freely from it in several passages.[75]

Back to the Tanakh

It is sometimes argued that since Jesus cited books from each of the three-fold collections of the Hebrew Bible—namely, the Law (*Torah*), Prophets (*Nebiim*), and Writings (*Ketubim*); altogether, the *Tanakh*—he must have acknowledged all three parts of the Hebrew Bible and that they were complete and fixed in the time of Jesus.[76] The earliest and *only* New Testament reference

73. For a helpful discussion of the Enoch tradition at Qumran and the current status of the research on this subject, see the introduction and later summary of this discussion by Gabriele Boccaccini (1–14 and 417–25) and the summary chapter by James H. Charlesworth (436–54) in Gabriele Boccaccini, ed., *Enoch and Qumran Origins*. See also James VanderKam, "1 Enoch, Enochic Motifs, and Enoch in Early Christian Literature," in *The Jewish Apocalyptic Heritage in Early Christianity* (ed. James C. VanderKam and William Adler; CRINT; Minneapolis: Fortress, 1996), 33–101. See also James C. VanderKam, *From Revelation to Canon: Studies in the Hebrew Bible and Second Temple Literature* (Boston/Leiden: Brill, 2002), 19–27, for several examples of the influence of the Enoch tradition both at Qumran and in early Christianity.

74. There are some twenty-four parallels in Matthew (e.g., 1:18–21, cf. *Jos. Asen* 21:1; 5:13, cf. *Jos. Asen* 11:4; 5:43–48, cf. *Jos. Asen* 29:5; 6:19–21, cf. *Jos. Asen* 12:15; 6:23, cf. *Jos. Asen* 6:6); twenty-three in Mark (e.g., 1:10, cf. *Jos. Asen* 14:2; 1:17, cf. *Jos. Asen* 21:21; 6:3, cf. *Jos. Asen* 4:10; 10:21, cf. *Jos. Asen* 10:11); fifty-four in Luke (e.g., 1:5, cf. *Jos. Asen* 1:1; 1:48, cf. *Jos. Asen* 11:12; 2:52, cf. *Jos. Asen* 4:7; 7:44, cf. *Jos. Asen* 7:1; 11:7, cf. *Jos. Asen* 10:2; 15:18, cf. *Jos. Asen* 7:4); and twenty-eight in John (e.g., 1:4, cf. *Jos. Asen* 12:2; 1:10, cf. *Jos. Asen* 12:2; 1:27, cf. *Jos. Asen* 12:5; 3:5, cf. *Jos. Asen* 8:9; 13:23, cf. *Jos. Asen* 10:4; 20:22, cf. *Jos. Asen* 19:11; 20:28, cf. *Jos. Asen* 22:3). See Steve Delamarter, *A Scripture Index to Charlesworth's "The Old Testament Pseudepigrapha"* (Sheffield: Sheffield Academic Press, 2002), 90–93, for the additional texts. He lists even more parallels throughout the rest of the New Testament.

75. For a discussion of the date of this document, see Ross Shepherd Kraemer, *When Aseneth Met Joseph: A Late Antique Tale of the Biblical Patriarch and His Egyptian Wife, Reconsidered* (Oxford: Oxford University Press, 1998), 5 and 225–28, who challenges the consensus on the date for *Aseneth*, namely, 100 BC–AD 135, saying there is no support for it and it is based on assumptions rather than fact. On the other hand, Gideon Bohak has reviewed Kraemer's book in the *Review of Biblical Literature* [http://www.bookreviews.org] (2000) and concludes that Kraemer's arguments have not overturned the consensus. Bohak's book, *"Joseph and Aseneth" and the Jewish Temple in Heliopolis* (Society of Biblical Literature: Early Judaism and Its Literature 10; Atlanta: Scholars Press, 1996), presents the consensus position.

76. E. E. Ellis argues this in his *The Old Testament in Early Christianity: Canon and Interpretation in the Light of Modern Research* (Grand Rapids: Baker, 1991), 37–46 and 125–30;

to three collections of Jewish Scriptures is in Luke 24:44, when Jesus speaks of the "law of Moses, the prophets, and the psalms," but "psalms" is not the same as the third category of the Hebrew Bible. Although Beckwith argues that this refers to the later, well-defined Law, Prophets, and Writings,[77] there is nothing in the text to suggest that the reference to "psalms" is anything more than a reference to psalms that were in circulation in the time of Jesus. Which psalms Jesus has in mind is not clear to us today. Similarly, there is nothing in the New Testament or first-century Jewish literature that clearly identifies the books that make up the Prophets. Scholarly attempts to identify "psalms" as the complete collection of all of the books that are later called Writings (*Ketubim* or *Hagiographa*) in *b. Baba Batra* 14b or in later rabbinic traditions are only speculation. It is not uncommon in New Testament and early church literature to find Hebrew Bible books called "prophets" in the time of Jesus that were later placed in the Writings identified in Jewish literature, as we will show presently. The notion that "psalms" in Luke 24:44 is a clear reference to the third division of the Hebrew Bible is both anachronistic and flawed.[78] Luke 24:44 is best seen as a parallel to 24:47.

There are no *clear* references to the later three-part Hebrew Bible that now exists either in the New Testament or elsewhere before the middle to end of the second century AD. The limited twenty-four sacred books of the Hebrew Bible are identified for the first time only in a Babylonian *baraita*,[79] namely, *b. Baba Batra* 14b, where for the first known time they are grouped into the three distinct sections identified as *Torah* (Law), *Nebiim* (Law), and *Ketubim* (Writings, also *Hagiographa*, that is, "sacred writings"). There is no evidence that a majority of Jewish rabbis agreed on these matters until centuries later.

Particular Passages

The following list of parallels between Jesus' teaching and both biblical and nonbiblical books clearly suggests that the later notions of a fixed biblical canon did not exist in the time of Jesus and that he did not hand on to his disciples a fixed list of sacred books.

---

see also Roger Beckwith, *The Old Testament Canon of the New Testament Church*, 111–15 and 221–22.

77. Beckwith, *Old Testament Canon*, 111–15. For a related topic, see also his discussion of "fifths" in ibid., 438–47.

78. See Lee Martin McDonald, *The Biblical Canon: Its Origin, Transmission, and Authority* (Peabody, MA: Hendrickson, 2006), 103–13.

79. A baraita (Hebrew = "external"; pl. *baraitot.*) is a rabbinic tradition (writing) not included in the Mishnah by R. Judah ha-Nasi (*Nasi* = "the Prince," "chief," or "president") ca. AD 200–220. It is unclear the extent to which this material was widely known or acknowledged as authoritative in the second century AD or before.

A. Jesus' Citations of Biblical Books in the Synoptic Gospels

Gen. 1:27 (Mark 10:6/Matt. 19:4); 2:24 (Mark 10:7–8/Matt. 19:5); 4:1–16 (Matt. 23:35/Luke 11:51); 4:24 (Matt. 18:22); 6–7 (Matt. 24:37–39/Luke 17:26–27); 19 (Matt. 10:15/11:23–24/Luke 10:12); **Exod.** 3:6 (Mark 12:26/Matt. 22:32/Luke 20:37); 20:7 (Matt. 5:33); 20:7 (Matt. 5:33); 20:12 (Mark 7:10/Matt. 15:4); 20:12–16 (Mark 10:19/Matt. 19:18–19/Luke 18:20); 20:13 (Matt. 5:21); 20:14 (Matt. 5:27); 21:12 (Matt. 5:21); 21:17 (Mark 7:10/Matt. 15:4); 21:24 (Matt. 5:38); 23:20 (Mark 1:2/Matt. 11:10/Luke 7:27); 24:8 (Mark 14:24; Matt. 26:28); 29:37 (Matt. 23:17, 19); 30:29 (Matt. 23:17, 19); **Lev.** 13–14 (Luke 17:14); 14:2–32 (Mark 1:44/Matt. 8:4/Luke 5:14); 19:2 (Matt. 5:48/Luke 6:36); 19:12 (Matt. 5:33); 19:18 (Mark 12:31/Matt. 5:43; 19:18; 22:39/Luke 10:27); 24:9 (Mark 2:25–26/Matt. 12:3–4/Luke 6:3–4); 24:17 (Matt. 5:21); 24:20 (Matt. 5:38); **Num.** 28:9–10 (Matt. 12:5); **Deut.** 5:16–20 (Mark 10:19/Matt. 19:18–19/Luke 18:20); 5:17 (Matt. 5:21); 5:18 (Matt. 5:21); 6:4–5 (Mark 12:29–30/Matt. 22:37/Luke 10:27); 6:13 (Matt. 4:10/Luke 4:8); 6:16 (Matt. 4:7/Luke 4:12); 8:3 (Matt. 4:4/Luke 4:4); 13:2 (Matt. 24:24); 19:15 (Matt. 18:16); 23:22 (Matt. 5:33); 24:1 (Mark 10:5/Matt. 5:31; 19:8); 30:4 (Matt. 24:31); **1 Sam.** 21:2–7 (Mark 2:25–26/Matt. 12:4/Luke 6:3–4); **1 Kings** 10:4–7 (Matt. 6:29/Luke 12:27); 10:13 (Matt. 12:42/Luke 11:31); 17:1–24 (Luke 4:25–26); **2 Kings** 5 (Luke 4:27); **2 Chron.** 24:20–22 (Matt. 23:35/Luke 11:51); **Pss.** 6:9 (Matt. 7:23/Luke 13:27); 8:3 (Matt. 21:16); 22:2 (Mark 15:34/Matt. 27:46); 24:4 (Matt. 5:8); 31:6 (Luke 23:46); 37:11 (Matt. 5:5); 48:3 (Matt. 5:35); 50:14 (Matt. 5:33); 110:1 (Mark 12:36; 14:62/Matt. 22:44; 26:64/Luke 20:42–43; 22:69); 118:22–23 (Mark 12:10–11/Matt. 21:42/Luke 20:17); 118:26 (Matt. 23:39/Luke 13:35); **Isa.** 5:1–2 (Mark 12:1/Matt. 21:33/Luke 20:9); 6:9–10 (Mark 4:12/Matt. 12:4; 13:14–15/Luke 6:4); 8:14–15 (Matt. 21:44/Luke 20:18); 13:10 (Mark 13:24–25/Matt. 24:39/Luke 21:25–26); 14:13, 15 (Matt. 11:23/Luke 10:15); 23 (Matt. 11:21–22/Luke 10:13–14); 29:13 (Mark 7:6–7/Matt. 15:8–9); 32:15 (Luke 24:49); 34:4 (Mark 13:24–25/Matt. 24:29/Luke 21:25–26); 35:5–6 (Matt. 11:5/Luke 7:27); 53:10–12 (Mark 10:45/Matt. 20:28); 53:12 (Luke 22:37); 56:7 (Mark 11:17/Matt. 21:13/Luke 19:46); 58:6 (Luke 4:18); 66:1 (Matt. 5:34–35; 11:5/Luke 7:22); 61:1–2 (Luke 4:18–19); **Jer.** 6:16 (Matt. 11:29); 7:11 (Mark 11:17); **Ezek.** 26–28 (Matt. 11:21–22; Luke 10:13–14); **Dan.** 7:13 (Mark 13:26; 14:62/Matt. 24:30; 26:64/Luke 21:27; 22:69); 11:31 (Mark 13:14/Matt. 24:15); 12:11, cf. 9:27 (Mark 13:14/Matt. 24:15); **Joel** 3:13 (Mark 4:29); **Hosea** 6:6 (Matt. 9:13); 10:8 (Matt. 23:30); **Mic.** 7:6 (Matt. 10:35–36/Luke 12:53); **Jon.** (Matt. 16:4; cf. 12:39); 2:1 (Mark 8:31); 3:5–9 (Matt. 12:41/Luke 11:32); **Zech.** 9:9 (Mark 11:1./Matt. 21:1./Luke 19:29.); 13:7 (Mark 14:27/Matt. 26:31); **Mal.** 3:1 (Matt. 11:10/Luke 7:27); 3:23–24 (Mark 9:12–13; 11:14/Matt. 11:10/Luke 7:27; 17:11–12); 12:12 (Matt. 24:30).[80]

---

80. What we see from this survey is that the evangelists attribute to Jesus the use of the Pentateuch—especially Deuteronomy—the Psalms, and Isaiah but others as well.

B. Jesus' Citations of Biblical Books in the Gospel of John

According to John, Jesus was partial to the Psalms, Deuteronomy, and Isaiah, and he was also acquainted with many other Hebrew Bible/Old Testament books. The biblical books cited in the Gospel of John include the following:

Gen. 1:1 (John 1:1); 4:7 (John 8:34); 17:10–12 (John 7:22); 21:17 (John 12:29); 21:19 (John 4:11); 26:19 (John 4:10); 28:12 (John 1:51); 40:55 (John 2:5); 48:22 (John 4:5); **Exod.** 7:1 (John 10:34); 12:10 and 46 (John 19:36); 14:21 (John 14:1); 16:4 and 15 (John 6:32); 22:27 (John 10:34 and 18:22); 28:30 (John 11:51); 33:11 (John 15:15); 34:6 (John 1:17); **Lev.** 17:10–14 (John 6:53); 20:10 (John 8:5); 23:34 (John 7:2); 23:36 (John 7:37); 23:40 (John 12:13); 24:16 (John 10:33); **Num.** 5:12 (John 8:3); 9:12 (John 19:36); 12:2 (John 9:29); 12:8 (John 9:29); 14:23 (John 6:49); 16:28 (John 5:30 and 7:17); 21:8 (John 3:14); 27:21 (John 11:51); **Deut.** 1:16 (John 7:51); 1:35 (John 6:49); 2:14 (John 5:5); 4:12 (John 5:37); 11:29 (John 4:20); 12:5 (John 4:20); 17:7 (John 8:7); 18:15 (John 1:21 and 5:46); 19:18 (John 7:51); 21:23 (John 19:31); 22:22–24 (John 8:5); 24:16 (John 8:21); 27:12 (John 4:20); 27:26 (John 7:49); 30:6 (John 3:13); **Josh.** 7:19 (John 9:24); **2 Sam.** 7:12 (John 7:42); 13:25? (John 11:54); **2 Kings** 5:7 (John 5:21); 10:16 (John 1:46); 14:25 (John 7:52); 19:15 (John 5:44); 19:19 (John 5:44); **Neh.** 12:39 (John 5:2); **Job** 24:13–17 (John 3:20); 31:8 (John 4:37); 37:5 (John 12:29); **Pss.** 2:2 (John 1:41); 2:7 (John 1:49); 15:2 (John 8:40); 22:19 (John 19:24); 22:23 (John 20:17); 25:5 (John 16:13); 31:10 (John 12:27); 32:2 (John 1:47); 33:6 (John 1:3); 35:19 (John 15:25); 35:23 (John 20:28); 40:11 (John 1:17); 41:10 (John 13:18); 51:7 (John 9:34); 63:2 (John 19:28); 66:18 (John 9:31); 69:5 (John 15:25); 69:10 (John 2:17); 78:24 (John 6:31); 78:71 (John 21:16); 80:2 (John 10:4); 82:6 (John 10:34); 85:11 (John 1:17); 89:4 (John 7:42); 89:27 (John 12:34); 92:16 (John 7:18); 95:7 (John 10:3); 107:30 (John 6:21); 118:20 (John 10:9); 119:142 and 160 (John 17:17); 122:1. (John 4:20); 132:16 (John 5:35); 145:19 (John 9:31); **Prov.** 1:28 (John 7:34); 8:22 (John 1:2); 15:8 (John 9:31); 15:29 (John 9:31); 18:4 (John 7:38); John 24:22 (John 17:12); 30:4 (John 3:13); **Eccles.** 11:5 (John 7:38); **Isa.** 2:3 (John 4:22); 6:1 (John 12:41); 6:10 (John 12:40); 8:6 (John 9:7); 8:23 [9:1] (John 2:11); 9:2 (John 4:36); 11:2 (John 1:32); 12:3 (John 7:37); 26:17 (John 16:21); 35:4 (John 12:15); 37:20 (John 5:44); 40:3 (John 1:23); 40:9 (John 12:15); 42:8 (John 8:12); 43:10 (John 8:28, 58); 43:13 (John 8:58); 43:19 (John 7:38); 45:19 (John 18:20); 46:10 (John 13:19); 52:13 (John 12:38); 53:7 (John 8:32); 54:13 (John 6:45); 55:1 (John 7:37); 57:4 (John 17:12); 58:11 (John 4:14); 60:1 and 3 (John 8:12); 66:14 (John 16:22); **Jer.** 1:5 (John 10:36); 2:13 (John 4:10); 11:19 (John 1:29); 13:16 (John 9:4); 17:21 (John 5:10); **Ezek.** 15:1–8 (John 15:6); 34:11–16 (John 10:11); 34:23 (John 10:11, 16); 36:25–27 (John 3:5); 37:24 (John 10:11, 16); 37:25 (John 12:34); 37:27 (John 1:14); 47:1–12 (John 7:38); **Dan.** 1:2 (John 3:35); **Hosea** 4:18 (John 7:38); 6:2 (John 5:21); **Obad.** 12–14

223

(John 11:50); **Mic.** 5:1 (John 7:42); 6:15 (John 4:37); **Zeph.** 3:13 (John 1:47);
3:14 (John 12:15); 3:15 (John 1:49); **Hag.** 2:9 (John 14:27); **Zech.** 1:5 (John
8:52); 9:9 (John 12:15); 12:10 (John 19:37); 13:7 (John 16:32); 14:8 (John 4:10
and 7:38); **Mal.** 1:6 (John 8:49); 3:23 (John 1:21).

C. Allusions to or Verbal and Subject Parallels with Apocryphal and Pseudepigraphal Texts Attributed to Jesus in the Synoptic Gospels

3 Ezra 1:3 (Matt. 6:29); **4 Ezra** 6:25 (Matt. 10:22); 7:14 (Matt. 5:1); 7:36 (Luke
16:26); 7:77 (Matt. 6:20); 7:113 (Matt. 13:39); 8:3 (Matt. 22:14); 8:41 (Matt.
13:3; 22:14); **1 Macc.** 1:54 (Matt. 24:15); 2:21 (Matt. 16:22); 2:28 (Matt. 24:16);
3:6 (Luke 13:27); 3:60 (Matt. 6:10); 5:15 (Matt. 4:15); 10:29 (Luke 15:12); 12:17
(Matt. 9:38); **2 Macc.** 3:26 (Luke 24:4); 8:17 (Matt. 24:15); 10:3 (Matt. 12:4);
4 Macc. 3:13–19 (Luke 6:12); 7:19 (Matt. 22:32/Luke 20:37); 13:14 (Matt.
10:28); 13:15 (Luke 16:23); 13:17 (Matt. 8:11); 16:25 (Matt. 22:32/Luke 20:37);
Tob. 2:2 (Luke 14:13); 3:17 (Luke 15:12); 4:3 (Matt. 8:21); 4:15 (Matt. 7:12);
4:17 (Matt. 25:35); 5:15 (Matt. 20:2); 7:10 (Luke 12:19); 7:17 (Matt. 11:25/Luke
10:17); 11:9 (Luke 2:29); 12:15 (Matt. 18:10/Luke 1:19); 14:4 (Matt. 23:38/
Luke 21:24); **Jdt.** 11:19 (Matt. 9:36); 13:18 (Luke 1:42); 16:17 (Matt. 11:22);
Sus. 46 (Matt. 27:24); **Bar.** 4:1 (Matt. 5:18); 4:37 (Matt. 8:11/Luke 13:29); **Let.
Jer.** 6:24, 28 (Matt. 11:29); 7:14 (Matt. 6:7); 7:32–35 (Matt. 25:36); 9:8 (Matt.
5:28); 10:14 (Luke 1:52); 11:19 (Luke 10:19); 13:17 (Matt. 10:16); 14:10 (Matt.
6:23); 20:30 (Matt. 13:44); 23:1.4 (Matt. 6:9); 24:19 (Matt. 11:28); 25:7–12
(Matt. 5:2); 27:6 (Matt. 6:12); 28:18 (Luke 21:24); 29:10 (Matt. 6:20); 31:15
(Matt. 7:12); 33:1 (Matt. 6:13); 35:22 (Matt. 16:27/Luke 18:7); 37:2 (Matt.
26:38); 40:15 (Matt. 13:5); 48:5 (Luke 7:22); 48:10 (Matt. 11:14; 17:11/Luke
1:17; 9:8); 48:24 (Matt. 5:4); 50:20 (Luke 24:50); 50:22 (Luke 24:53); 51:1
(Matt. 11:25/Luke 10:21); 51:23 (Matt. 11:28); 51:26 (Matt. 11:29); **Wis.** 2:13
(Matt. 27:43); 2:18–20 (Matt. 27:43); 3:7 (Luke 19:44); 5:22 (Luke 21:25);
7:11 (Matt. 6:33); 15:1 (Luke 6:35); 15:8 (Luke 12:20); 16:13 (Matt. 16:18);
16:26 (Matt. 4:4); 17:2 (Matt. 22:13); **Pss. Sol.** 1:5 (Matt. 11:23); 5:9 (Matt.
6:26); 16:5 (Luke 22:37); 17:25 (Luke 21:24); 17:26, 29 (Matt. 19:28); 17:30
(Matt. 21:12); 17:32 (Luke 2:11); 18:6 (Matt. 13:6); 18:10 (Luke 2:14); **1 En.**
5:7 (Matt. 5:5); 16:1 (Matt. 13:39); 22:9 (Luke 16:26); 38:2 (Matt. 26:24);
39:4 (Luke 16:9); 51:2 (Luke 21:28); 61:8 (Matt. 25:31); 62:2 (Matt. 25:31);
63:10 (Luke 16:9); 69:27 (Matt. 25:31/26:64); 94:8 (Luke 6:24); 97:8–10 (Luke
12:19); 103:4 (Matt. 26:13).[81]

---

81. Peter Stuhlmacher adds some other parallels to this list in his "The Significance of the
Old Testament Apocrypha and Pseudepigrapha for Understanding of Jesus and Christology," in
*The Apocrypha among the Biblical Writings and Their Significance in the Eastern and Western
Church Traditions* (ed. S. Meuer; trans. P. Ellingworth; UBS Monograph Series 6; New York:
United Bible Societies, 1991), 1–15, here 8–10. Stuhlmacher also identifies the parallels between
Matt. 11:25–28 and the apocryphal Psalm 11QPs 154 (11Q5 18, 3–6).

D. Allusions to or Verbal and Subject Parallels with Apocryphal and Pseudepigraphal Texts Attributed to Jesus in the Gospel of John

4 Ezra 1:37 (John 20:29); 4:8 (John 3:13); 1 Macc. 4:59 (John 10:22); 9:39 (John 3:29); 10:7 (John 12:13); 4 Macc. 17:20 (John 12:26); Tob. 4:6 (John 3:21); Bar. 3:29 (John 3:13); 2 Bar. 18:9 (John 1:9; 3:19; 5:35); 39:7 (John 15:1); Sir. 16:21 (John 3:8); 24:21 (John 6:35); 24:40, 43 (John 7:38); 44:19 (John 8:53); 50:25–26 (John 4:9); Wis. 2:16 (John 5:18); 2:24 (John 8:44); 3:9 (John 15:9–10); 5:4 (John 10:20); 6:18 (John 14:15); 8:8 (John 4:48); 9:1 (John 1:3); 9:16 (John 3:12); 15:3 (John 17:3); 15:11 (John 20:22); 18:14–16 (John 3:12); Pss. Sol. 5:3 (John 3:27); 7:1 (John 15:25); 7:6 (John 1:14); 17:21 (John 7:42); 1 En. 69:27 (John 5:22).

5

The Story of Jesus in History

From the Transfiguration to His Burial

||||||||||||||||||||||||||||||||||||||||||||||||||||||||||

As readers will recognize, there are several stories about Jesus that are not in the above or following list, such as the calling of the Twelve, the cleansing of the temple, and the Last Supper. Because of space restrictions, these cannot be fully discussed here, though several of these are mentioned briefly in various parts of the story of Jesus. What follows here are the most prominent events that have significant bearing on the church's proclamation about Jesus, but this does not exclude the fact that other stories that impact our understanding of Jesus are also in the Gospels.

The Transfiguration of Jesus

The remarkable story of the transfiguration is found only in the Synoptic Gospels (Mark 9:2–8; Matt. 17:1–8; Luke 9:28–36), although it is referred to one other time in the New Testament (2 Pet. 1:16–18). Since the transfiguration is beyond normal human experience and appears to function theologically in the Gospels, most scholars have either written this event off as a "transposed resurrection narrative" (that is, it is a resurrection appearance story that the authors of the Synoptics inserted back into the ministry of Jesus) or dismissed it altogether. It is seldom discussed in historical Jesus studies because, like the virginal conception stories, the transfiguration simply does not fit into normal or natural human activity or experience. But is there more to this story? How does it function in the Synoptic narratives? This story tells how Jesus' appearance was changed or transformed in front of his inner circle of disciples (Peter, James, and John) into the appearance of one who reflected the glory of God. Such an appearance is not unlike that of others who have experienced the divine presence, whom we see in Daniel 7:9; 12:3; and Revelation 3:5; 4:4; and 7:9, and, as we will soon see, in the story of Moses' encounter with God on Sinai.

The Transfiguration Story

This story is laden with several important theological motifs that, following the confession of Peter, seem to function as a foreshadowing of the coming kingdom and also as an encouragement to that inner circle of disciples who witnessed it. It is also wrapped up with Mark's "messianic secret" motif (discussed earlier in chap. 4).[1] In the transfiguration story, the evangelists describe Jesus in his heavenly glory as the Messiah, the Son of God. Matthew calls this a vision (Greek, *horama*, 17:9), but the exact nature of the experience appears to go beyond other visionary experiences mentioned in the Old or New Testament. In other passages, brilliance is associated with visionary experiences, as in the case of Paul's encounter with the risen Christ on the Damascus Road (Acts 9:3), but more likely here is the parallel of Moses' experience with God on Mount Sinai (Exod. 34:29–35). The fact that Moses is described in this passage makes the parallel of the Mount Sinai experience all the more likely. In Exodus 24:12–18, we see that Moses was on Mount Sinai for forty days while he encountered God and was given assurances that God was with him as he continued his journey of taking the children of Israel through the wilderness (Exod. 33:7–23; 34:29–35). His appearance was changed as a result of this encounter. A few other parallels are worth noting as well. For example, Mark refers to "six days" (Mark 9:2; cf. Exod. 24:16), the cloud covering the mountain (Mark 9:7; cf. Exod. 24:16), God's voice coming from the cloud (Mark 9:7; cf. Exod. 24:16), three companions taken on the journey (Mark 9:2; cf. Exod. 24:1), a transformed appearance (Mark 9:3; cf. Exod. 34:30), the experience taking place on a mountain (Mark 9:2; Matt. 17:1; Luke 9:28; cf. Exod. 24:12), and a fearful reaction (Mark 9:6; cf. Exod. 34:30). In Exodus 24:13 Moses takes Joshua up the mountain with him. In Hebrew the name "Jesus" is Joshua. Whether this was an intended *veiled* typology is not certain, but multiple parallels make it appear as such. Luke makes an obvious connection with Moses in his tell-

---

1. This motif, associated with the scholar W. Wrede (*The Messianic Secret* [Cambridge: J. Clarke, 1971], a translation of a book first published in 1901), recognizes that Jesus at several places in Mark's Gospel instructs the disciples and others not to tell anyone about what they have seen him do. Explanations of the origins and meaning of this motif vary considerably.

ing of this story and includes a few additions to it. He reverses Mark's order in the names (Luke 9:30) and emphasizes the discussion about Jesus' *exodus* or departure (Luke 9:31). Also, Luke tells of the disciples seeing Jesus' glory (9:32), a familiar parallel with Exodus 24:16, where the glory of the Lord was on the mountain, and with Exodus 33:18–23, where Moses asked to see God's glory. Luke adds that Jesus' face or countenance was changed (Luke 9:29; cf. Exod. 34:30, 35). Only Luke mentions the "eight days after," instead of the six days in Mark and Matthew. There is a parallel with Leviticus 23:33–44: there are seven days of offerings for the Feast of Tabernacles, or booths, and *on the eighth day*, a holy convocation, during which time the people are to dwell in booths or tents to remind them of the exodus from Egypt (Lev. 23:42–43). This "holy convocation" in Luke includes Moses the lawgiver, Elijah the first of the prophets, and Jesus, God's Son. The return of Elijah was anticipated at the end of the age, that is, before the coming of the day of the Lord (Mal. 4:5–6).

To the heavenly voice announcing Jesus as God's Son, Luke adds the words "my chosen," a possible reference to Isaiah 42:1. "Listen to him" is probably a reference to Deuteronomy 18:15, where Moses commanded the people to listen to the prophet that God would one day raise up. These parallels appear to be quite extensive and too obvious to be coincidental. Luke seems to have a "Moses motif" running throughout this passage. In Luke 16:16, Jesus says that the day of the Law and the Prophets concluded with the ministry of John the Baptist, and since then the good news of the kingdom was preached. The implication is that in Jesus a new day has dawned. In Luke 24:27, Jesus says that Moses and the Prophets spoke of him. In his appearance to the disciples, he shows references to himself in Moses (the Law), the Prophets, and the Psalms (Luke 24:44–45).

Table 5.1
The Transfiguration of Jesus: *Parallel Accounts*

Mark 9:2–13	Luke 9:28–36	Matthew 17:1–8
1. After six days . . .	About eight days after . . .	After six days . . .
2. Peter, James, and John accompany Jesus.	same	same
3. Jesus takes the three to a high mountain.	Jesus takes the three to a mountain to pray.	Jesus takes the three to a high mountain.
4. Jesus is transfigured before them.	As he was praying, his countenance is altered.	Jesus is transfigured before them.
5. His garments become intensely white.	same	same
6. Moses and Elijah appear, talking to Jesus.	Moses and Elijah appear and speak of Jesus' departure (exodus).	Moses and Elijah appear, talking to Jesus.

In the resurrection of Jesus, after he had appeared to his disciples for forty days, he was taken up in a cloud (Acts 1:3, 9). It is difficult not to draw a parallel to Moses, who also entered the cloud and was with God on the mountain for forty days (Exod. 24:15–18). The cloud reflected the presence of the glory of God (Exod. 13:21–22; 33:9–10; Isa. 6:4–5). Did Luke anticipate Jesus' ascension into heaven with the transfiguration story? Does this passage focus on Jesus' glory, which later was seen in his resurrection? Was the transfiguration intended by the evangelists as a foreshadowing of the resurrection that Jesus had predicted (Mark 8:31; 9:1; Luke 9:22, 27; and Matt. 16:21, 28)? There are many questions about this story that are unclear, but the many parallels with earlier biblical stories are suggestive.

The climax of the transfiguration story is the divine identification of Jesus—namely, "This is my Son, the Beloved" (Mark 9:7; Matt. 17:5; in Luke 9:35 "beloved" is omitted and "my Chosen" is used instead; cf. Mark 1:11; Matt. 3:17; Luke 3:22). What are the implications of this story in the Synoptics? The announcement by God of his special relationship with Jesus is either to the disciples ("this is" instead of "you are") or to Moses and Elijah. It is probably the former who are intended.

The Meaning of the Transfiguration in the Synoptic Gospels

How does this event contribute to the message of the Synoptics? Was it understood as a fulfillment of Mark 8:38–9:1 (see Matt. 16:28 and Luke 9:27)—namely, that this was a foretaste of the "coming of the Son of Man in his glory" that was shared with all of the disciples to encourage them as they began their journey to Jerusalem? Is Mark 9:1 a reference to the resurrection of Jesus? If so, why does Jesus say only "some" will witness it, since all but Judas witnessed his resurrection? Does the transfiguration highlight the coming of the kingdom of God that Jesus proclaimed, as suggested by some scholars, who also add that Jesus was wrong in his prediction of its soon arrival? Again, this would seem a strange meaning of the text, since all of Jesus' disciples would have witnessed the resurrection of Jesus (except Judas) if it were imminent and initiated that kingdom. Some have suggested that Jesus was referring to the destruction of Jerusalem that took place in AD 70, as Jesus may have believed that the nation stood under the condemnation of God and would be destroyed for its faithlessness (Luke 13:34–35; Matt. 23:37–39). The passage, however, does not require that Mark 9:1 and its parallels refer to the destruction of Jerusalem. Some scholars have argued that this was a reference to the coming of the Holy Spirit as seen in Luke 24:49 (cf. Acts 1:8 and 2:1–42). Again, the word "some" is not an easy fit here since all but Judas Iscariot experienced the coming of the Holy Spirit. It is more likely that the evangelists have the transfiguration in mind, as that takes place immediately in the context and in front of only a few. This interpretation is supported by the only New Testament passage that offers an interpretation of the transfiguration (2 Pet. 1:16–18). There it has to do with the glory and honor of Jesus and the majesty of God.

It appears then that the evangelists were drawing parallels to the transformation of Jesus, with the Moses motif in mind. The glory of Jesus was revealed in each of the accounts of the story, perhaps with the purpose of assuring and encouraging Jesus' disciples as they began their journey toward Jerusalem and all that would occur there (Mark 8:31; Matt. 16:21; Luke 9:44–45). As Peter's quick challenge to Jesus' prediction of his impending rejection and death—a response that was probably shared by other disciples—shows, one can understand the need for Jesus to give them some comfort and hope. This does not make this story an easy one to understand, but it does allow the reader to understand better why it took place.

What can historians make of this event? Could it have happened, or is it intended to be a theological reflection of the significance of Jesus on the part of some of his disciples? Dale Allison suggests that the story may have more historical credibility than many have supposed and that it does have some notable parallels in human experience, some fairly contemporary. He cites some examples of more recent experiences that others have testified to. He acknowledges that people judge such matters based on their own experience, and since this is not a "normal" experience, they conclude that it must be myth. However, he suggests that experience shows now and then that we must be open to the remarkable because it does happen. He cautions those who make their own experience normative for all reported events and for all people, concluding that "miracles associated with Jesus need not be late or secondary inventions."[2]

The Triumphal Entry

After his transfiguration, Jesus proceeded toward Jerusalem, and all four Gospels tell the story of the people's enthusiastic welcome of him by laying down cloaks and palm branches for him as he rode by them on a donkey (Mark 11:1–10; Matt. 21:1–9;[3] Luke 19:28–38; John 12:12–15). The evan-

---

2. Dale C. Allison, *The Historical Christ and the Theological Jesus* (Grand Rapids: Eerdmans, 2009), 72–76.

3. Matthew has Jesus' disciples secure two animals for this occasion (Matt. 21:2, 7), whereas the other evangelists mention only one animal. It appears that Matthew took the Hebrew

gelists see this event as a fulfillment of prophecy that they cite in telling this story. This event takes place in the last week of Jesus' ministry in Jerusalem just a few days before his arrest, trial, and execution. Because this story has multiple attestations, it does not appear to be a creation of the evangelists, but focuses on Jesus' awareness of his mission as king of a renewed Israel in which his relationship to God is recognized by the crowds. The same Scriptures are cited by the evangelists as Jesus' fulfillment of earlier promises; namely, Zechariah 9:9 is in all four Gospels, along with Psalm 118:26 (Synoptics). Isaiah 62:11 is also cited in Matthew's telling of this story. The objections by the Pharisees in Luke's account show that what was done and said on this occasion was considered blasphemous, and John 12:19 records a response of exasperation by the Pharisees over what was done. These references cohere with the record of Jesus' trial, where the charge of blasphemy is raised against him (Mark 14:61–64).[4]

The Passion Predictions of Jesus

Several times during his ministry, the evangelists note that Jesus predicted his own death (Mark 8:31; 9:10–12, 31; 10:45; Luke 9:44; John 2:21; 12:32–33). It is not difficult to see that Jesus might have understood the natural consequences of his teaching, especially his challenging the religious structures of his day, but one of the problems with the predictions is that the disciples seem unprepared to understand or accept Jesus' arrest and crucifixion in Jerusalem when it actually happens. If Jesus predicted his death so clearly, why is there an apparent lapse of faith by his disciples when he dies? And why is there an apparent lapse of faith on the part of Jesus when he cries out on the cross, "My God, my God! Why have you forsaken me?" (Mark 15:34).

Many scholars have understood this reference as pointing to Jesus' lapse on the cross. As a result, some have suggested that Jesus did not predict his death, but that the predictions were later attributed to him by the early church to help them deal with the scandal of the cross and the embarrassment that a crucified Messiah caused them. Others have argued that Jesus' predictions of

---

letter *waw* in the Hebrew of Zech. 9:9 to be a connective ("and") rather than an explicative ("even"). Even in the Greek text the problem would be the same—understanding *kai* ("and") as a connective rather than an explicative ("even"). Remarkably, Matthew has Jesus riding on "them"—on two animals!

4. A number of scholars have rejected the authenticity of the trial of Jesus before Caiaphas, especially the response of Jesus (Mark 14:62). However, this story fits with the rest of the pattern of Jesus' career and message, and is a part of the frequently attested and authentic tradition about him.

his death were more abbreviated than they appear in the Gospels, and not as clear as they were made out to be by the early church. In other words, the Gospel writers had the advantage of hindsight, and we should not expect them to be more obscure about what they understood more clearly at a later time. One could also say that the disciples heard Jesus' predictions but, because of their excitement about going to the city of fulfillment, Jerusalem, in anticipation of their roles in the coming kingdom of God, they were simply not attuned to understand them. They expected a ruling king who would establish a political kingdom, not a crucified Messiah.

Whatever the solution to the problem, it is clear that nothing that Jesus said to his disciples gave them confidence at the time of his arrest or changed their minds about what was taking place until after his resurrection.[5] This might be the key for understanding the earliest preaching in the book of Acts, where the cross does not play a significant role, but rather the crucifixion of Jesus is simply in the plan of God that death cannot destroy (Acts 2:23). The resurrection of Jesus, and not the cross, was at the heart of the earliest Christian preaching. A short time later the cross became central to Paul's preaching (1 Cor. 1:17–18, 23–24).[6]

The Arrest and Trial of Jesus

The setting for the arrest of Jesus has five important factors: (1) Jesus made personal claims to have a special relationship with God, claims that include his acceptance of the acclaim of the people in the triumphal entry (see Luke 19:39–40). (2) Jesus cleansed the temple. (3) Jesus rejected the traditional and legalistic application of the law to daily practice; for instance, he healed on the Sabbath (Mark 3:1–6), he allowed his disciples to collect grain on the Sabbath (Mark 2:23–28), and he rejected the traditional days of fasting, typically Mondays and Thursdays (it was believed that Moses ascended and descended Mount Sinai on those days; see Mark 2:18–22). (4) The charge of insurrection against Rome was brought against Jesus; that is, his accusers said that he had become a political threat to Rome by presenting himself as king (Mark 15:1–3;

5. C. A. Evans, in his helpful essay "Did Jesus Predict His Death and Resurrection?," in *Resurrection* (ed. S. E. Porter, Michael A. Hayes, and D. Tombs; New York: T&T Clark, 1999), 82–97, deals with the problem of Jesus' predictions of his death and resurrection and concludes that he did predict them, but this did not take away his anxiety about his impending death.

6. Although the book of Acts was written years after the epistles of Paul, it is nonetheless an accurate summary of the preaching of the early church. The fact that Acts presents a simple and idealistic view of the early church in summary form does not take away from this conclusion about the essence of early Christian preaching.

Luke 23:1–5; Matt. 27:11–14; John 19:12, 19). That one of Jesus' disciples was called a Zealot has led some to conclude that this revolutionary party that sought the overthrow of Roman domination of Palestine had influenced Jesus. That one of Jesus' disciples was carrying a sword when Jesus was arrested in the garden (Mark 14:47) has also led to the speculation that his followers were not so passive as tradition has led us to believe, but that they could be quite reactionary. These were characteristics of the zealotic movement that eventually prompted a confrontation with Rome in AD 66, and led to the destruction of the temple and the city of Jerusalem in AD 70. Finally, (5) Jesus' popularity among the people was a growing concern to the leaders in Jerusalem. It was for this reason that caution had to be taken when Jesus was arrested, and why they chose to arrest him and bring charges against him late in the evening (Mark 14:2; Matt. 26:5). According to John 6:15, the people even wanted to force him to be their king, perhaps seeing him as a liberator from oppression, as well as one who would care for the hungry and homeless, and correct the abusive system that kept so many in poverty.

Jesus' Claims and Actions

Scholars debate the merits of each of these factors, but there is little question that Jesus' neglect of the oral traditions that focused on keeping the law (for example, how far one could walk on the Sabbath, healing on the Sabbath, various kinds of ritual cleansings, and keeping the letter of the law) eventually led the religious leaders in Jerusalem to see Jesus as a threat. Consequently, they sought to destroy him (e.g., Mark 3:1–6). All the evangelists agree on this point. Whether Jesus made remarkable claims about himself and his relationship to God is more debated among historical Jesus scholars. Did Jesus make such claims? What passages suggest this, and to what extent might these passages be considered later church additions to the story of Jesus? There is no question that the Gospels report that Jesus made such claims. See, for example, John 20:26–29, where Jesus accepted such recognition from Thomas. Jesus' special relationship with God is reported in the earliest Christian proclamation (Rom. 1:3–4; 10:9–10; Phil. 2:11; 1 Cor. 16:22), but how soon was this recognized by the followers of Jesus? I suggest that these acclamations stem from the ministry and teaching of Jesus himself and the evangelists accurately reflect Jesus' claims. Without such claims it would be difficult to account for his crucifixion and opposition by religious leaders of his day.

For one known to have performed exorcisms, healings, and nature miracles (such as reports of him calming a storm or producing from five loaves and two fish enough food to feed a multitude of thousands, etc.), and to have proclaimed the coming kingdom of God, the question must surely have arisen, "Who is this man?" His actions understandably provoked questions from those who witnessed them and especially among the religious leaders of the day (Mark 4:41; Luke 8:25; Matt. 8:27). Along with his ministry of healing and exorcisms, Jesus was known as a teacher and proclaimer of God's kingdom, as well as one who received the outcasts of society. Who was he? According to the synoptic tradition, Jesus himself raised the question with his disciples (Mark 8:27–30; Matt. 16:13–20; Luke 9:20). He appears to have accepted acclaim from his disciples (see also John 20:28–29), and the early church itself soon acknowledged him as "Lord." This confession is found in the earliest known Christian confession (Rom. 10:9–10), and in an earlier form of this confession that told of the early church's hope for the return of the risen Christ who is Lord (1 Cor. 16:22).[7] It is likely that these acclamations did not originate in their current form until after the Easter event, but where did such ideas come from? Are they a reasonable inference of what Jesus himself taught, and could they be deduced from his performance of various miracles? Given Jesus' teachings and remarkable activities in healings and exorcisms, it is not surprising that such acclamation emerged early on, even before the death of Jesus, but after his resurrection (Rom. 1:3–4) they were once again at the heart of early Christian acclaim for him. The titles attributed to Jesus and those he used of himself may be helpful here. The following are the most frequent designations of Jesus, along with their use in the Old Testament and noncanonical Jewish literature.

Titles for Jesus

1. "Christ," "Anointed One" (2 Sam. 22:51; Pss. 2:2; 18:50; Dan. 9:25–26; *1 En.* 52:4) Mark 8:29; Luke 4:18; John 1:41

2. "King" (2 Sam. 7:8–16; Ps. 89:19–37; Zech. 9:9) Matt. 2:2; 21:5; Mark 15:32; Luke 19:38; John 18:33, passim

3. "Son of David" (Prov. 1:1; Eccles. 1:1; *Pss. Sol.* 17:21) Matt. 1:1; Mark 10:47–48

4. "Son" (Ps. 2:7; Isa. 7:14; 9:6) Mark 1:1, 11; 3:11; 5:7; 9:7; 13:32, passim

5. "Son of Man" (In the Old Testament there are some eighty references in Ezekiel to a human "son of man," but also to a messianic figure in Ps. 8:4 and especially Dan.

---

7. The words "Our Lord Come!" originally were written in Aramaic and transliterated into Greek as *marana tha* (or possibly, *maran atha*, "Our Lord *has* come"). The fact that Paul shares these words in Aramaic with Greeks from Corinth strongly indicates that the words had an earlier history in Palestine and did not originate on Hellenistic soil, as some scholars have earlier argued.

7:13–14; cf. *1 En.* 48:2; 62:7; 71:17.) In the New Testament this is the most common self-designation of Jesus in the Gospels. See, for example, Matt. 12:8, 32; 13:37; 19:28; Mark 2:10, 28; 8:38; 9:12; 13:26; 14:62; Luke 12:8, 10, 40, passim.

6. "Servant" (Isa. 42:1–4; 49:1–13; 50:1–11; 52:13–53:12) Matt. 12:18 (Isa. 42:1); Mark 10:45; Acts 4:27, 30

7. "Branch" (Isa. 11:1; Jer. 23:5; 33:15; Zech. 3:8; 6:12) In the New Testament this may be an equivalent to Jesus being a Nazarene (Matt. 2:23).

8. "Prophet" (Deut. 18:15–18) Matt. 11:9; 21:11, 46; Mark 6:4, 15; 8:28; Luke 7:16; 24:19; John 6:14; 7:40; Acts 3:22–23; 7:37

9. "Priest" (Gen. 14:18; Ps. 110:4; *T. Sim.* 7:2; *T. Jud.* 21:2; *T. Jos.* 19:6) In the New Testament, the focus on Jesus as priest is found explicitly only in Heb. 5:5–10 and 7:1–10:18, but also by implication in the ministry of Jesus, as in his forgiving of sin (Mark 2:5; Luke 7:47–48), shedding his blood for a new covenant (Mark 14:24), promising a "new temple" (Mark 14:58; John 2:19), and his role as mediator (1 Tim. 2:5–6).

10. "Holy One" (2 Kings 19:22; Isa. 5:24; 43:3, 15; 45:11; Jer. 50:29) Mark 1:24; Luke 4:34; John 6:69

11. "Chosen/Elect One" and "Righteous" (Isa. 42:1; 45:4; 53:11; Jer. 23:5; Zech. 9:9; *1 En.* 53:6) In the New Testament see the "righteous one" in Luke 23:47; Acts 3:14; 1 John 2:1; 3:7.

12. "Lord" (*Pss. Sol.* 17:32; 18:7) In the New Testament, see Mark 2:28. Note: Even though it is not a messianic title, Jesus was called "Lord of the Sabbath" in Mark 2:28; but "Lord" in Matt. 14:30; 15:22; John 20:28, passim.

13. "Rabbi" or "Teacher," John 1:38; 3:2, 26 (cf. Matt. 23:7–8, and "the Word" in John 1:1, 14; cf. *1 En.* 61:7)

14. "Son of God," Matt. 3:17; 4:3, 6; Mark 1:1; 3:11; 9:7; 14:61; 15:39; passim

What do these titles imply about Jesus' early followers' understanding of him? Does Jesus' reference to himself as the Son of Man imply anything more than that he was a part of the human race, such as we see in the some eighty uses of the term in Ezekiel (2:1, 3, 6, 8; 3:1, 3, 17, etc.)? Does the designation refer instead to a *divine* man who comes as the representative of God at the end of the age to bring the salvation of God—an eschatological figure, as we can infer from Daniel 7:13–14? Some of the references in the New Testament could have both meanings, but it is the reference to a divine man with which we are most concerned. If Jesus had this understanding in mind, then his self-awareness of being in a special, if not unique, relation to God is quite certain (see, for example, Mark 2:10, 28; 8:38; 9:9; 13:26; 14:62; Matt. 13:41; 16:27; 24:27, 30, 37; 25:31; Luke 12:40; 17:24; 21:27; John 3:13; 12:23; 13:31).

In each of these instances, as well as the others in the Gospels, it is Jesus who is speaking. The early church did not use this term in reference to Jesus, and, outside of the Gospels, it is found only in Acts 7:56 and Revelation 1:13 and 14:14. It is hardly possible that the term was an invention by the church since the followers of Jesus did not generally refer to him this way, but there is widespread attestation that Jesus used it in reference to himself. Did Jesus have in mind the eschatological figure mentioned in Daniel 7:13–14 and in most of the examples cited above, as well as in the pseudepigraphal *Parables of Enoch* (1 *En.* 37–71, see especially the vision of 46:1–8; and 4 *Ezra* 13:3–4, 25–32, 51–52), where such references are to a messianic and eschatological figure? In many of the passages noted above where Jesus speaks of himself as the Son of Man, it appears that he has this apocalyptic and authoritative messianic figure in mind. Was part of the rejection of Jesus precisely because he appeared to the religious leaders of his day to be a blasphemer, that is, speaking of a special relationship with God, his Father? That he should on occasion say to others that the kingdom of God was present in his activity of healing and preaching suggests this very thing.

Following Jesus' entry into Jerusalem, in which some Pharisees were troubled by the acclaim he had received and evidently accepted (Luke 19:39), he entered the temple and overturned the tables of the money changers in the outer court-yard (Mark 11:15–17). As a result, when the chief priests and scribes heard of this, they began to look for ways to kill him (Mark 11:18). After leaving the temple with his disciples, Jesus also predicted its destruction (Mark 13:1–2). Did others hear him make this pronouncement? Just prior to the outbreak of the war against Rome in AD 66, there was another man by the name of Jesus, son of Ananus, who pronounced woes against Jerusalem and against the temple (the "holy house"). As a result of this he was beaten several times and eventually killed with a stone (Josephus, *J.W.* 6.300–309). To say something against the temple or the city of Jerusalem, or even the religious leaders of Jerusalem, was serious (see also Jesus' woes pronounced against the religious leaders of Jerusalem in Matt. 23:13–36).

Obviously, Jesus was on a collision course with the religious leaders of his day, but the evangelists all say that he was aware of the consequences of his behavior (Mark 8:31; Matt. 16:21; see also Luke 9:21–22 and similar predictions in Mark 9:30–32; 10:33–34; and parallels; and in John 12:27–36). In Mark 10:44–45, Jesus made reference to giving his life as "a ransom for many," and at his Last Supper with his disciples, he referred to the cup as his "blood of the covenant, which is poured out for many" (Matt. 26:28; Mark 14:24; see also Luke 22:20). Later he made an apparent farewell statement, saying that he would not drink of the fruit of the vine again until he did so in the kingdom of God (Luke 22:15–18). The independent tradition in John is considerably different. Even stripped of its theological meaning, which speaks to the concerns of the church of a later generation, this tradition still attests to Jesus sharing a meal with his followers and speaking of his own personal sacrifice. In this final Passover meal (John 13:1–38) before his arrest in the garden, Jesus appears to have been aware that Judas has betrayed him (13:21–30). Supporting this is the tradition in Paul, who speaks about the supper of the Lord in which Jesus himself spoke of the elements of bread and wine as representing his body and blood (1 Cor. 11:25). These various strands of tradition, when combined, strongly suggest that Jesus knew he was in conflict in Jerusalem and would soon die (see also Matt. 23:37–39; Luke 13:31–34). After he predicts his death in Mark 10:32–34, the disciples obviously do not grasp what Jesus has said, and two of them, James and John, approach him to ask for places of prominence in his kingdom. He then asks them if they are able to drink from the cup that he drinks from and be baptized with the baptism that he is baptized with, speaking about his death. According to the Gospel tradition, Jesus was not taken unawares when he was arrested and brought to death.

If this is so, why then does Jesus apparently suffer a lapse on the cross, as some scholars have argued? His words on the cross are, "My God, my God, why have you forsaken me?" (Mark 15:34; Matt. 27:46). Although this cry is only found in two of the four evangelists, it is unlikely that the early churches invented it, since it makes it appear as if Jesus faced death believing that God had forsaken him and that something tragic had happened to his plans. Jesus' cry of despair, however, may in fact be more of an affirmation of hope, since what he says are the opening words of Psalm 22. Years ago, Martin Dibelius argued that an ancient manner of citing Scripture was to give the opening of the first verse with the rest of the passage understood. Since Psalm 22 finishes with great confidence in the faithfulness of God (vv. 25–31), Dibelius concluded that "no pious Jew dying with these words on his lips could have thought himself abandoned by God."[8]

Whether Jesus was an insurrectionist needs little comment. There are no elements in Jesus' behavior or teachings that would suggest he was a revolutionary anxious to overthrow the Roman government. He only asked that his followers should give to the emperor what belonged to the emperor (taxes) and to God what belonged to God (Mark 12:17). This teaching was carried on in the earliest Christian churches (Rom. 13:7). If Jesus was a revolutionary, he had no army, and his followers never created an army.

8. M. Dibelius, *From Tradition to Gospel* (London: Nicholson & Watson, 1934), 193–94. See also his *Jesus* (trans. C. B. Hedrick and F. C. Grant; Philadelphia: Westminster, 1949).

The arrest and trial of Jesus, therefore, was caused by several factors. Chief among them were his claims to be in a special relationship with God, his cleansing of the temple, his rejection of many of the religious traditions of his day (especially when they interfered with human need), and his growing popularity with the people. He was perceived as a threat, was arrested, tried, and crucified.

Betrayal and Trial

Jesus was betrayed by one of his own followers, Judas Iscariot, who gave information to the chief priests on Jesus' whereabouts (Mark 14:10–11).[9] Judas knew where to find Jesus (John 18:2; see also Luke 22:39) and brought the temple guards to him. Perhaps out of fear of the reprisals from Rome that Jesus could bring upon the Jewish people, the religious leaders determined to kill him (John 18:14), but because of his popularity with the people, that was not an easy job. Also, their formal grievances against him were not legally sufficient to have him killed. Further, convicting Jesus on a minor charge would not have stopped him.

It is fairly certain that it was Judas Iscariot who betrayed Jesus and turned him over to the Jewish religious authorities (the Sanhedrin and the temple guard). The tradition is too widespread in the Gospel narratives and is not the kind of story that the church would fabricate—that is, that one of Jesus' most trusted followers betrayed him for money. The question is, however, why did Judas betray Jesus? Was it because of the rebuke that Jesus gave to him earlier (Mark 14:4–8; Matt. 26:8–10; see also John 12:4–8) when Judas rebuked Mary? Did Judas simply want to force Jesus' hand to take a more prominent role in Israel, as he had come to expect? The evangelists have little good to say about Judas and focus on the money he received as his incentive. Judas's remorse is mentioned in Matthew 27:3–10, and, although there is no reference to his guilt in the different account in Acts 1:18, both stories connect Judas's death with a cemetery for foreigners.

In terms of the trial, it is probably safest to say that no *formal trial* as such took place, but rather there was a time set up before the religious leaders to bring accusations against Jesus. According to Mark 14:43–53, after Jesus was arrested, he was taken before the Sanhedrin by night or in the early morning hours (Matt. 26:31, 34, 75; John 18:27; but cf. Luke 22:66), evidently to allow religious leaders to deal with the matter as quickly and

---

9. An excellent work on this topic is R. E. Brown, *The Death of the Messiah* (2 vols.; New York: Doubleday, 1994). See also P. Benoit, *The Passion and Resurrection of Jesus Christ* (New York: Herder & Herder, 1969).

quietly as possible and to avoid conflict with Jesus' followers and admirers. Earlier a portion of the Sanhedrin, made up of chief priests, scribes, and elders, had met with Jesus to get him to condemn himself or to give them grounds to arrest him, but without success (Mark 11:27–33). This time they were more determined to convict him, and the whole Sanhedrin met (Mark 14:53–55). Although the time of the meeting was unusual, the concern they had over Jesus' arrest was great, and they wanted to deal with him quickly and privately. This meeting went on until past dawn (Mark 15:1). The solicited testimonies against Jesus did not agree (Mark 14:55–59), and according to Numbers 35:30, at least two witnesses were needed to condemn a person to death (Deut. 19:15–21). The lack of agreement among his accusers left the religious leaders with no alternative but to try to get Jesus to convict himself. At this point, according to Mark, the high priest, Caiaphas, asked Jesus if he was the Messiah, the son of the Blessed, that is, God (Mark 14:61). Jesus answered that he was, and began to quote Daniel 7:13, a messianic text that refers to the apocalyptic Son of Man, with Psalms 110:1 and possibly 110:5 in view. Although Jesus answered Caiaphas, we see in Mark 14:62 that he also included the whole Sanhedrin in his response as the change to a plural verb indicates (*opsesthe*, a second-person plural, literally "you [plural] will—or can expect to—see").

Much has been made of the irregularity of this trial and of Jesus' response. The point seems to be that if the trial did not take place as Mark claims—and since the trial appears to have violated the general laws governing its procedures—then Jesus' affirmation that he was indeed the Messiah and Son of God is also fabricated. There seems to be a shift in opinion taking place among New Testament scholars, however, and more credibility has been given to this trial or hearing before the Sanhedrin. Gundry, for instance, admits that the procedures that took place at the trial according to Mark are unusual, but maintains that they are not without precedent given the circumstances. To the extent that the Mishnaic legal regulations that were codified in the late second century and early third century AD were also in effect in the time of Jesus, as Gundry concludes is likely, Jesus' trial appears unjust and, in Mark's account, according to Gundry, also tendentious. Gundry argues that ancient texts like the book of Susannah (vv. 44–59) and 11QT 61:9 show the concern for justice at the time of Jesus, and provide early enough background to understand some of the concerns about the trial of Jesus. He acknowledges the irregularities in the passage; for example, the meeting place in the high priest's house rather than in the "Chamber of Hewn Stone," as called for in *m. Sanhedrin* 11:2, and the trial taking place on Passover eve, which is forbidden in *m. Sanhedrin* 4:1. Nevertheless, according to *b. Sanhedrin* 46a, allowances were made for emergencies when the protection of the Torah was in view.[10] In Jesus' case, the circumstances were unusual, and his actions were viewed as contrary to very important Jewish religious traditions since he both violated Jewish traditions about the Sabbath and interrupted temple activity. It is therefore understandable why such measures were taken in such an unusual manner.

The charge against Jesus was blasphemy (Mark 14:63–64), which meant that he was believed to have encroached upon an area reserved for God alone when he claimed to have a special relationship with him. However, as Evans has pointed out, it was not Jesus' claim to be the Messiah that warranted his condemnation. Others had made such a claim but had not been put to death. It was that Jesus, in citing Daniel 7:13 with Psalm 110:1, positioned himself on the throne of God, seated next to him when God comes in judgment against the Jewish people.[11] This was blasphemy, the penalty for which was death, but since the Sanhedrin did not have the authority to put persons to death in that political climate, they took Jesus before Pontius Pilate, the Roman prefect. They charged him with insurrection, that is, saying that he claimed to be a king (Mark 15:1–5; Luke 23:1–5), and with opposing paying taxes to Rome (Luke 23:2). These charges were supported by the *titulus*, or sign above the cross, mentioned in each of the four Gospels, which Pilate had placed over Jesus' head indicating his accusation (Mark 15:26, 32; Matt. 27:37, 39–42; Luke 23:36–37, 38; John 19:1–3, 15–16, 19). What adds credibility to this report is that the "Jews" (Sanhedrin?) contested this title and asked that it be changed. It is likely that the charge that Jesus claimed to be both king and Messiah is authentic. Supporting this is Pilate's question to Jesus asking whether he was the king of the Jews (Matt. 27:11–12; Mark 15:2–3; Luke 23:3; John 18:29–33). It is not likely that the reference to Jesus as Messiah came after his death, but rather that he was acknowledged as such by his disciples during his ministry (Mark 8:29; Matt. 16:16; Luke 9:20; cf. John 1:41–42). Although some scholars have rejected the authenticity of this confession and Jesus' acceptance of it, when placed in the context of the disciples leaving their businesses and following him to Jerusalem, even debating among themselves who would be greatest in his kingdom, it surely reflects their view that he had a special relationship with God, and their anticipation that he would soon establish the kingdom of God that he had proclaimed (Mark 10:35–40; Matt. 20:20–28; Luke 22:24–27). There can be little question that Jesus' disciples believed that he was the expected Messiah

10. R. H. Gundry, *Mark: A Commentary on His Apology for the Cross* (Grand Rapids: Eerdmans, 1993), 893.

11. See C. A. Evans, *Jesus and His Contemporaries: Comparative Studies* (AGJU 25; Leiden: Brill, 1995), 407–34, where he also defends the authenticity of the trial scene.

who had already begun to establish God's kingdom among them and that its arrival was imminent. The fact that Jesus chose twelve disciples, even if we are uncertain of their names, indicates that he believed he was going to establish a renewed people of Israel for the new day of the coming kingdom of God. Although Jesus accepted the messianic title from his followers in private, he did not use the title of himself in his public ministry, except once: at the point of his appearance before Caiaphas and the Sanhedrin (Mark 14:60–62).

Pilate was evidently unconvinced that Jesus had done anything worthy of death (Luke 23:1–5; John 18:33–38) and wanted the Jews to handle the matter themselves (John 18:30–31). Perhaps seeking to find an easy way to deal with the matter, he tried to pass the problem over to Herod Antipas, who was likely in Jerusalem for the Passover celebration (Luke 23:6–12). Antipas likewise found no fault in Jesus that was worthy of death (Luke 23:13–16) and sent him back to Pilate. Pilate therefore gave the Jews a choice of releasing either Jesus or the convicted criminal named Barabbas, but the "Jews" (likely the Sanhedrin, but possibly also the crowds that had been incited by the religious leaders at this time) chose to have Barabbas released (Mark 15:6–15; Luke 23:25). Pilate then had Jesus handed over to his guards for crucifixion as an insurrectionist, as the title over his cross ("King of the Jews") shows. Jesus was beaten, humiliated by soldiers (Mark 15:16–20), and prepared for crucifixion.

Who Executed Jesus and Why?

For years scholars have given significant attention to the question of who was responsible for the crucifixion of Jesus and why he was executed. Some have tried to eliminate Jewish complicity altogether by placing blame solely on the "Roman imperial system,"[12] while others have unjustly blamed the whole Jewish race for the death of Jesus. Neither position has credible support. The question, however, has been so emotionally packed that clarity has not been easy.

Roman and Jewish Authority in Palestine

In the time of Jesus, it was the official responsibility of Pontius Pilate, the Roman prefect from AD 26 to 36, to keep order in Judea. The actual indirect authority for keeping peace in Judea and making sure that the Jews were

---

12. See E. Rivkin, *What Crucified Jesus? The Political Execution of a Charismatic* (Nashville: Abingdon, 1984), and H. Cohn, *The Trial and Death of Jesus* (New York: Harper & Row, 1971).

obedient to Roman authority was given to the high priest in Jerusalem. For almost five hundred years before the Roman conquest of Palestine, the Jews were governed by a high priest. During the final eighty years of the Hasmonean Dynasty (ca. 140–63 BC), a king who was also the high priest ruled the Jewish nation. After Rome intervened in Judean affairs in 63 BC, Herod the Great became the client king who was responsible to Rome for the governance of the region, but he was not a high priest. After his death, Herod's territory was divided among his sons. One son, Herod Archelaus, did so poorly as a ruler that he was replaced by Roman prefects, who governed Judea from AD 6 on, with the brief exception of the years AD 41–44 when Agrippa I ruled until his untimely death (Acts 12:20–23; cf. Josephus, *Ant.* 19.343–50).

Pontius Pilate ruled Judea from the coastal city of Caesarea-Maritima, and was known for his ruthless dealings with rebellion and maintaining a strong posture with regard to the inhabitants of his region. In the day-to-day control of the region, the high priest had the right to make recommendations to the prefect, including for capital punishment, but neither he nor any other Jew had the authority to carry out executions. In the eyes of the Romans, Caiaphas, the high priest in Jerusalem, evidently did such a good job that he was allowed to serve eighteen years in that role, longer than any other high priest of the first century.

Table 5.2
The Death of Jesus in the Gospels

Event	Matthew 27:32–54	Mark 15:21–39	Luke 23:26–49	John 19:17–37
Thieves	Both thieves revile Jesus.	Both thieves revile Jesus.	One thief reviles Jesus and one asks to be remembered. Request granted.	Thieves are mentioned, but no reviling.
Time	From sixth to ninth hour	From sixth to ninth hour	From sixth to ninth hour	About sixth hour when Jesus stands before Pilate (v. 14)
Jesus' cry	*Eli, Eli, lema sabachthani* (Hebrew)	*Eloi, Eloi, lema sabachthani* (Aramaic)	Father, into your hands I commit my spirit!	Reference to Jesus' mother; "I thirst"; "It is finished."
Jesus offered a drink	Sponge with vinegar	Sponge with vinegar	Vinegar, but offered at a different time	Sponge full of vinegar on hyssop

Event	Matthew 27:32–54	Mark 15:21–39	Luke 23:26–49	John 19:17–37
Accompanying phenomena	*Darkness *Temple curtain torn in two from top to bottom *Earthquake *Tombs of dead opened and dead rise to life. *Centurion: "Truly this was the Son of God!"	*Darkness *Temple curtain torn in two from top to bottom *Centurion: "Truly this man was the Son of God!"	*Darkness *Temple curtain torn in two *Centurion: "Certainly this man was innocent!"	*Scripture fulfilled: 19:24, 28, 36, 37
Sign over Jesus	This is Jesus, the King of the Jews	The King of the Jews	This is the King of the Jews	Jesus of Nazareth, the King of the Jews

Circumstances Surrounding Jesus' Death

The immediate factors that led to the arrest and death of Jesus probably included his triumphal entry, when the Pharisees told Jesus to stop his disciples from their confession of him as king (Mark 11:1–11; Luke 19:38–40), the so-called cleansing of the temple (Mark 11:15–19), and his prediction of the demise of the temple (Mark 13:1–2; cf. 14:56–59 and Matt. 26:59–61). As Jesus came out of the temple, he said to his disciples that there would not be one stone on another that would not be torn down (Mark 13:1–2).[13] Sanders notes that many in antiquity claimed that the temple would be replaced or destroyed, such as one of the authors of *1 Enoch* and the author of the Qumran *Temple Scroll* (11QT 29:8–10). But Jesus' actions and words, combined with the fact that he had a following, caused alarm among the religious and political leaders. Sanders concludes that Caiaphas had Jesus arrested because he had mistakenly thought that Jesus had personally threatened or posed a threat to the temple.[14] Did Jesus threaten to destroy the temple? Probably not, but his accusers brought this charge against him (Mark 15:29–30). The importance of such allegations must be understood in light of the significance the temple had at that time. Its centrality in the political, social, and religious life of first-century Judaism cannot be overestimated.[15]

13. E. P. Sanders, *The Historical Figure of Jesus* (London: Allen Lane / Penguin, 1993), 257, says that the fact that this did not literally happen shows that the prediction predates the destruction of the temple and may well go back to Jesus himself.

14. Sanders, *Historical Figure*, 262, 271.

15. For a brief discussion of the function and importance of the Jewish temple in the time of Jesus, see E. Ferguson, *Backgrounds of Early Christianity* (3rd ed.; Grand Rapids: Eerdmans,

The religious authorities and Pilate as well considered Jesus' actions and teachings a threat to the stability of the region, so Caiaphas had Jesus arrested. He apparently believed that the death of one person was far better than the destruction of the whole land (John 11:50). Upon his recommendation, Pilate had Jesus beaten and crucified. Sanders argues that the New Testament references to Pilate's hesitation to have Jesus put to death (Matt. 27:24–25; Mark 15:6–15; Luke 23:4; John 18:38) were the word of a later generation of Christians trying to reduce conflict between Rome and the early Christian movement.[16] Although it is reasonable that later generations of Christians went to considerable lengths to show that the church was not in conflict with Rome, and thereby wanted to reduce the causes that would lead to the harm of their community, the reliability of the evangelists' report nevertheless has considerable support, especially since this tradition is found in all four Gospels.

Carroll and Green more carefully state that, while the Gospels are correct in Pilate's conclusion that the charges against Jesus were baseless and that Jesus posed no serious threat to Rome, Pilate's reputation in noncanonical sources (Philo, *Embassy* 302) and in the New Testament (Luke 13:1) shows that he needed little or no persuasion to move against Jesus.[17] Philo, for instance, spoke of Pilate's corruption, insolence, habit of insulting people, and cruelty and torture of innocent people without trial. Philo, for instance, says that Pilate outraged the Jewish nation and that his conduct included

> briberies, the insults, the robberies, the outrages and wanton injuries, the executions without trial constantly repeated, the ceaseless and supremely grievous cruelty. So with all his vindictiveness and furious temper, he was in a difficult position. . . . The violence of his anger, though he was not easily roused to anger, it is needless to describe since the facts speak for themselves" (*Embassy* 301–4, LCL)

Josephus observes that Pilate was removed from office by the Syrian governor Vitellius and returned to Rome "because of the matters with which he was charged" (*Ant.* 18.89), and adds that in conjunction with this, Vitellius

---

2003), 562–67, but also M. O. Wise, "Temple," in *Dictionary of Jesus and the Gospels* (ed. Joel B. Green, Scot McKnight, and I. Howard Marshall; Downers Grove, IL: InterVarsity, 1992), 811–17, and the instructive discussion of the significance of the cleansing incident in W. R. Herzog II, "Temple Cleansing," in Green, Mcnight, and Marshall, *Dictionary of Jesus and the Gospels*, 817–21, and especially in Sanders, *Historical Figure*, 35–43, 254–62, and 270–73.

16. Sanders, *Historical Figure*, 274.

17. J. T. Carroll and J. B Green, *The Death of Jesus in Early Christianity* (Peabody, MA: Hendrickson, 1995), 202–3.

also removed Caiaphas from office and appointed Jonathan in his place (*Ant.* 18.95). Crossan notes that Pilate's and Caiaphas's tenures in Judea overlapped by ten years and that the close cooperation between them probably offended Jewish sensibilities and made it necessary to remove them both.[18]

The Key Factors

The key factors that led to the death of Jesus likely included his earlier conflicts with Jewish religious teachers, especially the Pharisees, during his public career in Galilee (Mark 3:1–6). Jesus was a charismatic figure who challenged the religious and social norms of his day and, as a result, had a large following.[19] Along with this, if Jesus was a messianic claimant, we have a further reason for his downfall. He did not normally refer to himself as a messiah or king in public, but in his questioning by Caiaphas in Mark 14:61–62, Jesus acknowledged that he was the Messiah—a king, "the Son of the Blessed One." This fits with a number of clues in the Gospels. According to Matthew 11:4–6 and Luke 7:22–23, when John's disciples questioned Jesus about his identity, he answered with a reference to Isaiah 29:18–19 and 35:5–6. Jesus' response appears to make a messianic claim. As we observed earlier, the messianic text from the Dead Sea Scrolls, 4Q521, has twelve lines that refer to the role of the messiah. The first line indicates, "For the heavens and the earth will listen *to his Messiah*," who will care for the pious, the poor, the captives, and the blind, and, another line says that "*he will heal the badly wounded and will make the dead live, he will proclaim good news to the meek*" (4Q521 2 II, 1, 12, italics added).[20] Since this text reflects a first-century Jewish understanding of the role of the messiah, Jesus likely made a claim to be the expected messiah to John's disciples.[21] Jesus' reference to the nature of his ministry in Luke 4:18–19, when he cites Isaiah 61:1–2 (see also Isa. 58:6), also suggests that he at least saw himself as an eschatological prophet, if not a messianic figure. Stanton, citing the Qumran text 11Q13, in conjunction with 4Q521, contends that Jesus' reference to Isaiah 61:1–2 shows that he was making an indirect messianic claim.[22]

---

18. J. D. Crossan, *Who Killed Jesus? Exposing the Roots of Anti-Judaism in the Gospel Story of the Death of Jesus* (San Francisco: HarperSanFrancisco, 1996), 148.

19. Carroll and Green, *Death of Jesus*, 201–2, and G. Stanton, *Gospel Truth? New Light on Jesus and the Gospels* (Edinburgh: T&T Clark, 1995), 183–87.

20. Martínez, *Dead Sea Scrolls*, 394. For the complete translation of this document, see p. 340 above.

21. Stanton (*Gospel Truth?*, 185–87) makes this claim.

22. Ibid., 187.

While the term "messiah" does not necessarily refer to a king, had Jesus openly claimed to be a king early in his ministry, it could have been fatal.[23] Interestingly, even a non-kingly messianic reference is difficult to find on the lips of Jesus in the Gospels. Jesus seldom referred to the title "messiah" during his ministry, and he did not affirm the acclamation, but instead predicted his rejection and death (Mark 8:29–31). Suffering and rejection were not a part of Jewish messianic expectations in the first century. The despair of the disciples after Jesus' death is therefore understandable; they did not expect a crucified messiah. When Pilate ordered that Jesus be crucified and placed the sign "King of the Jews" over his head, we have some indication at least that his actions had been interpreted by his followers as well as by his enemies to mean that Jesus was viewed as a messianic figure or claimant.[24] Sanders argues that Jesus' three symbolic acts just prior to his death (triumphal entry into Jerusalem, cleansing of the temple, and transforming the Passover meal into a religious ceremony with a different significance) all point to Jesus' belief in the coming of a new kingdom and his leadership role within it.[25]

Jesus' temple cleansing and his predictions against the temple were likely the immediate causes for his arrest (Mark 11:15–18; 13:1–2; 14:1–2), but he also had opposition from both the Pharisees and the scribes dating back to the early days of his ministry in Galilee when they took exception to him for not agreeing with them on their views of keeping the Sabbath, the various purification laws, and fasting laws (Mark 2:18–3:6; 7:1–23). The Pharisees generally disappear as opponents of Jesus following his ministry in Galilee. After the chief priests, scribes, and elders confronted Jesus about his authority (Mark 11:27–33), they sent some Pharisees and Herodians to try to trap him in what he said in the temple precincts (Mark 12:13–17). The Pharisees' opposition evidently followed him from the early days of his ministry (Mark 3:6), when Jesus was also accused of being a magician who cast out demons by the power of the devil, or Beelzebub (Matt. 9:34; 10:25; 12:24, 27; and see Jesus' response in 12:25–32), and of being a false prophet who led the people astray (Luke 23:2, 5, 14). Early opposition to Jesus cannot be a negligible factor among those that brought Jesus to the cross. It may be that news of the growing opposition to his ministry, even in Galilee, contributed to Jesus' rejection in Jerusalem, even if the decisive events that led to his arrest were the temple cleansing, his predictions about its destruction, and his acclamation as Messiah at his triumphal entry. The so-called temple cleansing itself

23. Ibid., 179.
24. Ibid.
25. Sanders, *Historical Figure*, 253–64.

247

was probably more of a prophetic act intended to make a statement about Jesus' mission than simply a cleaning up of the temple. Stanton notes that it would have taken an army to halt the buying and selling in the temple and that therefore Jesus' actions are better understood to be not so much a protest against the money changers in the temple area as "a prophetic gesture against the temple itself."[26]

The religious leaders in Jerusalem perceived a threat in Jesus from his actions and feared that he could disrupt the stability and tenuous peace with Rome, which could lead to Roman intervention. Adding to this, though Jesus never enlisted an army to accomplish his ends, the size of his following at the time of his death was noticeable (Mark 11:18; Luke 19:39). Because of this, both the Jewish religious leaders and Pilate decided that Jesus posed too great a threat to the stability of the region, and they could not allow him to continue.

The Cause of Execution and Jesus' Defense

Jesus evidently had the opportunity to defend himself to Caiaphas and also to Pilate, who could essentially have dismissed the charges against him but chose not to do so (Matt. 26:62–64; 27:11–14; Mark 14:60–61; 15:1–5; Luke 22:66–70; 23:3–4, 8–9; John 18:19–24, 28–38). Sanders affirms the historicity of the Gospel reports, claiming that Jesus conceivably "could have talked his way out of execution had he promised to take his disciples, return to Galilee and keep his mouth shut. He seems not to have tried."[27]

Some years ago, S. G. F. Brandon wrote a controversial book saying that Jesus was sympathetic to the so-called freedom fighters of his day, the Zealots, and he concluded that this activity led to Jesus' untimely death.[28] On the contrary, there is no evidence that Jesus was ever a member of such a party or even sympathetic to such a group. His association with tax collectors (Mark 2:13–17), which would have been intolerable to many of his day, argues against this since the "freedom fighters" were opposed to Roman tax collectors. That both a tax collector and a zealot could be his disciples suggests significant changes in the outlook of both disciples. Jesus had no army, and since only he was arrested in Jerusalem, his disciples were not perceived to pose a threat to Rome or the Jewish nation at that time. The charge or accusation against Jesus in the superscription over the cross ("King of the Jews") expresses the concern that Jesus was perceived by some to be a king, even if the nature of his kingdom was misunderstood by the religious leadership of his day and probably also by Pilate.

26. Stanton, *Gospel Truth?*, 182–83.
27. Sanders, *Historical Figure*, 267.
28. S. G. F. Brandon, *Jesus and the Zealots* (Manchester: Manchester University Press, 1967).

Who Was Responsible?

Crossan does not believe that the New Testament writings present generally historically accurate information about the life and ministry of Jesus, but it is surprising that he also dismisses the historical accuracy of the passion narratives and their implication that there was *some* Jewish participation, even at the religious leadership level, in Jesus' condemnation and death.[29] He calls the information about Jesus in the Gospels "prophecy historicized rather than history recalled."[30] He rightly rejects the notion that the whole Jewish nation was responsible and that Rome was innocent, but he fails to satisfy the question of why there was such strong reaction against the Jewish people in early Christian writings. It did not happen in a vacuum. All of the Jews of Palestine could not possibly be held accountable for the death of Jesus, not even a sizeable percentage of them. No doubt there were some Jews who did not accept Jesus as a messianic figure and perceived him as some kind of charlatan. Some wanted to dismiss him, and others even wanted to execute him, while some believed in him. In no case, however, were all the Jewish people guilty of or responsible for his death. There is no good reason to deny, however, that certain Jewish religious leaders in Jerusalem believed that the death of one person who threatened the religious and social structure of the region could possibly keep the nation safe from Roman interference in their affairs (John 11:49–53).

Since the Jewish authorities did not have the authority to execute, the local Roman prefect, Pilate, and the soldiers under his command were responsible for the actual death itself. The execution came as a recommendation from the high priest, but Pilate was under no mandate to carry out the high priest's wishes. Pilate made the final decision, and evidently in a rather quick manner, since none of the Gospels indicate that he tarried long in his deliberation. The execution itself took place on the same day, within a few hours of the time when Jesus was brought to him.

The number of those responsible for Jesus' death was eventually and unfortunately expanded by the church to include the whole Jewish nation and eventually all Jews of all time. For example, the genre identified as "adversus *Judaeos*" literature often reflects Christian debates with Jews, and with one exception (Justin's *Dialogue with Trypho*), the Jew always loses the argument, even if occasionally praised by his Christian opponent. By the second and third centuries, it is not uncommon to hear prominent Christian teachers condemn all Jews instead of merely those that were responsible for

---

29. Crossan, *Who Killed Jesus?*, 147–59.
30. Ibid., 159.

his death.[31] Some references in the New Testament probably contributed to that conclusion—for example, John 8:34–59 and 1 Thessalonians 2:13–16. Gentile misunderstanding of Jewish texts in a later era was both an unfortunate and an unreasonable conclusion that has led to many tragedies for the Jewish people throughout history. It is an overstatement to say that no Jews in authoritative places were responsible for the death of Jesus, but on the other hand unreasonable to say that all of Israel should therefore be held accountable. There was no vote on the part of all of the Jewish people on this matter. The decision was made only by a handful of religious leaders, and the New Testament Gospels make this clear.

What most likely led to the expansion of Jewish responsibility for the death of Jesus is the fact that the Jews did not convert to Christianity and that many early Christians still found Judaism attractive well into the fifth century AD. Also, there appears to have been some Jewish involvement in the persecution of the Christians, such as their turning Christians over to Roman authorities after the Christian faith had been outlawed in certain sectors of the empire. In some cases, Jews were no doubt responsible for turning in Christians to Roman authorities who punished Christians for their faith, as in the case of the death of Polycarp (*Mart. Pol.* 12.2; 13.1; 17.2; 18.1).[32] That no doubt led to some of the hostile attitudes of the early Christians toward Jews, but this does not excuse Christians for unchristian attitudes or actions against their ancient siblings, especially because of Jesus' call to love even those considered one's enemies (Matt. 5:43–48; John 13:34–35).

Jesus' Death "Divinely" Ordered

From a biblical perspective, early Christian writers began to argue that the death of Jesus was in the plan of God (Acts 2:23) and that his death was for "our sins"; that is, he died in the place of sinners (Rom. 5:8; 2 Cor. 5:19–21). Stein is certainly correct in asserting that the historic Christian theological perspective is that "Christians know that *they* are the cause

31. E.g., Origen, *Hom. Jer. 5*, but also 4.73 and 5.8. Cyprian, *The Lord's Prayer*, in treatise 10, states, "In condemnation of these [Jews] we Christians say, when we pray, 'Our Father,' because He now has begun to be ours and has ceased to be of the Jews who have forsaken Him." As late as the eighth century, Prudentius called on all Jews to convert to faith in Christ, but was extremely negative against the Jews. See also Tertullian, *Adversus Judaeos* 13, for a similar view. For other examples, see Lee Martin McDonald, "Anti-Judaism in the Early Church Fathers," in *Anti-Semitism and Early Christianity: Issues of Polemic and Faith* (eds. Craig A. Evans and Donald A. Hagner; Minneapolis: Fortress, 1993), 215–52.

32. For a more detailed discussion of this, see chap. 7, and L. M. McDonald, "Anti-Judaism in the Early Church Fathers," especially 236–49.

for Jesus' death. Ultimately it is the believer, for whom Christ died, who is responsible for his death." He adds that those who need a scapegoat "need only look in the mirror."[33] The time for blaming the whole nation for the crimes against Jesus is long since over, and Christians should consider Stein's timely advice.

The Death and Burial of Jesus

The Practice of Crucifixion[34]

The Roman practice of execution by crucifixion may have been learned from the Carthaginians. Its practice dates from at least the sixth century BC and was banned in the Roman Empire by Constantine in AD 337 out of respect for Jesus. Crucifixion was normally reserved for slaves and subject peoples and only used on Roman citizens in cases of very serious crimes such as high treason.[35] Josephus reports that crucifixion was one of the most horrible manners of death and reports that Alexander Jannaeus, the Jewish Hasmonean king (reigned 103–76 BC), used it as punishment for his Jewish enemies (Pharisees). He writes:

> The most powerful among them, however, he shut up and besieged in the city of Bethoma, and after taking the city and getting them into his power, he brought them back to Jerusalem; and there he did a thing that was as cruel as could be: while he feasted with his concubines in a conspicuous place, he ordered some eight hundred of the Jews to be crucified, and slaughtered their children and wives before the eyes of the still living wretches. This was the revenge he took for the injuries he had suffered; but the penalty he exacted was inhuman for all. (*Ant.* 13.380–81, LCL)

33. R. Stein, *Jesus the Messiah: A Survey of the Life of Christ* (Downers Grove, IL: InterVarsity, 1996), 239.

34. The standard resource on Roman crucifixions with all of the pertinent data listed is that of Martin Hengel, *Crucifixion in the Ancient World and the Folly of the Message of the Cross* (Philadelphia: Fortress, 1977). See especially pp. 22–50 for an extensive discussion of Roman crucifixions. More recently, an excellent resource on the practice of crucifixion in antiquity is David W. Chapman, *Ancient Jewish and Christian Perceptions of Crucifixion* (Tübingen: Mohr Siebeck, 2008; Grand Rapids: Baker Academic, 2010). Similarly, Gunnar Samuelsson's *Crucifixion in Antiquity: An Inquiry into the Background and Significance of the New Testament Terminology of Crucifixion* (WUNT 2. R 310; Tübingen: Mohr Siebeck, 2011) is a helpful addition to Hengel's masterful work. Samuelsson focuses especially on the terminology of crucifixion, but also its history and practice in the ancient world.

35. See Hengel, *Crucifixion*, 39–45, who cites several examples of Romans who were crucified. He summarizes the practice of crucifixion on pp. 86–90.

Later the Pharisees, under the protection of Queen Alexandra Salome, the successor of Alexander Jannaeus, persuaded the queen to crucify those who had persuaded Alexander Jannaeus to crucify these eight hundred men (Josephus, *Ant.* 13.410).

Roman executions were generally done in the daytime and in public places to instill fear in all who observed the execution and to deter actions similar to those that led to the crucifixion. Torture, humiliations, and beatings were common in both Carthaginian and Roman crucifixions (see Livy 22.13.9; 28.37.3; Josephus, *Ant.* 19.94; and *Digesta* 48.19.8.3).[36] Crucifixions were considered more horrible than hangings, since hanging was quick but crucifixion took much longer and involved much torment and pain before death. Besides the usual beatings that preceded such executions, those crucified were often hung naked to add to their humiliation. Hengel observes the comment of Melito (ca. 170), in his *Homily on the Passion*, bemoaning the fact that Jesus was so displayed at his crucifixion. Melito writes: "The Master has been treated in unseemly fashion, his body naked, and not even deemed worthy of a covering, that [his nakedness] might not be seen. Therefore the lights [of heaven] turned away, and the day darkened, that it might hide him who was stripped upon the cross."[37] Also, victims of Roman crucifixion were often not buried, but rather left to decompose on their crosses and/or be devoured by birds and wild animals. In the land of Israel and during peacetime, however, considerations were given to the Jews, who were often allowed to bury their dead. The relevant question for our purposes is whether Jesus' body received a proper burial according to Jewish standards, or whether the Romans left it to decompose on the cross or discarded it in an open grave. Both Josephus (*Life* 75.420–21) and Roman law (*Digesta* 48.24.1–3) reflect the Roman practice of allowing bodies to be removed from their crosses and buried. Philo was also aware of this practice and complained that Flaccus, Roman governor of Egypt, did not allow for the burial of the bodies of those persons executed by crucifixion on the eve of a holiday (*Flaccus* 10.83).

While the Romans wanted to frighten the Jews into submission during the AD 66–70 war, and consequently left the bodies of crucified victims on the crosses in clear view of the Jews in the city (Josephus, *J.W.* 5.450–51), this was not the normal practice in Palestine. This is similar to the testimony of

36. *Digesta* (begun in AD 530 and completed in 533) is a summary of Roman law up to the time of the Emperor Justinian, who called for its composition. Most of the *Digesta* focuses on Roman law from roughly AD 100 to 250. Seldom is it a simple matter to discern between earlier and later Roman law in this document, but *Digesta* is often instructive of legal notions prevalent within sixty to seventy years after the time of Jesus.

37. Hengel, *Crucifixion*, 21.

Pseudo-Quintilian, who agrees that the Romans' practice of crucifixion was intended to terrify. Crucifixions, consequently, were placed on the most crowded roads so that large numbers of people could see them and be "moved by this terror." He adds: "For penalties relate not so much to retribution as to their exemplary effect" (*Decl.* 274).

In the time of Jesus there was relative peace in the land, and when he approached Jerusalem, a Passover holy day was about to begin, with the area crowded with Jewish pilgrims. It is unlikely, given the potential for riots in Jerusalem, that the Romans would deny the Jews their sacred duty of burying the dead in accordance with their religious traditions. Philo and Josephus both claim that in general the Romans honored the Jewish customs (Philo, *Embassy* 300; *Flaccus* 83; Josephus, *Ag. Ap.* 2.73), and this is similar to the Roman law cited in the *Digesta*. The relevant text for exceptions to the usual practice reads as follows:

> The bodies of those who are condemned to death should not be refused [to] their relatives; and the Divine Augustus, in the Tenth Book of his Life, said that this rule has been observed. At present, the bodies of those who have been punished are only buried when this has been requested and permission granted; and sometimes it is not permitted, especially where persons have been convicted of high treason. . . . The bodies of persons who have been punished should be given to whoever requests them for the purpose of burial. (*Digesta* 48.24.1–3)

From this it is clear that the Roman practice of allowing the burial of the bodies of crucifixion victims was common if the body was requested. Joseph of Arimathea's request to bury the body of Jesus following the crucifixion (Mark 15:42–45 and parallels) does have precedent in Roman law. Biblical scholars know well that the skeletal remains of a crucified man named Yehoḥanan were discovered in his family tomb at Giv'at ha-Mivtar. Because of the difficulty of extracting the spike from his ankle, it was left in the ankle, along with some of the wood pieces to which it was attached, and placed in the ossuary (bone box) with his bones.

Crossan, who argues that Jesus' body was put in a garbage dump and devoured by animals, claims that this one example shows that the practice of burying criminals was exceptional given the large number of crucifixions in the land of Israel in those days and that most of the bodies were left unburied.[38] Crossan, however, does not take into account that nails were normally extracted from the victims of crucifixion by the Roman soldiers themselves and often sold as amulets. The extraction of the nails is supported by the apocryphal *Gospel of Peter* 6:21, which indicates that the soldiers removed

---

38. Crossan, *Excavating Jesus*, 290–91.

the nails from Jesus' body: "And then the Jews drew the nails from the hands of the Lord and laid him on the earth." Because extracting the nails was a normal practice, and because of physical decay, we simply cannot tell how many persons who were placed in the ossuaries were crucified. Similarly, Crossan's argument does not take into account that many of the crucifixions did not include the use of nails, but ropes.[39] Yehoḥanan's was not a typical case, since the nail could not be removed from his foot, but the rarity of the case does support the usual practice of removing the nails following crucifixion.[40]

Although crucifixion was practiced in the Hasmonean period (165–63 BC), Herod the Great did not use it against the Jews. The Romans, however, did not hesitate to use crucifixion in order to pacify the people after the invasion of Pompey in 63 BC. The pseudepigraphal book *Assumption of Moses* (6:8–9) relates the practice of crucifixion (possibly by Pompey) as follows: "There will come into their land a powerful king of the West who will subdue them; and he will take captives, and a part of their temple he will burn with fire. He will crucify some of them around the city."[41] This was a hated form of death among the Jews, and the reference in Deuteronomy 21:23 (see also Gal. 3:13) helps explain why a crucified messiah was such a stumbling block to them (1 Cor. 1:23).

Crucifixion was normally preceded by scourging, after which criminals would sometimes carry their own crosses or the cross bar from the place of judgment to the place of execution. More notorious criminals were often hung higher than others. It is also possible that Jesus took the place of Barabbas, a convicted robber (John 18:38b–40).

Nails were normally driven through the wrists, and the feet were fastened on a peg either by nails or cords. Generally the crucified person died of exposure to heat and the elements, as well as from a lack of oxygen due to asphyxiation when the legs gave out. Death often took a day or two. Jesus did not spend much time on the cross—perhaps only three to six hours at the most—before

---

39. Dale C. Allison, *Resurrecting Jesus: The Earliest Christian Tradition and Its Interpreters* (New York: T&T Clark, 2005), 361. Allison also mentions the reference in the Mishnah to this practice among the heathen, but the Mishnah condemns the practice. The text reads: "Men may go out with a locust's egg, or a jackal's tooth or with a nail of [the gallows of] one that was crucified, as a means of healing . . . but the Sages say: Even on ordinary days this is forbidden as following in the ways of the Amorite" (*m. Šabb.* 6.10 [trans. Danby]).

40. C. A. Evans has produced a very helpful volume on Jewish burial practices, including the use of ossuaries in and around Jerusalem in the time of Jesus. See his *Jesus and the Ossuaries: What Jewish Burial Practices Reveal about the Beginning of Christianity* (Waco: Baylor University Press, 2003).

41. Trans. J. H. Charlesworth in *The Old Testament Pseudepigrapha* (ed. J. H. Charlesworth; Garden City, NY: Doubleday, 1983), 1:930.

he died. This likely reflects the severity of the beating prior to his crucifixion. Observe that even Pilate was surprised that it took so little time for Jesus to die (Mark 15:44–45).

In telling the story of Jesus' crucifixion, each evangelist also made important theological points. Matthew, for instance, includes the story of an earthquake (27:51), the temple curtain torn in two (27:51), and bodies rising out of their graves and going through the streets of Jerusalem (27:52–53—a likely reference to the resurrection at the end of the age that Matthew believed was at hand). This shows that for Matthew, the death of Jesus signified that the end of the age had come (see Matt. 24:7–8) and that through the death of Jesus, access to God was made possible for all persons, not just the high priest. Matthew also indicates that, in Jesus' death, he was acknowledged to be the Son of God (27:54). Table 5.2 shows how each evangelist listed accompanying phenomena at the death of Jesus. Each phenomenon appears laden with theological significance.

Burial Narratives

Jesus was taken from the cross and buried by Joseph of Arimathea to complete the requirements of Jewish tradition, but the purchase and use of a linen cloth suggests that Joseph had more than a religious motivation to keep the land undefiled. He was apparently concerned about Jesus himself. It is quite possible that at first Joseph was only an upstanding citizen known for his piety, and not yet a disciple when Mark and Luke produced their Gospels; but perhaps he became one by the time Matthew and John were written. The Gospels also agree that the tomb of Jesus was empty on the morning of the first day of the week, implying that Jesus, who was buried, was also raised from the dead, or someone removed his body to another place. His body was no longer where Joseph of Arimathea had placed it. This does not resolve all of the questions in the biblical narratives, but the burial of Jesus is in agreement with the earliest testimony on the matter as well as with early Jewish burial practices. For those who contend that the burial story was an early church invention to avoid the final shameful act toward Jesus, it is hard to believe that the act of crucifixion, the most shameful death imaginable in the ancient world, could have been surpassed by a shameful burial. As noted above, Jesus' burial is also in keeping with ancient Roman practices, which sought, in nonrebellious times, to allow Jewish customs of burial on the day of one's death to take place, even for those crucified for crimes of blasphemy according to Jewish beliefs.

Every known society in history has taken special measures to bury its dead with some form of dignity and honor. This is also true in the biblical traditions.

For Jews, the appropriate methods of acceptable care for the dead included placing the body in the earth or in a sepulcher. Biblical descriptions of burials are to be found in formulas such as "he lay with his fathers" (1 Kings 14:31; 2 Chron. 12:16) or "he was gathered to his people" (Gen. 25:8; Deut. 32:50). For the Jews, the burial of the dead was a religious obligation that extended even to the burial of criminals executed for major crimes (Deut. 21:22–23). The reason had to do chiefly with the belief that leaving any corpse on the ground brought impurity to the land (Deut. 21:23). Occasionally, and for the most serious offenses against God, a corpse was left exposed or experienced a dishonorable disposal (Deut. 28:25–26; 1 Kings 14:10–11; see especially Jer. 7:33; 8:2; 14:16; 16:4; 20:6;[42] 22:19; 25:33; Ps. 79:2–3; Ezek. 29:5).[43] While there were occasional exceptions, the usual practice was to bury the dead, even those who had committed crimes or were so accused. Indeed, according to the apocryphal book of Tobit, burying the dead was considered a special act of kindness, demonstrating the most charitable act that one could practice (1:18–20; 2:3–8; 4:3–4; 6:15; 14:10–13), and Tobit himself was the outstanding model of this kind of piety. This is also illustrated in Philo (*Joseph* 22–23).

From roughly 30 BC to AD 70, a common form of Palestinian Jewish burials, especially for the wealthy or those with appropriate means, was the practice of secondary burial called *ossilegium*. This meant that a body was placed in a tomb, normally a cave, for a year. After the body had decomposed, the bones were placed in an ossuary (a bone box hewn out of limestone) and left in the family tomb. These ossuaries were usually around 60 x 35 x 30 cm for adults and smaller for children. Some of the ossuaries were highly decorated, as in the case of the famous Caiaphas ossuary; but most were rather plain, with simple etchings of the name of the deceased and the family name, sometimes also with the deceased's profession or trade, and occasionally other information such as place of origin or age. Sometimes the deceased person's status was also mentioned; namely, whether the person was a "freedman" or related to others in the same tomb, or perhaps other matters deemed relevant about the person. After AD 70 this practice became less common until around AD 135, but possibly continued as late as the third century in some instances.[44]

This practice of secondary burials may be something like what is pictured in 2 Kings 22:20; namely, being gathered to one's ancestors—a practice that may

---

42. For these false prophets to be buried in a foreign land and not in their homeland was considered dishonorable. For this reason, Jacob's and Joseph's bones were brought from Egypt to the land of Canaan (e.g., Gen. 49:29–50:7, 24–26; Josh. 24:32).

43. For a discussion of ancient Jewish burial practices, see Elizabeth Bloch-Smith, "Burials," *ABD* 1:785–89.

44. See Rachael Hachlili, "Burials, Ancient Jewish," *ABD* 1:789–94.

have its roots in the story of Joseph transferring the body (bones?) of Jacob from Egypt to the burial site of his ancestors (Gen. 47:29–30; 50:4–14), and subsequently also of Joseph requesting that his bones be carried to the land God had promised Abraham. This was done when the Israelites left Egypt (Gen. 50:24–25; Exod. 13:19; Josh. 24:32; see also 1 Sam. 31:12–19). Jesus' word to a man who wanted to be his disciple to "let the dead bury the dead" likely assumes the practice of placing bones into an ossuary in the family tomb (Matt. 8:21–22; Luke 9:59–60).[45] The practice of *Shiv'ah*, seven days of mourning begun after the body was interred, may have roots in the mourning of seven days that Joseph observed for his father (Gen. 50:10), or perhaps even in the death of Moses as we see in *y. Ketub.* 1. The location of such burial sites was, according to Jewish law, outside the city limits or city wall (*m. B. Bat.* 2:9). In Jerusalem, as well as elsewhere in Jewish communities such as Hierapolis and Antioch on the Orontes, tombs were located outside the city walls.

Émile Puech contends that similar burial practices based on Deuteronomy 21:22–23 took place at Qumran, and that the Essenes, like the Pharisees, believed in the resurrection of the body, so care was given to burial procedures.[46]

As a general practice, secondary burials took place, as noted above, outside the walls of Jerusalem or in that vicinity from roughly 30 BC to AD 70. Although, again, as mentioned above, some secondary burials were practiced in other places where Jews resided until around the third century AD, this practice was never as common elsewhere as it was in the vicinity of Jerusalem.[47] The majority of Jewish burials would have been in trench graves rather than in hewn-out caves, which were more common among the rich.

According to Josephus, the Jewish customs of the day required that all persons who died be buried, whether they were enemies (*J.W.* 3.377; 4.317) or those condemned to death by Jewish law (*Ant.* 4.264–65). Occasionally

45. For a more full discussion of this, see B. R. McCane, *Roll Back the Stone: Death and Burial in the World of Jesus* (Edinburgh: T&T Clark, 2003); and his "Burial," *NIDB* 1:509–10; Rachel Hachlili, "Burials, Ancient Jewish"; Elizabeth Bloch-Smith, *Judahite Burial Practices and Beliefs about the Dead* (Sheffield: Sheffield University Press, 1992); and Bloch-Smith, "Burials, Israelite." A more comprehensive discussion of such practices is R. Hachlili, *Jewish Funerary Customs, Practices, and Rites in the Second Temple Period* (JSJSup 94; Leiden: Brill, 2005). Similarly, any study of the use of ossuaries is now also heavily dependent on L. Y. Rahmani, *A Catalogue of Jewish Ossuaries in the Collections of the State of Israel* (Jerusalem: Israel Antiquities Authority, 1994).

46. Émile Puech, "Resurrection: The Bible and Qumran," in *The Dead Sea Scrolls and the Qumran Community* (vol. 2 of *The Bible and the Dead Sea Scrolls: The Princeton Symposium on the Dead Sea Scrolls*; ed. J. H. Charlesworth; Waco: Baylor University Press, 2006), 277–81. See also Joe Zias, "The Cemeteries of Qumran and Celibacy: Confusion Laid to Rest?," *DSD* 7 (2000): 220–53.

47. Hachlili, "Burials, Ancient Jewish," 790–91.

one sees an exception to this practice among Jews who allowed the "wicked who rejoice in the death of the righteous" to be left to decompose on the ground. Josephus observes that Achar (Achan; cf. Josh. 7:18–26) was given an "ignominious burial proper to the condemned" (*Ant.* 5.44; cf. 4.264), but this was unusual. More common was his reference to activities of pious Jews who "furnish fire, water, food to all who ask for them, point out the road, [do] not leave a corpse unburied, show consideration even to declared enemies" (*Ag. Ap.* 2.211; cf. 2.205). Despised persons would normally not be placed in their family tombs, but rather in a common place for persons of low esteem (criminals); they would nevertheless be buried, and in time their bones could be placed in family tombs.[48] This tradition is also found in the Mishnah (*m. Sanh.* 6.5) and later in the Tosefta (*t. Sanh.* 9.8). The Mishnah allows that in some cases the body of the deceased criminal could be placed in the family tomb (*m. Sanh.* 6.6).

Later the rabbis questioned whether a good person who was executed by a wicked empire could be buried in a family tomb or given an honorable burial. The answer was that that person could be buried in the family tomb (*b. Sanh.* 47a–47b). Brown describes this situation in the circumstance of the Maccabean martyrs receiving honorable burials.[49] Jesus was accused of blasphemy by the Jews, however, and was, according to Jewish tradition, worthy of death. Josephus indicates that blasphemers would be hanged, stoned, and buried "ignominiously and in obscurity" (*Ant.* 4.202). In the *Martyrdom of Polycarp* 17:2 (ca. AD 150), the story is told of Jews objecting to giving the body of the martyred bishop Polycarp of Smyrna to his friends and followers for an honorable burial. When the centurion in charge of the execution "saw the contentiousness caused by the Jews, he put the body [of Polycarp] in the midst, as was their custom, and burned it. Thus we [his followers], at last, took up his bones, more precious than precious stones . . . and put them where it was appropriate" (18:1–2). Brown observes that Jesus was crucified by the Romans, not for blasphemy, but for the charge of being the king of the Jews. He asks whether this might have opened the possibility for an honorable burial.[50]

Why is all of this information about Jewish burial practices important? The answer is that some scholars have argued that Jesus was not buried by his followers, but by his enemies, based on what these scholars contend is an earlier tradition used by Luke in Acts 13:29 that claims Jesus was buried by his enemies. If this is so, then all of the stories about an elaborate burial and subsequent empty tomb are simply late additions added to the Easter stories

48. Brown, *Death of the Messiah*, 2:1209–11.
49. Ibid., 2:1210.
50. Ibid., 2:1211.

for apologetic purposes. Was Jesus, therefore, placed in a *loculus* tomb (a small chamber or cell in an ancient tomb), or some other kind of interment after his crucifixion? Since he was crucified under Roman rule as a traitor to the empire, would Jewish custom be overridden and his body be allowed to decompose on the cross, or was Jesus' body placed in an open grave with bodies of criminals? Jewish custom is clear: dead bodies were buried—even those of criminals.

Those who point to the secondary nature of the burial and empty-tomb narratives also tend to emphasize the differences in Gospel stories of the burial of Jesus. We will look at some of them shortly, but I should also point out many consistencies in these reports that suggest a common origin. In all four narratives, for instance, it is Joseph of Arimathea who requests and receives permission from Pilate to bury the body of Jesus. It is also Joseph who reportedly prepared Jesus' body with a linen shroud and placed the body of Jesus in the tomb. John indicates that Nicodemus helped (John 19:39–40). All four evangelists agree that the day of the burial was the day of preparation (Friday), just prior to the beginning of the Sabbath at sundown.

Beyond these agreements, Mark and Matthew say that Joseph (alone?) rolled the stone against the door of the tomb after the body was placed inside (Mark 15:46; Matt. 27:59–60). Luke and John make no mention of Joseph rolling the stone against the tomb, but the possibility that someone had sealed up the tomb could be inferred from the surprise of the women in the next chapter (Luke 24:2–4)—or from Mary's surprise in John 20:1—at the stone being rolled away. It is strange that Luke and John would mention the stone being rolled away since neither records that the tomb was sealed. This could be an indication of Luke's and John's dependence upon a common source or that both assumed the tomb was sealed.

Mark says Jesus' body was placed in a tomb (15:46), but Matthew adds that it was Joseph's own tomb that "he had hewn in the rock" (27:60). Luke and John are in agreement when they describe the tomb as one "where no one had ever been laid" (Luke 23:53; John 19:41). Luke and John differ at this point only in that Luke calls the tomb a "rock-hewn" tomb and John calls it a "new" tomb, although these descriptions are not incompatible.

Furthermore, in John 19:38, Joseph asks for the body *in secret*, but Mark (15:43) says Joseph "went boldly" to Pilate to request the body. The secret nature of the request in John is different from Mark. Matthew shows that the Roman guard and Jewish leaders knew the whereabouts of the tomb in which Jesus' body was placed (27:62–66). According to John, however, Mary, who was a Galilean, evidently knew where to go to find the body of Jesus (20:1). Further, the Synoptics make no mention of Joseph adding spices or ointments to the body during the preparation for burial. John alone introduces this thought, along with the only mention of Nicodemus's helping Joseph prepare the body (John 19:39–42). John alone does not mention the women at the burial of Jesus. Since none of the Gospel writers indicates that the women saw the preparation for Jesus' burial, it may be that the women were unaware of the specific preparations, but this is not explicitly stated. Mark says Mary Magdalene and Mary the mother of Joses saw where the body of Jesus was laid (15:47). Matthew simply says Mary Magdalene and the "other Mary" were there sitting opposite the tomb (27:61), while Luke says that the women who came with Jesus from Galilee followed and saw the tomb and how the body was laid and that they returned and prepared spices and ointments (23:55–56).

In the burial stories, Luke and John tend to have many agreements, and the same is true between Matthew and Mark. There is no mention of a new tomb "where no one had ever been laid" in Mark or Matthew, nor reference to the linen clothes in the empty tomb, which are mentioned in Luke and John. These similarities may provide evidence for a common source behind Luke and John.

Perhaps the more obvious problems of harmony in the burial stories are the following: Who provided the spices? Did Nicodemus provide them (John 19:39) or the women (Luke 23:55–56)? The answer may lie in the ignorance of the women regarding how the body was prepared for burial. Having seen only the burial itself and not the preparation of the body, they might well have considered coming back to prepare the body appropriately for burial. Can much be made of the silence of Mark and Matthew about the women preparing the spices but rather observing the burial, and what of John's failure to mention the women at the burial of Jesus? Should it be assumed that in all four Gospels the purpose of the coming of the women (or woman, in John) to the tomb on the first day of the week was to anoint the body with spices or simply to pay respects? Making that conjecture goes beyond what we know from the sources, though it is not impossible, as some have suggested.

Bultmann concluded that Mark 15:46 indicates that the burial of Jesus was complete and needed nothing further,[51] but he does not take into consideration the possible ignorance of the women regarding what had already occurred and does not allow that the women's act was simply an act of devotion on their part, not something required to make it a proper burial. Because of the lateness of the day when Jesus was buried, the women may not have had time to pay their final respects of devotion and honor to their fallen Master. On the day of preparation (*paraskeuē*), or Friday, there was only enough time to

---

51. Rudolf Bultmann, *The History of the Synoptic Tradition* (trans. J. Marsh; 2nd ed.; Oxford: Blackwell, 1972), 274.

perform the most necessary of obligations, and any further acts of devotion had to be postponed until after the Sabbath.

Burial Procedures

All of the evangelists indicate that a rather elaborate preparing, or wrapping, of Jesus' body in a shroud took place, and that the Sabbath was fast approaching, forcing those who prepared the body to do so somewhat hastily (see Matt. 27:57; Mark 15:42; Luke 23:54; John 19:42). Long ago Lilly noted that the Talmud, in the treatise dealing with Sabbath rest, permits all necessary steps to be taken for a decent burial on the Sabbath, and that "the duty of burying the dead was thus regarded as taking precedence over other laws whenever there should be a conflict."[52] It may well be that, as Lilly argues, what had obtained in Judaism in a later generation was also true during the time of Jesus. Since Deuteronomy 21:23 expressly states that the body of a condemned man cannot hang upon a tree all night but has to be buried "that same day," there seems to be no contradiction in Jesus' burial story taking place on a late Friday afternoon as the Sabbath was approaching. Also, the elaborate burial given to Jesus (Mark 15:46; John 19:39–41) is not necessarily in conflict with the lateness of the day of preparation or with the fact that Jesus died a criminal's death, since according to the Mishnah those who buried a person "may make ready (on the Sabbath or on a feast day) all that is needful for the dead, and anoint it and wash it, provided they do not move any member of it" (*m. Šabb.* 23.5). Therefore everything necessary for a decent burial, including the washing and anointing of a body, as the evangelists mention, was certainly possible within the proper keeping of the law by the Jews.

For this reason Lilly concludes that the evangelists, who were familiar with Palestinian Jewish conditions and customs, could not have attributed to the women the intention of coming to embalm the body of Jesus three days after burial. The intention of the women, he argues, was in keeping with an ancient Palestinian Jewish custom of visiting graves for three days after burial. This custom stemmed from the belief that the soul of the deceased remained in or near the body for three days. The custom of bringing spices and ointments for anointing was similar to the modern custom of bringing flowers or wreaths to the graveside of loved ones. Lilly cites as proof examples from Josephus (*Ant.* 17.196–99) in which there were some five hundred pounds of perfumes brought for the burial of Herod the Great, which were used quite apart from

---

52. J. L. Lilly, "Alleged Discrepancies in the Gospel Accounts of the Resurrection," *CBQ* 2 (1940): 103–4.

those used to embalm the body.[53] Although we may agree that according to Mark 15:46 the burial of Jesus was complete, we should ask whether Mark 16:1 and Luke 24:1 suggest otherwise or simply refer to an act of devotion on the part of Jesus' followers. If Lilly is correct, it is possible that Nicodemus supplied all the necessary spices for the burial (John 19:39) and that the women only intended to offer their spices and ointments out of love and devotion (Luke 23:56).

This is speculation, of course, and we may be reading something into the biblical narratives that is not explicitly there, but it does offer a possible solution. Whether the women's visit to the tomb on the first day of the week was to anoint the body of Jesus, as in Luke, or just to visit the tomb, as in Mark, Matthew, and John, this does not detract significantly from the message of the evangelists. Several motivations for the women coming to the tomb are plausible, but the important fact is, as Bode puts it, "the women came and that is enough."[54] I should add, however, all four evangelists say that Jesus was buried in a tomb.

Who Buried Jesus?

I return to the question posed earlier that asks who buried Jesus—his followers or enemies. All four Gospels state quite clearly that it was Joseph of Arimathea, but Acts 13:29 strangely appears to attribute this act to the enemies of Jesus, the Jews. According to Bultmann, Hans Grass, and subsequently Crossan, the purpose of the burial stories in the Gospels is to prevent Jesus from suffering the shame of an improper burial.[55] Fuller concludes that Mark 16:1–8 is more naturally an earlier part of the Gospel tradition.[56] For him, the stories of the women coming to the tomb complete the ordinary burial rites since, before then, the body of Jesus had simply been buried by those who wanted to ensure that proper Jewish burial was done, and this, he claims, fits with Acts 13:29. The women coming to the tomb was to make the final act

53. Lilly, "Alleged Discrepancies," 104–5.
54. E. L. Bode, *The First Easter Morning: The Gospel Accounts of the Women's Visit to the Tomb of Jesus* (Rome: Biblical Institute Press, 1970), 173.
55. H. Grass, *Ostergeschehen und Osterberichte* (Göttingen: Vandenhoeck & Ruprecht, 1962), 179–80.
56. R. H. Fuller, *Formation of the Resurrection Narratives* (London: SCM, 1972), 54–56. Bultmann argued that the story of the women coming to the tomb on Easter morning was secondary because it did not fit with the previous section in Mark. After giving the names in 15:40, 47, it would not be necessary to do so again as in 16:1; also their intention to embalm the body does not agree with 15:46, where there is no indication that the burial was incomplete. See Bultmann, *Synoptic Tradition*, 284–85.

toward Jesus one of charity. Mark's statement that Joseph of Arimathea was a respected member of the council and one who was looking for the kingdom of God (15:43) was, according to Fuller, later developed in the Gospel tradition to the point where Joseph eventually was even called a "disciple" (Matt. 27:57). Fuller suggests that the difference in the names of the women in the burial and empty-tomb stories can be attributed to later attempts to square the empty-tomb tradition with the names in the burial story. He claims that originally there was only Mary Magdalene at the tomb (John 20:1) and agrees with Wilckens's thesis that when the disciples returned from Galilee after receiving their visions, they heard the report from Mary Magdalene about the empty tomb and were pleased with it because it was in accord with their experience.[57] For him, Mary's report was later attached to the Passion Narrative as a vehicle for proclaiming the resurrection of Jesus.

F. F. Bruce suggests that it is not necessary to opt for one tradition (the Gospels) over another (Acts 13:29), suggesting a harmony of the two stories that allows the enemies of Jesus to remove the body from the cross, as seems possible from John 19:31, and yet to allow Joseph (and Nicodemus) at the same time to take care of the burial itself. He argues that both verbs in Acts 13:29 are "generalizing" plurals; that is, Luke does not specifically wish to say that the enemies of Jesus actually buried him.[58] Hanson apparently agrees, saying that Luke's representation of the Jews as burying Jesus is a result of his "condensed style" and not his deliberate intention.[59] He claims that the author of Luke-Acts probably would not have had Joseph of Arimathea perform the burial rites in one part of his work (Luke) and then be inconsistent with that in the second part of his work (Acts).

Despite the several variations in the Gospel accounts of the burial story, all agree, including Acts 13:29, that Jesus of Nazareth was buried. This is also supported by the earliest New Testament reference to Jesus' burial in 1 Corinthians 15:4, a tradition that precedes Paul and was handed down to him (1 Cor. 15:3). Because the death and burial of Jesus are so central to early Christian proclamation, it is important to take the time to be clear on the New Testament's certain affirmation of the matter.

How do the New Testament narratives regarding the crucifixion and burial of Jesus stand up in light of Jewish burial practices and Roman crucifixions? Although there are a number of variations in New Testament traditions, the writers of the New Testament are agreed that following his death, Jesus was

---

57. Fuller, *Formation of the Resurrection Narratives*, 54–55.
58. F. F. Bruce, *The Acts of the Apostles* (3rd ed.; Grand Rapids: Eerdmans, 1990), 308.
59. R. P. C. Hanson, *The Acts* (Oxford: Clarendon, 1967), 143.

buried (Mark 15:42–47; 16:1–3; Luke 23:50–56; 24:1–3; Acts 13:28–29; Matt. 27:57–66; 28:1; John 19:31, 39–42; 20:1; 1 Cor. 15:3–4). The canonical Gospels, the *Gospel of Peter* 2:3–4 and 6:23–24 (mid-second century AD?), and the *Acts of Pilate* 15:5–6 (perhaps as early as the late second century or even as late as the fourth century AD) agree that Joseph of Arimathea buried the body of Jesus.[60] It is possible that Joseph acted at the behest of the Sanhedrin to keep Jewish law and ensure that the body would not defile the land (Deut. 21:22–23; cf. Ezek. 39:14–16). This may be implied in John 19:31 and Acts 13:29—that is, the Jewish leaders were concerned about burial practices, and the law led them to request the body of Jesus for burial—but if so, it is strange that John reports that Joseph went to Pilate secretly for *fear* of the Jews (John 19:38). If he went to Pilate as a member of the Sanhedrin (Mark 15:43; Luke 23:50) at the behest of the Jews (John 19:31), his discipleship did not have to be declared, and there would be no need for a private meeting with Pilate as well as no occasion for fear. On the other hand, if Joseph was a secret disciple of Jesus, or eventually became one, that could account for his name being included in the biblical narratives and in subsequent Christian sources (*Gos. Pet.* and *Acts Pil.*). The multiplicity of reports about Joseph's participation in the burial of Jesus in both the canonical and noncanonical traditions strongly suggests the authenticity of that report.

Evidence from the *Gospel of Peter*?

Crossan calls the *Gospel of Peter* the "*Cross Gospel*" and contends that all other gospels are dependent upon it, but there are serious objections to his view.[61] Crossan's position has gained little support among New Testament

60. The *Gospel of Peter* (ca. AD 100–130) has some interesting parallels with the Gospel traditions, as well as several differences. Although this gospel has been accused of containing a Docetic heresy that denied the physical body of Jesus (Eusebius, *Hist. eccl.* 6.12.3–6), there is nothing in the surviving fragment of that Gospel that indicates this aside from an easily explained "My power, O power, you have forsaken me" (5:19), though this does not preclude something else in the document that has not survived that was contrary to the common Christian tradition circulating at the end of the second century. It could be that such traditions were popular in some churches at that time, but were later seen by Serapion and others to be contrary to the received traditions found in the canonical Gospels or in oral tradition. As a result, those traditions were excluded from churches; but that is not clear. As for the document's similarities with the canonical Gospels, they could be explained on the basis of shared oral or written traditions in the churches rather than direct dependence.

The author of the *Gospel of Peter* is clearly not as familiar with the Jewish traditions, the land, or the circumstances in Israel in the first century, but that does not detract from the fact that the author shows an awareness of some of the important traditions surrounding the death and burial of Jesus.

61. For J. D. Crossan's view that this gospel was the source for all four canonical Gospels, see his *The Cross That Spoke: The Origins of the Passion Narrative* (San Francisco: Harper & Row, 1988).

scholars, and it is unlikely that a careful evaluation of this fragmented gospel will support his proposal. Helmut Koester, for example, concludes that this document has independent traditions not found in the canonical Gospels, and raises three important arguments against Crossan's thesis; namely, (1) the surviving text is not reliable, (2) Crossan presumes major literary activity at a time when it is not present in the early church and also ignores the presence of oral tradition in the churches for many decades after the emergence of the early church, and (3) the variety of traditions in the Easter proclamation of the canonical Gospels cannot be reduced to one common source as Crossan supposes.[62] Further, an evaluation of the parallels between the canonical Gospels and the *Gospel of Peter* makes much more sense if the author of the *Gospel of Peter* depends on the canonical Gospels.[63] Some of the story that it shares is clearly not historically credible, especially that Pilate was submissive to the will of Herod, and also the famous speaking cross.

N. T. Wright lists eight telling arguments against an early dating of this document and also its credibility: (1) the sensational appearance of two enormous angels coming out of the tomb followed by a speaking cross; (2) it is easier to see that the *Gospel of Peter* depends on the canonical Gospels, which have no biblical references, than to explain why, if the canonical Gospels were dependent upon the *Gospel of Peter*, they eliminated biblical exegesis and Scripture references that are present in the *Gospel of Peter*;[64] (3) the strong anti-Jewish bias in the *Gospel of Peter* is more at home with a development later than in the first century; (4) that a large crowd of soldiers and Jewish leaders actually witnesses the resurrection is contrary to all four canonical Gospels; (5) historical details of Herod sending Jesus to his death instead of Pilate are historically indefensible; (6) the text speaks of the resurrection on the "Lord's Day," a term developed later and only in the New Testament at Revelation 1:10; (7) if all the canonical Gospels used the *Gospel of Peter*, it is remarkable that all of them omitted several of the same elements in the story, such as three men coming out of the tomb, two of whom had descended from heaven; and it suggests a resuscitation rather than a resurrection; and (8) the meaning of the speaking cross is obscure and reflects later theological thinking

62. Helmut Koester, *Ancient Christian Gospels: Their History and Development* (Philadelphia: Trinity Press, 1990), 216–20.

63. These parallels are conveniently listed in Christian Maurer's translation of the Akhmim Fragment of the *Gospel of Peter* in *New Testament Apocrypha* (ed. Wilhelm Schneemelcher; trans. R. McL. Wilson; rev. ed.; Louisville: Westminster John Knox, 1991), 1:226–27. See also Maurer's and Schneemelcher's discussions of the origin and date of this document in 1:216–22.

64. N. T. Wright, *The Resurrection of the Son of God* (Christian Origins and the Question of God 3; Minneapolis: Fortress, 2003), 594–95.

in the church.[65] It is more likely that a *largely* independent witness supports the traditional burial stories of Jesus in the canonical Gospels; namely, that Jesus was buried following his death and that Joseph of Arimathea was instrumental in that burial. I contend that Mark 15:42–47 is the earliest story of the burial of Jesus and that all seven traditions (all four canonical Gospels, 1 Cor. 15:4; Acts 13:29; and *Gos. Pet.* 2:3 and 6:23–24) agree that Jesus was appropriately buried in accordance with Jewish custom. Attempts to deny the burial of Jesus, the empty tomb, and ultimately the resurrection of Jesus go against the multiple attestation of this tradition in antiquity.

Who Was Joseph of Arimathea?

Was Joseph of Arimathea a disciple of Jesus? The problem here is that if Joseph was not a disciple of Jesus, why would he have provided such an expensive burial place for him and a new tomb? John and Matthew, however, call Joseph a "disciple" of Jesus, and John includes another disciple (Nicodemus) in the burial story. Luke says that Joseph was a member of the Sanhedrin, which makes him both a Jew and one with sufficient clout to ask for the body of Jesus. Joseph of Arimathea may eventually have become a disciple of Jesus, and because of this his actions would have been especially valuable to the evangelists, who wanted to have an adequate preparation of Jesus for burial as a final act of love and respect, but we cannot be sure of this.[66] That he was a righteous man looking forward to the kingdom of God (Mark 15:43) may give us the reason that he risked (although he "feared" the Jews, John 19:38) going to Pilate privately to ask for the body of Jesus. If his concern was preserving the sanctity of the land and therefore wanting to bury Jesus out of respect for Jewish law (Deut. 21:22–23), why would he fear the Jews when asking for permission to follow Jewish law in burying a fellow Jew? Likewise, if Jesus were placed in Joseph's family tomb, there is no reason to suppose that the tomb was lost or unknown. All of the biblical and nonbiblical traditions conclude that Jesus was indeed buried, whether by a member of the Sanhedrin interested in maintaining Jewish purity of the land or by a secret disciple of Jesus. Since nothing more is said about Joseph in the rest of the New Testament, he probably had little influence on the emerging life and growth of the early church. The story of Joseph of Arimathea was passed on in later traditions of the church, not only in the *Gospel of Peter*, but also in

---

65. Allison, *Resurrecting Jesus*, 356, also makes the important observation that if the early Christians had wanted to make the death of Jesus and his burial fit with Scripture, they would surely have cited Isa. 53:9 ("they made his grave with the wicked"), but they did not.

66. For a careful discussion of the Joseph of Arimathea tradition, see Stanley E. Porter, "Joseph of Arimathea," *ABD* 3:971–72.

the apocryphal *Acts of Pilate* (= *Gospel of Nicodemus*), where he is arrested for burying Jesus[67] and defends himself by indicating how Jesus appeared to him during his (Joseph's) imprisonment (*Acts Pil.* 15:5–6).[68] While this story is certainly legend, it is interesting that the legend of Joseph of Arimathea continued and expanded in the early churches. In the canonical Gospels, however, Joseph is not a legendary figure. He is simply there and provides a proper burial for Jesus.

Historical Conclusions

All four Gospels agree that Joseph requested and was granted permission to bury Jesus. They all agree that the day of the burial was late on the day of preparation prior to the beginning of the Sabbath, and all four mention the presence of women (or just Mary Magdalene, as in John 20) at the tomb on the first day of the week, though there is variation in the names of the women. There are many variations in the burial traditions in the New Testament, more than were mentioned here, but the most important question is whether Jesus was buried appropriately or in disgrace. David Daube has discussed the importance of the burial clothes in the Gospels, as well as the breaking of the legs and other disrespectful acts done to the bodies of criminals who were executed. He observes that Mark only mentions that Joseph of Arimathea wrapped Jesus in a "linen cloth" (15:46), a sign, according to some, that Jesus' burial was "disreputable" based on the Jewish traditions about *niwwul*, a term roughly from the time of Jesus used by the Jewish Tannaitic teachers for disgrace. When a criminal died, proper burial preparation was not ordinarily given, including placing the body in a common grave for criminals, in order to show disrespect or disgrace.[69] He observes that the term used for Jesus' body was *ptōma* instead of the usual *sōma*. According to Daube, *ptōma* was used

---

67. "We were very angry because you asked for the body of Jesus, and wrapped it in a clean linen cloth, and you placed it in a tomb. And for this reason we secured you in a house with no window, and locked and sealed the door, and guards watched where you were shut up" (*Acts Pil.* 15:5, in Schneemelcher, *New Testament Apocrypha*, 1:518).

68. After Joseph is arrested and called on to defend himself, the text reads, in part: "And Joseph said: 'On the day of preparation about the tenth hour you shut me in, and I remained the whole sabbath. And at midnight as I stood and prayed, the house where you shut me in was raised up by the four corners, and I saw as it were a lightning flash in my eyes. Full of fear I fell to the ground and someone took me by the hand and raised me up from the place where I had fallen, something moist like water flowed from my head to my feet, and the smell of fragrant oil reached my nostrils. And he wiped my face and kissed me and said to me: Do not fear, Joseph. Open your eyes and see who it is who speaks with you. I looked up and saw Jesus" (trans. Felix Scheidweiler, in Schneemelcher, *New Testament Apocrypha*, 1:518). See also R. Brown, *Death of the Messiah*, 2:1232–34.

69. David Daube, *The New Testament and Rabbinic Judaism* (Peabody, MA: Hendrickson, 1956, 1998), 301–24.

of those whose bodies were desecrated, as in the case of the beheading of John the Baptist (see Matt. 14:12; Mark 6:29). The earliest tradition about the burial of Jesus in Mark uses the same term, but Matthew uses the term *sōma* for the body of Jesus and adds that the linen cloth was a "clean linen cloth" (27:58–59). Likewise, he emphasizes that Jesus was placed in a "new tomb" in which no other had been placed—unlike the common grave for criminals. John also has the more favorable term for Jesus' body (*sōma*) and honorable burial rites for Jesus; namely, the anointing of his body with spices (19:38–40) and the placing of it in a new tomb (19:41). Luke also uses the more favorable term for Jesus' body (*sōma*) in 23:52, where it is wrapped in a linen cloth and put in a rock-hewn tomb *in which no one had ever been laid* (v. 53). Joseph does not apply the appropriate spices for an honorable burial, but the women prepare the spices and return after the Sabbath is over (23:56–24:1). Mark says nothing about the anointing of Jesus' body following his burial, but he does earlier when a woman anoints him before his burial (12:3–8). All of this suggests that the later evangelists made sure that Jesus received honor at his burial, rather than the *niwwul* or disgrace that was afforded to criminals or disreputable persons. John makes sure that his readers know that no bones were broken, which would thereby render him unfit for resurrection according to Jewish law. It is interesting that in the second century, during Justin's debate with Trypho, Trypho speaks of the disgraceful death of Jesus (*Dial.* 32.89).[70] Does Mark, who only mentions the use of a linen cloth—the lowest level of burial preparation—and only that Jesus was placed in a rock-hewn tomb, reflect a disgraceful burial that simply carried out Jewish law, but not a service for an honorable person such as we see in the later Gospels? There seems to have been a growth in the burial traditions, but, again, all evangelists agree that Jesus was buried by Joseph of Arimathea.

According to the Mishnah, preparing the body even late on the Day of Preparation is in keeping with Jewish sentiment, and even if a person had been executed and his body decomposed, his bones could be interred in his family's tomb:

> R. Meir said: When a man is sore troubled, what says the Shekinah? My Head is ill at ease, my arm is ill at ease. If God is sore troubled at the blood of the ungodly that is shed, how much more at the blood of the righteous? Furthermore, every one that suffers his dead to remain over-night transgresses a negative command;

70. Ibid., 308. Daube also mentions the goal of the Jews to have Polycarp burned at the stake, but when that did not work, he was stabbed and his body was burned (*Mart. Pol.* 13). Such desecration of a body in death and burial indicated that the dead person had no hope for the resurrection of the body (ibid., 301–2).

but if he had suffered it to remain by reason of the honour due to it, to bring for it a coffin and burial clothes, he does not thereby commit transgression. . . . When the flesh had wasted away they gathered together the bones and buried them in their own place [the family burying place]. (*m. Sanh.* 6.5–6 [trans. Danby])

It normally took about two hours to prepare a body for entombment, depending on how many persons were helping with preparations and how elaborate a procedure was followed. The fact that Jesus died a criminal's death does not conflict with his receiving a proper burial according to Jewish tradition in the Mishnah cited above (see *m. Šabb.* 23.5). Therefore everything necessary for a decent burial was normally possible and within the proper keeping of the law by the Jews. The evangelists, who were familiar with Palestinian Jewish conditions and customs, would not have attributed to the women the intention of coming to *embalm* the body of Jesus three days after burial, but only to anoint it according to custom and respect. The intention of the women was in keeping with the ancient Palestinian custom of visiting graves for three days after burial. This custom stemmed from the belief that the soul of the deceased remained in or near the body for three days.[71] The Palestinian custom of bringing spices and ointments for anointing was similar to the modern custom of bringing flowers or wreaths to the graveside of loved ones. Evidence of this can be seen in Josephus's story of the burial of Herod the Great, in which there were some five hundred pounds of perfumes that were brought for his burial but they were not used to embalm his body (*Ant.* 17.196–99). Crossan's complaint, that the amount of spices for Jesus' burial in John not only parallels that of a king but of the divine, is without merit.[72]

Although we may agree with Bultmann that according to Mark 15:46 the burial of Jesus appeared complete, do Mark 16:1 and Luke 24:1 really suggest otherwise? It is possible that Nicodemus supplied all the necessary spices for the burial of Jesus but that the women, perhaps unaware of this, only intended to offer their spices and ointments out of love and devotion. This is all speculation, of course, but within the boundaries of custom and activity in the time of Jesus.

Despite several variations in the accounts of the burial story, one basic message is found in all of them; namely, it was Jesus of Nazareth who died on a cross and was buried in accordance with Jewish burial practices. Since there was no war or civil uprising going on at the time of Jesus' death, it would not

---

71. This tradition is reflected in *Gos. Pet.* 8:30, which has the scribes and Pharisees coming to Pilate asking him for a guard to watch the tomb for three days ("Give us soldiers that we may watch his sepulcher for three days").

72. Crossan, *Excavating Jesus*, 291–92.

have been unusual for Roman authorities to be sensitive to the Jewish concerns about burial practices, as we have seen in both Philo and Josephus. The only known ancient text that suggests that Jesus did not receive a proper burial is in the *Apocryphon of James,* which concludes with Jesus saying: "Or do you not know that you have yet to be abused, to be unjustly accused, to be shut up in prison, to be unlawfully condemned, to be crucified <without> reason and to be <shamefully> buried, just like myself, by the evil one?" (5:19–21).[73] There is nothing that supports this later tradition about Jesus' burial and nothing that supports that he was shut up in prison either. Since it is late and stands alone in antiquity, it is hardly a reliable witness to the burial of Jesus.

73. Trans. Einar Thomassen, in Schneemelcher, *New Testament Apocrypha,* 1:292. This source is noted in Allison, *Resurrecting Jesus,* 359.

6

Easter

The Story of Jesus within History and Faith

IIIIIIIIIIIIIIIIIIIIIIIIIIIIIIIIIIIIIIIIIIIIIIIIIIIIIIIII

The most important New Testament event, which is foundational for Christian faith and the establishment of the church, is the resurrection of Jesus from the dead. The message that God raised Jesus from the dead gave rise to Christian faith (Rom. 10:9). The earliest New Testament Christology (see Rom. 1:3–4), eschatology (1 Cor. 15:20–28; Phil. 3:21; Rom. 8:9–11, 22–24), and other doctrines, especially the salvation of humanity (1 Cor. 15:12–20), are all firmly anchored in Jesus' resurrection. If Jesus has only been raised in the faith of the early followers of Jesus, as some scholars have argued, then the resurrection of Jesus did not happen and, according to Paul, there is no basis for Christian proclamation or for understanding how the proclaimer (Jesus) became the proclaimed in the Christian tradition. Faith would then be vain and futile, believers would still be in their sins, and they would be a most pitied community (1 Cor. 15:14–19). It was in his resurrection that Jesus' message was authenticated and faith was born in his disciples (Acts 2:22–36). In the proclamation of the resurrection of Jesus, forgiveness of sins and hope beyond the grave were extended to all who believed in him.

A Challenged but Central Affirmation

There are many challenges in understanding the Easter narratives, especially in knowing precisely what happened in Jesus' resurrection, where his appearances

271

took place, and the nature of those appearances. Some challenges arise from comparing Paul's letters with the Gospels. Paul's letters, which were written earlier, do not speak of an empty tomb—though to be sure the empty tomb was not the object or initiation of faith even in the Gospels. It raised a question that the resurrection appearances answered. I will discuss this in more detail below. Paul's testimony to the resurrection of Jesus seems to suggest a more visionary experience than what we find in the Gospels (1 Cor. 15:3–8; Acts 9:1–9; 22:6–11; 26:12–18; Gal. 1:15–16). Moreover, Paul places his encounter with the risen Lord on par with that of the other apostles (1 Cor. 9:1–2; 15:3–8). Some biblical scholars therefore argue that the original experiences were more visionary and the later Gospels made them more physical (Luke 24:38–43). Other challenges arise from observing the differences between the resurrection narratives in the Gospels, especially in the angelic reports, the number and names of the women who came to the tomb, the time of their arrival, the nature and location of the resurrection appearances, and the message of the risen Lord to his followers. Those who deny the possibility of a resurrection from the dead do not believe it is possible to harmonize the apparent discrepancies or identify clearly what it was that gave rise to Christian faith.[1] They often account for the Easter stories in terms of psychological issues facing the apostles or, more specifically, Peter and Paul.

Facing the Challenges

While scholars who reject the resurrection of Jesus as an event of history tend to emphasize variants in the resurrection narratives, those who accept the resurrection of Jesus tend to minimize the variants. This chapter presupposes that it is important to discuss the differences and tries to demonstrate that it is not necessary to harmonize all of the differences in order to present a plausible explanation of what actually happened in Jesus' resurrection. Although some changes are discernible in the Easter traditions, it does not follow that the basic

---

1. X. Léon-Dufour (*The Gospels and the Jesus of History* [ed. and trans. J. McHugh; London: Collins, 1968], 254) makes this observation. It is borne out in the writings of conservative scholars like C. Pinnock in his "On the Third Day," in *Jesus of Nazareth: Saviour and Lord* (ed. C. F. H. Henry; London: Tyndale, 1966), 147–55; and "In Defense of the Resurrection," *Christianity Today* 9 (1965): 6–8. On the other hand, those who emphasize the differences in the narratives and the difficulty of knowing what happened in the resurrection of Jesus include Rudolf Bultmann, *Theology of the New Testament* (trans. K. Grobel; New York: Scribner, 1951), 1:45; Willi Marxsen, *Jesus and Easter: Did God Raise the Historical Jesus from the Dead?* (trans. V. P. Furnish; Nashville: Abingdon, 1990); and his *The Resurrection of Jesus of Nazareth* (trans. M. Kohl; London: SCM, 1970). Finally, Gerd Lüdemann, *The Resurrection of Jesus: History, Experience, and Theology* (Minneapolis: Fortress, 1994), and A. J. N. Wedderburn, *Beyond Resurrection* (Peabody, MA: Hendrickson, 1999), both posit some sort of psychological challenges that the apostles were facing to account for the rise of Easter faith.

core that initiated faith in the earliest followers of Jesus and the birth of the church has been lost or obscured. There is little doubt that the kingdom of God and its coming played a significant role in the thinking of Jesus' disciples, and indeed in the thinking of Jesus himself. The disciples anticipated an early establishment of the kingdom of God, and even quarreled among themselves over who would be greatest in that kingdom (Mark 10:35–41; Matt. 18:1). They believed that Jesus was the one who would initiate the coming of that kingdom (Acts 1:6–7). After Jesus was arrested, his disciples abandoned him and fled (Mark 14:50) and understandably were filled with discouragement (Luke 24:17–21). The death of Jesus must certainly have shattered their hopes and led them to doubt his identity. Rudolf Bultmann rightly perceived that the death of Jesus raised a question to the disciples that had to be answered.[2] Paul agreed that the cross was the major stumbling block that Jews had to overcome (1 Cor. 1:23). How could confidence be restored in Jesus in such a short space of time after his ignoble death? The New Testament writers contend that it was because Jesus was raised from the dead and exalted by God that faith became a possibility and the church was born.

Several historical facts surrounding the resurrection of Jesus are generally accepted: (1) Jesus was arrested and executed on a cross in Jerusalem, (2) his disciples were filled with doubt and despair over this unexpected turn of events, (3) within a relatively short period of time the disciples had a renewed faith and confidence in Jesus as the bringer of God's salvation, and (4) the Christian community grew as a result of the disciples' preaching about the resurrection of Jesus. A more frequently disputed, but also well-argued, fact is the report of the empty tomb in which Jesus' body was placed after his crucifixion. All of these facts listed are consistent with some first-century Jewish notions of life after death, but also with early Christian preaching that God raised Jesus from the dead.

The evangelists do not describe the resurrection of Jesus itself but only relay early reports that Jesus was raised from the dead and that he appeared on eleven or twelve occasions to his disciples. There were no eyewitnesses to the Easter event, and unlike the *Gospel of Peter*,[3] the four canonical Gospels

---

2. R. Bultmann, "The New Testament and Mythology," in *Kerygma and Myth* (ed. H.-W. Bartsch; trans. R. H. Fuller; New York: Harper & Row, 1961), 1:38.

3. In an enlargement of Matthew's account, the author of this apocryphal gospel has the resurrection of Jesus take place in front of the guard at the tomb and the Jewish authorities. The author lays blame for the crucifixion at the feet of the Jews, and abandons the eschatological focus of the Synoptic Gospels. This suggests a second-century dating of that Gospel, since the flavor of the writing is similar to Gnostic teaching of the second century and reflects the later developed anti-Jewish sentiment in the Christian community. For a description and translation of this gospel, see C. Maurer and W. Schneemelcher, "The Gospel of Peter," in *New Testament Apocrypha* (ed. W. Schneemelcher; trans. R. McL. Wilson; Louisville: Westminster John Knox, 1991), 1:216–27.

do not describe it. The evangelists do not doubt that Jesus was alive after his execution. Their belief is based not on the empty tomb but rather on the resurrection appearances.[4] The bodily nature of the appearances is reflected in the empty-tomb stories but also in several of the appearances. Gerd Lüdemann agrees that the empty tomb tradition was a part of the beliefs of the earliest Christian community, though he himself does not accept that the tomb of Jesus had been vacated through a miracle from God.[5] The earliest Christian proclamation only declares the resurrection of Jesus without any narration, and Jesus' resurrection called for a confession of his lordship (see Rom. 10:9). Paul, for instance, includes affirmation of the resurrection of Jesus when introducing his letters to Christians (see Gal. 1:1; Rom. 1:3–4). Similarly, in several early Christian affirmations, the exaltation of Jesus was seen in his resurrection, and this is at the core of early Christian belief (Phil. 2:6–11; Acts 2:32–36). At the heart of early proclamation, God did not allow Jesus' *flesh* to see corruption (Acts 2:24–31), but rather God raised him up and exalted him (Acts 2:32–33). This, of course, suggests a bodily resurrection as we see earlier in Luke.

Despite the many unsettled questions about the nature of this event and the differences between the Gospel accounts, the united testimony from the early church follows the Gospels, and indeed the rest of the New Testament, in affirming that Jesus of Nazareth was crucified, buried, raised from the dead, and seen (or will be seen—see Mark 16:7) by witnesses. This message is at the heart of the entire New Testament witness to the glorification of Jesus and Christian hope (see also 1 Pet. 1:3–5; Rev. 1:5; passim).

The Appearances and the Empty Tomb

I indicated above that from Paul's and the evangelists' perspective, the basis for proclaiming Easter faith was the postresurrection appearances of Jesus and not the empty tomb. Without the resurrection appearances, it is difficult to account for the birth of Christianity. The earliest Christian message is that God raised Jesus from the dead and exalted him, and as a result there is forgiveness of sins and participation in the coming kingdom of God (Acts 2:38; 3:19; 5:30–31; 13:39; passim).[6] That Jesus was seen alive after his death

---

4. Except in 16:9–20, which is widely acknowledged as a later addition to the Gospel, Mark does not record postresurrection appearances. It is unlikely, however, that the original ending of Mark was at 16:8. It is also possible that Mark, due to unknown circumstances, was unable to finish it or that the original ending was lost.

5. G. Lüdemann, *What Really Happened to Jesus? A Historical Approach to the Resurrection* (trans. J. Bowden; Louisville: Westminster John Knox, 1995), 134.

6. While scholars debate the dating of Luke-Acts, Luke likely made use of sources that reflect the nature and substance of early Christian preaching.

is reported in three of the four Gospels and presumed in Mark 16:7, and Paul also affirms this (1 Cor. 9:1–2; 15:3–8) and assures readers of the aliveness of Jesus *on the basis of his appearances.*

All of the evangelists employ the empty-tomb story as a means of proclaiming the resurrection of Jesus—or at least clarifying what was involved in the resurrection; namely, the *complete* disappearance of Jesus from the grave.[7] Although in the resurrection narratives the angelic acknowledgment of the meaning of the empty tomb is not lost (Mark 16:6; Luke 24:4–7; Matt. 28:1–7; and, in a different way, John 20:1–18), still the tomb was not the catalyst for faith, but rather the resurrection appearances. The empty tomb also pointed to the meaning of the resurrection; namely, Jesus was not there, but risen. His body was gone, and the appearances were bodily, or corporeal. Easter faith proclaims, then, that God raised Jesus from the dead, but specifically how that happened remains a mystery, though clearly it was a bodily resurrection even if the raised body was a different kind of "transformed body" (1 Cor. 15:42–44, 50–53).

Another difficulty in determining what happened in the resurrection of Jesus is that the earliest narratives reporting it date some thirty or more years later, and all reflect some growth in that intervening time. The Gospels are clearly based on earlier traditions circulating in churches (1 Cor. 15:1–11). The earliest traditions about Easter were passed on by word of mouth, no doubt with some alterations or expansions, such as the inclusion of the empty-tomb story into the proclamation of Easter. The earliest Easter traditions in the New Testament (1 Cor. 15:3–8; Rom. 10:9–10) do not employ the empty-tomb story, but they are also not Easter narratives, but rather summaries of early Christian belief.

I am not suggesting that the empty-tomb tradition is a later invention of the early church, as many scholars have argued, but only that its inclusion in the mainstream of the Easter tradition was not in the earliest preaching of the resurrection of Jesus. The emptiness of Jesus' tomb could have been assumed, given the current views of resurrection among many (not all) Jews in Palestine in the time of Jesus. Again, this does not mean that the empty-tomb story was unknown or unimportant to the earliest Christians, but only that

7. Like many others, Daniel A. Smith, *Revisiting the Empty Tomb: The Early History of Easter* (Minneapolis: Fortress, 2010), 153–84, argues that the empty tomb is a late addition to the Easter tradition and reflects ancient apotheosis (exaltation or glorification) similar to the exalted departures of prominent and ancient persons such as Romulus, Enoch, Moses, Elijah, and others. Although we will return to this and these parallels in the Roman world when we focus on the ascension of Jesus in Luke and John, for now we note that Smith's argument depends heavily on dating Q (Luke 13:34–35). Smith assumes the postmortem story of Jesus is an early reference to Jesus' eventual exaltation, and that it is combined with the appearance stories. He is right that the evangelists do not base faith on the tomb, but instead on the appearance stories as evidence of the Easter proclamation.

it was not reflected in early Christian preaching. In time, what was assumed was included in the Easter narratives, but not initially. The addition of the empty-tomb stories to the Easter tradition suggests that the early churches needed to show that Jesus' resurrection was not simply a spiritual vision, but rather a bodily event. This does not imply, however, that the empty tomb was added because of Gnostic or Docetic tendencies in early churches.[8] Matthew 28:11–15 reflects a Jewish polemic that the disciples stole Jesus' body, but this polemic nevertheless assumes that the tomb was empty, and accounts for how it got that way. This, of course, adds credibility to the emptiness of Jesus' tomb.

Origins of the Notion of Resurrection

No single understanding of life after death was accepted by all Jews in the time of Jesus, even though the view that eventually prevailed was the resurrection of the body at the end of the ages. Nickelsburg has shown that belief in a meaningful life after death was a later development in the history of Israelite religion.[9] Notions of life after death appear to begin with the Jewish understanding of theodicy; that is, God's justice and power must ultimately deal with the problem of evil in the world. It was believed that the all-loving and all-powerful God had to address the apparent triumph of evil in the world over those who faithfully followed God. Speculation that there was life beyond this life despite physical death can be seen in many Old Testament passages (Pss. 16; 49; 73; and Isa. 24–27, but especially 25:6–8 and 26:14–19). Scholars often debate the dating of all of these texts, but most put them late in Old Testament history.

Persecution and Vindication

The persecution of the people of God and belief in God's vindication may be the source of such early notions of life after death. What form will life after death take? How could God and the people of God *not* be vindicated? And

---

8. J. D. G. Dunn has discussed the weakness of that view. See his *The Evidence for Jesus* (Philadelphia: Westminster, 1985), 77–78. The inclusion of the empty-tomb tradition came well *before* Docetic and gnosticizing issues became problematic for the early churches. See also Dunn's more recent discussion in *Jesus Remembered* (Grand Rapids: Eerdmans, 2003), 828–40, where he observes that the early churches remarkably did not venerate the tomb where Jesus was placed (837), but that the empty tomb emphasized that Jesus had been buried. Jesus' body was buried and so also it was raised. While this *implies* an empty tomb, the tomb itself was not the focus of the earliest Christian preaching.

9. G. W. Nickelsburg, "Resurrection (Early Judaism and Christianity)," *ABD* 5:685–91, here 685.

what form will that vindication or theodicy take? The case for vindication is made, for instance, in *1 Enoch* 22–27, where the blessing of God comes to the righteous even after death, as does the eternal judgment against evil and all who perpetrate it. The nature of existence in the afterlife is not fully described here, but appears to be in nonphysical terms (e.g., 22:3–14, except in 22:13), where the souls of the righteous, but not the unrighteous, are assumed to rise on judgment day. However, in *1 Enoch* 25:6 the "fragrance" of the holy place "shall (penetrate) their [the righteous's] bones," and "long life will they live on earth such as your fathers lived in their days."[10] Here the mode of life after death, if it is like the life of the fathers before them, appears to be a physical one. These, and other, similar passages, may depend on Isaiah 65–66 (written perhaps late fifth century or early fifth century BC), which focuses on the blessings of the faithful and a judgment of sinners.

This notion of the blessing and judgment of God is also present in *Jubilees* 23:11–31 and 2 Maccabees 7:9–14. In 4 Maccabees 2:23 (ca. late first century BC or early first century AD), the writer mentions the blessing that God promises to those who are faithful and live by the law. Later, in 17:11–12, following the martyrdoms of an aged priest, a mother, and her seven sons, it is reported that the prize for victory is "incorruption in long-lasting life." Finally, in 18:23 they win the "victor's prize" and "are gathered in the choir of their fathers, having received pure and deathless souls from God."[11] In the first-century-BC book the Wisdom of Solomon, the blessing of God after death comes in the form of immortality of the soul (see 1:15; 2:22–23; 3:1, 8; 5:15). The late-first-century-AD book *4 Ezra* speaks of immortality of the soul for the righteous (7:13), who escape what is corruptible in order "to receive and enjoy immortality" (7:96–99), while the wicked face the judgment of God (7:76–87). Qumran literature also refers to rewards for godly living and punishment for the unjust in the life to come (e.g., 1QH [*Hymn Scroll*] 3:19–23 and 11:3–14; 1QS 3:13–4:26; cf. *T. Ab.* 11–12).[12]

Old Testament and Second-Temple Views

As J. I. H. McDonald has correctly observed, there is very little language about the notion of resurrection from the dead in the Old Testament, and what is there is late in the history of Israel and appears in a context of suffering. He also claims that the idea of resurrection of the body emerges in the context of

10. Trans. E. Isaac, in *The Old Testament Pseudepigrapha* (ed. James H. Charlesworth; Garden City, NY: Doubleday, 1983), 1:26.
11. Trans. H. A. Anderson, in Charlesworth, *Old Testament Pseudepigrapha*, 2:562, 564.
12. Nickelsburg, "Resurrection," 686–88.

"theodicy" or the "attempt to affirm the goodness and omnipotence of God in the face of evil in the world."[13] When so much of the promise of God to Israel was voiced in terms of possession of the land of Palestine, how could it be that the people of God, even if a remnant, could die in captivity in Babylon following the destruction of their homeland and temple? A time came among the Jews when they had to face the issue of God's goodness in the face of evil. Ezekiel was one of the first to speak of God reconstituting the nation in terms of a resurrection of "dry bones" (Ezek. 37:1–14). In symbolic language, the nation is reconstituted. Similarly, Isaiah 26:19 (see the whole passage in Isa. 24–27) makes this same point using resurrection imagery. These may be the earliest texts that discuss the notion of a bodily resurrection and reward of the righteous (Isaiah scholars dispute the dating of Isa. 24–27, but many claim that they are postexilic in origin).

The notion of the resurrection of the righteous is more clearly seen in references to the notion of resurrection *from the grave*, as in the case of Daniel 12:2 (ca. 150 BC) where we see a reference to a dual resurrection for the faithful *and the unfaithful*, to both blessing and condemnation. Daniel focuses on the persecution of the righteous, and resurrection is the means by which God corrects injustice and vindicates the righteous (Dan. 9–10). Daniel 12:2 can be compared with *Assumption of Moses* 10 (ca. first century AD) and *Jubilees* 23:27–31 (ca. 135–107 BC), which reflect similar interests in resurrection as a means of both reward and punishment. *Testament of Judah* 25 (ca. 150 BC) is also a close parallel. In 2 Maccabees 7:7–23, we see a description of the physical tortures of the Jews by Antiochus (167–165 BC) but also an affirmation that God will "raise us up to an everlasting renewal of life, because we have died for his laws" (v. 9). Similar perspectives are in *Psalms of Solomon* 3:11 (ca. 50 BC) and *1 Enoch* 22, which focus on rewards and punishments of the righteous and sinners. *First Enoch* 25:6 anticipates the righteous rising to new life in the new Jerusalem, but it is not clear whether the unrighteous will rise for punishment. These passages witness a belief in a resurrection from the grave, but this view was not uniform in the "intertestamental" (or apocryphal and pseudepigraphal) literature. Wisdom of Solomon, for instance, does not speak of resurrection, but rather of immortality of the soul (2:23–24; 3:1; see also *Jub.* 23:32; *1 En.* 103; cf. Ps. 73:24–26). On the other hand, *1 Enoch* 102:4–104:8 (ca. early second century BC) argues that a day of judgment will come to those who oppress the poor, and the souls of the righteous who grieve in Sheol will come back to life and receive the reward that their fleshly bodies missed. On the basis of these passages, J. I. H. McDonald concludes

13. J. I. H. McDonald, *The Resurrection: Narrative and Belief* (London: SPCK, 1989), 5–24.

that resurrection language is essentially eschatological and is related to an apocalyptic worldview.[14]

The lack of unanimity in Jewish teaching about life after death is well illustrated by Josephus, who claims that Pharisees believed in the resurrection of the body, Sadducees did not hold to any view of life after death whether for rewards or punishments, and Essenes held to the immortality of the soul (*J.W.* 2.154–66; *Ant.* 18.12–20; see also 13.171–73).[15] The New Testament agrees that this was one of the points of contention between the Sadducees and the Pharisees (Matt. 22:23–33; Mark 12:18–23; Luke 20:27–39; Acts 23:6–8). New Testament writers, however, side with the Pharisees, who say that those who have faith in God will experience life after death in a resurrected body (1 Cor. 15:3–5, 35–58; 1 Thess. 4:13–17; Rev. 20:4). A possible exception to this is in Hebrews, where the author does not use the typical resurrection language in reference to Jesus' exaltation, but does affirm the notion of resurrection from the dead (Heb. 6:2; 13:20).

The nature of the resurrection is described differently in Luke (24:36–43) and Paul (1 Cor. 15:38–45, 50), but both focus on a *bodily* resurrection from the grave, even if Paul emphasizes a *transformed bodily resurrection* (1 Cor. 15:51–54) and that "flesh and blood cannot inherit the kingdom of God" (15:50). Although rabbinic Judaism of the second century AD and later concluded that "all Israelites have a share in the world to come" *except* those who say "that there is no resurrection of the dead prescribed in the Law" (*m. Sanh.* 10.1),[16] this does not tell us what the views of Judaism were between 100 BC and AD 100.[17]

The Empty-Tomb Tradition

Do the differences in the empty-tomb tradition lead to a denial of its historicity? Scholars often disagree on the answer to that question. I will begin our inquiry by identifying the most important differences and the most important consistencies. While I have placed this tradition in the "Within History and Faith" chapter, that is only because it also has to do with the resurrection of

14. Ibid., 16. An excellent resource on understanding the origin of Jewish notions of resurrection and subsequent Christian notions as well is Claudia Setzer, *Resurrection of the Body in Early Judaism and Early Christianity: Doctrine, Community and Self-Definition* (Leiden: Brill Academic, 2004).

15. See D. J. Goergen, *The Death and Resurrection of Jesus* (Wilmington, DE: Michael Glazier, 1988), 78–79.

16. Trans. H. Danby, *The Mishnah* (Oxford: Oxford University Press, 1980), 397.

17. For further examples see Goergen, *Death and Resurrection of Jesus*, 71–85.

Jesus. The empty tomb, as we will see, is nevertheless capable of *historical* defense, but it did not in itself initiate faith and it could be explained in a variety of ways (someone stole the body or the women went to the wrong tomb, or the body was moved, perhaps by a gardener). So from the beginning, it was not a part of the Easter proclamation, but pointed to the nature of the resurrection (it was bodily) and raised a question that the appearance stories answered.

The Time of the Discovery

All four Gospels agree that the time the women (or Mary) discovered the empty tomb was early on the first day of the week. The actual time of the morning varies in Mark ("when the sun had risen," 16:2) and John ("while it was still dark," 20:1). Matthew, similar to Mark, says it was "toward the dawn of the first day" (28:1), and Luke, closer to John, says it was "at early dawn" (24:1). Matthew and Luke could fit with either Mark or John, but not both. Matthew and Luke are also quite similar, but closer to John than Mark.

According to Lilly, it is possible that the women needed to purchase the spices while they were on their way to the tomb. Mary Magdalene, he says, left this task to the other women and went to the tomb by herself, and the others came later, "when the sun had risen," to join her. He says this is possible because John 20:1 says Mary "is on her way before daylight" (*erchetai prōi skotias eti ousēs*), and the emphasis is on the *beginning* of the journey to the tomb while it was still dark.[18] His explanation, however, is foreign to Mark, who says all of the women went (third-person-plural verb, *erchontai*, "they went") to the tomb when the sun had risen. Mark makes no room for a separation or parting of the women. Lilly's focus on the present tense of *erchetai* (John 20:1) suggests that he should translate the same verb in Mark 16:2 the same way, but he does not.[19] If this were done in Mark, the women would *begin* their trip "when the sun had risen," and Mary in John would begin her journey "while it was still dark." Such explanations are not convincing and do not seem to clarify the situation.

Jeremias claims that in Mark, when two references to time are given and one appears unnecessary, there seems to be a tendency for the latter to explain the former. Thus, in Mark 16:2, "very early" (*lian prōi*) could be before the sun had risen or even afterwards, but here "when the sun had risen" is intended

---

18. J. L. Lilly, "Alleged Discrepancies in the Gospel Accounts of the Resurrection," *CBQ* 2 (1940): 99–111.

19. The tenses in Greek are not to be equated with temporal values, apart from a consideration of context.

to clarify the "very early."[20] Brown suggests that "darkness" is appropriate for John's theological emphasis because the empty tomb to Mary meant that someone had stolen the body of Jesus.[21] John does frequently use signs or themes in his Gospel to point to the significance of the work of Christ, but it cannot be argued convincingly that John had anything else in mind than that the women came to the tomb "while it was still dark." John frequently uses the term "light" (*phōs*) in reference to Christ (e.g., 8:12; 9:5; 12:35), or "darkness" (*skotia*) in contrast to the "light" (see, e.g., 1:5; 3:19; and 12:35, where "darkness" is a reference to unrighteousness or evil), but that bears no parallel to his description in 20:1.

While there is difficulty in reconciling the time of the discovery of the empty tomb in John and Mark, all of the evangelists agree that it took place early in the morning on the first day of the week, that is, Sunday. Mark and John both use *prōi* ("early"), though it is not clear how early. Both Luke's "at early dawn" (*orthrou batheōs*) in 24:1 and Matthew's "after the sabbath" (*opse . . . sabbatōn*) in 28:1 do not make the matter more clear, especially Matthew's repetition of the word *sabbatōn* in 28:1, where it literally means "first (day) of the Sabbath." It is unlikely that his "at the dawn of the first day of the sabbath she came" (*tē epiphōskousē eis mian sabbatōn ēlthen*) refers to "late on the sabbath," especially because of his "break of dawn" (*epiphōskousē*, or "nearing of dawn"). It is more likely that Matthew, like the other evangelists, is saying that the discovery took place early on the first day of the week *near dawn*.

The Number and Names of the Women

A simple reading of the four Gospels shows that the evangelists differ on which women came to the tomb. Mark says three women made the journey to the tomb (Mary Magdalene, Mary the mother of James, and Salome, 16:1). Matthew mentions only Mary Magdalene and "the other Mary" (28:1), while Luke says that it was Mary Magdalene, Joanna, and Mary the mother of James, as well as "the other women with them" (24:10). Perhaps Luke wanted to include all the women who came with Jesus from Galilee who are mentioned earlier in his passion report (23:55). John only mentions Mary Magdalene (20:1–2, 11–18) in his empty-tomb story, but the first-person-plural "we" in "we know" (*oidamen*) in 20:2 may bring John in line with the other evangelists.[22]

20. J. Jeremias, *New Testament Theology* (trans. J. Bowden; London: SCM, 1971), 17–18. For other references in Mark, see 1:32, 35; 4:35; 10:30; 13:24; 14:12, etc.

21. R. E. Brown, *The Gospel of John* (2 vols.; AB 29, 29A; Garden City, NY: Doubleday, 1966, 1970), 2:981.

22. Lilly, "Alleged Discrepancies," 105, makes this point.

Jeremias is not convinced and says that the "we" is simply the influence of Galilean Aramaic, in which the "we" is idiomatic for "I" (= *oidamen* for *oida*). He points to the return to the singular "I" (*oida*) in 20:13 but allows that the "we" could be the result of some synoptic influence on John.[23] Bultmann calls John 20:2 an "editorial connective" for the purpose of joining 20:1, 11–18, with 20:3–10, and he agrees with Jeremias that the "we" is a Semitic way of speaking and not a genuine plural.[24] Brown, on the other hand, disagrees because this does not adequately explain the switch back to *oida* ("I know") in verse 13. If the "we" was used for the first-person singular, he asks, why go back to the singular in verse 13? Brown concludes that the "we" of John 20:2 refers to the other women present with Mary at the tomb.[25] Eduard Schweizer suggests that the Synoptics expanded the earlier tradition that is preserved in John—namely, that only Mary Magdalene came to the tomb, as she is the one constant in all four evangelists. He adds that if John's story were a late fabrication to prove the reality of the resurrection of the body, then it would probably have included more witnesses who could "testify" to that fact.[26]

John obviously wished to highlight Mary Magdalene in his empty-tomb story. If there were other women present, John only pays a passing reference to them (i.e., *oidamen* in 20:2). It is puzzling why Matthew, who drew upon Mark, omitted Salome from his list of women and why all three Synoptics mention Mary Magdalene and Mary the mother of James (or the "other Mary"; see Matt. 28:1), but only Mark mentions "Salome" (16:1) and only Luke mentions "Joanna" instead (24:10). The "other women with them" in Luke may be in some sense parallel to John's "we" (20:2), but this is uncertain. If the expanding tendency in the early church is correct, and the original story involved only Mary being present at the tomb (John), and Mark added Mary the mother of James and Salome, then we must ask, why does Matthew reduce the number of women coming to the tomb to Mary Magdalene and "the other Mary" (28:1)? The answer is not clear. We either admit with

23. Jeremias, *Theology*, 304–5n. C. K. Barrett also believes the *oidamen* is an example of synoptic influence on John, but is careful to mention that the word itself does not stem from that tradition. He admits that no such report of the "stolen" body exists in the synoptic tradition, but does not consider that tradition in Matt. 28:11–13, where the notion of the disciples stealing the body is set forth. Cf. Barrett, *The Gospel according to St. John* (2nd ed.; Philadelphia: Westminster, 1978), 563.

24. R. Bultmann, *The Gospel of John* (ed. G. R. Beasley-Murray; trans. G. R. Beasley-Murray, R. W. N. Hoare, and J. K. Riches; Philadelphia: Westminster, 1971), 684.

25. Brown, *Gospel of John*, 984.

26. E. Schweizer, *Jesus* (trans. D. E. Green; London: SCM, 1968), 48. He also adds that it is highly unlikely that Jesus' resurrection could have been preached in Jerusalem if anyone knew of a tomb containing the body of Jesus.

Schweizer that only Mary Magdalene was present and the Synoptic Gospels expanded this tradition, *or* admit to the possibility that several other women were also present with Mary Magdalene at the tomb but were not mentioned in John. It is doubtful that the women—whether one or more—would have been called upon for apologetic purposes, since in ancient times the supporting testimony of women would likely not have settled such an important matter.[27] It is possible that the earlier synoptic tradition including several women coming to the tomb is original, but since Mary Magdalene was the leading figure among them, John gave priority to her.

Whatever the solution, all evangelists agree that Jesus' tomb was discovered empty on the first day, not by the Twelve (or Eleven), but by Mary and possibly other women who accompanied Jesus from Galilee. The disciples subsequently confirmed their report (Peter in Luke 24:12; and Peter and the Beloved Disciple in John 20:2–10).

Bultmann contends that the discrepancies in the empty-tomb stories, especially in the Synoptics, point to the lateness of that tradition. He says the cumbersome repetition of the women's names in Mark 16:1 from 15:40 and 47 demonstrates this.[28] This repetition of names in Mark may only reflect his faithfulness to the source(s) he uses. In 15:40 the women accompanying Mary Magdalene were Mary, the mother of James the younger and of Joses, and Salome. In 15:47 it was only Mary Magdalene and Mary the mother of Joses who saw the burial. Mark says that all three of the women (16:1; cf. 15:40) went to anoint Jesus' body, rather than just the two women who saw Jesus buried the Friday before. That Mary the mother of James and Joses is mentioned as only the mother of Joses in 15:47 but of James in 16:1 should not cause concern since it is clear that the same Mary is in mind in both places. Perhaps the names are reintroduced in 16:1 because Salome, who did not see the burial (15:47), joined the two Marys for the subsequent planned anointing, and Mark wanted to express her devotion along with that of the other two

---

27. E. L. Bode (*The First Easter Morning: The Gospel Accounts of the Women's Visit to the Tomb of Jesus* [Rome: Biblical Institute Press, 1970], 169; see also 168–70) contends that the development of the tradition of the angelic appearance at the tomb came about because the Jewish polemic against the resurrection of Jesus required Christians to adduce more support than the testimony of some women. He concludes that the angelic appearances are separate from and secondary to the historical nucleus of the empty-tomb narrative.

28. R. Bultmann, *The History of the Synoptic Tradition* (trans. J. Marsh; rev. ed.; Oxford: Blackwell, 1972), 285n. Jeremias (*Theology*, 304) agrees with Bultmann at this point. G. O'Collins (*The Easter Jesus* [London: Darton, Longman, & Todd, 1973], 21) also thinks that the repetition of the names is a clear indication of an editorial hand involved in Mark 16:1–8 in an effort to link the passion and burial of Jesus to the resurrection narratives. He sees Mark 16:7 as another attempt to do the same thing. See p. 40 for those elements in 16:1–8 that he argues are late additions to the passage.

women. This is admittedly a strict reconstruction of the text, but it opens up possibilities for understanding the duplication of names.

Someone to Open the Tomb

The women's failure to consider in advance who would open the tomb (Mark 16:3) points, for Bultmann, to the lateness of that tradition.[29] It is only in Mark 16:3 that the women worry about opening the tomb for the purpose of anointing the body of Jesus. Is this why Matthew has no mention of spices and says only that the women went *to see* the sepulcher where Jesus was placed (28:1)? Luke simply states that the women brought spices to the tomb and that they found the stone rolled away (24:2). John, like Matthew and Luke, does not mention the difficulty of moving the stone. C. F. Evans notes that in Matthew the women knew of the sealing of the tomb and only came to visit the tomb, not anoint the body.[30]

The problem here does not appear so great since both Mark (15:46) and Matthew (27:60) indicate that Joseph of Arimathea *himself* closed the tomb by rolling the stone against it. To this should be added that, since one man closed the tomb, it might well be possible for one man (or two women) to open it. When Jesus appears to Mary in John 20:15, she supposes him to be a gardener who may have *himself* taken the body away. Also, is it possible that the women knew that someone in the vicinity could have opened the tomb? This appears to be a hope, but not a certainty, in Mark 16:3. Could it be that this hope was sufficiently strong that the women began their journey to the tomb anxious to find someone (a gardener?) to open it? Since these women came from Galilee (Luke 23:55), they likely had few friends in Jerusalem on whom they could call for help other than the disciples, who were in hiding. It is possible, therefore, that the only chance of receiving help was from someone in the neighborhood of the tomb itself, such as a gardener. Mark 16:3 allows for that possibility.

The Actual Opening of the Tomb

According to Mark 16:4, the stone was already rolled back when the women arrived. Luke and John also say that the women found the stone rolled away from the tomb (Luke 24:2; John 20:1). Matthew, however, reports that the women and the guards actually saw an "angel of the Lord" descend from heaven

---

29. Bultmann, *Synoptic Tradition*, 285.
30. C. F. Evans, *Resurrection and the New Testament* (London: SCM, 1970), 82.

and roll back the stone (28:2–4), adding that there was "a great earthquake" that preceded the opening. How can such differences between Matthew and the other evangelists be reconciled? Was Matthew's description of the opening of the tomb his attempt to increase the testimony supporting the resurrection of Jesus by including the guards as witnesses, thereby strengthening the women's testimony? Matthew's apologetic interests are reflected in the fact that he alone has a guard at the tomb and points to the significance of Jesus' resurrection through the earthquake, the "angel of the Lord" descending, and both followers and nonfollowers of Jesus witnessing the opening. Apologetic concerns obviously are intended to dispel the Jewish polemic against the resurrection of Jesus that claimed that the disciples stole the body (28:4, 11–15). Perhaps the key to understanding Matthew's intentions is in his reference to the "great earthquake" that was a mark of Yahweh's presence for revelation (Exod. 19:18) and of destructive judgment (Isa. 29:6). Earlier in Matthew earthquakes are among the catastrophic phenomena of the last days (Matt. 24:7; see also Zech. 14:4–5). It is thus likely that Matthew used the earthquake not found in the other Gospels to emphasize the revelatory and apocalyptic nature of Easter and that in the death and resurrection of Jesus the end times had arrived.[31] The description of the "angel of the Lord" (28:2–3) and the results of his activity (28:4) are almost direct parallels to Daniel 10:5–7. This can be seen in the "appearance like lightning" (compare 28:3 and Dan. 10:6), the fear of those present (28:4 and Dan. 10:7), and the admonition not to fear (28:5 and Dan. 10:12). The Daniel passage (10:2–21) is an apocalyptic passage focusing on the approaching activity of Yahweh. At the death of Jesus, the synoptic evangelists record accompanying miraculous phenomena as in the tearing of the temple curtain (Mark 15:38; Matt. 27:51–54; Luke 23:45). Only Matthew adds an earthquake and the unusual story of the resurrection of the bodies of many saints who went walking through the streets of Jerusalem (27:51–54). Matthew apparently wanted his readers to know that in the death and resurrection of Jesus the dawn of a new age had begun. Notice that Matthew 24:7; Mark 13:8; and Luke 21:11 all mention earthquakes in the last days before God's coming judgment and kingdom, but unlike Mark and Luke, Matthew includes them at the death and resurrection of Jesus (27:51 and 28:2). Jeremias adds that Matthew 28:18–20 is not unlike Daniel 7:13–15, which also speaks of the kingdom and dominion of the Son of Man. He says Matthew means to say that the hope "that the Son of Man would one day be

---

31. Dunn, *Jesus Remembered*, 830n16, is similar in his interpretation of the earthquakes in Matthew's account, and adds that Matthew's "readers of the time would be familiar with the device (used also in Scripture) of signaling epochal events by referring to such perturbations in heaven or on earth."

enthroned as ruler of the world was fulfilled in the resurrection."[32] Matthew presents supernatural phenomena not only for apologetic purposes, but also to point to the significance of the events he is describing. The dawning of a new age dominates Matthew's empty-tomb story and his appearance stories.

Entering the Tomb

The synoptic evangelists indicate that the women entered the tomb when they saw that it was open (Mark 16:5; Luke 24:3; and, by implication, Matt. 28:6, where the women are invited to "Come, see the place where he lay"). John, however, says Mary Magdalene saw the stone had been rolled away and then ran to tell Peter and the "other disciple" (presumably John), stating that the body was missing (20:1–2). John assumes that Mary had at least peered into the tomb; otherwise her report to Peter makes little sense. While she only sees the stone rolled away and tells the disciples Jesus' body has been taken, in 20:11 she stoops to look into the tomb *after* Peter and the "other disciple" have entered it (20:3–10). Is John simply connecting two different stories here, namely the story of Mary with another story about Peter and the "other disciple" sandwiched in the middle?[33]

The difference between John and the Synoptics may well lie in John's emphasis on preserving the priority of Peter in his narrative (see also 1 Cor. 15:5). Does he prevent Mary from entering the tomb until after Peter has done so? See also the unusual waiting of the Beloved Disciple until *after* Peter has entered the tomb (20:5, 8). Mary's looking into the tomb *at her first visit* seems assumed without being expressly stated, since otherwise it makes Mary's comment about the missing body (20:2) difficult to follow. If she had looked in at her first visit to the tomb, why did she not see the grave clothes (20:6–7)? John's story is problematic, and there may be several motives for its form; namely, affirming the priority of Peter, sewing together two distinct traditions, and/or stressing the special nature of the resurrection itself (see 20:24–27).

But why did Mary not see the grave clothes that earlier impressed the "other disciple" (vv. 6–8) as she looked into the tomb in verse 11? She saw only the angels (v. 12), who communicated nothing significant to her, unlike in the other Gospels. Is John relating two different empty-tomb stories in John 20:1–18? The rough composite nature of John's resurrection narrative may offer a clue. According to Brown, several awkward things are in John's account: (1) Mary comes to the tomb alone, but speaks of "we" in 20:2; (2) she states that the

---

32. Jeremias, *Theology*, 310.
33. Bultmann, *Gospel of John*, 681–84, makes this argument.

body was stolen (v. 2), but fails to look into the tomb until 20:11; (3) frequent duplication occurs in the story about Peter and the Beloved Disciple—for example, two "to" phrases in 20:2 and a repetition in what was seen in 20:5 and 20:6; (4) the belief of the Beloved Disciple (20:8) apparently has no effect on anyone else until the risen Jesus shows the disciples his pierced hands and side (20:19–20); (5) it is not clear how or when Mary returns to the tomb (20:11); (6) it is not clear why Mary sees angels, but not the grave clothes (20:12); (7) in 20:13 the message of the angels reveals nothing about the fate of Jesus (or anything else, for that matter); and (8) Mary is said to have turned to Jesus two times (20:14, 16).[34] These oddities likely show the bringing together of two separate Easter stories.

The Angels: Location and Message

The story of the angels at the tomb varies in the Gospels. First, how many angels were involved? Mark says there was only a young man in a white robe.[35] Matthew agrees with Mark (Matt. 28:2), but Luke indicates that there were *two* men "in dazzling clothes" who appeared to the women (24:4). John agrees with Luke on the number of angels (John 20:12), but why is there a difference between Mark and Matthew on the one hand and Luke and John on the other?

The almost identical words "suddenly two men" (Luke 24:4) are found in the story of the transfiguration in Luke 9:30, but not in Mark 9:4. Two angels are also found in the ascension story of Acts 1:10. Was Luke trying to connect Moses and Elijah (Luke 9:30) with these three events, the transfiguration, the resurrection, and the ascension, as van Daalen suggests?[36] Or is the reference to *two* angels an indication of a common tradition behind Luke and John (see John 20:12)? As we saw earlier, parallels between Luke and John are not necessarily insignificant.[37]

34. Brown, *Gospel of John*, 995.

35. Greek *neaniskos* (literally "a young man") is used here, but his description leaves little doubt that an angelic figure is intended. The white robe is the dress used elsewhere to refer to the glory of the wearer. Cf. Mark 9:3; Luke 9:29; 24:4; John 20:12; and Acts 1:10. In Rev. 3:18; 4:4; 6:11; 7:9, 14; and especially 19:8, 14, white clothing refers to various inhabitants of heaven. Mark is probably referring to an angel, since angelic apparel is spoken of as white robes elsewhere in the New Testament. Also, the two men in dazzling apparel in Luke 24:4 are understood to be angels in 24:23. Mark therefore probably understood the young man dressed in a white robe (16:5) to be an angel. It would otherwise be difficult to explain why the women were amazed (v. 5b) and afraid (16:8) if the young man were in fact only a young man.

36. So D. H. van Daalen, *The Real Resurrection* (London: Collins, 1972), 22.

37. Another interesting parallel is that in each of these references in Luke the two men "stood by"; that is, in Luke 9:30 they "stood with" Jesus (the perfect participle of *sunistēmi*), in Luke 24:4 they "stood by" the women (the aorist indicative of *ephistēmi*), and in Acts 1:10

Another way of accounting for the differences in the number of angels at the tomb is that Luke usually has two witnesses at major events, for example, Simeon and Anna witnessing the dedication of Jesus (2:25–38); Herod Antipas and Pilate attesting to the innocence of Jesus (23:1–25); two men observing the transfiguration (9:30–34); two men attending the empty tomb (24:4); two men walking on the road to Emmaus (24:13–32); and the sending out of the disciples two by two (10:1). Elsewhere Luke uses numbers to make a significant point beyond the number itself. For example, he uses the number "forty" days for the length of Jesus' temptations (Luke 4:2) and "forty" days for the length of the appearances (Acts 1:3). This parallels earlier uses of "forty" in several Old Testament passages where God is actively involved (Noah's flood, the giving of the law, Moses at Sinai, the length of the wilderness wanderings, Elijah at Mount Horeb). The number "two" is one of the most commonly used numbers in the Gospels and, along with the number "seven," is one of the most popular numbers in the New Testament. Luke-Acts refers to it more than any other book in the New Testament, although it is quite common in the other Gospels. It is difficult to find a consistent use of "two," but it is frequently found in Jesus' parables or in stories where Jesus makes pronouncements. Lillie concludes that originally only one angel was mentioned, but Luke and John, perhaps following an earlier tradition that is also found in the later Christian document *Ascension of Isaiah,* where two angels (Michael and "the angel of the Holy Spirit") are identified at the tomb of Jesus, introduced the second angel because the Jews were accustomed to the idea of angels participating in a resurrection.[38]

Whether some special significance is to be attached to the number two in the empty-tomb narratives is not clear, but the above examples may suggest the direction in which one might pursue the question. The frequency of the number "two" in Luke may be an indication of theological significance that is not in Mark's and Matthew's orientation. Both Luke and John mention two angels at the empty tomb; Luke has them interpret the importance of the empty tomb, but John does not. Does the number "two" alone suggest the significance of the resurrection?

In John, Mary's lack of surprise or amazement when she encounters the angels is strange (20:12–14). In Mark the women express amazement and fear (16:6, 8), in Matthew they express fear and joy (28:5), and in Luke there is fear (24:5). John subdued the role of the angels in his story, but were angels

---

they "stood by" the apostles (the pluperfect of *paristēmi*). Such similarities may or may not be easily dismissed as unintentional or insignificant trivia.

38. W. Lillie, "The Empty Tomb and the Resurrection," in *Historicity and Chronology in the New Testament* (ed. M. C. Perry; London: SPCK, 1965), 6:106–8.

too significant to dismiss them altogether? For John, the angels only occasion Mary's encounter with the risen Lord. Luke and John may depend on a common tradition for their information on the number of angels at the tomb.

Second, aside from the question of how many angels there were, *where* were the angels? Mark's angel was inside, evidently sitting on "the right side" of where Jesus' body was placed (16:5). Matthew's angel descended from heaven, rolled back the stone from before the tomb, and sat down outside, on the stone (28:2). Luke's angels are inside and standing (24:4), but John's angels were inside and sitting "where the body of Jesus had lain, one at the head and one at the foot" (20:12).

Third, what did the angels say? In Mark the angel tells the women, "Do not be alarmed; you are looking for Jesus of Nazareth, who was crucified" (16:6). Matthew is quite similar: "Do not be afraid; I know that you are looking for Jesus who was crucified" (28:5). Luke's angels say nothing to dispel the fear of the women, but ask, "Why do you look for the living among the dead?" (24:5). John's angels only ask Mary, "Woman, why are you weeping?" (20:13). In John, Jesus combines the question of the angels with one similar to the angelic statement in the Synoptics; namely, "Woman, why are you weeping? Whom are you looking for?" (20:15). In John the initial revelation about the emptiness of the tomb comes from Jesus himself. In the Synoptics the angel(s) give(s) the answer: he has risen; he is not here (Mark 16:6; Matt. 28:6; Luke 24:5).

The angelic messages reflect interesting differences. In Mark 16:6, the angel invites the women to look at the location where Jesus was placed. In Matthew, the angel tells the women, "Come, see the place where he lay" (28:6), indicating that they have not yet entered the tomb, but are invited to do so. Mark's angel then tells the women, "Tell the disciples *and Peter* that he is going ahead of you to Galilee; there you will see him, *just as he told you*" (16:7, italics added). Matthew's version of the angelic command expands by telling the women, "Go quickly and tell his disciples, 'He has been raised from the dead, and indeed, he is going ahead of you to Galilee; there you will see him'" (28:7), but Matthew omits Peter from the angelic command. Luke's angels do not give a command to go to Galilee or even to tell the disciples, but call instead on the women to remember Jesus' words "while he was still in Galilee" concerning his crucifixion and subsequent resurrection (24:6–7; cf. 1 Cor. 15:4). These differences may stem from Luke's theological preference for Jerusalem as the center of the church and its missionary endeavors.[39] John also says nothing about going to Galilee except

---

39. This will be discussed further below when we look at the problem of the location of the appearances.

in the appendix in John 21, but rather reports that Jesus, after telling Mary about his ascension, commands her to report his ascension to the disciples who are still in Jerusalem (20:17).

The problems concerning the angels at the tomb initially seem trivial but, taken together, suggest apologetic motifs and possibly also a lack of attention to detail. Do the evangelists have theological emphases that are not altogether clear to modern interpreters? How can we account for these differences? Were the angels a part of the original story, and what is their role in the Easter traditions? Matthew speaks of an "angel of the Lord" to point to the eschatological nature of the events he describes, namely, that the future has broken into the present through the death and resurrection of Jesus. Mark and Luke employ the angel(s) to interpret the significance of the empty tomb to the women and report the resurrection of Jesus. John uses the angels to point to the importance of Jesus' resurrection, but Mary does not understand this until Jesus speaks to her. In John the angels do not advance the message of or about the risen Lord as they do in the Synoptic Gospels. The angels in John's empty-tomb tradition point to the significance of the resurrection itself. There may have been no angels present in the earliest form of the empty-tomb tradition, but they appear to have been later employed to heighten the significance of the empty tomb. The presence of the angel(s) in all four Gospels has multiple and varied attestation in the tradition, but the differences about them in the narratives may suggest their lateness and apologetic purposes.

The Response to the Angelic Message

In the Synoptic Gospels, the women's (or Mary's) response to the angelic presence is mixed. In Mark 16:8, the women left the tomb and said "nothing to anyone, for they were afraid." Matthew says the women departed from the tomb "with fear and great joy, and ran to tell his disciples" (28:8). Luke says nothing about the joy of the women, but after the women were told of the meaning of the empty tomb, they "remembered his [Jesus'] words, and returning from the tomb, they told all this to the eleven and to all the rest" (24:8–9). Luke 24:10 seems like an afterthought to make sure the women are identified. Was this Luke's attempt to make his Gospel correspond to the other evangelists, since he adds "the other women with them" (24:10)? Luke departs from Mark and seems to add several women besides Mary Magdalene, Joanna, and Mary the mother of James (see 23:55 and 24:10). It may also be significant that Luke introduces the title "apostle" in his Easter story (24:10), a term that has greater significance in Acts.

The Disciples' Response to the Women

Mark says nothing of the disciples' response to the message of the women since his Gospel ends so abruptly, but Matthew says the women went to tell the disciples (28:11) and that the disciples responded to their message by going to Galilee (28:16). Matthew intends for his readers to understand that the disciples believed the women and went back to Galilee. Luke, however, says that the apostles did not believe the women's report because "these words seemed to them an idle tale" (24:11). While Peter visits the tomb, he leaves with questions, not faith (24:12). Matthew does not reflect a lack of belief in the women's report, though after Jesus met with the disciples in Galilee, some of them believed and worshiped him, but "some doubted" even after they had seen Jesus (28:17). Luke reserves faith for when Jesus appears to the disciples and breaks bread with them (24:30–34). John says nothing about the disciples' response to Mary's second report of her encounter with Jesus (20:12–18). He only mentions their response to her report about the absence of Jesus' body, and they went to investigate it for themselves (20:2–10).

The Grave Clothes

In John, upon receiving news from Mary Magdalene that Jesus' body was missing, Peter and the "other disciple" ran to the tomb to check out her report (20:1–10). In this scene, the "other disciple" reached the tomb first and looked inside without entering, but he saw the grave clothes ("linen wrappings"). Peter entered the tomb and saw the clothes lying in their (evidently) peculiar position. Then the "other disciple" entered the tomb and "believed" based on what he saw (20:8). Here and later there is a parallel between "saw" and "believed" (20:29). The faith of the "other disciple," however, does not fit well with the statement in verse 9: "for as yet *they* did not know the Scripture, that he must rise from the dead" (italics added). If the "other disciple" had faith at the tomb, why is it that this faith was not shared with Mary, who is left standing at the entrance of the tomb weeping (v. 11), or, for that matter, with the rest of the disciples (vv. 19–23)? It apparently had no effect on the other disciples or anyone else.

In Luke 24:12, faith was not achieved at the discovery of the empty tomb. Luke does not mention the "other disciple" accompanying Peter to the tomb, but he does say that Peter saw the grave clothes lying by themselves, and "he went home amazed at what had happened" (24:12). The word "amazed" (Greek = *thaumazōn*) can refer to surprise or wonder, as in confusion, or that one is significantly impressed or overwhelmed. The latter does not fit what follows, because there is no faith expressed here and the rest of the apostles do not express faith. The same word for "amazed" is also found in 24:41 when some of the disciples were "disbelieving and wondering [Greek = *thaumazontōn*]" even after an appearance by the risen Lord. After he ate with them and taught them, they worshiped him (24:52). The point here is that no one in Luke's account believed until Jesus broke bread with the two disciples on the road to Emmaus (24:32–34).

In John's story, he may be highlighting the "other disciple" coming to faith if the story of the "other disciple" was intended to show how an ideal disciple of Jesus ought to respond. If this is correct, then the conflict in John's story between believing in 20:8 and not believing in verse 9, with no mention of it to Mary (v. 11) or the other disciples (vv. 19–23), is more understandable. In the original story no one believed when they saw the grave clothes or an empty tomb. The two disciples "not yet" (*oudepō*) understanding the Scriptures about Jesus' resurrection (v. 9) parallels somewhat Luke's version of the same story, where Peter ran to the tomb after the women's report and stooped down looking in and "saw the linen cloths by themselves; then he went home, amazed at what had happened" (*pros heauton thaumazōn to gegonos*, 24:12).[40] If this is correct, John's narrative becomes more consistent with itself, as well as with Luke's. This possibility does not suggest that all of the problems noted above are resolved.

If the above is correct, why did John insert the story of an ideal disciple into his narrative? Was he trying to shape a well-known tradition—the story of the grave clothes—into a vehicle for expressing that which the other Gospels express through the angels, namely the interpretation of the empty tomb? If so, why did Peter and Mary not come to faith like the "other disciple"? Brown posits that John tried to introduce here not only the significance of the empty tomb, but also a loving relation to Jesus that Peter did not have. He says that John was not necessarily trying to detract from Peter as much as trying to build up the image of the "other disciple" (the Beloved Disciple). Brown also discredits the notion that John pointed to the blessedness of the Beloved Disciple because he believed without seeing (contrast 20:29) and agrees with Cullmann that the "other disciple" who saw and believed (20:8) could not have been one of those in 20:29 who had not seen and yet believed. Brown concludes that John was making a special hero of the Beloved Disciple, who was closely connected to Jesus. He argues that John used the story of the race to the tomb to show that

---

40. Luke 24:12 is well attested in the manuscript evidence even though classified as a "Western non-interpolation"—that is, an instance where the Western manuscript tradition has not expanded a reading and is stronger than the Alexandrian text.

the "other disciple" was bound closest to Jesus in love, and was the "quickest to look for him and the first to believe in him."[41] John's interpretation of the empty tomb and focus on the faith of the "other disciple" are probably later additions to the grave-clothes tradition seen more clearly in Luke 24:12.

The reference in Luke 24:24 to "some of those who were with us" going to the tomb stands in opposition to the implication from 24:12 that only Peter went to the tomb. This may be resolved if Luke's point in the text was to emphasize the priority of Peter (see also 24:34) and not to rule out the possibility of others being present at the tomb. It is possible that in Luke 24:12, another disciple may have been with Peter on his visit to the tomb and perhaps even more than two at a later time, as Luke 24:24 suggests.

The double witness to the grave clothes suggests that a common early tradition was available to both Luke and John. John introduces a new element into the story—the faith of the "other disciple"—in order to express both the *meaning* of the empty tomb and the exalted status of that disciple. If this disciple's act of believing is deleted from the passage, there are fewer problems in understanding the continuing sorrow of Mary (v. 11) and the failure of the "other disciple" to tell the other disciples of his discovery and his faith in his risen Lord.

The Guard at the Tomb

Many biblical scholars regard the story of the guard at the tomb in Matthew 27:62–66 and 28:11–15 as a late addition to the Easter traditions. This is largely because of the clear apologetic purpose of the story, the apocalyptic coloring throughout the passage (for example, the earthquake and the angel of the Lord), and the fact that no other Gospel mentions the soldiers at the tomb. Fuller accepts that the story is an "apologetic legend," but contends that it helps establish the Jewish understanding of resurrection from the dead; namely, that the popular notion of resurrection at that time was *bodily*. He explains:

> The rise of the Jewish polemic is of considerable importance, for it shows that "resurrection" to the Jewish mind naturally suggested resurrection *from the grave*. It was to the Christian kerygma that Christ "had been raised from the dead" that they [the Jews] replied by the allegation that the empty tomb was a fraud. It never occurred to them, apparently, to separate the concept of resurrection from the concept of the empty tomb.[42]

41. Brown, *Gospel of John*, 1004–7. See also O. Cullmann, *Salvation in History* (trans. S. K. Stowers; London: SCM, 1967), 273.

42. R. Fuller, *The Formation of the Resurrection Narratives* (London: SPCK, 1972), 73 (italics original).

Fuller also believes that this story supports the church's *earliest* belief about the time of Jesus' resurrection; namely, it was on the "third day" (1 Cor. 15:4) or "after three days" (Matt. 27:63–64). Others argue that this story contradicts itself. For example: (1) When the guards experience the opening of the tomb (Matt. 28:2–4), they return to tell the chief priest (v. 11). Why would they report to the Jewish authorities if they were Romans? If, however, Pilate placed the guard at the disposal of the chief priest, why would the guards not have reported back to him? (2) How can anyone say what happened while he was asleep?[43] These inner challenges in the story force one to say that the story of the guard at the tomb needs reconsideration, though it does reflect two important matters. First, it apparently was not in dispute that the tomb of Jesus was empty on the first day of the week. Both the early church and the enemies of the church agreed that the tomb was empty, and the only disagreement was how it got that way. Second, the tradition points to the nature of the resurrection of Jesus—namely, that it was a bodily resurrection. The body of Jesus was not in the tomb where he was buried.

The basic reliability of the empty-tomb tradition as part of the early church's Easter proclamation is attested by the early church's decision not to tamper with the many variations in the details of these stories.[44] These variations did not escape the notice of the ancient Christians who received them.[45]

Consistencies in the Empty-Tomb Tradition

The consistencies in the empty-tomb tradition are often overlooked, as is their significance for understanding what happened in the resurrection of Jesus. First, all of the evangelists are clear that the tomb in which Jesus' body was placed was empty early on the first day of the week, and several witnesses testified to this. This was witnessed not only by women (or Mary in the case of John), but also by at least two of Jesus' disciples. While Matthew and Mark do not claim that the disciples examined the tomb, neither do they deny it. If the disciples were in Jerusalem when they received the women's report, it should not be thought unusual for them to check out the tomb *if they knew of its whereabouts*, especially given the report by the women.

43. W. Marxsen, *The Resurrection of Jesus of Nazareth* (trans. M. Kohl; London: SCM, 1970), 46.
44. Dunn, *Evidence for Jesus*, 63–66.
45. See, for instance, how Eusebius of Caesarea wrestles with the challenges in the resurrection narratives in Eusebius, *Gospel Problems and Solutions* (*Quaestiones Ad Stephanum et Marinum*, CPG 3470; ed. Roger Pearse; trans. D. J. Miller, A. C. McCollum, and Carol Downer; Ipswich, UK: Chieftain Publishing, 2010), 10.147–84. He deals with the time of the women coming to the tomb, which women, the location of the appearances, and other problems in the resurrection narratives. See pp. 287–95.

Secondly, in all four Gospels there is an angelic presence at the site of the tomb on Easter morning. In the Synoptics, the angels interpret the significance of the tomb by saying that Jesus is risen, even though the angels in John only ask a question, leaving the explanation of the empty tomb to the risen Lord himself (John 20:11–18; cf. Matt. 28:8–10). The message of the angel(s) varies according to each evangelist, but their very presence indicates that the empty tomb and events surrounding it were perceived to have far-reaching, if not eschatological, implications. Angels (or men in white robes) are also present at the ascension of Jesus in Acts 1:10–11, reflecting on the return of the risen Lord in triumph. Through the angelic presence, the evangelists wanted readers to understand the significance of what occurred at the tomb. Perhaps because the empty tomb by itself could only lead to wonder or doubt, the evangelists saw that the empty tomb needed to be interpreted—whether by angelic reports (Mark and Luke), the grave clothes (Luke and John), the appearance of Jesus (John), or the angelic reports and appearances of Jesus (Matthew).

Bode omits all angelic appearances from the historical nucleus of the empty-tomb tradition because he finds too many kerygmatic and redactional elements in the angelic message. He asks: "How could the angel have spoken in the kerygmatic language of the primitive church according to Mark, with the authority of God as his messenger to announce the predicted resurrection according to Matthew, with the themes of Lukan theology according to the third gospel and without any message according to John?"[46] He concludes that the angelic appearance and messages can be dismissed from the historical nucleus of the empty-tomb tradition because angels constitute a biblically acceptable literary motif for presenting a divinely authoritative message. He adds that the exclusion of the angel(s) from the empty-tomb tradition gives better insight into the tradition and its development. The women, he claims, came to the tomb early on the first day of the week and found the tomb empty. For them and all who visited the tomb, its significance remained ambiguous until the appearance of Jesus to his disciples. Bode rejects the authenticity of the account of the disciples going to the tomb (Luke 24:12, 24; John 20:3–9) and argues instead that the women kept silent about the tomb until the resurrection proclamation began to be preached. Bode concludes that the virtual silence about the empty tomb in all of the appearance stories, except the Emmaus account (Luke 24:22–24), argues for an independent origin of both traditions.[47]

Lüdemann says all reports of the corporeality of the resurrection of Jesus are late and legendary and that their purpose was to answer the objection that

46. Bode, *Easter Morning*, 178; see also 166–70.
47. Ibid., 178, 182.

Jesus was not raised from the dead and that the disciples only experienced a phantom or a spirit.[48] He says that the revival of a corpse is "*not a historical fact, but a verdict of faith*," and that Jesus' tomb "*was not empty, but full, and his body did not disappear, but rotted away*." He goes on to say that "with the scientific view of the world, the statements about the resurrection of Jesus have irrevocably lost their literal meaning."[49] These conclusions, however, are based on an argument from silence that also involves an assumption about what is generally accepted as a modern worldview.

Simply because the empty-tomb tradition is not found in Paul's epistles or elsewhere outside of the Gospels does not prove that the tradition of the bodily resurrection of Jesus was unknown to the writers of the epistles. Lüdemann presupposes that during Paul's visits to Jerusalem (Gal. 1:18; 2:1–10), he did not come in contact with any presynoptic traditions about Jesus, or that if he did, they did not interest him.[50] His view assumes that the empty-tomb tradition emerged in the middle to late 60s at the earliest, and was well entrenched in the church by the early 70s, the latest presumed date for the writing of Mark's Gospel. This cannot be sustained, as Dunn shows.[51] Lüdemann believes that Paul was unaware of the empty-tomb tradition and that the tomb was not empty, but nevertheless claims that Paul "imagines the resurrection of Jesus in bodily form, which seems to require the emergence of the body of Jesus from the empty tomb." Lüdemann states that "the fate of the physical body of Jesus cannot have been unimportant to Paul."[52]

The empty-tomb tradition is absent from the oldest tradition about the resurrection in the New Testament (1 Cor. 15:3–8), but the independence of this tradition from the appearance stories would still, if Bode is correct, *only be short-lived*. It makes sense that the disciples also visited the empty tomb (so Luke and John). Because all four Gospels agree that the tomb was discovered early on the first day of the week, the disciples were probably still in Jerusalem at the time, since otherwise they would have had to leave Jerusalem on the Sabbath—quite an unlikely scenario. The disciples would more than likely have heard from the women (or Mary) about the empty tomb. Not only do Luke 24:12, 24 and John 20:1–2 give this impression, but all of the evangelists

48. Lüdemann, *What Really Happened to Jesus?*, 79–80.

49. Ibid., 134–35 (italics original).

50. See instead G. Delling, "The Significance of the Resurrection of Jesus for Faith in Jesus Christ," in *The Significance of the Message of the Resurrection for Faith in Jesus Christ* (ed. C. F. D. Moule; trans. D. M. Barton and R. A. Wilson; London: SCM, 1968), 81–82, who believes that Paul probably was aware of the empty-tomb tradition as well as the corporeality of the resurrection of Jesus. Note the arguments on pp. 83–88.

51. See Dunn's arguments against this view in *Evidence for Jesus*, 77–78.

52. Lüdemann, *Resurrection of Jesus*, 46.

say that the angels (or Jesus, as in John) commanded the women to tell the disciples, who were still in Jerusalem, about the tomb. The message that "he [Jesus] is not here" must refer to the tomb (see Mark 16:6 and Matt. 28:6, but also John 20:13 and Luke 24:3). In every Gospel account the women (or just Mary) tell the disciples about their experience at the tomb.[53] Consequently, the empty-tomb story could not have been separated long from the proclamation of the resurrection of Jesus. The disciples therefore likely knew of the tomb when Jesus appeared to them.

The argument for the separation of the empty-tomb stories from the appearance stories is not as convincing as it first appears, since neither the evangelists nor the earliest Christian writers make the tomb an object of faith. The early followers of Jesus did not venerate the empty tomb, and unlike the tombs of many of the early martyrs of the church, it was not initially an object of worship.[54] Only after the fourth-century building of the Church of the Holy Sepulchre by Constantine's mother did the burial place of Jesus become an icon for Christian faith.

Further, why should the empty tomb be recalled in the appearance stories or in the epistles that were giving only a summary of early Christian beliefs about the resurrection of Jesus (1 Cor. 15:3–8)? The appearances, not the tomb, assured the disciples of the reality of Jesus' aliveness after his death and gave to them their mission. In his proclamation of the resurrection of Jesus, Paul and the other New Testament writers had no need to give a narration of a tomb since this was not the basis for their Easter faith.

Nevertheless, it could well be that at the time when the evangelists wrote their stories about Jesus, there was a need to be more specific about the corporeality of the resurrection appearances. Where could the evangelists more appropriately include the tradition of the empty tomb, which by their time was common knowledge, than by including it in their narratives about the life, death, and resurrection of Jesus? Since all four evangelists include this story, and in light of their free handling of empty-tomb traditions, why would all of them include the story of the tomb unless it had occupied an important place in the Easter traditions well before them?

J. I. H. McDonald cites Jewish beliefs about the physical nature of resurrection hope, but rightly observes that not all Jews in the time of Jesus held to

---

53. Mark 16:7 is a command for the women to tell the disciples about the resurrection of Jesus, even though the present ending of the Gospel does not indicate that they complied with the angelic command. It should be noted that this command, found in all four Gospels, would be superfluous if the disciples had already fled or departed Jerusalem. The fourfold testimony to tell the disciples at the least implies their presence in Jerusalem at the time of the discovery of the tomb.

54. Dunn, *Evidence for Jesus*, 63–66.

this. He considers that the examples of the translation of elevated persons—Enoch, Elijah, and Moses, who left no human remains on earth—are more to the point. Instead, he claims that the empty tomb is a basic presupposition of early Christian preaching that is "not in itself explained, though it is verified."[55] He cites an interview that he had with J. C. O'Neill, who also stated that "the preaching of the resurrection could not have arisen on any basis other than the empty tomb. There is positive evidence that the tomb was empty. . . . Negatively, nobody produced the body, although it would have been required for any refutation of the resurrection claims that a body be produced."[56] Davis similarly concludes that the empty tomb is not only compatible with Christian preaching about the resurrection; it is required by it! Although competing theories about life after death circulated in the first century, the New Testament writers had bodily resurrection in mind. Davis writes that "resurrection from the grave is what Jews of Jesus' day *would naturally have meant* by the term 'raised from the dead' (even though they could have *understood* alternative theories). And in the absence of compelling evidence for the claim that they had some other theory in mind . . . the proper conclusion is that the New Testament writers had bodily resurrection in mind."[57] He contends that all New Testament accounts of Jesus' resurrection present it as a bodily transformation rather than a resuscitation or spiritual resurrection, even in 1 Corinthians 15. He asks why, if the empty-tomb stories are a late tradition, early Jewish tradition did not dispute them. Their question was not whether the tomb was empty, but how it got that way, and this, according to Davis, strongly suggests "that the empty tomb was a fact agreed upon by all parties early in the game."[58]

Despite the variations in the empty-tomb tradition, all of the evangelists agree that Jesus' body was no longer in the tomb. This cannot be considered inconsequential. The angelic message to the women at the tomb was seen as a heavenly vision (Luke 24:23) and was later included in the church's proclamation. Dodd, trying to account for the presence of the angels in the Easter proclamations, suggests that whenever angels are introduced in biblical narratives, it is frequently a sign that a truth is being conveyed that is beyond the reach of the senses—a "revelation." Concerning the angelic visit to the empty tomb, he explains that "what the women saw [the empty tomb] brought only

55. McDonald, *Resurrection*, 141; see also 5–16, 140–41.
56. Ibid., 143n2. See also J. C. O'Neill, "On the Resurrection as a Historical Question," in *Christ, Faith and History* (ed. S. Sykes and J. P. Clayton; London: Cambridge University Press, 1972), 205–19.
57. S. T. Davis, *Risen Indeed: Making Sense of the Resurrection* (Grand Rapids: Eerdmans, 1993), 61.
58. Ibid., 71.

perplexity; then by a leap beyond the evidence of the senses, they knew what it meant. But it still awaited verification from later experience."[59] The variation in the angels' message in the Synoptics is evidence for an early dating of that tradition, if traditions tend to expand as they are passed along over time. John's rather different role for the angels is difficult to understand, and perhaps he included the story of the angels at the tomb because it was imbedded in the tradition that he received, but he focused instead on the fact that the first appearance of Jesus was to Mary, rather than to Peter. Matthew, the only Gospel that does not mention Peter by name (28:9–10), is also apparently trying to establish this point. The reason John dispensed with an angelic message is not clear, but the presence of the angels adds to the story of Jesus' resurrection that something divinely significant occurred. It is a wonder why John chose to include them at all, unless the tradition he had received was sufficiently strong that he thought it necessary to include them.

While it appears that the empty-tomb tradition in the Gospels allows for Easter faith apart from having received an appearance from the risen Lord (Matt. 28:8; Luke 24:8–11; John 20:8), such faith does not come until after the appearances of Jesus. Mark also allows for this possibility (16:6–7), but in his account the women do not believe, at least not up to the point where his Gospel breaks off in 16:8; rather, they leave in fear and say nothing. In Matthew, the disciples evidently believe the women's report and set off for Galilee (28:16), but, again, the women, who have both fear and joy at what the angel tells them, make no report to the disciples before they have an appearance from the risen Jesus (28:8–10). It seems that in their joy (did they believe already?), they ran to tell the disciples, but Jesus interrupted them with an appearance and the repetition of the angelic message to tell the disciples to go to Galilee. In the other Gospels and in the story of Paul, Easter faith is a result of meeting the risen Lord, not viewing an empty tomb. The significance of the empty tomb was at first probably ambiguous, causing only confusion (so Mark 16:8; Luke 24:12, 24; John 20:1–2), but after the appearances, it became a signpost that pointed to the great anticipated eschatological act of God that began in the resurrection of Jesus. The empty tomb certainly pointed them to the bodily nature of the resurrection, but that was likely already assumed. It is difficult to imagine how Jesus' resurrection could be proclaimed in Jerusalem or elsewhere if someone could point to the body of Jesus. The empty-tomb story itself eventually, though not at first, became a vehicle for proclaiming the resurrection of Jesus.[60]

59. C. H. Dodd, *The Founder of Christianity* (London: Collins, 1971), 165.
60. Cf. J. F. Jansen, *The Resurrection of Jesus Christ in New Testament Theology* (Philadelphia: Westminster, 1980), 43–44. See also his balanced discussion of the historicity of the Easter proclamation on pp. 31–75. For a careful interpretation of the resurrection narratives,

Finally, after surveying the conflicting stories about the empty tomb, Dunn maintains that the empty-tomb tradition is both early and accurate; the body of Jesus was not in the tomb in which he had been buried. In light of the arguments for the authenticity of this tradition, he concludes that "as a matter of historical reconstruction, the weight of evidence points firmly to the conclusion that Jesus' tomb was found empty and that its emptiness was a factor in the first Christians' belief in the resurrection of Jesus." He adds that "those who were involved in the episode, those who experienced the impact of the event, those who in speaking of what they had thus seen and heard gave the tradition its definitive and lasting shape." [61] Those individuals, he claims, were the women who visited the tomb, or those others who saw it, and those who heard about it. Early Christian claims that the tomb of Jesus was empty were not challenged even by their enemies. Wright also correctly comments that the empty tomb by itself, or the appearances by themselves, would only have led to the conclusion of visions that were common in the ancient world; but the combination of the empty tomb and the appearances of "a living Jesus, taken together, would have presented a powerful reason for the emergence of the belief" that Jesus was alive. He adds that "the meaning of resurrection within second-Temple Judaism makes it impossible to conceive of this reshaped resurrection belief emerging without it being known that a body had disappeared, and that the person had been discovered to be thoroughly alive again." [62] He concludes by saying, "It is therefore historically highly probable that Jesus' tomb was indeed empty on the third day after his execution, and that the disciples did indeed encounter him giving every appearance of being well and truly alive." [63] Johnson thus correctly concludes that what empowered the community of faith was not the absence of a body from the tomb, but a new form of presence that needed explanation: "Whatever the character of the ministry of Jesus for the 'Jesus movement' before his death, it is the experience of the transformed Jesus as Lord that begins the 'Christian movement.'" [64] I agree.

From this brief survey of the biblical texts, it seems clear that the emptiness of the tomb, although ambiguous by itself, was well established quite early in both Christian and non-Christian communities, and elicited numerous interpretations. For example, some thought that the disciples had taken the body

---

along with their theological significance for early Christianity, see J. Neyrey, *The Resurrection Stories* (Wilmington, DE: Michael Glazier, 1988).

61. Dunn, *Jesus Remembered*, 830–32.

62. N. T. Wright, *The Resurrection of the Son of God* (Christian Origins and the Question of God 3; Minneapolis: Fortress, 2003), 686.

63. Ibid., 687.

64. Luke Timothy Johnson, *The Real Jesus: The Misguided Quest for the Historical Jesus and the Truth of the Traditional Gospels* (San Francisco: HarperSanFrancisco, 1996), 135–36.

(Matt. 28:11–15), and Mary thought that someone else had taken it (John 20:13). No evidence shows that anyone went to the tomb of Jesus anticipating an empty tomb or a resurrected Lord. The story of the empty tomb did not lead to Easter faith, but to fear, despair, and doubt. It is likely that because of this the emphasis in the narratives shifted from the ambiguity of the tomb to the appearances of Jesus as confirmation of the fact of the resurrection. The vacant tomb could never stand on its own as evidence of the resurrection of Jesus, but it could help corroborate the conclusions drawn from the appearances and point to the nature of the event—namely, that it was a bodily resurrection and not a vision, apparition, or dream.

While I support the authenticity of the empty-tomb reports in the Gospels, I am mindful of the equally strong opposition to their inclusion in the story of the historical Jesus. Allison has rightly pointed to this enigma in historical Jesus scholarship and the tendency for scholars on opposite sides to argue past what the evidence shows.[65] He acknowledges that often those who oppose the authenticity and originality of the empty-tomb tradition also tend to oppose the miraculous activity of God in history.[66] There is room for debate in this matter, and I have not tried to hide the many obvious differences in the empty-tomb narratives, but I believe that the empty-tomb tradition "fits" well with the earliest Easter proclamations and notions of life after death current in the time of Jesus. The empty tomb is a historical fact, but the interpretation of the fact is strongly debated.

The Appearance Stories

When it comes to the resurrection appearances, the primary cohesion in the Gospels seems to be their order and pattern. For example, all of the appearances follow the discovery of the empty tomb, and, as Dodd observes, there is a basic pattern in them that includes the situation (generally the disciples' state of gloom, despair, and unbelief), the appearance of Jesus, his greeting, the disciples' recognition of Jesus, and a word of command.[67] But even though a pattern can be found, there are striking differences in the persons involved in the appearances, the circumstances surrounding the appearances, and their various locations. These differences suggest that while several of

65. Dale Allison, *Resurrecting Jesus: The Earliest Christian Tradition and Its Interpreters* (New York: T&T Clark, 2005), 299–300.

66. Ibid., 304–5.

67. C. H. Dodd, "Appearances of the Risen Christ: An Essay in Form-Criticism of the Gospels," in *Studies in the Gospels* (ed. D. E. Nineham; Oxford: Blackwell, 1957), 9–35.

the early church fathers recognized them, the early churches did not go to great lengths to harmonize the Gospels. When Tatian made such an attempt in his second-century *Diatessaron*, the majority of the early churches eventually rejected his efforts. Denying that such problems exist in the narratives is not honest, but harmonizing them can also be a major challenge. We cannot ignore the inconsistencies in the resurrection narratives, but because of the fundamental significance of the resurrection of Jesus for Christian faith, every attempt should be made to clarify their meaning. Sometimes these differences can be understood as reflecting the theological stance of the evangelists. After examining the differences in the narratives, I will focus on their cohesion. The following chart lists the reported postresurrection appearances of Jesus.

|||||||||||||||||||||||||||||||||||||||||||||||||||||||||||||||||||||||||||||||||||||||||||||||||||||||||||||||||||||||||||||||||||||||||||||||||||||||||||||||||||||||||||||||||||||||||||||||

The Appearance Stories

There are at least eleven distinguishable appearance stories in the Gospel narratives (including Mark 16:9–20 and John 21), plus the one to Paul in Acts 9 (see also Gal. 1:15; 1 Cor. 9:1; 15:8). The asterisks (*) below indicate which passages were probably *not* an original part of the Gospels in which they appear, but incorporated at a later time. The appearance stories include the following:

1. Matthew 28:9–10, to the women at the tomb.

2. Matthew 28:16–20, to the eleven disciples in Galilee.

3. Luke 24:13–35, to the two disciples on the road to Emmaus. (The appearance to Peter in Luke 24:34 is only stated and not narrated.)

4. Luke 24:36–53, to the disciples in Jerusalem (vv. 50–53 are treated as part of the same appearance).

5. John 20:11–18, to Mary Magdalene at the tomb.

6. John 20:19–23, to the disciples without Thomas in Jerusalem.

7. John 20:26–29, to the disciples with Thomas in Jerusalem.

*8. John 21:1–22, to the seven disciples at the Sea of Tiberias (the dialogue with Peter, vv. 15–22, is evidently in the presence of the others).

*9. Mark 16:9–11, to Mary Magdalene.

*10. Mark 16:12–13, to the two disciples walking in the country (Emmaus?).

*11. Mark 16:14–20, to the eleven disciples in Jerusalem (?) (this was concluded with Jesus' ascension).

To these we add Paul's list that included not only appearances to Cephas and the "Twelve," but also the appearance to some "five hundred" followers of Jesus, James the brother of Jesus, "then to all the apostles," and then Paul himself (1 Cor. 15:5–8; also 9:1; Gal. 1:15–16; plus Acts 9:1–19 and parallels).

|||||||||||||||||||||||||||||||||||||||||||||||||||||||||||||||||||||||||||||||||||||||||||||||||||||||||||||||||||||||||||||||||||||||||||||||||||||||||||||||||||||||||||||||||||||||||||||||

The Location of the Appearances

One of the major challenges in reconstructing the events of the first Easter is the problem of locating the resurrection appearances of Jesus. Mark says that the forthcoming appearances will take place in Galilee (Mark 14:28; 16:7). Could this be "footnotes" that Mark took from an older tradition telling of the disciples' flight to Galilee? Bultmann reasons that since Mark had dispensed with the story of the disciples' flight, he found it "necessary to have the disciples artificially dispatched to Galilee in order to achieve congruity with the old Easter tradition."[68] Matthew, following Mark, places the appearance of Jesus to the disciples in Galilee (28:16–20), though he has an appearance to the women ("Mary Magdalene and the other Mary") in Jerusalem (28:9–10). The close parallels between Mark 14:28; 16:7; and Matthew 28:7 show Matthew's dependence on Mark. As we have already observed, Luke and John do not mention any appearances of Jesus in Galilee. For them, the appearances all took place in and around Jerusalem. Luke includes the appearance on the road to Emmaus, as well as appearances in Jerusalem and Bethany (see Luke 24:13–52). John mentions only Jerusalem. The Galilean appearances of Jesus in John 21 are not included here since, as I argued earlier, they were not an original part of John's Gospel. As Mark 16:9–20 is generally recognized by biblical scholars as a late addition to Mark, so also John 21 is generally considered by many scholars to be an epilogue added by someone in the early church sometime after the original work (chaps. 1–20) had been composed (see 21:24). No doubt these additions were an attempt to harmonize existing traditions and possibly to answer later questions.

How do we bring these two traditions together? In current scholarly opinion, there appear to be three possibilities: (1) the appearances of Jesus took place both in Galilee and in Jerusalem; (2) the appearances took place solely in Galilee; or (3) the appearances took place solely in and around Jerusalem. If we add the later (last) appearance that Paul claims came to him, then we have another possibility that took place while Paul was on his way to Damascus (Acts 9). Biblical scholars have long attempted to reconcile the geographical differences in the appearance stories. Some have emphasized that the appearances occurred in only one of the two locations, but this raises questions of why two locations are mentioned in the Easter traditions and what significance may be connected with either place.

Long ago, Ernst Lohmeyer suggested that differences in the location of the appearances may be answered by recognizing that the appearances were

---

68. Bultmann, *Synoptic Tradition*, 285–86.

visionary experiences of the disciples, and physical location would not be a problem in such instances. On the other hand, he raised the question of the theological significance of the two locations and suggested that the reason for the variation in the tradition is that Galilee represented the place of preaching and origin of the "Son of Man christology" as well as the land of fulfillment. On the other hand, Jerusalem represented the place of the "messiah christology."[69] Some scholars today often support Lohmeyer's contention that there may be theological reasons these two locations are mentioned, but few agree precisely what those theological reasons are. O'Collins has noted that since the 1930s, when Lohmeyer first published his work, scholars have not always considered Mark's references to Galilee in a geographical sense. Some have urged instead that Galilee denotes the place of preaching or even the land of the gentiles, which would point instead to the worldwide mission of the church.[70] If Mark does not intend Galilee to be taken literally in a geographical sense, then it may be best to accept Jerusalem as the place for all of the appearances.

O'Collins suggests that Mark uses the term "Galilee" with some theological value in mind, but also says that it is still better to follow Mark rather than Luke and John, and place all of the appearances in Galilee. He thinks it is more likely that Luke altered Mark's text for theological reasons than the other way around.[71] Marxsen takes Mark 14:28 and 16:7 not as references to a resurrection appearance, but rather to the soon approaching return or *parousia* of Christ that Mark expected to occur in Galilee. He argues that in the Gospels and in Paul (1 Cor. 15:3–8), the term *ōphthē* ("he was seen" or "he appeared") and not *opsesthe* ("you will see") is used for the resurrection appearances, and that Mark refers not to a resurrection appearance but to the *parousia*, or coming of Christ, which did not happen. Mark, therefore, was pointing to the location of where the disciples would see Jesus in his coming (*parousia*), not simply a resurrection appearance.[72] This is not likely, however, since Paul and John both use *opsomai* ("will see") for a resurrection appearance (1 Cor. 9:1; John 20:18, 25, 29), and Matthew undoubtedly understood Mark 16:7 as a resurrection appearance and not the *parousia* (Matt. 28:7, 10, 16–20). Also, Mark names Peter and the other disciples in the appearances,

69. E. Lohmeyer, *Galiläe und Jerusalem* (Göttingen: Vandenhoeck & Ruprecht, 1956), 34–42. See also H. A. Anderson, *Jesus and Christian Origins* (New York: Oxford University Press, 1964), 197–98.

70. O'Collins, *Easter Jesus*, 36.

71. Ibid., 37.

72. W. Marxsen, *Mark the Evangelist* (Nashville: Abingdon, 1969), 83–92. See also Marxsen, *Resurrection of Jesus*, 141–43 and 163–64.

and so does Paul in his listing of appearances (1 Cor. 15:5). Fuller explains that "if Mark 16:7 were pointing forward to the *parousia* it is hard to see why Peter should be singled out for special mention. But if it points to resurrection appearances, the reason for the mention of Peter is obvious."[73]

So did the appearances of the risen Christ take place in Galilee or Jerusalem, or in both places? There have been several major attempts to resolve this difficulty. Moule asks whether it is possible to hold that the appearances took place first in Jerusalem and then in Galilee. He explains that the location of the resurrection appearances might be understood in terms of the festival pilgrimages. The disciples of Jesus were all Galileans and consequently were in Judea only as pilgrims for the Passover festival, just as Jesus had been. Within a week after the end of Passover they naturally returned to Galilee. During that week some of the disciples could have seen Jesus in Jerusalem and then later also in Galilee. Accepting that the appearances were spread over a longer period of time—that is, for some forty or fifty days (Acts 1:3)—Moule thinks it is quite possible that the disciples returned to Jerusalem for the next pilgrim festival, Pentecost, and there Jesus appeared to them again in Jerusalem.[74] He admits that this is a rather rigid interpretation of the narratives, but believes that it makes sense of Mark 16:7 and of Luke's recorded admonition from the risen Christ to the disciples to remain in Jerusalem (Luke 24:49; Acts 1:4). He says that "such literalism may seem absurd; but it seems to make sense of the Marcan 'he goes before you into Galilee' (16:7)—it would mean, when you return home you will find him already there—and of the injunction in Luke-Acts not to leave Jerusalem after Pentecost (Luke 24:49; Acts 1:4)—it would mean, this time, do not return to Galilee, as you did after Passover."[75] Moule's proposal, while unique and interesting, is not supported by the resurrection narratives themselves, and this raises the difficult problem of separating Luke 24:36–53 (presumably between vv. 43 and 44) in order to allow for a Galilean appearance before the command of 24:48 to remain in Jerusalem. It is therefore questionable whether Moule's interpretation comes to grips with the fact that Mark and Matthew have opted so strongly for Galilee but Luke and John for Jerusalem.

---

73. Fuller, *Formation of the Resurrection Narratives*, 63–64. Peter's prominence among the apostles, his denial of Jesus after his arrest and the need for reconciliation such as we see in John 21, his role in the establishment of the church, and his leadership among the disciples make a special appearance to him obvious if not necessary. If the reference were to the *parousia* or coming of Christ, then the reference to Peter in the narrative, as Fuller observes, does not make much sense.

74. Moule, *Significance of the Message*, 4–6.

75. Ibid., 5. See also his "The Post-Resurrection Appearances in the Light of Festival Pilgrimages," *NTS* 4 (1957): 58–61.

The same can be said about Lilly's somewhat traditional solution to the problem based on the refusal of the disciples to believe the women's report of the empty tomb, and their report of the angelic command to go to Galilee. He says that at first Jesus intended for the disciples to leave the hostile atmosphere of Jerusalem for the more tranquil territory of Galilee, where he would reveal himself to them and give his final commission. Because, Lilly says, the women delayed their report to the disciples, the disciples did not believe it, and the only way to overcome their disbelief was for Jesus to appear to them in Jerusalem, establish their faith there, and prepare them for more appearances in Jerusalem.[76] His attempt to harmonize, like Moule's, is fanciful and does not square with Luke's and John's clear preference for Jerusalem as the location for all of the appearances, nor for Luke (24:49), who may have been aware of the Markan tradition but simply rejected it (see 24:6). Also, it is an argument from silence. The evangelists do not say that the disciples rejected the women's report (not even Luke 24:11–12, as we see in 24:24) and that therefore Jesus had to appear to the disciples in Jerusalem to get them to go to Galilee!

C. F. Evans translated *proagein* as "lead" (normally it is "precede" or "go before") in Mark 14:28 and 16:7, based on Mark's earlier use of this term in 10:32. If the word means "lead," would Jesus have had to lead his disciples from Jerusalem all the way to Galilee?[77] This translation, however well suited for Mark 10:32 or 14:28, is not useful for 16:7, where the angel says, "There (*ekei*) you will see him."

Paul's reference to an appearance to "more than five hundred brothers and sisters" may suggest Galilee, since Jesus' largest following was there. Von Campenhausen may be right that Jesus made an appearance in Galilee to many of his followers (more than 500? See 1 Cor. 15:6), but to his disciples only in Jerusalem. Von Campenhausen claims that there would hardly have been a place available in Jerusalem for such a large crowd to meet. Only in Galilee, where he had a longer tenure of ministry, would Jesus have had more than five hundred disciples. His relatively brief tenure of ministry in Jerusalem (one week according to the Synoptics) does not suggest large numbers of followers there.[78] The same could be said of the appearance to James (and possibly to "all the apostles"), since James (also of Nazareth) was not one of the original Twelve, and would not likely have traveled to Jerusalem with Jesus. Paul indicates that James also received an appearance from Jesus, which

76. Lilly, "Alleged Discrepancies," 103–4.

77. C. F. Evans, "I Will Go before You into Galilee," *JTS* NS 5 (1954): 3–18.

78. H. von Campenhausen, *Tradition and Life in the Church* (trans. A. V. Littledale; London: Collins, 1968), 47–48. It may be that John's longer tenure of Jesus' ministry (some three years), which also includes several visits to Jerusalem, is more accurate than the Synoptic accounts, which report only on Jesus' Galilean ministry for about a year.

presumably led to his faith, and that would likely be in the region of Galilee. Because the majority of Jesus' ministry was in Galilee, it is likely that some resurrection appearances took place there. A large gathering of followers of Jesus is more likely in Galilee because the atmosphere there would have been less hostile than in Jerusalem. The Pharisees, who were among Jesus' strongest opponents in Jerusalem, had very little influence in Galilee.[79]

The earliest known church was in Jerusalem, where the first council took place (Acts 15) and where Paul visited the "pillars" of the church (Gal. 2:1–10). Since the death and resurrection of Jesus occurred there, as well as the earliest known Christian missionary activity, Luke and John may have chosen to emphasize Jerusalem over Galilee to stress the missionary activity to which Jesus had called the disciples. Jerusalem, the city of promise and fulfillment, became the place where the Jesus movement was firmly established. But also, since Jesus' preaching, teaching, and healing ministry took place primarily in Galilee and the majority of his followers were from there, including all of his disciples (apostles), Mark and Matthew may have chosen to emphasize Galilean appearances.

The differences in the location of the appearances, like the nature of the resurrection (bodily, physical, transformed body), were understandably less important to the earliest followers of Jesus than they are for biblical scholars today. That community was more excited about reports that Jesus was alive than in some of the details that became more important as the early churches had more time to reflect on what happened. This is exactly what we might expect with any remarkable event in history. Initial reports are often conflicted, but generally reflect the basic truth of the matter—here, the basic truth is that Jesus is alive!

Most harmonizations of the two locations are strained and fail to appreciate what may have been at the heart of the evangelists' intentions. The earliest attempt to bring the Jerusalem and Galilee traditions together is the Johannine "appendix" (chap. 21), and it both is awkward and leaves questions unanswered. For example, if the disciples saw the risen Jesus in John 20 in Jerusalem, why do they not recognize him in John 21 in Galilee? More troubling, if Jesus' commission of the disciples took place in 20:22–23, why are the disciples back *fishing* in John 21 rather than carrying out their commission?

The difficulty in bringing the Galilee and Jerusalem traditions together suggests that more than geography is involved. Luke clearly chose Jerusalem over Galilee, especially in light of 24:6, and apparently rejected Galilean appearances (Mark 16:7). Most harmonizing proposals, and there are many,

---

79. See E. P. Sanders, *Jesus and Judaism* (Philadelphia: Fortress, 1985), 198n90.

ignore details in the resurrection narratives. Even attributing variations in the narratives to their visionary nature does not solve the problem. In some instances, as we have already seen in the birth narratives and genealogies in Matthew and Luke and also in the earthquake stories in Matthew, there is a combination of historical and theological motivation present. It should not be so unusual to find this to be true in the resurrection narratives when so much of early Christian faith focuses and depends on this event, however it is reported.

Should we therefore accept one tradition over another, say Mark and Matthew over Luke and John? The data is insufficient to make a final decision, and such questions may have to remain unanswered. As the narratives stand, there are apparent discrepancies, but is there more to the matter? Do Luke and John absolutely reject the possibility that any appearances took place in Galilee? Do Mark and Matthew intend to exclude any appearances to the disciples in Jerusalem? Matthew does have an appearance of Jesus *to the women* at the tomb, but not to the disciples. Mark's Gospel ends abruptly, and the conclusion of it appears to have been lost.

At present, aside from positing differing theological motives, no one seems to have found *the* connecting link that brings the Galilee and Jerusalem appearances together, nor have they identified clearly the theological motives that may have been present in the minds of the evangelists. These are still matters of debate with no consensus emerging on the horizon. The location of the appearances of Jesus continues to be an important matter in any harmonization of the Easter traditions.

To Whom Did Jesus First Appear?

Matthew says that Jesus' first appearance was to the women (Matt. 28:9–10), and John indicates that it was to Mary alone (John 20:14–18). Mark and Luke have no such appearance of Jesus to the women, only an angelic report at the tomb letting them know that Jesus had risen and would appear to the disciples in Galilee (Mark 16:7), or an evangelist's report that the women simply told the disciples in Jerusalem what they saw at the empty tomb (Luke 24:2–9). Whether Mark intends that Peter will be the first or last to see the risen Jesus is not clear, but Peter is singled out for special mention ("tell his disciples and Peter," 16:7; cf. Luke 24:12; John 20:3–8; 1 Cor. 15:5). The women in Luke reported what had happened to the *initially* unbelieving disciples (24:9–12, 24). Luke then reports an appearance to the two disciples on the road to Emmaus. Following that occasion, *they* also told "the Eleven" that Jesus had risen and "appeared to Simon" (Luke 24:33–35). Exactly when the appearance to Peter occurred is not noted in Luke, but evidently it was before the appearance to the two disciples on the way to Emmaus, though the text does not explicitly say this. Luke seems to be following the Pauline tradition (1 Cor. 15:5) that Peter received the first appearance. All four Gospels mention the angelic appearance to the women, but differ on who received the first appearance. Mark implies that it was the disciples and Peter (16:7 [note the order]); Matthew says it was the women (28:9); John says it was Mary Magdalene (20:14–18); and Luke says it was Peter (24:34), but the two on the way to Emmaus are the first reported.

If Mark's Gospel had continued past 16:8, would he have included a story of an appearance of Jesus to the women or to the disciples in Jerusalem? Both Matthew (28:9–10) and John (20:11–18) say that an appearance to Mary (or the women) came immediately after the angelic appearance. Whether the original text of Mark would have included an appearance of Jesus to the women is speculation based on an elusive argument from silence. Since Matthew, who elsewhere seems to have followed Mark rather closely, has such an appearance, and since John, who followed another tradition, agrees with him by reporting an appearance to Mary, this may not be too far-fetched.

But why does Luke not mention an appearance to the women? Was he trying to set forth the best defense for his Gospel, and the mention of women in the story in that day appeared to weaken his argument? In Acts 1:3 he summarizes his case for the resurrection, stating that there were "many proofs" (*pollois tekmēriois*) of Jesus' aliveness after his death. Is this why Paul does not mention an appearance of the women in 1 Corinthians 15:5–8 "to more than five hundred brothers and sisters [Greek, *adelphois*]"? Since women were not deemed competent to testify under Jewish law (see *m. Roš. Haš.* 1.8),[80] did Luke and Paul omit mentioning them in their cases for the resurrection of Jesus?[81] Owing to the problem of the credibility of women among the Jews at that time, would an appearance to women have been readily accepted into the resurrection traditions of John and Matthew, two very Jewish Gospels, had there not been an element of credibility to the reports? What motive could be advanced for the inclusion of the appearances to the women in such an important tradition in the ancient *patriarchal* documents? It is more reasonable to conclude that such stories were excluded, as in the case of 1 Corinthians 15:5–8, than that they were added later to the Gospel traditions. Peter's prominence in the formation of the early church probably led to the special priority given to him in the Easter traditions, rather than to the women who had also claimed such an appearance.

Matthew's and John's omission of special references to Peter (Matt. 28:10; John 20:17) may indicate that portions of their Easter sources were earlier

---

80. Von Campenhausen, *Tradition and Life*, 75, presents a number of arguments for this.
81. Ibid., 85.

than Mark's or Luke's. A good reason can be suggested for adding Peter's name to the resurrection traditions and also giving priority to him, but not for deleting references to him. Conversely, apologetic reasons can be found for omitting the story of the appearance to the women, but not for introducing them into the resurrection narratives. Moreover, one became an apostle by virtue of having received an appearance from the risen Lord (1 Cor. 9:1), and therefore, when in Romans 16:7 Paul greets Andronicus and Junia, who "are prominent among the apostles," the implication is that Junia, a woman, was acknowledged to have received an appearance from the risen Lord. If this is so, it is likely that other women did as well!

The Ascension of Jesus

Biblical scholars have known for some time that there are parallel ascension stories in antiquity. For example, in the Roman tradition the most famous emperors were seen by credible witnesses as they ascended to heaven following their deaths (see Plutarch, *Rom.* 27.5–28.2; *Num.* 2.1–3; Livy 1.16; Ovid, *Metam.* 14.805; *Fast.* 2.475; Cicero, *Rep.* 1.16.25; 2.10.17–20; Suetonius, *Aug.* 97.1–3; 100.4; cf. Justin, *1 Apol.* 21.3). Clouds commonly played a role in several ascension stories, as in the case of Plutarch's *Parallel Lives* when he speaks of Romulus's ascension. He writes:

> Suddenly there was a great commotion in the air, and a cloud descended upon the earth bringing with it blasts of wind and rain. The throng of common folk were terrified and fled in all directions, but Romulus disappeared, and was never found again either alive or dead. . . . And Proculus, a man of eminence, took oath that he had seen Romulus ascending to heaven in full armor, and had heard his voice commanding that he be called Quirinius. (*Num.* 11:2, 3, LCL)

It is interesting that Tertullian, who knew this tradition well, compared Romulus's ascension to Jesus' ascension (Tertullian, *Apol.* 21.23). Ascension stories in the Greco-Roman world generally told of the prominence and significant achievements of emperors or other famous persons. Suetonius says that after Octavian (Augustus) died, a person testified to his ascension into heaven. He reports that following the emperor's death and cremation, "an ex-praetor [a person of distinction and highly thought of] took an oath that he had seen the form of the Emperor after he had been reduced to ashes, on its way to heaven" (*Aug.* 1.100.4–5, LCL). An emperor who was not well thought of (as in the cases of Nero and Domitian) did not have such reports by a credible person saying that he had witnessed his ascension!

Biblical scholars have observed the parallels with the ascension story in Luke (24:50–53) and Acts (1:9–11). An important distinction between the Greco-Roman stories and those in the New Testament, however, is that the bodies of the emperors were destroyed or buried and were not a part of the ascensions. In John and Luke, the tomb was empty and the body was taken up into heaven. Such stories suggest that the ascension was intended by Luke and John to proclaim the exaltation of Jesus in his resurrection. The divine nature of the event in Luke is attested by the apostles and by the interpreting angels.

One of the more intriguing and complicated passages in the resurrection narratives is John 20:17, in which the risen Jesus forbids Mary to touch him because he has "not yet ascended" to his Father, but she is to go and tell his "brothers" (disciples) that he is (now?) ascending to "my Father and your Father, to my God and your God." In 20:24–29, he invites Thomas to touch him, and this suggests that the ascension has already taken place. The difficulty here is that we tend to understand "ascension" from the perspective of Luke 24:50–53 and Acts 1:6–11—namely, as the *final* appearance of Jesus to the disciples before he returns to heaven. John emphasizes the exaltation of Jesus to the Father as the fulfillment of his Gospel of divine Sonship (see John 1:11–12). For John, the ascension of Jesus took place on Easter morning after the appearance to Mary but *before* the appearances to the disciples. Since earlier the Spirit had not been given because Jesus had not yet been glorified (John 7:39), and in 20:22–23 Jesus gives the Spirit, it appears that John uses the appearance to Mary as a way to introduce the exaltation of Jesus and therefore the giving of the Spirit to the disciples to accomplish their ministry. John understood the resurrection appearances as the means of exaltation and includes a reference to the ascension in the appearance to Mary before his appearance to the disciples.[82] Obviously, this needs some unpacking!

John seems to equate the ascension with Jesus' glorification that takes place in the resurrection *before* his appearance to the disciples and the giving of the Spirit, but Luke-Acts has the ascension *after* the appearances and before the giving of the Spirit (24:50–53 and Acts 1:9–11)—namely, as a separate and subsequent event to the resurrection of Jesus. A. M. Ramsey believes that John introduces the "touch me not" story to emphasize the importance of the ascension (or exaltation) of Jesus, which, though important to the resurrection of Jesus, is nevertheless subsequent to it. He admits that his interpretation is difficult to square with other New Testament passages that link the exaltation

82. Evans, *Resurrection*, 119, 123–24, 140. Cf. Brown, *Gospel of John*, 992.

of Jesus to his resurrection; that is, by means of the resurrection from the dead, Jesus has been exalted or glorified.[83]

Dodd connects this story not so much with exaltation as with the picture of the high priest going into the Holy of Holies to offer his sacrifice. Only after his offering for the people has been made will Jesus, the high priest, be touchable.[84] But if that is the case, John uses the story as a picture to emphasize a point he nowhere else explicitly makes. Porter emphasizes the linguistic elements in John's account, seeing Jesus as exalted in the resurrection but still in the process of moving toward the ascension. In John 20:17 Jesus tells Mary "do not to touch me" (*mē mou haptou*) since he has not yet ascended (*anabebēka*), but to go and tell the disciples that he is in the process of ascending (*anabainō*)—something that occurs subsequent to the resurrection and before the other appearances. The contrast is between the resurrection *having begun a process*, and its culmination in the ascension.[85] Another explanation requires considerable theological and ecclesiastical input emphasizing the "cling" (or "touch")—namely, that Mary may no longer cling to Jesus' earthly existence, but must look for another way of experiencing his presence. This interpretation recognizes that the passage intends more than what a mere physical touch might suggest (there is no problem with the women touching Jesus in Matt. 28:9), but is nevertheless unjustified and foreign to the context. Its proponents suggest that 20:17 is simply a Johannine redaction designed to have Mary tell the disciples, but there appears to be something more important than that in this passage.[86] John uses the appearance to Mary to make clear that Jesus is now exalted and he can now send the Holy Spirit. By this reckoning, the ascension in John takes place before Jesus' appearance to the disciples in 20:19. After that, it is now appropriate for Thomas to touch him (20:27), even though Thomas does not actually touch him. The implication from the passage is that Jesus had ascended between the first and second appearances.

Elsewhere John seems to make the exaltation of Jesus synonymous with his crucifixion and gives more attention to the significance of the death of Jesus

---

83. A. M. Ramsey, "What Was the Ascension?," in Perry, *Historicity and Chronology in the New Testament*, 139, 144. Paul, for example, assumes that the glorification of Jesus took place in his resurrection, without any separate event like the ascension (see Rom. 1:3–4 and Phil. 2:8–11), and this understanding is similar to Peter's speech in Acts 2:17–36.

84. Dodd, "Appearances of the Risen Christ," 19n. Fuller, *Formation of the Resurrection Narratives*, 138–39, also mentions this as a possible interpretation.

85. See S. E. Porter, *Verbal Aspect in the Greek of the New Testament, with Reference to Tense and Mood* (SBG 1; New York: Lang, 1989), 356.

86. Fuller, *Formation of the Resurrection Narratives*, 138, raises the question of whether the first "father" (*patera*) of this passage should be followed by "my" (*mou*), suggesting there is also fairly good evidence for it to be excluded.

than do the Synoptics (10:11–18; 11:49–53;[87] 12:32–33) and Acts (2:22–23). Similarly, Paul emphasizes the importance of the death of Jesus for sins followed by his exaltation (Phil. 2:6–11). He isolates the proclamation of the death of Jesus from his resurrection (1 Cor. 1:22–24 and 2:2), even though, like John, he knew the importance of Jesus' resurrection (1 Cor. 15:3–5, 12–20). The author of Hebrews also is aware of the resurrection (6:2), but because some of his readers were returning to Judaism and abandoning their faith, he emphasized the superiority of Jesus' priesthood over that of Aaron, and the exaltation of Jesus in his death by going into the Holy of Holies (2:5–11; 9:11–14; 10:12–13; 12:2). For John, exaltation may come for Jesus through the cross, but this exaltation is not acknowledged before the resurrection. Faith in John comes not at the cross (19:35 does not contradict this), but only in Jesus' resurrection. John 20 was not a later attachment to John by a final redactor, but was an integral part of it. In John, the disciples feared for their lives and fled when Jesus was arrested. There was no faith expressed by them at his death. Peter denied knowing Jesus, and the others scattered. At Jesus' death there was no faith, as Bultmann earlier has argued, but only pain and despair. With the exception of the "other disciple" who "believed" at the gravesite when he saw the grave clothes (following the resurrection) and the empty tomb, Mary believed only on the basis of a resurrection appearance (20:18: "I have seen the Lord!"). Thomas was distraught and disbelieving until he saw the risen Lord (20:28). Although John paves the way for understanding the exaltation of Jesus on the cross, that exaltation was not perceived apart from the resurrection of Jesus. The cross did not disclose its meaning to the disciples apart from the resurrection, and faith was not born at the cross, as others have argued.[88]

Brown says that John dramatizes the resurrection to make it part of the ascension, and he uses the appearance to Mary Magdalene as a vehicle to explain that only after the ascension, of which the resurrection is a part, can the enduring presence of Jesus in the Spirit be given. He notes that earlier John

---

87. John reports this as a prophecy; that is, Caiaphas the high priest tells the people what the will of God is regarding the death of Jesus!

88. It is difficult to follow Lüdemann (*Resurrection of Jesus*, 180–82), who argues that everything that was finally proclaimed after Easter was already contained in the sayings and history of Jesus. He, like Bultmann before him, finds the basis for the proclamation of the early church in a new understanding of the cross of Jesus. For him the decision of faith is focused on the historical person (Jesus) and not on the risen Christ. He rejects the notion that the figure of the historical Jesus had to be "raised to that of the mythical Christ . . . in order to have the well-known great effect" (252n702). This, of course, goes against the New Testament testimony, as we have seen. There is no theology of the cross in the New Testament that overcomes the scandal of the cross without the resurrection of Jesus from the dead.

states that only after Jesus' glorification could the gift of the Spirit be given (7:39). Consequently, when Jesus offers the Spirit in 20:22, John is saying that Jesus has already been exalted and glorified; that is, he has already ascended to the Father. For John, it is only the ascended and thereby glorified Jesus who appears to the disciples. But what can we make of the appearance to Mary? It happened before the ascension, and the appearance to the disciples took place after the ascension! Brown says that at face value the resurrection is not the same event as the ascension or exaltation, but this also implies that the appearance to Mary was of inferior status.[89]

Unlike Luke's ascension, John's comes not at the end of the earthly appearances but before they began. Brown believes that an understanding of John's technique may provide a solution to this issue. John tries to fit a theology of resurrection and ascension that has no dimensions of time and space into a narrative that is necessarily sequential and spatial.

> If John's purpose is forgotten, the attempt to dramatize in temporal scenes what is *sub specie aeternitatis* [in the category of eternal] creates confusion. When the risen Jesus has to explain to Mary Magdalene that he is about to ascend, the emphasis is on the identification of the resurrection and the ascension, not on the accidental time lag. In Johannine thought there is only one risen Jesus, and he appears in glory in all his appearances.[90]

Here the controlling interest in John is not the sequence of events, but his theological motive for explaining the meaning of the resurrection and the fact that Jesus gave the disciples the continuing presence of the Spirit. That interest or theme in John's resurrection narrative is the intimate connection between the ascension of the Son of Man and the giving of the Spirit. He recalls in 16:7 that Jesus says, "If I do not go away, the Advocate will not come to you; but if I go, I will send him to you." In 20:17 and 22, John fulfills this promise by associating the resurrection, the ascension, and the giving of the Spirit.[91]

From the time of the arrest and crucifixion (18:1–19:42) to the discovery of the empty tomb (20:10), there is no note of victory in John.[92] Jesus' disciples abandon him, and Peter even denies knowing him. Although John finds the manner of Jesus' death a fulfillment of Scripture (19:24, 36–37), the sound of joy or triumph found in 20:18 ("I have seen the Lord") or 20:28 ("My Lord

89. Brown, *Gospel of John*, 992–94, 1011–17.
90. Ibid., 1015.
91. Ibid., 1015–16.
92. Most scholars consider John 19:35 to be a redactional or authorial insertion, and this seems obvious from the verse itself.

and my God") is completely missing in John's story of Jesus' passion. The exaltation (or glorification) of Jesus comes only *after* the resurrection in John.

In John, the ascension is a part of the resurrection story that, from a temporal point of view, takes place awkwardly between the appearance to Mary and the appearance to the rest of the disciples. As with the story about the disciples' visit to the tomb (20:3–10), John makes use of the appearance to Mary Magdalene to point to a very important theological matter—the presence of the Spirit and the exaltation (glorification) of Jesus in his resurrection.

But what was the ascension? In the New Testament the ascension of Jesus is only mentioned in John and Luke-Acts. Because in Luke-Acts the ascension was the last appearance of Jesus, it is appropriate to view it as an appearance story, but John places the ascension in a different sequence. Matthew closes his Gospel emphasizing Jesus' abiding presence (28:20; cf. 1:23) and has no ascension story.

So what can we say about the nature of the ascension? Does the tendency in the early church to make the resurrection of Jesus more physical than spiritual necessitate the removal of Jesus' body from the earth with an ascension? After Jesus' body was raised from the dead and seen, what happened to it? Lampe says when the resurrection of Jesus came to be thought of in physical-materialistic terms, it was natural to believe that the tomb was empty; and because of the belief in the materialistic conception of the resurrection of Jesus, the ascension story naturally developed to answer the question of what happened to Jesus' body of flesh and bones.[93] He does not discuss the various possible meanings of the ascension in Luke and John, nor does he observe that John has no mention of the final state of Jesus' resurrection body after the appearances. He understands that this was not a question that John entertained, nor was it the motivating factor behind John's ascension story. Luke, on the other hand, may have had several meanings behind his ascension story; namely, the final completion of the appearances (Luke 24:50–53), the exaltation of Jesus (Acts 1:9–11; 13:30–39), and/or the introduction to the coming of the Holy Spirit (Luke 24:49; Acts 1:8).[94] For Ramsey, "There is nothing incredible in an event whereby Jesus assured the disciples that the appearances were ended and that His sovereignty and His presence must henceforth be sought in new ways."[95] John and Luke more likely used a well-known tradition in the early church, each modifying it, to point to the exaltation of Jesus in his resurrection (see John 20:24–27; Luke 24:51–53).[96] Attempts to bring John and Luke together

93. G. W. H. Lampe and D. M. MacKinnon, *The Resurrection* (London: Mowbray, 1966), 54.
94. D. P. Fuller, *Easter Faith and History* (London: Tyndale, 1968), 197–98.
95. A. M. Ramsey, *The Resurrection of Christ* (London: Collins-Fontana, 1966), 123.
96. Manuscript evidence supports this reading of Luke 24:51.

on the chronology of the ascension appear futile, and it is more useful to focus on how each writer understood it.

John offers an important theological truth in the appearance of Jesus to Mary at the tomb—namely, that the exaltation of Jesus is to be understood through a pattern of death, resurrection, and the giving of the Holy Spirit. According to Brown, John may have tried to answer an issue raised by the Docetists, who favored an ascension into heaven at the moment of Jesus' death on the cross. John was opposed to such a view, since for him Jesus is the Christ who experienced death and was exalted or glorified in his resurrection before the giving of the Spirit.[97] Brown is probably right when he notes the difficulty of having an "unglorified" appearance of Jesus to Mary (before his ascension), and when he suggests this should be subdued in light of John's purpose of showing that the exaltation of Jesus to the Father came by way of the cross and resurrection. Consequently, the appearances in John are of an exalted Jesus, even if the appearance came when Jesus had not yet ascended. This is supported by Mary's second report to the disciples in John 20:18 that she had "seen the *Lord*." If Jesus' glorification in John is equated with his resurrection, then all of the appearances are by the exalted Lord because the Holy Spirit can only come after the glorification of Jesus (7:39; 20:17–23).

This also seems true for Luke. In 24:49, the promise of the Father—the "power from on high"—is given with the purpose of enabling the disciples to witness. After the promise is given, Luke depicts Jesus' ascension in the familiar Old Testament imagery of Elijah in 2 Kings 2:11. Shortly after Jesus' departure, the Holy Spirit comes (Acts 2). In both John and Luke, the exaltation of Jesus is conveyed through the ascension followed by the giving of the Holy Spirit. In the rest of the New Testament, Jesus' resurrection is indistinguishable from his exalted status (Acts 2:32–33; 5:30–31; Rom. 8:34; Col. 3:1; Phil. 2:8–9; Eph. 1:19–20; 1 Tim. 3:16; 1 Pet. 3:21–22).

There is yet another question concerning the time of the ascension in Luke. This has to do with the difference between Luke 24, where the ascension apparently takes place late on the same day as the resurrection, and Acts, where the ascension occurs only after "forty days" of appearances. As we noted above, the number "forty" is a special "holy" number that is probably not to be taken literally. The frequency of this number in Scripture probably suggests it means more than a literal forty days. Anderson sees a theological significance in the forty days, representing a special "holy interval" in sacred history in which the apostles are prepared by the coming of the Holy Spirit for the

---

97. Brown, *Gospel of John*, 1014.

forthcoming task of witness.[98] O'Collins, however, contends that the mention of the forty days in Acts 1:3 is Luke's attempt, like John's and Paul's, to link the resurrection of Jesus and the coming of the Holy Spirit: "His 'forty days' helps to ensure that his readers will understand Pentecost as the extension of Easter and the manifest outpouring of the Holy Spirit as the gift of the risen Christ."[99] But if this is so, why does Luke stop at "forty days"? Why not "fifty days" to coincide with Pentecost? Anderson says that the "forty days" in Acts 1:3 implies that there was also a "specific and limited time for the Resurrection appearances."[100] Paul agrees that the Easter appearances ceased after a period of time (1 Cor. 15:3–8), stating he received the last such appearance. If the "forty days" are taken literally, then there is a clear discrepancy between Luke 24 and Acts 1 regarding the length of the appearances and the time of the ascension. But if "forty" is a holy number, as Anderson claims, the conflict on the length of the resurrection appearances is resolved. The number is not repeated in Acts in reference to the length of the appearances (see 10:41 and 13:31), but since the presence and power of God are referred to in all the places where the number forty occurs in Scripture (even in the temptation story of Luke 4:1–2; see also the reference to forty days in 4 Ezra 14:42–45, in which God restores the Jewish Scriptures through Ezra and his scribes), this is the likely intention of Luke in Acts 1:3. One need only be reminded of the forty days of the rains in the flooding of the earth during the days of Noah, the forty years of the children of Israel in the wilderness, the forty days that Moses spent on Mount Sinai, and Elijah at Mount Horeb to understand the significance of this number in the Scriptures. The length of the appearances was most likely something other than a literal forty days.

Another explanation for the difference in Luke 24 and Acts 1 may lie in the changing of Luke's purpose. In Luke 24, Jesus apparently offers a final appearance to the disciples, the purpose of which is to indicate the cessation of his resurrection appearances and to focus on his commission to the disciples. He then departs and is "carried up into heaven." The point is that the appearances as such cease, and the disciples are to look forward to a new manifestation of the presence of God in their midst: "And see, I am sending upon you what my Father promised; so stay here in the city until you have been clothed with power from on high" (Luke 24:49). In Acts 1:3, however, "forty" probably indicates that Luke emphasized the presence of God in the appearances, rather than their length.

98. H. Anderson, *Jesus* (New York: Oxford University Press, 1964), 232.
99. O'Collins, *Easter Jesus*, 87.
100. Anderson, *Jesus*, 232.

In Acts 1:6–11, Luke has not eliminated the apocalyptic nature of the kingdom while emphasizing the ministry of the Spirit in evangelizing. The kingdom is still coming, but the timing of it is not for the disciples to know. They are reassured by the promise of the return of the risen Christ (1:11), but the dominant theme is the exaltation of Jesus in his resurrection. The disciples got the idea and worshiped him (Luke 24:52).

The ascension story was essentially the early church's understanding of the meaning of the resurrection of Jesus. In his resurrection, he was exalted, glorified, and made worthy of worship and service. John's story of the ascension emphasizes that Jesus, the risen Lord, is glorified (7:39) and worthy of worship (20:17–28). John and Luke have the ascension of Jesus in different places, but they agree on the broad sequence of the primary events of Easter; namely, resurrection, ascension, and the giving of the Holy Spirit. The chronology of the ascension story for both John and Luke is not as important as the fact that the ascension in both points to the exaltation of Jesus in his resurrection.

The Nature of Jesus' Resurrection Appearances

One of the most challenging aspects of the post-Easter appearances has to do with their nature. Were they subjective visions or hallucinations born out of the faith of the earliest disciples in their departed Lord (or their collective grief and guilt), as some claim, or were they actually physical and/or transformed bodily manifestations? Was Jesus only raised in the apostles' faith, or if he was raised from the dead, how should we describe it? What can we discern from the biblical narratives and reports?

Lüdemann rejects the empty-tomb tradition as a secondary development in the early church and contends that the whole Easter experience was psychologically self-induced, first by a visionary experience of Peter in Galilee that Lüdemann says led to an "incomparable chain reaction," and then later by a similar experience of Paul that came from his guilt over persecuting the early followers of Jesus. It was from these two primary visionary experiences, Lüdemann concludes, that Easter faith began. On the basis of Paul's conversion (c. AD 33), he locates all of the appearances between AD 30 (the time of Jesus' death) and AD 33 (Paul's conversion).[101] From his examination of the resurrection narratives, he is led "to the insight that the structural characteristics of the Easter experience indicated above, of the forgiveness of sins, the experience of life, the experience of eternity, are contained in the words

---

101. Lüdemann, *What Really Happened to Jesus?*, 14–15.

Table 6.1
Easter Appearances in the Gospels and Paul

Major Sources	Matthew	Mark	Luke-Acts	John	Mark 16:9–20	John 21	1 Cor. 15
Location	Jerusalem + Galilee	Galilee	Jerusalem	Jerusalem	Jerusalem + Galilee	Galilee: Sea of Tiberias	Not clear, but possibly Galilee (500+) Damascus Rd. to Paul
Number of Women at tomb	2	3	3 + others	1 (Mary)	1 (Mary)	none	None, but possibly 500+
Women's/Mary's report	Evidently told disciples, who went to Galilee	Fled, said nothing because fearful	Joy, reported empty tomb to disciples, who did not believe	Mary reported empty tomb to disciples	Reported empty tomb to disciples, who did not believe		
Touching Jesus	Allowed to touch		To all: "Touch me and see" (Luke 24:39)	Mary: "Do not touch"; later to Thomas: "Touch"			Blinding light, voice (Acts 9:3–6; 22:6–10; 26:13–18)
Appearance	To women in Jerusalem; to disciples in Galilee	Promise to appear to disciples in Galilee	To 2 disciples on road to Emmaus; to disciples during meal in evening; ascension	To Mary in Jerusalem; to disciples in Jerusalem	To Mary; ascension; to 2 disciples in country (Emmaus); to Eleven at table; to Eleven	To 7 disciples in Galilee; to Peter (this was 3rd appearance, 21:14)	Peter, Twelve, 500+; James + rest of apostles; Paul (Acts 9:3–6; 22:6–10; 26:13–18; Gal. 1:15–16; 1 Cor. 9:1)
Greeting	To women: "Greetings! Do not be afraid; go and tell my brothers" (28:9–10).		"Peace be with you" (24:36).	"Peace be with you" (20:19).	Chided for their lack of faith		"Why are you persecuting me? … I am Jesus" (Acts 9:4–5).

(continued on next page)

Major Sources	Matthew	Mark	Luke-Acts	John	Mark 16:9–20	John 21	1 Cor. 15
Command/ commission	To disciples: "All authority . . . given to me. Go . . . make disciples. . . . I am with you always" (28:18–20).		Wait for Holy Spirit, witness	To Mary: Do not touch, go to brothers & tell he is ascending; to disciples: "As the Father has sent me, so I send you" (20:21); receive Holy Spirit, forgive sins; to Thomas: Touch	"Go . . . proclaim the good news" (16:15), and signs will accompany you.	Feed my sheep; follow me	"Enter the city, and you will be told what to do" (Acts 9:6).
Response	Worship by women; worship and doubt		Startled and afraid; thought they saw a ghost	Thomas: "My Lord and my God!" (20:28); Jesus: "Blessed are those who have not seen and yet have come to believe."		"It is the Lord!" (v. 7).	
Ascension	"I am with you always" (28:20).		Final appearance: resurrection, appearance, sending Holy Spirit	Between 1st and 2nd appearance: resurrection, appearance, giving Holy Spirit	Final appearance & ascension		

and story of Jesus. So we have to say that before Easter, everything that was finally recognized after Easter was already present."[102] There was for him no necessity for the Easter tradition.

Some scholars say Jesus was alive after his death, but they deny that his physical body was raised from the grave. They speak of the appearances in terms of "objective visions"—that is, that Jesus was alive after his death and manifested his aliveness to his disciples in a way that was unmistakable to them. The visions were not induced by psychological experience in the apostles, but were objective experiences that came to them. Jesus' body, however, decomposed somewhere in Palestine. They claim that his resurrection was of a different sort than the physical resurrection or resuscitation described in the Gospels, especially in Luke 24:39–43.

Any examination of the nature of the appearances in the Gospel narratives and comparison to Paul's encounters reported in his epistles and in the book of Acts reflects many perplexing problems. Those who take the "objective visions" position argue that the language Paul uses to describe his experience with the risen Lord (1 Cor. 15:3–11; Gal. 1:15–16), or the language used of Paul's experience in Acts (9:1–9; 22:6–11; 26:12–16), is normally used to depict visionary experiences. They note that, if all the testimony we had on the nature of the appearances came from Paul or the book of Acts, then we might well conclude that the resurrection appearances were visionary experiences.

The two verbs most frequently used in the New Testament in reference to the resurrection of Jesus are *egeirō* ("I raise," or "I raise up") and *anistēmi* ("I raise up," or "I rise"), both of which appear in earlier Jewish apocryphal literature. *Egeirō* was used very little in secular Greek for the resurrection of the dead, probably because most ancient Greeks did not believe in a bodily resurrection, and instead referred most often to an awakening (see Eph. 5:14), lifting up, or raising. *Anistanai* (the infinitive form) was sometimes used in reference to the raising of the dead, but its use is not always clear. C. F. Evans believes that the New Testament understanding of resurrection is better conveyed by the words "to live," "to make alive," and "to glorify":

The resurrection of Christ is a living after death, and the conquest of death, so that he has dominion over all men (Rom. 14:9), and being the conquest of sin is a life lived permanently to God (Rom. 6:13; 14:8; 2 Cor. 13:4; Phil. 1:21;

102. Lüdemann, *Resurrection of Jesus*, 181–82. He tries to account for Paul's and Peter's experience with the risen Christ in psychoanalytical terms of guilt on the part of both. He goes on to cite Ernst Fuchs saying that there were no differences between Jesus of Nazareth, the historical Jesus, and the "Risen Lord" (cf. n699 on p. 232). See his discussion of the resurrection on pp. 79–100, but especially his conclusions on 174–75.

Col. 3:1f.), and who will be "made alive" (see *zoopoiei* in John 5:21). Since the word "glory" is the biblical word that comes nearest to expressing the being and nature of God himself, it is inevitably connected with the thought of resurrection as entry into the divine life.[103]

As we saw earlier, not all of the Jews in the time of Jesus accepted a belief in the bodily resurrection of the dead. However, many Jews at that time accepted varying notions of the resurrection of the dead.

Some scholars argue that Paul's use of the verb *ōphthē* ("appeared," or "was seen"), an aorist passive indicative of *horaō* ("see") in 1 Corinthians 15:5–8, is a technical term used primarily for visionary experiences with God in biblical writings.[104] If used in this sense in Paul, this implies that those who experienced resurrection appearances had visionary experiences or some special revelations from God. When this passage is compared to others in Paul that do not emphasize the physical nature of the appearances or his encounter with God (Gal. 1:15–17; 2 Cor. 9:1; 12:2–4), it is understandable that some interpreters conclude that the earliest appearances were visionary in nature and that only *after* the Gospels began circulating did that view change to something more physical. This interpretation allows that the body of Jesus decomposed somewhere in Palestine (the absence of the body from the tomb is explained in natural terms—namely that someone stole the body, the disciples went to the wrong tomb, or its emptiness is denied altogether), and yet these scholars maintain that the disciples experienced something apart from their own longings that initiated their Easter faith. This is the "objective vision" theory.

Since Paul places his seeing of the risen Lord on par with the other apostles' seeing of him (1 Cor. 9:1; 15:5–8), the argument goes that all of Christ's postresurrection appearances were of the same nature—namely, visionary experiences. Scholars holding this view typically argue that because of later apologetic needs in the church, the Easter experiences were recast into a more concrete form such as we see in Luke's and John's resurrection narratives.

However, the verb *ōphthē* and its various forms are not so much technical designations but rather neutral terms denoting sight. The use of the aorist passive of *horaō* ("see") in both Matthew 17:3 and Luke 9:31 leaves open the question of the form of seeing. There is not just one use of *ōphthē* in biblical and extrabiblical literature, and so arguments about the nature or form of the appearances based on this term alone seem unwarranted. Bultmann argues that the disciples experienced hallucinations or *subjective* visions, but

---

103. Evans, *Resurrection*, 126.
104. See Lampe and MacKinnon, *Resurrection*, 36, and H. Grass, *Ostergeschehen und Osterberichte* (Göttingen: Vandenhoeck & Ruprecht, 1962), 186–232.

nevertheless rightly concludes that "neither vision nor objective fact can be deduced from *ōphthē* in this passage."[105] Michaelis's investigation of *ōphthē* in 1 Corinthians 15 is worthy of note:

> It thus seems that when *ōphthē* is used as a t.t. [technical term] to denote the resurrection appearances there is no primary emphasis on seeing as sensual or mental perception. The dominant thought is that the appearances are revelations, encounters with the risen Lord who herein reveals Himself or is revealed, cf. Gal. 1:16. . . . The relation of *ōphthē* in 1 Cor. 15:5 ff. to the act of 9:1 does not involve a simple replacing of the act by the corresponding form. If so, the significance attached to seeing would be the same in both instances. The important point about the dative, however, is that the one who constitutes the subject is the one who acts, i.e., appears, shows himself, with no special emphasis on the resultant action of the person in the dative, namely that he sees or perceives. . . . ["He appeared to Cephas,"] etc., does not mean in the first instance that they saw Him, with an emphasis on seeing, e.g., in contrast to hearing. It means rather: . . . ["he himself stood among them living"] (cf. Acts 1:3), or even better: . . . ["God revealed him among them"] (Gal. 1:16). He encountered them as risen, living Lord; they experienced His presence. In the last resort even active forms like *heoraka* in 1 Cor. 9:1 mean the same thing."[106]

Lüdemann, while agreeing with the visionary nature of the appearances, rejects their objectivity. He appeals to Paul, whose sightings of the risen Christ were visionary rather than real (Gal. 1:15–16; Phil. 3:8; 2 Cor. 4:6; 12:1–10), and bases this conclusion on his interpretation of the visionary type of experiences mentioned in Acts (9:1–19; 22:4–16; 26:9–18) and Paul.[107] He argues that these visions were subjectively induced from Paul's guilt and an "inner personal inability which depth psychology has established to be a frequent cause of aggressive behavior."[108] He concludes the same is true of Peter. Peter was guilt laden because of his denial of Jesus, but under the impact of Jesus' preaching and death, and through an appearance of the "risen Christ," Peter accepted God's forgiveness, which was already present in the earlier ministry and activity of Jesus (Mark 2:5). For Lüdemann, the other visions (e.g., 1 Cor. 15:5–8) were also produced through mass psychosis or hysteria. As a result, God must not be considered the author of these visions, but rather "they were

---

105. R. Bultmann, *Faith and Understanding* (ed. R. W. Funk; trans. L. P. Smith; London: SCM, 1966), 83.

106. W. Michaelis, "Horaō," *TDNT* (1968) 5:358.

107. Lüdemann, *What Really Happened to Jesus?*, 102–28. See also his more complete discussion of the visionary nature of the appearances to Paul in his *Resurrection of Jesus*, 47–87, and for Peter on 84–108.

108. Lüdemann, *What Really Happened to Jesus?*, 128–30.

psychological processes which ran their course with a degree of regularity—completely without divine intervention."[109]

Confusion over the nature of the resurrection appearances stems from the fact that Paul apparently does not describe his encounter with the risen Lord in the same concrete terms that are in the Gospels and does not mention the empty-tomb tradition. Luke describes Paul's encounter with the risen Christ as a "light from heaven" (*phōs ek tou ouranou*; see Acts 9:3; 22:6; 26:13) accompanied by a "voice" (*phōnēn*; 9:4; 22:7; 26:14) that was intelligible only to Paul. In Acts 26:19 the same encounter is described as a "heavenly appearing" (*tē ouraniō optasia*). The appearance (*optasia*) here is not necessarily a vision, since Luke's normal word for "vision" is *horama* (see Acts 10:17), and the normal understanding of *optasia* is of a nonvisionary appearance.[110] It is difficult to conclude that all appearances were visionary based solely on Paul's use of *ōphthē*. Nevertheless, if the only evidence that we had was Paul's testimony about his experience with the risen Lord (Gal. 1:12, 15–16) and the witness of Acts (9:3; 22:6; 26:13), we would be hard pressed to speak of more than visionary encounters.

Since Paul's writings are earlier than the Gospels, what can we conclude from him about the nature or form of the resurrection appearances? His argument in 1 Corinthians 15:42–54 indicates that in the resurrection, the body is transformed. Although the presence of Christ in the appearances seems nonvisionary in the Gospels, there are, as Michaelis observes, no adequate categories to explain them, and he concludes that the appearances are "manifestations in the sense of revelation rather than making visible."[111] We have no evidence that Paul rejected a bodily resurrection of Jesus nor that he simply accepted a physical or fleshly resurrected body. He states that the resurrection for Christians will be like that of Jesus (Rom. 8:9–11; Phil. 3:21), and it will evidently be a *transformed bodily resurrection* (1 Cor. 15:52–54). In other words, the present physical body is transformed into a new, resurrected body.

According to Lampe, objections to a visionary encounter with the risen Christ stem from a failure to understand the nature of Christian faith, which involves risk and cannot seek refuge in the security of demonstrable facts. Lampe says objections to the visionary nature of Jesus' resurrection are from those who seek guarantees for faith, but God "makes his activity known to faith, and faith is not compatible with unmistakable proofs."[112] Faith is indeed

---

109. Ibid., 130.
110. See Michaelis, "*Horaō*," *TDNT* 5:353, 357, 372. An exception to this is in the plural *optasias* ("appearances") in 2 Cor. 12:1, but, as Michaelis shows, the usage is different from that of the singular (357).
111. Ibid., 5:359.
112. Lampe and MacKinnon, *Resurrection*, 37.

faith rather than sight, and Christian faith cannot advance beyond the faith of the earliest disciples or verify the testimonies of those disciples through historical-critical inquiry; but is Lampe's alternative the only option?

Paul's experience with the risen Lord seems "visionary," but were all resurrection appearances like his? Is his experience as one "untimely born" (1 Cor. 15:8) the same as earlier encounters with the risen Christ, or is Paul simply trying to say that the same risen Christ appeared to him as to the others and he is not focusing on the nature of those appearances? We may be missing the character of the appearances of Jesus to the disciples *even in the Gospels.* Recall that some of the disciples failed to recognize Jesus in his appearances. Is it because of the revelatory nature of the appearances that some "doubted" after they saw the risen Lord (see Matt. 28:17), even though Matthew does not initially mention any difficulty in recognizing the risen Jesus? Also, in Luke's story about the disciples on the road to Emmaus, they did not recognize Jesus until he broke bread with them (24:30–34). In Luke's next appearance, Jesus had to demonstrate to the disciples that he was not a ghost or a spirit, but a real person with an ability to eat fish (24:37–43). In John 20:14–16, Mary did not recognize Jesus until he spoke her name. The Johannine "appendix" is also quite similar; it is only after a miracle is performed that the Beloved Disciple recognizes it is Jesus standing on the beach (21:4–7). Even John's story of Jesus' appearance to the disciples, without Thomas, suggests the need for him to show some sign to prove that he was the same as the one who was crucified (20:20), such as showing them his hands and side.

The difficulty in recognizing the resurrected Jesus may signal that his appearances were more than physical occurrences and could only be perceived by those whose eyes were open to such things.[113] Those who think only in physical categories often overlook these *less*-than-physical manifestations of the risen Lord in the Gospel narratives. While it is true that Luke takes the time to describe Jesus' appearances in a more physical way (24:37–42), his purpose for doing so is to dispel the notion that Jesus was merely a spirit or ghost (24:37, 39). Jesus' ability to disappear (24:31) and then to reappear (24:36) might lead some early Christians to conclude that only a spirit was in their midst, but Luke emphasizes that this was not so; Jesus' new mode of existence was *bodily, but not limited by the physical realm* of this-worldly existence. John, who along with Luke describes the resurrection of Jesus in physical fashion, also depicts the risen Christ as having no physical limitations in his bodily existence. In John 20:19 the disciples were huddled together, and "the doors of the house where the disciples had met were locked for fear of the

113. Fuller, *Formation of the Resurrection Narratives,* 75.

Jews," yet Jesus came in and stood in their midst, evidently passing through the walls or doors. This seems especially clear in the following appearance to Thomas eight days later: "*Although* the doors were shut, Jesus came and stood among them" (20:26), yet in the Thomas story Jesus invites Thomas to touch his hands and side. This new mode of existence of the resurrected Lord was not simply spirit, but a new bodily existence not governed by the limitations of the physical body, even though some form of a body was manifested in the appearance (John 20:20, 27). In Matthew, the stone is rolled away by the angel of the Lord *not to let Jesus out, but to let the women in* (28:2–6)! Jesus was already out, evidently having come through the walls of the tomb. On the other hand, Matthew shows that the risen Lord could be touched as well as heard (28:9–10), but even after seeing him "some doubted" (28:17). What appears to have happened to Jesus in his resurrection is beyond the experience of historians and what we would normally anticipate. His resurrection was not a resuscitation to the same limitations of physical life that he had experienced before, but to a new mode of life. In a real sense, what the biblical affirmations reflect is beyond historical inquiry, but not beyond the realm of faith. Jesus' new mode of existence was a first among human beings and yet for those who follow him, as we have seen above, not the last!

The problems of doubt and the difficulties in the initial recognition of Jesus in some of the narratives are likely due to the unique revelatory nature of the appearances. The resurrection of Jesus was bodily (the old taken up into the new), yet beyond the normal understanding of "physical." Doubt is a common theme in the appearance narratives (see especially Matt. 28:17; Luke 24:11, 38–42; John 20:24–29; Mark 16:12–14). In Matthew, those who doubted did so even after Jesus appeared to them, while in John, Jesus rebuked those who refused to believe the *reports* that he was indeed alive (20:26–29). In Matthew, the doubt was not rebuked, but was evidently dismissed with Jesus' reference to his own authority.

It is likely that the element of doubt in the narratives reflects the questionings of the later church "about a new Easter certainty and conviction."[114] Thomas may be representative of the doubting element in the church who needed reassuring that the blessing of God comes to those who have not seen, yet believe (John 20:24–29). Perhaps some of the resurrection appearances should be understood in this context. Each evangelist in his own way seeks to establish continuity between the crucified Jesus and the risen Lord. For them and for Paul, the one who died is the same as the one who has appeared to his followers—but doubt lingered in some. The appearance of Jesus was coupled with the charge of evangelism (the missionary motif), most clearly

114. Anderson, *Jesus*, 224.

seen in Matthew 28:19–20; Luke 24:45–49; Acts 1:8; and John 20:19–23. The redactional sections of Mark (16:15–18) and John (21:15–22) where doubt is expressed should also be added to this collection.

Even if Jesus' appearances in the Gospels seem more physical or bodily than we see in Paul (so Luke 24:39 and John 20:27), they reflect a revelatory nature different from what a mere resuscitation suggests. The appearances of Jesus were not just physical manifestations, but appearances of a different order than has been generally understood. Even without 1 Corinthians 15 and reports of Paul's encounter with the risen Lord in Acts, a careful look at the Gospels demonstrates that more than physical appearances were intended. The ascension story in Luke and Acts says, however, that the appearances of Jesus ceased after a brief time, and whatever their nature, they were encountered by several persons. In Acts 1:21–25, the basis for selecting an apostolic replacement for Judas was that the candidate had to be a witness from Jesus' baptism until his ascension (Acts 1:22). For Paul, the revelatory encounters with the risen Lord concluded with his experience (1 Cor. 15:8). What is common in all of these stories is that what the apostles and Paul experienced was more than a physical encounter, that it transformed their lives, and it also ceased to occur after a short period of time.

Paul reflects the church's hope about resurrection in terms of the bodily resurrection of Jesus (see Rom. 8:9–11; see also 8:22–23; Phil. 3:21). We have seen the same in the Gospels. The nature of Jesus' resurrection and his appearances to the disciples was spiritual-bodily (transformed-bodily), *whatever sort that may be*. In Paul, the "old body" of flesh was transformed and incorporated into the new. The old puts on the new body and the old is transformed (1 Cor. 15:42–54). How this happened or happens remains a mystery, but it is significant that all of the New Testament data surrounding Easter coincides with Paul's view of a transformed-bodily resurrection. The empty tomb supports the conclusion that Jesus' resurrection was a bodily one and his body was incorporated into his new, resurrected body; and the various reports of him going through doors or suddenly appearing and vanishing support the conclusion that his appearances were more than mere physical manifestations, but also more than visions.

There are no parallels to this kind of a manifestation, and Jesus' resurrection appearances are unique and revelatory. He is the "first fruits of those who have died"(1 Cor. 15:20). Transformed-bodily resurrection appearances appear to answer many questions about the nature of the events themselves, and may be a clue to understanding their various locations (Jerusalem, Galilee, Damascus Road). The appearances were not a product of the disciples' faith, but rather of the activity of God coming to those who were in despair and without faith.

The oldest Christian confession of faith acknowledges the risen Christ (Rom. 10:9–10). That confession may be stated more precisely: Christians confess that Jesus of Nazareth rose from the dead. The nature of that event is no more clear to the person of faith than to a critical historian, since its nature is unique and for the time being lies beyond our experience, knowledge, and scope of inquiry—it is "beyond history." The historian may claim that something happened, and the Christian may claim to know what happened (Jesus was raised from the dead and appeared to others), but how it happened escapes both. Whatever a "transformed-bodily" resurrection is cannot be known since it is without parallel in human experience. There are no adequate human expressions available for a description of this event, though for the Christian that inexperience of the "beyond" is only temporary (Rom. 8:11; Phil. 3:21).

A Summary of the Events of Easter

From our limited discussion of the Easter traditions, some conclusions may be drawn. The evangelists agree that after Jesus' crucifixion, he was buried by Joseph of Arimathea in a tomb near the city of Jerusalem on the day of preparation (Friday) as the Sabbath was approaching. When the Sabbath was over, a group of women from Galilee (or perhaps just Mary) came to the tomb where Jesus was buried to pay their final respects. Upon reaching the tomb, they found it empty. The women reported this to Jesus' disciples, who were still in Jerusalem, possibly hiding out of fear of arrest. Some of the disciples examined the tomb and confirmed the report that the tomb was empty. This raised questions among the disciples, because as yet they were uncertain about the empty tomb's meaning. They may have returned to Galilee, where they saw the risen Lord, but perhaps they remained in Jerusalem until they had received an appearance from him there.

If the disciples went to Galilee (Mark and Matthew), or if they stayed in Jerusalem (Luke and John), they saw the risen Jesus. His final appearance(s) may have been in Jerusalem or just outside of Jerusalem. Although the location of the appearances varies in the Gospels, it is clear that Jesus who died was raised from the dead and appeared to them. Belief in Jesus' resurrection from the dead and the conviction that he had indeed appeared to the disciples after his resurrection was central to early Christian preaching.

While there is no doubt about the earliest Christians' belief in the resurrection of Jesus, the nature of his resurrection remains unclear. The empty tomb pointed to the mode of his resurrection—that it was bodily—but Jesus' appearances did not have physical limitations characteristic of human beings.

The appearances were more than simple physical manifestations and also more than merely subjective or objective visionary experiences. They were "revelatory" or "revelational," and retain something of the unique and mysterious character that surrounds them in the New Testament narratives.

Relations between the Gospel Narratives

Although Luke records no appearance of Jesus to the women as do Matthew (28:9–10) and John (20:11–18), what is disclosed in Matthew's and John's narrations of Jesus' appearances is also discernible in what the angels revealed to the women at the tomb. Matthew's account of the appearance of Jesus to the women adds little to the story already told by the angel (28:5–7), unless its purpose was to indicate to the women that, in their ability to touch Jesus' feet, they were encountering a "real" person.[115] This point is also clear in the angelic message, and it is difficult to see why Matthew added this appearance unless it was present in his sources. The similar passage in John where Jesus appears to Mary also appears to be an early tradition. John has no message of the angels to Mary in favor of making the disclosure of the meaning of the empty tomb come from the risen Lord himself.

Matthew and John agree that Jesus appeared to the women (in John, it is a woman; but see the "we know" in John 20:2) at the tomb, and both passages agree that the woman/women touched Jesus (Matt. 28:9) or that Mary attempted to do so (maybe did? see John 20:17) and that Thomas was invited to do so. John uses this tradition to illustrate that the exaltation of Jesus came in his resurrection from the dead. Nevertheless, Matthew's reference to the women worshiping the risen Christ (28:9) may not be far from John's focus. Could this be the same reason behind John's story of the grave clothes (20:3–10; cf. Luke 24:12)? In all four Gospels there are references to appearances of Jesus or the promise of such (Mark 16:7).

The mutual-appearance pattern in John's and Luke's appearance narratives suggests a common tradition behind them. Dodd distinguishes this tradition from folklore, claiming that their story "has something indefinably first hand about it" that he says is a "reflective, subtle, most delicate approach to the depths of human experience."[116]

References to the resurrection of Jesus as a fulfillment of Scripture (see, for example, Luke 24:27, 44–46; Acts 2:25–36; 13:32–37; John 20:9; 1 Cor. 15:3–4) are problematic since sometimes it is difficult to determine which

115. C. H. Dodd argues this point in *More New Testament Studies* (Grand Rapids: Eerdmans, 1968), 106.
116. Ibid., 115.

Scriptures the writers had in mind. Since we cannot be certain, it is possible that the evangelists were thinking of the texts most commonly cited in early Christian preaching—namely, Deuteronomy 18:15 (the prophet like Moses), Psalms 22 and 69 (the Passion Psalms), Psalm 110 (the exaltation of Christ to the right hand of God), and Isaiah 42 and 53 (Jesus as the Suffering Servant of God). References to these and other passages do not suggest that the early followers of Jesus expected his resurrection because of their interpretation of the Scriptures. It took them all by surprise, but because of their commitment to the Jewish Scriptures, the early Christians were anxious "to find some scripture to fit a fact, and were far from inventing a fact to fit a scripture."[117] There is little doubt that Jesus powerfully influenced his followers' understanding of the Jewish Scriptures. The Scriptures cited by Luke, John, and Paul are correctly seen as indications that the early Christians' understanding of the Scriptures was radically altered by their encounter with the risen Christ. This apologetic use of Scripture was in existence well before Paul referred to it in 1 Corinthians 15:3–5, but finding Scripture to clarify what it was that Jesus' disciples experienced was a challenge since "resurrection is certainly not something which could have been arrived at by reflection on the Old Testament."[118] So vague are the references to resurrection in the Old Testament that, apart from the resurrection of Jesus actually taking place, it is difficult to account for the centrality of the resurrection in the thinking of the early followers of Jesus. Their attempts to establish Jesus' resurrection in their Scriptures point to its significance in their community as well as to the difficulty of locating the origins of resurrection faith in anything other than the Easter event itself. Apart from their strong belief that Jesus had in fact been raised from the dead, there appears to be no good reason for such attempts to use the Scriptures in this manner.

Finally, I will refer again to the so-called transposed resurrection narratives. It has long been supposed by some scholars that the Gospel reports about Jesus' remarkable activities during his earthly ministry are nothing more than "transposed" resurrection stories. Those passages include the miraculous draft of fishes (Luke 5:1–11), the stilling of the storm (Mark 4:35–41), the walking on the water (Mark 6:45–52), the feeding of the multitude (Mark 6:32–44; 8:1–10), the transfiguration (Mark 9:2–8), and the "you are Peter" saying (Matt. 16:17–19). Arguments for calling such passages resurrection encounters are not convincing. Not only do these supposed transposed appearance stories fail to

117. A. R. C. Leaney, "Theophany, Resurrection and History," in *Studia Evangelica* (ed. F. L. Cross; Berlin: Akademie-Verlag, 1968), 5:112.
118. Evans, *Resurrection*, 14.

conform to the usual pattern of the resurrection appearances mentioned above, but the motives of the evangelists in transposing them are also unclear. What different purpose would they have served by being transposed? The arguments of those who continue to make such assertions are unconvincing, and so I have omitted any significant discussion of them. Long ago C. H. Dodd effectively answered such arguments, showing that they do not conform to the pattern of the resurrection appearances.[119]

Guidelines for Further Study

Given the limitations of this volume, it is not possible to treat equally all of the many issues related to the resurrection of Jesus, but I have given considerable attention to some of the most important issues. For those interested in pursuing the study of the resurrection of Jesus further, I offer the following suggestions.

(1) Be mindful that the evangelists' faith perspectives and theologies played a significant role in their selection and shaping of their Easter proclamations, just as they did in the shaping of the rest of their Gospels. An examination of the reported phenomena occurring at the death and resurrection of Jesus— earthquakes, tearing of the temple curtain, bodies going through the streets of Jerusalem, confessions of faith, darkness over the land, fulfillment of the Scriptures, the length of the appearances of Jesus after his resurrection, the ascension story in Luke and John—*all* suggest that the evangelists' theological perspectives helped shape the traditions they passed along. In any study of the Gospels, just as it is important not to overtranslate the text or import foreign theology into the text, it is equally important to avoid *undertranslation*, that is, saying *less* than the evangelists intended to say. Although many Christians continue to affirm literal interpretations of the various phenomena that occurred at the death and resurrection of Jesus, the evangelists intended to say much more than merely literal interpretations are capable of saying. They all intended at the least to say that Jesus of Nazareth, who died, is now alive, but also that this has great significance for those who believe in him.

(2) Be cautious of a reductionist interpretation of the narratives. The resurrection narratives cannot be reduced to a new understanding of human existence, as some scholars have suggested (Bultmann, Marxsen, C. F. Evans), or traced back to some psychological guilt in Peter and/or Paul (Lüdemann, Wedderburn). The resurrection narratives are about the fate of the crucified Jesus. He who died is now alive, and the mode of his existence is a bodily one, however we might understand that.

119. Dodd, "Appearances of the Risen Christ," 9–35.

(3) In the resurrection narratives, we are dealing with a sphere of knowing and understanding that moves *beyond* the historical sphere of inquiry, and this complicates our understanding of these sources. As Johnson says, "some sort of powerful transformative experience is required to generate the sort of movement earliest Christianity was, and to necessitate the sort of literature the New Testament is."[120] It is infinitely more than something like a lightbulb going on in someone's head. What happened occurred in time and space, but also in a realm totally unfamiliar to traditional historical inquiry.

(4) Finally, be cautious about attempting to harmonize the resurrection narratives. There is a tendency in such reconstructions to minimize important theological distinctions intended by their authors. Throughout its history, the church has seen the wisdom of maintaining the integrity of each evangelist's message and rejected the temptation to adopt a single harmonized Gospel such as Tatian's *Diatessaron* (ca. AD 170).[121] Apart from the difficulty in harmonizing the Easter narratives, most such attempts are based on hypotheses that have little historical, rational, theological, or even narrative support. It is better to look at the differences in terms of each evangelist's purpose and to allow each narrative to stand by itself, except when there are obvious parallels that show dependence on other sources.

120. Johnson, *Real Jesus*, 136.
121. See J. H. Hill, *The Earliest Life of Christ Ever Compiled from the Four Gospels Being the Diatessaron of Tatian* (Edinburgh: T&T Clark, 1894).

Osborne, G. F. "Jesus' Empty Tomb and His Appearance in Jerusalem." In *Key Events in the Life of the Historical Jesus*, edited by D. L. Bock and R. L. Webb, 775–823. Wissenschaftliche Untersuchungen zum Neuen Testament 247. Tübingen: Mohr Siebeck, 2009.

———. *The Resurrection Narratives: A Redactional Study*. Grand Rapids: Baker, 1984.

Perkins, Pheme. *Resurrection: New Testament Witness and Contemporary Reflection*. Garden City, NY: Doubleday, 1984.

Porter, Stanley E., Michael A. Hayes, and David Tombs, eds. *Resurrection*. New York: T&T Clark, 2004.

Sawicki, M. *Seeing the Lord: Resurrection and Early Christian Practices*. Minneapolis: Fortress, 1994.

Setzer, Claudia. *Resurrection of the Body in Early Judaism and Early Christianity: Doctrine, Community and Self-Definition*. Leiden: Brill Academic, 2004.

Smith, Daniel A. *Revisiting the Empty Tomb: The Early History of Easter*. Minneapolis: Fortress, 2010.

Vinzent, Markus. *Christ's Resurrection in Early Christianity and the Making of the New Testament*. Surrey, England: Ashgate, 2011.

Wedderburn, A. J. M. *Baptism and Resurrection: Studies in Pauline Theology against Its Greco-Roman Background*. WUNT 44. Tübingen: Mohr Siebeck, 1987.

———. *Beyond Resurrection*. Peabody, MA: Hendrickson, 1999.

Wright, N. T. *The Challenge of Jesus: Rediscovering Who Jesus Was and Is*. Downers Grove, IL: InterVarsity Press, 1997

———. *The Resurrection of the Son of God*. Christian Origins and the Question of God 3. Minneapolis: Fortress, 2003.

Scripture Index

||||||||||||||||||||||||||||||||||||||||||||||||||||

Index of Modern Authors

||||||||||||||||||||||||||||||||||||||||||||||||||||||

Subject Index

||||||||||||||||||||||||||||||||||||||||||||||||||||||

385

Osborne, G. F. "Jesus' Empty Tomb and His Appearance in Jerusalem." In *Key Events in the Life of the Historical Jesus*, edited by D. L. Bock and R. L. Webb, 775–823. Wissenschaftliche Untersuchungen zum Neuen Testament 247. Tübingen: Mohr Siebeck, 2009.

———. *The Resurrection Narratives: A Redactional Study*. Grand Rapids: Baker, 1984.

Perkins, Pheme. *Resurrection: New Testament Witness and Contemporary Reflection*. Garden City, NY: Doubleday, 1984.

Porter, Stanley E., Michael A. Hayes, and David Tombs, eds. *Resurrection*. New York: T&T Clark, 2004.

Sawicki, M. *Seeing the Lord: Resurrection and Early Christian Practices*. Minneapolis: Fortress, 1994.

Setzer, Claudia. *Resurrection of the Body in Early Judaism and Early Christianity: Doctrine, Community and Self-Definition*. Leiden: Brill Academic, 2004.

Smith, Daniel A. *Revisiting the Empty Tomb: The Early History of Easter*. Minneapolis: Fortress, 2010.

Vinzent, Markus. *Christ's Resurrection in Early Christianity and the Making of the New Testament*. Surrey, England: Ashgate, 2011.

Wedderburn, A. J. M. *Baptism and Resurrection: Studies in Pauline Theology against Its Greco-Roman Background*. WUNT 44. Tübingen: Mohr Siebeck, 1987.

———. *Beyond Resurrection*. Peabody, MA: Hendrickson, 1999.

Wright, N. T. *The Challenge of Jesus: Rediscovering Who Jesus Was and Is*. Downers Grove, IL: InterVarsity Press, 1997

———. *The Resurrection of the Son of God*. Christian Origins and the Question of God 3. Minneapolis: Fortress, 2003.

Scripture Index

|||||||||||||||||||||||||||||||||||||||||||||||||||||||

Old Testament

Genesis

1:1 152, 223
1:26 152
1:26–27 152
1:27 222
2:24 222
4:1–16 222
4:7 223
4:24 222
6–7 222
14:18 236
14:18–20 168
17:10–12 223
19 222
21:17 223
21:19 223
25:8 256
26:19 223
28:10 152
28:12 223
36:9–14 191
36:15–19 191
39:2 151
40:55 223
46:8–27 193
46:9 191
46:12 191
46:17 191
47:29–30 257
48:22 223
49:24–26 256n42
49:29–50 256n42
50:10 257
50:24–25 257

Exodus

2:1–2 194
3:1 151
3:6 197, 222
4:19–20 179
6:14–27 194
7:1 223
9:12 223
12:2 223
12:8 223
12:10 223
12:46 152, 223
13:19 257
13:21–22 230
14:21 223
14:23 223
15 223
16:4 223
16:28 223
19:2 222
19:18 285
20:7 222
20:12 222
20:13 222
20:14 222
21:8 223
21:12 222
21:17 222
21:24 222
22:27 223
23:20 222
23:36 223
24:1 228
24:8 222
24:12–18 228

24:13 228
24:15–18 230
24:16 223, 228, 229
27:20 152
27:21 223
28:30 223
29:37 222
30:29 222
32:31 152
33:7–23 228
33:9–10 230
33:11 223
33:18–23 229
33:20 152
33:20–23 152
34:6 223
34:29–35 228
34:30 228, 229
34:35 229

Leviticus

12:6 152
13–14 222
14:2–32 222
17:10–14 223
19:2 150, 222
19:12 222
19:18 222
20:10 223
23:33–44 229
23:34 223
23:40 223
23:42–43 229
24:9 222
24:17 222
24:20 222

Numbers

5:6 151
5:12 223
6:3 152
6:25 152
11:1–15 204
13:25–38 204
22–24 187n24
24:16 168
24:17 151
28:9–10 217, 222
31:16 154
35:30 240

Deuteronomy

1:16 223
1:35 223
2:14 223
4:12 223
5:16–20 222
5:17 222
5:18 222
6:4–5 151, 222
6:13 222
6:16 222
8:3 222
10:1 151
11:29 223
12:5 223
13:2 222
13:25 223
18:15 229, 330
18:15–18 236
19:15 222

367

Romans

1 Corinthians

378

Index of Modern Authors

|||||||||||||||||||||||||||||||||||||||||||||||||||||||

Subject Index

||||||||||||||||||||||||||||||||||||||||||||||||||||||||||